Capitalist Restructuring and the Pacific Rim

I0126019

This book situates the evolution of the high growth economies along Asia's Pacific Rim after the Second World War within broader global political and economic changes. Specifically, it charts the growth of capitalist economies in the region throughout periodic crises and successive waves of restructuring, and links changes in the world economy to shifts in the domestic political economies of East and Southeast Asia. It suggests that the financial crisis of 1997–98 laid the basis for a new phase of regional economic integration in Pacific-Asia.

Key issues examined include:

- comparison of patterns of state intervention and industrial organization in individual countries
- history of US power in the region
- analysis of class and state–society relations
- how shifts in regional dynamics can effect changes in the world economy.

Through this detailed analysis of regional economic growth and integration since 1945, *Capitalist Restructuring and the Pacific Rim* concludes that the continued accumulation of capital in East and Southeast Asia is undermining the material foundations of US power.

This comprehensive survey of the emergence of Asia's Pacific Rim will intrigue and inform scholars of Asian Studies, Sociology, and Development Studies alike.

Ravi Arvind Palat is an Associate Professor of Sociology at the State University of New York at Binghamton and has previously taught at the Universities of Hawaii and Auckland.

RoutledgeCurzon Studies in the Modern History of Asia

Capitalist Restructuring and the Pacific Rim

Ravi Arvind Palat

Routledge
Taylor & Francis Group

LONDON AND NEW YORK

First published 2004
by RoutledgeCurzon
2 Park Square, Milton Park, Abingdon, Oxfordshire OX14 4RN

Simultaneously published in the USA and Canada
by RoutledgeCurzon
711 Third Avenue, New York, NY 10017

Routledge is an imprint of the Taylor & Francis Group, an informa business

First issued in paperback 2012

© 2004 Ravi Arvind Palat

Typeset in Baskerville by Wearset Ltd, Boldon, Tyne and Wear

All rights reserved. No part of this book may be reprinted or
reproduced or utilized in any form or by any electronic, mechanical,
or other means, now known or hereafter invented, including
photocopying and recording, or in any information storage or
retrieval system, without permission in writing from the publishers.

British Library Cataloguing in Publication Data
A catalogue record for this book is available from the British Library

Library of Congress Cataloging in Publication Data
Palat, Ravi Arvind.
Capitalist restructuring and the Pacific Rim/Ravi Arvind Palat.
   p. cm. – (RoutledgeCurzon studies in the modern history of Asia;
   19)
Includes bibliographical references and index.
1. Pacific Area – Economic conditions. 2. Financial crises – Pacific
Area. 3. Structural adjustment (Economic policy) – Pacific Area. 4.
Pacific Area – Economic integration. 5. United States – Foreign
economic relations – East Asia. 6. East Asia – Foreign economic
relations – United States. I. Title. II. Series.
   HC681.P35 2004
   330.95–dc22

                                                      2003016720

978-0-415-13074-5 (hb)
978-0-415-65371-8 (pb)

In memory of Amoma

Contents

Illustrations

Figures

Tables

Preface

I was instinctively suspicious of predictions that we were standing on the cusp of a new 'Pacific century' when I first seriously encountered them on joining the Asian Studies Program at the University of Hawaii in 1989. As I started reading and teaching about East and Southeast Asian economies, I found much evidence which seemed to go against the prevalent orthodoxy. But it was the invitation to give a lecture at the Department of Sociology at the University of Auckland in 1992 that irritated a suspicion into a research project. If the financial crisis of 1997–98 proved that my initial suspicions were right even before I completed writing up my findings, the savage intensity of the crisis led to regional initiatives that are obscured by triumphant proclamations of Western economists. These regional initiatives may yet turn Pacific-Asia into an economic superpower as the region metamorphoses from a low-cost exporter to the world to an area of higher mass consumption and its several economies are freed from their dependence on US markets.

I was privileged in being able to rehearse my arguments over the years with some extraordinary colleagues and students. Arriving in Honolulu, after just having completed a Ph.D. dissertation on the historical sociology of the Indian Ocean, I could ask for no better guides in helping me understand the political economy of East Asia than Hagen Koo and Alvin So. Over the years, they have generously read and commented on various pieces I have done on East and Southeast Asia including earlier drafts of this book, as has Mimi Sharma. Some of the ideas that have eventually worked their way here were first presented at the Political Economy Group at Hawaii, and I especially thank Harry Friedman, Benedict Kerkvliet, Peter Manicas, and Bob Stauffer. And above all at Hawaii, my greatest debt is to Cristina Bacchilega for her encouragement, the warmth of her friendship, and for the fun we have shared for over twenty years.

I can imagine no more collegial a place than the Department of Sociology at the University of Auckland when I arrived there in July 1993. Barry Smart first suggested I write this book and earlier versions have benefitted from discussions with David Bedggood, Charles Crothers, Cluny Macpherson, Tracey McIntosh, Kit Malalgoda, Nick Perry, and Ivanica

Vodanovich. Tracey Jones initiated me into Kiwiana and has been a very dear and caring friend for many years.

Over twenty years of conversations, arguments, and friendship with Giovanni Arrighi, Terence Hopkins, Caglar Keyder, Mark Selden, Beverly Silver, Faruk Tabak, and Immanuel Wallerstein have provided the basic framework for this book. Giovanni, Beverly, Caglar, and Fred Deyo read parts of the book, while Faruk read all of it – and some parts several times over! He constantly pushed me to go further than I had intended but he is well compensated by the pleasure he derived from me being forced to cut the length of this book by almost a third of its original size!

Among others, Mark Berger, Kyung-sup Chang, Vedi Hadiz, William Hayes, Kevin Hewison, Su-Hoon Lee, Philip McMichael, T. J. Pempel, and Lily Rahim have either shared their expertise with me or provided me with unpublished copies of their work. In 1995, Bruce Koppel arranged a small grant for me at the East-West Center to do some research for this book and work at the University of Hawaii Library. In the summer of 2001, Alvin So kindly arranged for me to spend five weeks at the Hong Kong University of Science and Technology. A research semester grant in the Fall of 2002 by the Harpur College dean provided relief from teaching to complete this manuscript. The final revisions on the first draft were completed in Istanbul, where Biray Kirli was a most generous host. But to Biray, I owe much more than that: when I came back to Binghamton in January 2001, she was the first new friend I made there and her loving comradeship lifted my spirits even in a Binghamton winter! She has been a constant source of warm encouragement and of emotional support.

My brother and sister-in-law, Raghu and Pushpa Palat and my nieces, Divya and Nikhila, in Bombay were always welcoming and provided a warm respite whenever I returned to India. I always enjoyed going back to the Nilgiri Hills where I had spent much of my youth. It was also where my grandmother lived and I deeply regret that she died just as I was putting the final touches on this book. I dedicate this book to her memory.

Acknowledgments

The authors and publishers would like to thank the following for granting permission to reproduce material in this work:

Center for Southeast Asian Studies, Kyoto University for use of Kunio Yoshihara, *Japanese Investment in Southeast Asia*, 1978, tables 2.3 and 2.4 (Tables 4.2a, 4.2b).

Cornell University Press for use of Stephen Haggard and Tun-jen Cheng, 'State and Foreign Capital in the East Asian NICs,' in *The Political Economy of the New Asian Industrialism* edited by Frederic C. Deyo, 1987, table 8 (Table 3.5).

Greenwood Press for use of Giovanni Arrighi, Satoshi Ikeda, and Alex Irwan, 'The Rise of East Asia: One Miracle or Many?' in *Pacific-Asia and the Future of the World-System* edited by Ravi Arvind Palat, 1993, table 3.3 (Table 3.1).

Institute of International Finance for use of 'External Financing for the Most Afflicted Asian Economies,' in *Capital Flows to Emerging Market Economies*, 1998 (Table 5.5).

Oxford University Press for use of Ann Markusen, Scott Campbell, Peter Hall, and Sabrina Dietrich, *The Rise of the Gunbelt: The Military Remapping of Industrial America*, 1991 (Table 1.1).

Oxford University Press for use of Alice Amsden, *Asia's Next Giant: South Korea and Late Industrialization*, 1989, table 5.1 (Table 3.2).

Pion, London for use of Manuel Castells, Lee Goh, and R. Y.-W. Kwok, *The Shek Kip Mai Syndrome: Economic Development and Public Housing in Hong Kong and Singapore*, 1990, p. 66, table 3.5 (Table 3.4).

Princeton University Press for use of Robert Wade, *Governing the Market: Economic Theory and the Role of Government in East Asian Industrialization*, 1990, table 3.6 (Table 3.3).

Routledge for use of Makato Itoh, 'The Japanese Model of "Post-Fordism,"' in M. Storper and Alan J. Scott, *Pathways to Industrialization and Regional Development*, 1992, table 5.3 (Table 2.1).

Every effort has been made to contact copyright holders for their permission to reprint material in this book. The publishers would be grateful to hear from any copyright holder who is not here acknowledged and will undertake to rectify any errors or omissions in future editions of this book.

Acknowledgments

The authors and publishers would like to thank the following for granting permission to reproduce material in this book:

Introduction

Dragons, tigers, and other myths of our time

Nothing illustrates the pervasiveness of a de-historicized economic rationality more than the debate over the causes of, and solutions to, the precipitous drop in East and Southeast Asian currency values in 1997 and the ensuing meltdown of some of the fastest growing economies in history. Led by Japan, economies along Asia's Pacific coasts had posted such spectacular growth rates that even the World Bank had been compelled to acknowledge the significance of macroeconomic planning and the centrality of industrial policy in the economic success of the 'East Asian model of growth' (World Bank, 1993: 5–6, 8–10, 83–4).[1] Just as the rapid growth of economies on Asia's Pacific perimeters had led to hagiographic evaluations of their performance, their headlong descent in 1997–98 prompted an equally sharp turnabout in assessments of their patterns of growth. Their overnight transformation from nimble tigers to debt-laden, lumbering elephants was attributed to 'crony capitalism': code for cozy arrangements between governments and entrepreneurs that led to ready infusions of cash to those with the right political connections while insulating them from shareholder scrutiny, the need to disclose embarrassing financial information, or exposure to serious foreign competition in their domestic markets.

The well-publicized venality of former Indonesian President Suharto's children and associates and the large, illegal payoffs made to former South Korean presidents Chun Doo Hwan and Roh Tae Woo by large industrial conglomerates gave this diagnosis an aura of plausibility and attracted support from prominent dissidents in each of the ailing economies. However, it ignored that close coordination between political and economic elites and the violation of Western practices of prudential lending were precisely the wellsprings for the remarkable performance of Japanese and South Korean enterprises over the previous quarter century. If they had merely relied on retained corporate earnings and equity markets for investment funds, it is hardly conceivable that they could have emerged as formidable competitors in the most exacting markets in so short a time (Wade and Veneroso, 1998a). From this perspective, the remarkable growth of small, resource-poor economies in East and

Southeast Asia had been due precisely to their violation of the market principles now being thrust on them by the International Monetary Fund (IMF) as a condition for emergency cash infusions and loan guarantees.

By focusing on the immediate triggers of the meltdown of 1997–98, this debate about the 'Asian model' of growth ignores the underlying causes of the economic collapse. While mainstream orthodoxy conveniently ignored the importance of national economic planning and close coordination between government and business elites for rapid economic growth in the East and Southeast Asian 'miracles,' theorists of the developmental state conveniently ignored that national economic planning had been rendered anachronistic by high-speed growth that had transformed production and procurement networks and social topographies all along Asia's Pacific coasts. After all, the crisis spread like bush-fire from Thailand across the region in large part because of the integrated character of regional production. By emphasizing the particular attributes of discrete states, the more empirically-grounded studies of national economy-making not only tend to routinely underplay the similarities shared by states located at comparable coordinates in the global hierarchy of wealth but also obscure the impact of wider global processes of change on individual states. By routinely extrapolating their findings on one economy to neighboring economies, they also tend to homogenize different constellations of class accommodations, patterns of resistance, and historical legacies.

Though economies in the region were marked by different patterns of socio-political relations and occupied different coordinates in the world hierarchy of wealth, the practice of treating each economy as a self-contained isolate had two further adverse consequences. First, the tendency to prescribe the same policies for each economy, as the IMF did in 1997–98 without regard to their internal constitutions, could have very different consequences, as we see in Chapter 6. Second, the fragmentation of production processes and their widespread dispersal across the region resulted in the adverse impacts of business failures in some locations cascading onto businesses in other locations. Trans-border integration of production operations implied that economies could not be easily insulated from the impact of policies implemented in neighboring economies: closure of insolvent enterprises in one economy led to shortages of key inputs in other economies.

Taking our cue from Bruce Cumings (1987: 46) who argued that 'a country-by-country approach' misses 'through a fallacy of disaggregation the fundamental unity and integrity of the regional effort,' we shall analyze economic growth along the Pacific coasts of Asia as a singular process rather than as multiple, parallel processes. Complementing Cumings' analysis of product cycles and power relations in the structuring of a regional economic formation, Giovanni Arrighi, Satoshi Ikeda, and Alex Irwan (1993) had highlighted the spatial expansion of Japanese production and procurement networks. The integration of select Southeast and East Asian economies into Japan-centered hierarchical subcontracting systems and the transfer of manufacturing operations to neighboring jurisdictions on the Pacific coasts of Asia had led to the formation of a regional economic structure. This enabled them not only to withstand the debt crisis of the early 1980s unlike most other low and middle-income economies, but also to register rates of growth that were the envy of the world. Building on these insights, we will argue that if the close coordination of the transborder expansion of corporate networks by elite economic agencies led to regional economic integration, it also simultaneously undermined the national foundations of accumulation and eroded the social coalitions of the developmental state. The subsequent unbridled expansion of production led to the meltdown of these 'miracle' economies in 1997. Paradoxically, even though the crisis gave Western governments and the IMF the leverage to weaken active state intervention, corporate bankruptcies and massive layoffs strengthened states in the region by weakening capital and organized labor. In this context, while the reintegration of China into the world market undermined patterns of intra-regional linkages by exerting a downward push on wages, Chinese participation in regional institutional arrangements provided a counterweight to Japan. Resentful of the draconian prescriptions imposed by the IMF, and with Chinese involvement in regional arrangements assuaging deep-seated suspicions about the 'land of the rising sun,' governments began to negotiate regional arrangements whereas previously economic integration had been largely driven by the transborder expansion of corporate networks. The coincidence of the emergence of an institutional framework for regional integration with the collapse of the US stock market bubble and the creation of the euro as a potential alternative to the dollar as world money offers the prospect of greater intra-regional flows of goods and investments, freeing economies in the region from their dependence on the United States. In short, if the transborder expansion of Japanese corporate networks was responsible for structuring a regional economy, it is the reintegration of China that will consolidate it.

We begin by tracing the origins of the extraordinary dynamism of several economies along Asia's Pacific seaboard to the reconfiguration of geopolitical alignments after the end of the Second World War. The reconstitution of the world market under US auspices, based on state-centered systems of regulation, revolved around military Keynesianism and the transnational expansion of vertically-integrated American enterprises, impacted differently on Western Europe and East Asia as we shall see in Chapter 1. While the United States pursued policies designed to foster regional integration in Western Europe, it established bilateral relations with its client states in East Asia and opened its markets to their products without requiring reciprocal access for US products to their domestic markets. Under the compulsions of the wars in Korea and

Vietnam, the US also channeled large doses of military and economic aid to its client states in Asia.

The strategic political and military arrangements of US hegemony also conditioned postwar rehabilitation and reconstruction of its client states along Asia's 'Pacific Rim.' Japanese defeat in the Second World War had fundamentally ruptured patterns of state–society relations all across the region. While the emerging geopolitical equations of the Cold War conferred considerable autonomy on the state apparatuses, as we see in Chapter 2, the new regimes were under immense pressure to transform the basis of their rule from coercion to consent. Massive US military procurements and large infusions of American aid led state machineries in Japan, South Korea, and Taiwan to decisively shape the direction of industrial production through the allocation of subsidized capital, credit guarantees, and favorable – even negative – interest rates to targeted firms and industries.

Though governing elites in Singapore and Hong Kong did not have access to large dollops of US aid, the loss of their hinterlands and the compulsion to transform their economies from entrepôts to off-shore manufacturing platforms also placed their governments under pressure to foster economic growth. Hence, Chapter 3 traces patterns of state intervention and structures of industrial organization in Japan and the Four Dragons (Hong Kong, Singapore, South Korea, and Taiwan) as their regimes sought to legitimize their rule by pursuing state-directed strategies of industrialization based on cheap labor and relatively unfettered access to high-income markets in the core. Despite differences in industrial structures in the several states, what is significant for the purposes of the present discussion is that their industrial structures were relatively independent of one another and their bilateral ties to the United States easily overshadowed all other linkages. Equally importantly, while these states were relatively autonomous from domestic constellations of power and privilege, different configurations of class alliances and resource endowments shaped the development of their industrial structures and modes of labor control. These differences, in turn, were to condition the differential impact of the crisis of 1997–98 on each of these economies.

Precisely because these trajectories – internal configurations of class and power relations, patterns of state intervention and forms of industrial organization, methods of labor control in each of these jurisdictions, and their location within larger political and socio-economic networks – were dynamic processes each of these chapters builds upon and augments the others. Constitutively, since our focus is on the local processing of larger systemic forces within the region, each of these chapters depict integral moments in the formation of an integrated nexus of production, trade, and investment along Asia's Pacific seaboard rather than the narrative of national economy-making in individual countries. Since economies located in this cartographic space did not equally participate in the evolving networks of regional integration, we begin by focusing on Japan and the Four Dragons and then expand our field of vision to other economies as they become integrated within this regional divisioning of labor.[2]

State-centered strategies of industrialization were not displaced even when narrow domestic markets, not only in South Korea and Taiwan but eventually also in other economies along Asia's Pacific coasts, began to constrain possibilities of import-substituting industrialization (ISI). As the saturation of domestic markets in light consumer goods in these locations coincided with rising wages in Japan, it led to their accommodation of declining Japanese labor-intensive light industries, producing largely for markets in the United States and other high-income economies as we shall see in Chapter 4. At the same time, internal political developments in Indonesia and Malaysia – respectively General Suharto's coup in 1965 and the 1969 riots against the Chinese ethnic minority in Malaysia – inclined their governments to facilitate foreign investments just as high rates of growth were pushing up labor costs in Japan and the dragon economies. After the US withdrawal from Vietnam and the consequent loss of revenue from its role as a rest and recreation center for American troops, just as oil price hikes and heightened security concerns led to increased government expenditures, the Thai government also began to court foreign investors.

The transborder expansion of Japanese corporate networks shielded economies along Asia's Pacific coasts from the debt crisis of the 1980s as we see in Chapter 4. While these chapters integrate material rehearsed elsewhere, they provide the backdrop to the central claims of this book: that the financial crisis was merely the surface manifestation of an underlying social crisis and that the expansion of production and procurement networks to China not only unraveled the regional divisioning of labor but also provides an opportunity to reconstruct it on an entirely new basis. In the first instance, high-speed growth rendered national economic planning anachronistic by transforming production and procurement networks and social topographies all along Asia's Pacific coasts. The progressive transnational expansion of Japanese, South Korean, and Taiwanese corporate networks eroded the national foundations of accumulation. The deregulation of capital flows and financial markets in high-income states and the resultant explosive increase in world liquidity emancipated large conglomerates in Northeast Asia from their dependence on state bureaucracies for access to capital at preferential rates. Without the administrative guidance provided by elite economic bureaucracies, the continued emphasis on capturing market share through debt-led patterns of industrial expansion led to rampant overproduction, often at the expense of technological innovation.

Equally significantly, the transborder expansion of corporate techno-structures undermined the social coalitions underpinning the developmental states, as we shall see in Chapter 5. As political changes were gradually being instituted to accommodate these new social forces, a realignment of the yen–dollar exchange-rates negotiated in 1985 at the Plaza Hotel in New York at the insistence of the United States government stimulated a new wave of transborder expansion of corporate networks that was significantly different. On the one hand, it signified the progressive erosion of national foundations of accumulation and on the other hand, the availability of large pools of low-wage labor in China implied that 'runaway' shops were accompanied by a hollowing out of industrial sectors not only in the high-income states but also in the 'Four Dragons.' As manufacturing profits plummeted and capital flowed into financial expansion, it aggravated the problem of overproduction and brought social conflicts in the open. Put differently, as geopolitical equations have changed over the last half-century, and especially after China's shift to market-oriented reforms and the end of the Cold War, economic recovery can only occur after the political order has been reshaped on a world scale. In the Asia-Pacific theater, this can be achieved most plausibly be reconstituting regional linkages and emancipating enterprises from their dependence on US markets – by forging closer intra-regional integration and by increasing consumption in the region. Such a move would divert capital flows away from the United States, which is chronically dependent on such inflows to compensate for its persistent balance of payments deficits. As we see in the Epilogue, resentment against the United States for the harsh measures it imposed on the ailing economies in 1997–98 has gone a long way to transcending regional obstacles toward closer integration and it has led to capital inflows to the United States in 2002 being only one-tenth their level two years earlier.

1   Geopolitical ecology of US hegemony

The Pacific Ocean is now our ocean. It never before was anybody's since the earth was formed. The Chinese of the great Central Kingdom never came down to the sea – they never built any ports, let alone ever set out across the stormy deeps. The British may have held a kind of sway as part of their Rule Britannia. The Japanese, with ferocious industry, pretty nearly held it commercially and made, as we recall, a bid to establish their imperial sun in all its skies, but they were doomed to fail because of the United States. Now the Pacific is America's.

Henry R. Luce, *Life*, February 23, 1953

If the Second World War transformed the Pacific Ocean into an 'American Lake,' not even the most audacious soothsayer would have forecast that economies on the Asian perimeters of the ocean would threaten the economic supremacy of the United States within 50 years.[1] So commanding was the financial, industrial, and military lead established by the United States over the other 'great powers' that Henry Luce's prophesy of an 'American Century' seemed far more plausible than any suggestion of a whittling away of US dominance in the ensuing postwar world order. By 1947, gold reserves of the United States accounted for 70 percent of the world total and – reflecting its role as the arsenal, banker, and breadbasket to the Allied war effort – for the first time US claims on incomes generated abroad substantially exceeded foreign claims on incomes produced in the United States (Arrighi, 1994: 275). Indeed, so impoverished were the other powers that the chief obstacle to a reconstitution of the world market was the virtual monopoly over world liquidity established by the United States. Equally impressive was the concentration and centralization of industrial capacity in the United States. While the United States had twice the share of industrial production of its closest rivals – Britain and Germany – as early as 1900, its dominance became even more pronounced during the Second World War when its GNP rose in real terms from $91 billion in 1939 to $210 billion in 1945. The extent of the concentration and centralization of industrial production in the United States can be gauged from the fact that it possessed 48 percent of the world's industrial capacity in 1948, whereas Britain, at the zenith of its power in 1870, had held a 'mere' 32 percent of the global share (Ikenberry, 1989: 380; Ingham, 1994: 40–1). Finally, the detonation of atomic bombs over Japan provided a vivid demonstration of the technological superiority of US military forces (McCormick, 1989: 45; LaFeber, 1980: 26).

Despite its unprecedented economic and military superiority, US plans for a new world order were repeatedly hamstrung by the sheer enormity of the task of postwar reconstruction, resistance by its key European allies, militant nationalism in the Asian peripheries, and the intransigence of an increasingly conservative Congress. These obstacles not only thwarted dominant visions for a new world order within the US administration, but also threatened the continued social and economic well-being of the United States itself. The eventual resolution of these difficulties by the bipartite division of the world into two competing and relatively impermeable blocs with the onset of the Cold War provided the structural and institutional scaffolding for the emergence and increasing interconnectedness of major nodes of accumulation along the Asian and North American seaboards of the Pacific.

Simply put, the rhetorical division of the world into two zones – one 'free' and the other 'unfree' – served to overcome the objections of isolationist 'America-firsters' and cajoled them into sanctioning the reconstruction of those parts of the world deemed to be 'free.' The reconstruction of a world market under American auspices through military Keynesianism, increased aid to friendly powers, and the expansion of the free enterprise system was a three-fold process chronicled in this chapter. If it was the inability of the British government to spearhead Western intervention in the Greek Civil War in 1947 that breached the walls of Congressional resistance to greater overseas involvement, the first section of this chapter demonstrates that it was the Korean War which opened the floodgates for the prodigious outflow of American military expenditures and economic aid and finally resolved the world liquidity crisis. By placing a large expanse of the world outside the pale of American responsibility, the Cold War legitimated military Keynesianism – the unprecedented garrisoning of large numbers of American troops in a network of bases circling the globe – and primed the world economic pump. The second section of this chapter traces the impact of military Keynesianism on the reconstruction of the world market under US auspices in Western Europe, in East Asia, and in the United States itself.

Korean War, military Keynesianism, and the new world order

Early in the Second World War, recognizing the massive tilt of economic and military power to the United States, President Franklin Roosevelt had envisioned the new world order as the New Deal writ large: 'that only big, benign, and professional government could assure people order, security, and justice.... Just as the New Deal brought "social security" to America, so "one world" would bring political security to the entire world' (Schurmann, 1974: 40–2). This eschatological vision entailed two policy prescriptions: the creation of a multilateral free trade system and an expansion of US government spending to aid the poorer countries (including the USSR), just as social welfare expenditures had helped revive the American economy and dampen revolutionary enthusiasms in the 1930s (Schurmann, 1974: 67). Economic assistance to the peoples of Asia and Africa would not only detach them from their orbits around European metropolitan states, but also secure supplies of strategic raw materials, particularly when the increased scale of US industrial production had steadily depleted conveniently located sources. Though the business community was opposed to increased government expenditures, there was unanimity among US policy makers on the importance of a multilateral free trade system. The wartime expansion in industrial capacity had created widespread anxieties that large-scale unemployment would return in the postwar period with the projected phaseout of military-related expenditures. A multilateral free trade system was expected to generate export surpluses that would avert the need to reorganize certain sectors overbuilt during the war (for example, machine tools) and thereby render high levels of government expenditure unnecessary to prevent the return of Depression-era rates of unemployment (Block, 1977: 33–4; Bunker and O'Hearn, 1993: 87–90). Finally, the development of industrial production, communications, and weaponry – the 'technology of power,' to employ Michael Mann's (1986) useful expression – had so eroded the geostrategic insularity of the United States that a return to a position of splendid isolation was virtually unthinkable, even if large isolationist constituencies existed both in the country and in Congress (Arrighi, 1994: 276; Goldstein and Rapkin, 1991).

However, the unprecedented concentration and centralization of productive capacity and effective demand in the United States was an obstacle to the reconstitution of the world market on the basis of multilateral free trade because other core states simply did not have the wherewithal to purchase the industrial goods and farm products they needed from the new hegemonic power. The liquidation of overseas assets, the accumulation of foreign debts, and the high costs of preserving their colonial empires had so disrupted prewar patterns of trade and monetary flows that European core states could no longer finance balance of payments deficits with the United States from surpluses with their colonies or from services such as shipping and insurance as they had done since 1914. As the small size of their domestic markets discouraged technological innovations and rendered their products increasingly uncompetitive against US goods, European industrialists were against a multilateral free trade order.

So too were the strong labor movements, given their aim of full employ-ment. Far from uniting America and its allies in Western Europe, free trade was the issue that divided them (Block, 1977: 60–1, 79–80; Calleo and Rowland, 1973: 39–43; van der Wee, 1986: 43).

The very weakness of European allies, however, made it difficult for them to either resist or meet US demands for free trade and fully con-vertible currencies, as illustrated by the US loan of $3.75 billion to Britain in 1946. The condition attached to this loan, that the pound be made convertible by 1947, reversed the respectable economic performance of Britain since the war – with exports in 1946 being 11 percent higher and imports 28 percent lower than prewar levels – as traders in a dollar-starved Europe hoarded pounds to convert them to dollars (Gardner, 1980; McCormick, 1989: 55–6; Calleo and Rowland, 1973: 40–1; Block, 1977: 55–73, 84–5; Ikenberry, 1989: 384; van der Wee, 1986: 39–40, 434–5).

Even as the depreciation of the pound revealed that the insolvency of its European partners made the vision of world-wide free trade an impossi-bility, a fiscally conservative Republican controlled Congress rendered a redistribution of world liquidity through massive government-sponsored programs to stimulate growth equally impracticable. Though Congress encouraged private foreign investment through a variety of schemes, since exchange controls by foreign governments discouraged such investments, the trickle of private US foreign investments proved wholly inadequate to the task of redistributing world liquidity and the lack of effective demand in Europe constrained the further expansion of US capital (Arrighi, 1994: 295; see also Block, 1977: 114).

Reconstruction in Asia faced obstacles of a different order and magni-tude. The Soviet preoccupation with their western frontiers and with the task of coping with the brutal human and material destruction they had faced at home led them to accept American dominance in the Pacific except in Korea, where the Soviets in fact arrived earlier than the Ameri-cans (Cumings, 1981: 120–221, 384–6). Despite the comparatively free hand the United States had, the relative backwardness of Asian states bor-dering the Pacific meant that the task of postwar reconstruction was in an entirely different category from the case of Western Europe.

The resumption of the Chinese Civil War also created new security con-cerns in the area – whereas reconstruction in Western Europe could be expected to create a rough parity between Britain, France, and West Germany, a revived Japan had no obvious counterweight in East Asia except China (McCormick, 1989: 57). And the record of Japan did not inspire great confidence that it would play the role of a loyal regional *gen-darme*. Consequently, US policy initially hinged not on the reconstruction of Japan but on dismantling its centralized industrial structure and foster-ing the growth of several competing industrial centers in Indonesia, the Philippines, Korea, and China, to be financed through war reparations.

This position was clearly articulated in a 1946 *Report on Japanese Reparations to the President of the United States*:

> The overall aim should be to raise and to even up the level of industrialization [in East Asia]. This aim can be served by considered allocation, to different countries, of industrial equipment exacted from Japan for reparations. Reconstruction is an urgent need of all the countries against which Japan committed aggression. Reconstruction is also needed in Japan. In the overall comparison of needs, Japan should have last priority.
>
> (quoted in Calleo and Rowland, 1973: 198; see also Itoh, 1990: 141, 245)

However, without an extensive program of economic aid that the 'meat-axe' 80th Congress was unlikely to enact, any prospect of the densely populated and impoverished states in Asia providing a large market for US manufactures was extremely remote, especially when a wave of anticolonial insurgencies in Southeast Asia (Indonesia, Malaya, Vietnam) and socialist revolution in China led to continued political instability.

When hopes for remaking the world in America's image foundered on the shoals of these circumstances, the growing confrontation between the United States and the Soviet Union provided a means to force the impasse in which US policy makers had been trapped. The indication by the British government in February 1947 that it was no longer able to bear the burden of intervention in the Greek Civil War provided an opportune moment for President Harry Truman to follow Arthur Vandenberg's advice and 'scare the hell out of the American people' by raising the prospect of a global conflict between 'freedom' and Soviet 'totalitarianism.' A Congress that had balked at aiding Clement Attlee's 'socialist welfare state' responded more positively to the task of rebuilding Western Europe and Japan as bulwarks of the 'free world' in the face of an encroaching communist menace.

Though the Marshall Plan inaugurated the reconstruction of Western Europe in America's image, it proved inadequate to the task both because of conservative opposition to American internationalism in Congress, and continued balance of payments difficulties and national parochialisms within the Organization for European Economic Cooperation. The Plan was innovative not because of its size – $17 billion over four years was hardly revolutionary when over the previous two years the US had already funneled almost $9 billion to Europe – but because it sought to change political and economic conditions in Europe by integrating Germany within a unified European market viable enough to reap economies of scale and remain competitive in the world market. Since the Plan was administered by a US agency – the Economic Cooperation Administration, which had veto powers over measures it deemed contrary to the

Plan's aims – considerable pressure was applied on social democratic governments to reduce debts, balance budgets, freeze wages and to commit themselves to a reduction in tariffs on intra-European trade (McCormick, 1989: 74–9; van der Wee, 1986: 353–5).

Despite its success in undermining the Left and controlling inflation in Europe, it was soon abundantly clear that the task of rebuilding Western European economies within the four-year term of the Plan was unrealistic. These anxieties were heightened by the American recession of 1948–49, when a small drop in the US GNP wiped out more than half the dollar exports of some West European states. This led Truman to caution, in his 1949 mid-year economic report, that 'If a severe shrinkage in the flow of dollars abroad occurred, it would not only reduce our exports now, but would also force other countries to try to save dollars by making discriminatory trading arrangements that would adversely affect the long run future of our foreign trade' (quoted in Borden, 1984: 30, 35).[2] Yet, Congressional suspicion toward the Plan made its extension beyond the original four-year period ending in 1952 equally unrealistic and the United States was once again faced with the prospects of declining exports, falling employment, and isolation from Europe (Block, 1977: 82–92; Arrighi, 1994: 296–7).

Mounting tensions with the Soviet Union and the gathering strength of the Chinese Communist Party (CCP) also led to staggering changes in US Occupation policies in Japan. Despite the USSR – for the sake of its own geopolitical interests – urging Mao Zedong and the CCP to reconcile with the Guomingdang (GMD), the resumption of full-scale war between the two contending parties in 1946 made it increasingly evident that, regardless of the outcome, no Chinese regime could or would play the role of an American surrogate in the 'Far East.' In the ensuing reassessment of US policy, the reconstruction of Japan catapulted to the top of the American agenda by late 1947.

This reversal of earlier Occupation plans was operationally embodied in the Dodge Plan, named after the American banker who formulated the blueprint, instituted in late 1948 and early 1949. It aimed at making Japanese light industrial products competitive on the world market by severely disciplining labor and restricting domestic demand. To achieve these ends, several measures were enacted to repress labor unions and reduce wages, control prices, allocate supplies to select exporters in preference to those producing for the domestic market, and to balance the budget by laying off a quarter-million government employees and severely curtailing social services (Borden, 1984: 163). In other words, whereas the European recovery program was financed both by American taxpayers and European workers, the Dodge Plan sought to reconstruct the Japanese economy largely by decreasing labor's share of the national income. Simultaneously, to speed up the process of economic recovery, the Occupation forces prematurely aborted the program of monopoly dissolution even though only 19 of the 325 *zaibatsu* (Japanese industrial conglomerates) targeted for dissolution had been broken up. To increase the competitiveness of Japanese exports, the exchange-rate was set at ¥360 to the dollar in April 1949 despite the US Treasury's recommendation of a rate closer to ¥250. Finally, in mid-May 1949, the US Occupation authorities unilaterally terminated the program to dismantle Japanese industries and transfer them to those Asian states that had been the victims of Japanese aggression as war reparations. However, in conditions of a world-wide liquidity shortage and protective tariffs, the dampening of domestic demand by the austerity measures imposed by the Dodge Plan led to a worsening of Japan's trade deficit with the United States by late 1949 and early 1950. Unemployment in April 1950 was double the 1948 mark. To compound matters, even as the strategic importance of Japan grew during the late 1940s, a Congress already troubled by the $17 billion committed to European reconstruction was being increasingly impatient with the slow pace of recovery in Japan and pressured the administration to make the occupation pay for itself (Schonberger, 1982: 46–51; Schonberger, 1989: 81, 176–8, 202–25; Borden, 1984: 92–102, 124–8; McCormick, 1989: 88–90; Yonekura, 1993: 207).

The solution to the continuing liquidity crisis was ultimately provided by a massive program of military rearmament to which Secretary of State Acheson and the head of his Policy Planning Staff, Paul Nitze, gave the most characteristic and distinguished expression:

> The new line of policy they [Acheson and Nitze] proposed – massive U.S. and European rearmament – provided a brilliant solution to the major problems of U.S. economic policy. Domestic rearmament would provide a new means to sustain demand so that the economy would no longer be dependent on maintaining an export surplus. Military aid to Europe would provide a means to continue providing aid to Europe after the expiration of the Marshall Plan. And close integration of European and American military forces would provide a means to prevent Europe as an economic region from closing itself off from the United States.
>
> (Block, 1977: 103–4)

The invasion of South Korea by North Korean forces in 1950, combined with the Soviet explosion of the atomic bomb and the 'loss' of China in 1949 provided an opportune moment for the Truman Administration to get authorization from a fiscally conservative Congress to solve the world liquidity crisis. Expenditures on national security programs rose dramatically from $13 billion in 1950 to $50.4 billion in 1953 and direct military expenditures in the US balance of payments skyrocketed from $570 million to $2.6 billion between 1949 and 1953 (McCormick, 1989: 94; Block, 1977: 115). In addition to expenditures incurred by the stationing of military personnel in a world-wide network of bases, US military aid was provided to NATO members and other client states including support for French and British efforts to combat nationalist/communist insurgencies in Indo-China and Malaya (Borden, 1984: 27, 121–3).[3] The channeling of dollars through military Keynesianism so stimulated economic growth in Europe that by 1951 the output of French industry was almost twice its prewar levels, while in West Germany a year later production was almost one-and-a-half times the prewar level (Wilkins, 1974: 310–11).

The economic boom sparked by the Korean War created a large demand for raw materials in the United States, leading to an escalation of imports from European dependencies and drove the prices of some commodities up by as much as 150 percent. The resulting increase in the triangular trade – US payments for raw materials to peripheral states led to an increase in their purchases from metropolitan states in Europe and thereby enabled the latter to balance deficits in their dollar trade – and the flood of military expenditures ensured the redistribution of world liquidity essential for the expansion of structures of capital accumulation (Borden, 1984: 50–1, 117). However, as the US moved simultaneously to prevent its European allies, during the term of the Marshall Plan, from drawing funds from the new international financial institutions set up at Bretton Woods – the International Monetary Fund (IMF) and the World Bank – the net effect was to subject international flows of liquidity to American control and increase the dependence of Western European states on the US (Block, 1977: 108–15; van der Wee, 1986: 437). Thus was initiated a period of 23 years, between the start of the Korean War and the Paris Peace Accords of 1973 which signaled the end of America's war with Asia, that has been termed the 'most sustained and profitable period in the history of world capitalism' (McCormick, 1989: 99).

Acheson was clearly not exaggerating when he stated in 1954 that 'Korea came along and saved us.' It is difficult to imagine how the United States would have resolved the problem of redistributing world liquidity without the massive military expenditures made possible by the Korean War. But the 'us' – as Bruce Cumings (1987: 63) has underscored – also included Japan, South Korea, and Taiwan since it is equally difficult to imagine the reconstruction of these states without the prodigious outflows of aid from, and military expenditures by, the United States. Put differently, despite the Atlantic orientation of most influential policy makers, events in the Pacific once again provided the context for a reintegration of the world market under US auspices, much as the bombing of Pearl Harbor had shattered America's geostrategic insularity. Yet the world market that emerged was very different from the idealistic vision of Roosevelt. Whereas his 'one worldism' had encompassed the Soviet Union among the poorer states to be incorporated into a global New Deal, the 'free worldism' of the Truman doctrine made containment of the Soviet Union the principal organizing basis of US hegemony (Calleo and Rowland, 1973: 42–3; Schurmann, 1974: 68–71; Arrighi, 1994: 67–8).

The Korean War legitimated the stationing of large garrisons in a network of military bases across the world: never before in history had a state permanently maintained garrisons in other sovereign states in peacetime. Military alliance and the expansion of US corporate networks across the Atlantic tethered West Germany to the rest of Western Europe and the United States. Increased military expenditures – as we shall see in the next section – transformed the geography of manufacture in the United States. And US military procurements jump-started economic reconstruction in Japan and subsequently, during America's Indochina War, elsewhere along Asia's Pacific Rim.

Just as the Korean War provided the ideological legitimation for military Keynesianism, militant nationalism in Asia – most notably in Malaya and in Indochina – transformed US support for anti-colonial movements to US opposition to such movements. Instead of seeking access to strategic raw materials in Asia and Africa through support for nationalist movements, the US sought to transform its relations with its European allies. At the same time, increased emphasis on defense production transformed the topography of manufacturing in the United States itself, as we see in the next section.

Free enterprise system and the changing socio-spatial dynamics of production

The two central policy derivatives of Roosevelt's vision of the new world order – a multilateral free trade system and massive doses of aid to the poorer countries to provide political security – were substantially transformed in the Cold War world order. In this debased but more workable political dispensation, the difficulties of reconstructing West European economies and the elevation of containing the Soviet Union as the main goal of US policy led to a substitution of the principle of universal free trade by a series of bilateral and commodity-specific regional and multilateral trading arrangements. This was symbolized by the substitution of the General Agreement on Tariffs and Trade (GATT) for the more ambitious International Trade Organization (ITO). Whereas the ITO had embodied the ideal of a suprastatal authority to promote a global, market-determined free trade system, GATT was a negotiating forum between member-states, without the power to enforce bilateral or multilateral agreements. Stated differently, GATT and the Bretton Woods twins, the World Bank and the IMF, gave governments the power to dictate the pace and direction of trade liberalization. This institutional framework enabled governments to accommodate their diverse constituencies within a unified trading system by permitting them to retain controls over capital movements and to institute different arrangements for the distribution of income between capital and labor within their jurisdictions (Arrighi, 1994: 67–8; Bienefeld, 1989: 20).

The massive outflows of military aid even shored up protectionist sentiments within the United States as it reduced dependence on an export
surplus to maintain domestic economic expansion and the US consequently opposed across-the-board tariff reductions in international trade
negotiations during much of the 1950s. A tripling of defense spending not
only revived those sectors of the economy that had fallen into the doldrums after the war (for example, machine tools, aircraft production), but
also provided a cushion against the adverse effects of downturns in the
business cycle and fluctuations in exports. As a substitute for an expanded
government role in the economy through public sector projects and
redistributive welfare programs, military spending did not threaten to dis-
place private capital or raise the cost of labor. Farming out defense contracts to private firms rather than expanding government-owned and
operated arsenals, aircraft factories, and submarine yards cloaked the
surge in public expenditure with impeccable free enterprise credentials.
Military Keynesianism was, in effect, the conservative counterpart to the
social welfare programs proposed by the more universalistic vision of
Roosevelt (Block, 1977: 34–5, 107, 119; McCormick, 1989: 94–7; Markusen
et al., 1991: 31, 96).

The abandonment of the ideal of universal free trade for a system of
state-centered regulation was accompanied by a diminution in American
insistence on the dismantling of the preferential access European core
states, particularly Britain, enjoyed to markets in their colonies or former
colonies (Block, 1977: 84, 131–2; van der Wee, 1986: 349). This was imperative since European states could ill afford to purchase US goods unless
they could obtain raw materials from non-Dollar Areas. Rather than
seeking to compete with European producers in the impoverished
markets of Africa and Asia, the US promoted a policy of free enterprise,
designed to permit US corporations to boost their competitive positions
by exploiting the wage and cost differentials between and among different
segments of the world market for labor and commodities by creating 'a
complex *organizational* network of productive and service activities spanning *across* national boundaries' (Arrighi, 1982: 76, emphases in the original; Arrighi, 1990). The resulting transnational expansion of US
enterprises also served to undermine the power of organized labor at
home, especially after the end of the Korean War boom (Davis, 1986). In
fact, by expanding the organizational web of US corporations across the
Atlantic, it was almost 'as if the United States, spurning Europe's colonies
had decided to annex the mother countries [*sic*] instead' (Calleo and
Rowland, 1973: 46).

Indeed, state-centered systems of regulation and the policy of free
enterprise soon corroded systems of imperial preference, particularly the
Sterling Area. The requirement that Britain maintain free access to its
capital markets as a reciprocal condition for privileged access to Commonwealth markets led to the outflow of capital sorely needed at home and

hampered postwar reconstruction in Britain. The responsibility to maintain security for its colonies and former colonies through a far-flung
network of military outposts represented an additional drain on the
British exchequer. The existence of large overseas markets also discouraged technical innovation and rendered British industry increasingly
uncompetitive in comparison with other European core states. Most
importantly, as industrialization was virtually synonymous with 'development' in the economic discourse of the time, state-centered systems of
regulation encouraged the pursuit of multiple, parallel strategies of industrialization which progressively closed large areas of the Commonwealth
to British products as newly decolonized states erected tariff barriers to
protect their infant industries.

A reorientation of US strategies from universal multilateral free trade
to the defense of a 'free world' had differential impacts on Western
Europe and along the Pacific perimeters of Asia due to differences in
their patterns of socio-historical evolution. Reflecting these differences, as
we see below, different policy tools were devised for dealing with each
area: promoting the *regional integration* of state structures in Western
Europe and the *bilateral linkage* of client states in Asia to the US (Arrighi,
1994: 340). Finally, policy choices made in the context of the Cold War –
particularly the 'militarization of manufacture,' or the rise of a 'military-
industrial complex' – not only reconfigured the social and spatial dynamics of industrial production within the United States as manufacturing
operations were spatially dispersed, but they also led to the development
of new forms of production networks, or rather the revival of old forms in
a new guise. When we are constantly told that small batch production and
long-term affiliative relationships with subcontractors are the *differentia
specifica* of postwar Japanese manufacturing – or 'Toyotism,' as it has often
been called to distinguish it from the 'Fordism' said to be characteristic of
US production – it is instructive to recall that precisely these organizational forms were pioneered independently under the impetus of military Keynesianism in the United States: new forms of organization are
born from the womb of the old, to paraphrase Marx.

As we will see below sequentially, the remaking of Western Europe in
the American image after the Second World War was accompanied by a
remapping of the geography of manufacture within the United States.
While the revival of demand for consumer durables revitalized industry in
its traditional homes in the midwestern and northeastern states, military
Keynesianism in the political calculus of the Cold War led to the construction of an entirely different organizational network in the western states.
Thus, when competition for low-waged sites – especially in Asia – corroded
the industrial foundations of the old heartland from the 1970s, California
and other 'sunbelt' states continued to post high rates of growth leading
to popular imaginaries of an impending 'Pacific century.' Finally, across
that ocean, along Asia's eastern coasts, widespread poverty and the

absence of stable markets precluded an expansion of US Foreign Direct Investment (FDI) parallel to the spread of US corporate networks across the Atlantic. Instead, economic reconstruction and growth were based on large doses of US aid and procurements.

'Second American invasion' and postwar reconstruction in Western Europe

The retreat from the expansive universalism of free trade to the shoddier defense of the 'free world' was accompanied by increased US support for the regional integration of West European economies – manifested most notably by the US insistence that subsidiaries of American corporations in Europe be treated as 'European' firms leading, in turn, to a steady erosion of tariffs on intra-European trade (Arrighi, 1994: 306). Regional economic integration within Western Europe was viewed as a device to tether these states, particularly West Germany, permanently to the United States in the context of the growing bipolar rivalry between the two superpowers, as well as a means to create liquidity to finance West European trade with the Dollar and Sterling Areas. Institutionally, the creation of a US-sponsored European Payments Union (EPU) in 1952 was designed to increase intra-European trade through the progressive reduction of tariffs between member-states and, as the development of a common market was permissible under GATT regulations, by discrimination against goods from outside the trading area during postwar reconstruction. However, as closer regional integration could potentially close off Western Europe to US goods in the long run, the United States repeatedly scuttled attempts in the 1950s to create a pan-European region in favor of a smaller nucleus of the six member states – France, West Germany, Italy and the Benelux countries – who would eventually sign the Treaty of Rome in 1957, creating the European Common Market (Block, 1977: 99–103, 106–8, 121–9).

Most importantly, once the Marshall Plan and US military aid had raised levels of effective demand in Western Europe, regional integration proved conducive to a prodigious transnational expansion of US capital. Though US FDI in Western Europe after the Second World War was initially designed to evade tariff barriers as well as to reduce transport and labor costs, the integration of jurisdictionally-segmented markets was particularly favorable to US corporations. The size, resource endowments, and autocentricity of the US domestic market had led to the internalization of transaction costs within vertically-integrated corporations in the half century following the American Civil War – the creation of 'economies of speed' rather than 'economies of size' in Alfred Chandler's (1977) terminology. They were, hence, endowed with several advantages over the highly specialized and differentiated networks of enterprises that characterized British industry or the horizontal combinations of German business as several scholars have underscored (Chandler, 1977; Chandler, 1990; Arrighi, 1994: 218–20, 239–44, 283–95; Morales, 1994; van der Wee, 1986: 213–25):

> By routinizing the transactions between units, the costs of the transactions were lowered. By linking the administration of producing units with buying and distributing units, costs of information on markets and sources of supply were reduced. Of much greater significance, the internalization of many units permitted the flow of goods from one unit to another to be administratively coordinated. More effective scheduling of flows achieved a more intensive use of facilities and personnel employed in the process of production and distribution and so increased productivity and reduced costs. In addition, administrative coordination provided a more certain cash flow and more rapid repayment for services rendered.
>
> (Chandler, 1977: 7)

The restoration of currency convertibility in Western Europe in 1958 and the formation of a Common Market provided additional stimuli to the transnational expansion of US capital into Europe and US FDI more than doubled between the mid-1950s and the mid-1960s (Dunning, 1988: 91; Chandler, 1990: 158–9, 613).

While US transnational penetration was most extensive in Britain where it has been estimated that subsidiaries of American corporations accounted for 14 percent of all production by 1969, the share of US transplants in the production of machine tools, refrigerators, and washing machines in France, for instance, was about a quarter of total production; of elevators, tires, and tractors about a third; and of safety razors and synthetic rubber over 80 percent by the mid-1960s (Wilkins, 1974: 402–4). Thus, as Robert Gilpin (1975: 11) observes, the 'essence of American direct investment has been the shift of managerial control over substantial sectors of foreign economies to American nationals.'

The transnational expansion of US capital was of course not a novel phenomenon – beginning in the 1850s as they were consolidating their continent-wide integration within the United States, American enterprises were establishing 'branches' in Europe and by 1914 US FDI amounted to 7 percent of the US gross national product (GNP), the same percentage as in 1966. Of course, the extraordinary increase in US GNP in the intervening period meant that US FDI in Europe in the mid-1960s was qualitatively different – accounting for a much larger volume of production than at the outbreak of the First World War. What was particularly new about the second 'American invasion' – Europeans had already characterized the earlier spurt of US investments as an 'invasion' as early as 1902 – were the changes in the conditions in which it occurred. The integration of jurisdictionally-segmented markets with the formation of the Common

Market had facilitated a transfer of the managerial hierarchies and bureaucratic structures pioneered and perfected by American businesses within the United States. This was what Jean-Jacques Servan-Schreiber had in mind when he spoke of an 'American challenge' in 1968 as being 'something quite new and considerably more serious' than the existence of a mere 'technological gap' between the US and Western Europe – 'the extension to Europe of an *organization* that is still a mystery to us' (quoted in Chandler, 1990: 615, emphasis in the original; see also Arrighi, 1994: 241, 304).

If the multi-unit, vertically-integrated structure of American enterprise was a 'mystery' to Servan-Schreiber, it was no mystery at all to European state and corporate bureaucracies. Realizing the decisive competitive advantages that accrue from the replacement of the invisible hand of market forces by the 'visible hand of managerial direction' through the internalization of a whole series of operations within a single organizational frame, European businesses responded to the transnational expansion of US capital by reorganizing their own structures and becoming transnational enterprises themselves (Chandler, 1977: 285–6; Arrighi, 1994: 240, 303; van der Wee, 1986: 217–22). Steps taken toward the integration of European markets created a propitious climate for the replication of the technostructures of US corporations by European firms. For instance, though cars produced in Europe – even by subsidiaries of US automakers – had virtually no interchangeable parts in the early 1950s, the creation of a common market promoted the increasing standardization and interchangeability of parts (Womack *et al.*, 1990: 45–7; Wilkins, 1980: 236–7; Morales, 1994: 66, 88–9). Government assistance in the form of subsidies, tax incentives, lucrative contracts, and even the establishment of state-owned enterprises or the nationalization of nearly insolvent corporations was vital to the restructuring of European industry. While American businesses could finance their transnational expansion through the abundant and reliable cash-flows they already generated in their domestic markets, European firms had to set up a competing network *before* they attained the unit cost reductions through high volume production (Chandler, 1977: 299).

The integration of fragmented markets with the formation of the Common Market and the restructuring of European industry along American organizational lines had an adverse impact on smaller manufacturers. In conditions of market segmentation when production for multiple, differentiated markets had been prohibitively expensive, small, innovative manufacturers had thrived as long production runs were required to reap profits at low volumes. The growth of mass production by large, vertically-integrated multi-unit enterprises made the smaller companies either vulnerable to take-overs, or forced them to join forces to remain competitive. In either case, a cost-squeeze was put on suppliers in the ancillary parts industry as standardization enabled the large corporations to source components from bigger, high-volume manufacturers, or set up their own subsidiaries to fabricate parts (Morales, 1994: 88–95).

By the late 1960s, European firms had substantially completed their restructuring, as indicated by the fact that the percentage of the leading 135 European firms having subsidiaries in more than six countries had risen from 24 in 1950 to 77 in 1970 (Lash and Urry, 1987: 90). The transnational expansion of European firms was accompanied by their internal restructuring along the lines of the multi-unit lines pioneered by American enterprises (van der Wee, 1986: 219–20).

This transformed the landscape of industrial relations and the geography of European manufacturing substantially. The smaller, more labor-intensive, and skilled nature of industrial enterprises in Europe meant that the laborforce had considerable control over the pace and content of their work, and as unions were organized around crafts the labor movement could more adamantly resist the introduction of any technology which would decrease shop-floor control or wages, reduce employment, or cause deskilling. Except for Volkswagen, European manufacturers in the automobile industry, for instance, produced well-crafted, expensive vehicles until the Second World War when civilian automobile production stopped altogether, in contrast to the mass-produced vehicles of US manufacture. The reliance on a highly-skilled workforce, versatile in a wide range of manufacturing operations, also led to the concentration of production in 'industrial districts' – locational clusters of single-unit enterprises engaged in the same line of production so that they could all benefit from localized external economies by drawing on a common repertoire of skills and business connections (Arrighi, 1994: 283–4; Morales, 1994: 91–4; Womack *et al.*, 1990; Wilkins, 1980: 223–33; Lash and Urry, 1987: 47).

The introduction of mass-production technologies by US manufacturers meant that they did not have to rely on the reservoirs of skilled workers in 'industrial districts,' but could construct factory complexes in 'greenfield' sites without a long history of labor struggles. In the case of the West German automobile industry, to take just one example, while production had been concentrated in the northeast and in the Rhine-Main area in the early 1950s, subsequent growth had been disproportionately biased toward the south – especially Bavaria and Baden-Wurtemberg – where Volkswagen, Opel, and Ford installed assembly plants due to the abundant availability of cheap, pliable labor (Lash and Urry, 1987: 147).[4] This pattern held so uniformly over Western Europe and was reflected in the demographic decline registered by the largest conurbations that Scott Lash and John Urry (1987: 101, 131, 147–8) have argued that since *circa* 1952 growth in manufacturing employment was inversely related to the size of a settlement.

Additionally, the Marshall Plan and the Cold War had crippled the Left in most European states through intimidation, corruption, and propaganda, as well as by buying the consent of workers through higher wages. The introduction and rapid expansion of mass production techniques, as

US transplants and state-sponsored European firms radically restructured their production facilities during the 1950s and 1960s following the 'second American invasion,' further marginalized the power of craft unions in Europe.

The power of unions was also diluted by a parallel remaking of metropolitan agriculture as liquidity shortages, decolonization, and peripheral industrialization fractured imperial trading arrangements. Postwar reconstruction in the West European countryside under the auspices of the Marshall Plan once again followed the American model by integrating intensive cropping with stock farming into complex transnational agrofood chains dominated by large conglomerates (Morgan, 1980; Friedmann, 1982; Friedmann and McMichael, 1989; van der Wee, 1986: 110–11, 167–9, 234–5). For the purposes of the present discussion, the most salient aspect of this remaking of the European rural landscape, with the mechanization of agriculture, the introduction of new and high-yielding varieties of crops, and the increasing use of chemical fertilizers, pesticides, and herbicides, was a dramatic increase in productivity and an even more dramatic decline in the numbers employed in agriculture. As overpopulation on land had been a long-standing feature of the European experience, the increased productivity of agriculture relieved chronic rural unemployment and provided a large army of previously non-proletarianized workers for expanding industries.

The largely unskilled labor force was also disproportionately drawn from migrants from the marcher zones of Europe (Eastern Europe, southern Italy, Spain, Portugal, Turkey, and Yugoslavia) who, like the migrants from Eastern and Southern Europe powering the automobile industry in Detroit in the 1920s and 1930s, rarely protested harsh working and living conditions (Castles, 1984; van der Wee, 1986: 160–4; Womack *et al.*, 1990: 47). The resultant shift of control to managements over work processes, job assignments and promotions, recruitment and retention of workers all contributed to higher profit margins and provided manufacturers a competitive weapon to counter the increased power of labor in the United States (Silver, 1997). By the late 1950s, General Motors and Ford, using cheaper European labor, could even import products they made abroad to the US to meet their domestic requirements and by 1957, the numbers of cars imported into the United States exceeded American exports for the first time (Wilkins, 1974: 377; Wilkins, 1980: 238–9).

The reconstruction of the European industrial landscape in the American image not only led to the realization of greater unit cost reductions through high volume production but the installation of continuous flow production processes also led to a pay explosion due to the increased 'workplace bargaining power of labor' (Arrighi and Silver, 1984: 193–5). From the late 1950s, the resultant rise in affluence led to the emergence of a mass market in durable consumer goods (refrigerators, washing machines, and above all, automobiles) for the first time in Western

Europe (Wilkins, 1980: 236; Itoh, 1990: 32–4). The increasing affluence not only narrowed the historical gap in income levels between West European states and the United States, but also more than compensated European businesses for the loss of their protected markets in the colonies.[5]

Once the reorganization of European industry, sheltered behind high tariff walls, had been completed and a large domestic market secured, European manufacturers of mass-produced automobiles and light machinery were able to compete with their American counterparts not only in Europe but also in the United States. A key element in the greater competitiveness of European automakers was the implementation of a series of innovations – including front-wheel drive, disc brakes, engines with high power-to-weight ratios, and five-speed transmissions – which enhanced performance, while American manufacturers concentrated on comfort features such as air-conditioning, power steering, and automatic transmissions (Friedman, 1983: 365–6; Womack *et al.*, 1990: 46). Thus, for instance, for the first time since 1906, the dollar value of US imports of motor vehicles, parts, and engines overshadowed exports of these goods in 1968. What is particularly striking is that in 1906 the imports had largely been expensive, hand-crafted vehicles. Sixty-two years later, the bulk of imports were economy cars – while no US-produced car had a manufacturer's recommended retail sales price of less than $1800, 17 different models of imports were priced less than $1800 (Chandler, 1990: 616; Wilkins, 1980: 239). The transformation had been complete.

Remapping the industrial geography of the United States

Just as the Marshall Plan and military aid precipitated a prodigious expansion of US FDI in Europe, the Cold War and America's renunciation of its isolationist stance profoundly revamped the industrial geography of the United States and eventually transformed the terrain of competitive struggles between enterprises. The choice of military expenditures and highway construction – respectively the largest rearmament program in peacetime until Reagan, and the largest domestic public works program in history (Mollenkopf, 1983: 116) – by the Truman and Eisenhower administrations as the preferred means to prime the pump of the US economy led to the decentralization of manufacturing from the industrial heartland of the northeastern and midwestern states and to the growth of a high technology based production complex along the Pacific coasts. If the origins of the eclipse of the 'Frostbelt' by the 'Sunbelt' can be traced to the decentralization of industrial production and to the 'militarization of manufacturing,' this was by no means apparent when the basis of what has been called a 'permanent war economy' was laid after the Soviet detonation of the hydrogen bomb in 1953.

On the contrary, though new production facilities were disproportionately sited in the West during the unprecedented expansion of investment during the Second World War – when the cumulative value of existing manufacturing investment in the United States in 1939 was estimated at $39.5 billion, $23.1 billion was spent on new manufacturing facilities between 1942 and 1945 – the Detroit area had received the largest share of new investments as the automobile industry produced the tanks and aircraft for the Allied war effort (Mollenkopf, 1983: 104–8). Even as Los Angeles emerged as the largest automotive manufacturing complex outside the Midwest by the late 1940s and California became the prime locus of aircraft production with 20 percent of all contracts, wartime production ensured the continued vitality of established industrial centers (Goldfield, 1982: 142; Davis, 1986: 75; Cobb, 1984: 34–5; van der Wee, 1986: 108; Buttel, 1989: 48–9). If anything, the outlook for manufacturers in the industrial heartland after the Second World War was particularly buoyant as wartime regulations had prohibited the production of a wide range of goods – automobiles, electric ranges and refrigerators, radios and phonographs, vacuum cleaners, sewing machines, and washing machines – and they prepared to meet pent-up demand (Markusen *et al.*, 1991: 238). Demand for these products, as well as for earth-moving equipment and building materials was also fueled by the allocation of billions of dollars to highway construction and suburban housing through federal subsidies – with homeownership rates spiraling upward from less than 50 percent of all households during the war to 60 percent by 1960 and consumer expenditures on automobiles rising even more impressively from an annual average of $7.5 billion in the 1930s to $22 billion in 1950 and to about $30 billion five years later (Mollenkopf, 1983: 111).

The steady expansion of demand for automobiles and consumer durables in the boom conditions of the early postwar years was so profitable that there was no incentive for producers of these typically Midwestern goods to bid aggressively for the huge military contracts in aerospace and electronics. Even when the Berlin airlift of 1948–49 brought rearmament back on the agenda, there appeared to be no reason to move away from the production of standardized goods, as military demand until the end of the Korean War continued to be for basic armaments for which factories in the industrial heartland were ideally equipped (Markusen *et al.*, 1991: 9). In retrospect, however lucrative an investment focus on standardized, mass-production may have been in the immediate postwar years, it completely underestimated the changed technological conditions of the Cold War to the detriment of the industrial heartland and was the taproot of its transformation into the 'Rustbelt' of the late 1970s and early 1980s.

Unlike any other period in history, a Cold War based on the presumption of 'mutually assured destruction' led to the development of weapons prized chiefly for their preemptive value. As the aim was to deter attacks by continually improving the technological sophistication of opposing arsenals, the new strategic imperatives minimized the importance of savings accruing from the mass-production of standardized armaments in favor of enhanced performance and the potential destructive capacity of weaponry in the calculus of military planning. Hence, though the greater prominence of cybernetics, and communications and radar guidance systems embedded in aircraft and missiles required very expensive production equipment – and US defense spending never fell below $150 billion (in 1982 dollars) annually since the end of the Korean War – they needed to be produced in small batches to unique design specifications. The technologies and production processes required for the manufacture of aircraft and missiles, often with designs modified in the production process itself, was characteristic of craft-production and very different from the mass production techniques and long production runs associated with the manufacture of automobiles and consumer durables (Markusen *et al.*, 1991: 9, 30, 78, 124; Henderson, 1989: 43).

If the business traditions of manufacturers in the Midwest were simply not suited to the Cold War imperatives of maintaining a technological lead over the Soviet Union, the creation of new production complexes in the industrial heartland was also impeded by the dominance of the area's resource and capital markets by strong, well-established industries flush with pent-up demand for their 'traditional' products. In contrast, the nascent aerospace companies of California were ideally positioned to exploit the increased strategic importance of automated warfare, especially since the development of jet engines and missiles required large open spaces for testing while low rainfall and good all-year flying weather provided ideal conditions. Thus, in the 1950s and 1960s, Los Angeles emerged as the most important center of the aerospace industry (Markusen *et al.*, 1991: 34–6, 75, 99, 105; Soja, 1989: 195–6).

The preoccupation with mass-produced, standardized commodities with long production runs not only made manufacturers in the industrial heartland reluctant to aggressively bid for military contracts as indicated by Table 1.1, but their focus on short-term profit margins also rendered Midwestern enterprises impervious to a fundamental shift in the terrain of competitive struggles. Whereas a mere ten states had accounted for over 75 percent of prime contracts in 1952, fifteen years later these contracts were much more widely distributed and *no* Midwestern state figured among the top ten. When prime contracts are broken down by weapons systems, the lead of the Pacific region in high technology sectors is even more impressive. Of the seven broad categories of weapons – missiles, aircraft, electronics and communications, ships, tanks, ammunition, and weapons – which accounted for more than 75 percent of all prime contracts since the end of the Second World War, aircraft was by far the largest category and the states on the Pacific coasts, California and Washington, recorded the largest share both in aircraft and missiles, though New England received the largest per capita shares in both categories. And reflecting the strategic importance of maintaining a technological lead over the Soviet Union, firms located in California secured 42 percent

Table 1.1 Prime military contracts: top ten states, 1945–82 (percent of total)

Second World War to June 1945		Korean War 1952		Cold War 1958		Post-Sputnik/Cuban missile crisis 1962		Vietnam War 1967		End Vietnam 1972		Begin Buildup 1977		Reagan Buildup 1982	
New York	11.0	New York	16.3	California	21.4	California	23.9	California	17.9	California	18.7	California	22.1	California	21.8
Michigan	10.9	Michigan	13.7	New York	11.6	New York	10.7	Texas	9.5	New York	11.0	New York	9.5	New York	7.5
California	8.7	California	12.8	Texas	6.9	Massachusetts	5.2	New York	8.7	Texas	7.7	Texas	6.1	Texas	6.6
Ohio	8.4	Ohio	6.2	Washington	5.8	Connecticut	4.8	Missouri	6.1	Missouri	5.4	Massachusetts	5.3	Connecticut	5.7
New Jersey	6.8	New Jersey	5.1	Kansas	5.6	Ohio	4.5	Connecticut	5.2	Massachusetts	4.5	Missouri	5.2	Missouri	5.2
Top 5	45.8	Top 5	54.1	Top 5	51.3	Top 5	49.1	Top 5	47.4	Top 5	47.3	Top 5	48.2	Top 5	46.8
Pennsylvania	6.6	Pennsylvania	5.0	Ohio	4.8	New Jersey	4.2	Pennsylvania	4.4	Connecticut	4.0	Virginia	4.5	Massachusetts	5.1
Illinois	6.1	Illinois	4.5	Connecticut	4.3	Texas	4.0	Ohio	4.3	Florida	3.6	Connecticut	4.3	Florida	4.0
Indiana	4.5	Washington	4.3	New Jersey	4.2	Pennsylvania	3.8	Massachusetts	3.8	Pennsylvania	3.5	Washington	3.8	Virginia	3.9
Connecticut	4.1	Indiana	4.1	Massachusetts	3.5	Washington	3.7	New Jersey	3.3	New Jersey	3.5	Pennsylvania	3.6	Ohio	3.2
Massachusetts	3.4	Texas	3.3	Pennsylvania	3.4	Michigan	2.7	Georgia	3.1	Virginia	3.2	Michigan	2.7	Maryland	3.0
Top 10	70.5	Top 10	75.3	Top 10	71.5	Top 10	67.5	Top 10	66.3	Top 10	65.1	Top 10	67.1	Top 10	66.0

Source: From *The Rise of the Gunbelt: The Military Remapping of Industrial America* by Ann Markusen and Peter Hall *et al.*, copyright – 1991 by Ann Markusen, Peter Hall, Scot Campbell, and Sabina Deitrick. Used by permission of Oxford University Press, Inc.

of all the federal research and development contracts awarded to business firms between 1962 and 1982 (Markusen *et al.*, 1991: 17–19).

Above all, the strategic imperative of continually making improvements in technology spawned a new organizational network of production, very different from the mass-production units archtypical of the Midwest which had propelled the United States to global hegemony. If the peculiarities of military production – the need for secrecy, for the construction of huge, expensive, experimental facilities to test aircraft and missiles away from prying eyes, small-batch production, experimental fabrication of materials and parts, and the emphasis on performance rather than costs – favored the distribution of prime contracts to a few major corporations, the pressure to innovate privileged small contractors who monopolized the manufacture of certain specialized parts. These factors promoted tendencies toward agglomeration and the development of long-term, affiliative relationships between major corporations – Hughes, McDonnell-Douglas, Rockwell, Grumman, Boeing, General Dynamics, and others – and their subcontractors rather than the multi-unit, vertically-integrated structure, oriented toward cost reductions typical of the industrial heartland. By sharing a research and supply infrastructure and a labor force of highly skilled engineers and craftsmen, aerospace and electronics firms were tied together into a single system of specialized production, especially since the project-oriented nature of defense production encouraged job swapping on a scale that would threaten mass-production industries (Markusen *et al.*, 1991: 35–6, 99–101; Henderson, 1989: 37–8, 42–3). Put differently, the 'post-Fordist, flexible accumulation,' based on flexible specialization, small batch production, with continuous improvement of manufacturing procedures that is often associated with Japanese corporations – as 'Toyotism,' or 'global Japanization' (Womack *et al.*, 1990; Elger and Smith, 1994b; Elger and Smith, 1994a; Markusen *et al.*, 1991: 248) – originated autonomously in the defense-based industries.

With the buoyant consumer demand for the mainstays of heartland industries, however, a far more immediate threat to the continued vitality of the manufacturing centers of the Northeast and the Midwest than that posed by the 'post-industrial' manufacturing networks associated with defense-production came from a progressive decentralization of industrial production due to the mechanization of agriculture and a reorientation of federal programs from public housing and welfare spending to assistance for suburban, single-family housing and the creation of a federally-subsidized interstate highway system. Cumulatively, as the conservative counterpart to the social programs of the New Deal, military Keynesianism and changing federal priorities directed toward subsidizing the private sector along with the mechanization of agriculture caused a tectonic shift in labor-markets and serially eroded the manufacturing base of many older urban centers.

The acceleration of the mechanization of agriculture in the southern states during the Second World War and federal programs to increase meat supplies during the war led to the transformation of the breeding and rearing of livestock and poultry from the 'extensive techniques of husbandry to intensive, scientifically-managed continuous production systems' (Friedmann and McMichael, 1989: 106). This transformation, in turn, led to rapid increase of acreage under crops like soybean and hybrid maize cultivated to support the growing integration of farming and stock-rearing by huge consolidated agro-food processing corporations, and swiftly transformed the rural landscape in the South during the 1950s (van der Wee, 1986: 108–10; Cobb, 1984: 52–3; Buttel, 1989: 48–50; Goldfield, 1982: 142).

These changes were accompanied by an unprecedented exodus to southern cities in the 1950s, and by 1960 over 50 percent of the population of Dixie were living in urban areas, up from 12.5 percent in 1940 (Goldfield, 1982: 143–4; cf. Cobb, 1984: 53). The massive displacement of labor, by providing a vast pool of low-wage workers, stimulated a wave of plant relocations particularly as the construction of the interstate system improved the accessibility of rural areas experiencing massive labor displacements (Goldfield, 1982: 166, 189; Cobb, 1984 #565: 38–50; 82–94; Blumberg, 1994 #666; Taplin, 1994 #667). The vigorous opposition of Southern politicians and business leaders to unionization – by 1954 every Southern state except Louisiana and Oklahoma had adopted 'right-to-work' legislation making it illegal to make union membership a prerequisite for employment – and massive subsidies by state governments created propitious conditions for a relocation of labor-intensive, low-skill manufacturing sectors such as textiles, footwear, apparel, hosiery, and furniture – from New England and other early centers of American industrialization. Low wages and business-friendly state governments also triggered, from the mid-1960s, a wave of investments to the South by European and Japanese firms seeking to evade US import quotas and tariff barriers on textiles, pharmaceuticals, and other commodities (Goldfield, 1982: 189–90; Cobb, 1984: 58–9, 90). Even in states without 'right-to-work' legislation, the recruitment of previously non-unionized or unwaged workers (displaced cultivators and agricultural workers, women) enabled firms to erode the power of organized labor, gain greater wage flexibility, and establish tighter controls over job specifications, especially after the restoration of currency convertibility in Western Europe and Japan in 1958 and the formation of a European Common Market increased competitive pressures (Cobb, 1984: 82; Davis, 1986; Henderson, 1989).

Precisely as low-skilled, labor-intensive manufacturing industries were fleeing the aging urban centers of the industrial heartland, federal assistance for downtown developers and businesses, and subsidies for private, single-family housing and for the interstate highway system under the Eisenhower administration sharply reversed housing commitments to central-city working populations characteristic of Democratic programs. Consequently, even though central cities grew by over 1.5 percent between 1950 and 1960 (on the basis of 1950 boundaries), the suburbs grew by 61.7 percent (Mollenkopf, 1983: 111, 117–22). The decline was even greater for the major urban centers of the industrial heartland which, with the singular exception of New York, lost blue-collar jobs. New York's exceptionalism was due to its ability to provide external economies, the Marshallian 'industrial districts,' as small firms developing non-standard, high-value added products (for example, expensive, high-quality clothing), experimenting with short-production runs, could avoid fixed costs by sharing facilities, labor, and materials with other producers in the unique ecology of Manhattan's Central Business District (Fitch, 1993: 104–7).

Ironically, then, just as European corporations were being remolded in the image of vertically-integrated, multi-unit enterprises typical of American heartland industries, these very organizational forms were being superseded by a revival of earlier forms in a new political and economic context. In both California and New York, industrial districts sharing a common infrastructure of specialized knowledge, skilled labor, and supply networks, more typical of nineteenth-century British industry, were reaping competitive advantages. Tellingly, even when established manufacturers – Ford Aerospace, for instance – entered high-technology fields, their organizational structures in the new ventures, often situated in California, bore no resemblance to the technostructures in their Midwestern home bases (Markusen *et al.*, 1991: 67). The creation of similar organizational forms, but oriented toward mass-production of standardized products, on the Asiatic coasts of the Pacific under the aegis of Japanese enterprises would, as we shall see later, be a crucial element in the emergence of new centers of accumulation on Asia's 'Pacific Rim.' But before we examine these processes, the peculiarities of socio-political and economic reconstruction along the Asian perimeters of the ocean that was the soil in which these processes germinated need to be investigated.

War and reconstruction along the Asian rimlands

As might be expected, the Korean War was even more significant a climacteric in the postwar reconstruction of states along the Pacific perimeters of Asia than it had been in the case of Europe. In the first instance, the Korean War effectively drew the lines of confrontation between the United States and the Soviet Union in Asia, and the principal prewar sources of raw materials and markets for Japanese industry – North Korea, Manchuria, and China – were outside the US 'sphere of influence.' This raised the specter of a resource-poor Japan and a China seeking technological assistance merging their complementary needs to form an Asian bloc closed and hostile to American interests. Spurred by this threat to US strategic interests, top priority was assigned to keep Japan wedded to the Western alliance. On analogy with the process of regional integration in

Western Europe, American planners sought to integrate Japan with South-east Asia, with the latter replacing Japan's traditional markets and sources of raw materials. These designs, however, bristled with formidable obstacles. War and revolution severely limited the ability of the area to provide stable markets or supplies of raw materials to Japan and this, more than any vital American interest, prompted the United States government to renege on its earlier support for decolonization and provide considerable support to the French in their colonial war in Vietnam. An integration of Southeast Asia with Japan also ran headlong into British opposition and the Attlee government sponsored an alternative policy – the Colombo Plan – to foster greater cooperation within the Commonwealth. Anglo-American differences were also reflected in policy cleavages within the US administration itself, as officials involved with European reconstruction saw Southeast Asia, much as their European counterparts did, as Europe's 'backyard.' Most notably, there was adamant resistance by Southeast Asian governments to Japanese domination, a sentiment forcefully expressed by the Manila *Times*:

> Why should the Philippine republic agree to a deal under which the Japanese will profit and prosper and the Philippines will remain on the old colonial basis of providing basic raw materials to a former enemy in exchange for the modern equivalent of glass beads, brass rings and hand mirrors? Especially when the Philippines can make its own?
>
> (quoted in McCormick, 1989: 116)

By denying large-scale aid to these states at the 1947 conference of the United Nations Economic Commission for Asia and the Far East, the United States government, in fact, had voluntarily renounced its strongest weapon to force them to cooperate in Japanese economic recovery. Finally, the lack of purchasing power in Southeast Asia meant that regional integration would be insufficient to generate an adequate expansion of markets to guarantee Japanese recovery (Iriye, 1974: 173–6, 187–8; Borden, 1984: 109–42, 192–5, 204–12; Cumings, 1987: 59–63; McCormick, 1989: 88; Calleo and Rowland, 1973: 198–202).

These circumstances conditioned a reversal of US occupation policies in Japan – the corralling of the labor movement, the early termination of the program to break up monopolies, the end of industrial reparations – though as we have seen the austerity measures imposed by the Dodge Plan did not stimulate an economic recovery. As the Japanese trade deficit with the United States continued to soar, the Korean War provided a providential deliverance from an increasingly untenable situation, by dramatically altering the geopolitical equation. Procurements of clothing, weapons, tents, trucks, jeeps, and ammunition for the US-led United Nations forces from Japan were so extensive that industrial production, which in 1948 had been little more than two-fifths of the 1937 level, was considerably higher than it had been in the late 1930s by the end of 1951. By another measure, between 1950 and 1954, the US spent approximately $3 billion in Japan for war-related supplies, tantamount to an almost $2 million per day subsidy. US procurements were particularly important for reviving vital industrial sectors like the automobile industry (Schonberger, 1989: 163; McCormick, 1989: 105; Borden, 1984: 145–7; Itoh, 1990: 142; van der Wee, 1986: 46).

Of greater long-term significance – the reason why Japanese business and government elites welcomed the steep escalation of US military procure-ments as a 'gift from heaven' – was the provision of extensive American technical assistance to modernize Japanese plant and equipment. The very causes that led to the increase in American procurements – Japan's strategic location as the nearest industrialized zone to the theater of conflict – also entailed a technological upgrade of production facilities because the US military required a higher product quality than Japanese industry was then capable of supplying. Confident of their technological superiority, the American government and enterprises had no fears of Japanese competi-tion and even collaborated with the Japanese government and private indus-try to set up the Japan Productivity Center in 1953 to disseminate new technology and managerial practices. Apart from financing visits by Japan-ese managers and technicians to American plants to study the latest tech-niques, American and West European enterprises freely licensed their technologies to Japanese corporations and as late as 1968 over one-third of these licenses had no conditions attached to them (Itoh, 1990: 143–4; Morris-Suzuki, 1994: 166–207; Bunker and Ciccantell, 1995).

The shift of production in the United States and Europe from goods for export to war-related manufacture also presented Japanese entre-preneurs with additional opportunities to increase their export earnings. The reliance of a recovery program on US military spending, however, raised fears that a tapering off of procurements with the cessation of hos-tilities in Korea would expose the underlying structural weakness of the Japanese economy. These concerns were heightened in 1953 when Japan-ese exports rose by a paltry $3 million while imports soared to $2.4 billion and the trade deficit correspondingly mushroomed from $150 million in 1950 to $1.1 billion in 1953 (Borden, 1984: 168). At the same time, a com-modities boom caused by a rapid escalation of demand for raw materials at the start of the Korean War had actually led to a price-depression as rubber prices slumped from 88 cents per pound in 1951 to 20 cents in 1954 and tin prices fell from $1.81 to 84 cents, and thereby further com-plicated the problem of Southeast Asia providing a market for Japanese industrial products. Conversely, Japanese manufacturers, who had stock-piled raw materials at the start of the war, were left holding overpriced raw materials which crippled their export competitiveness (Borden, 1984: 160, 214; van der Wee, 1986: 46).

The faltering progress of postwar reconstruction in Japan once again threatened to undermine US plans to contain Soviet expansion in Asia and unravel the Cold War world order, especially when the conservative Japanese elite advocated a resumption of trade links with China to obtain cheap raw materials and access to large markets. Consequently, to consolidate the process of economic recovery in Japan by developing it as a low-cost exporter, the Eisenhower administration was compelled to overrule protests by American manufacturers already hurt by cheap imports of toys, footware, canned fish, china, silk, novelties, and textiles and grant most-favored-nation status for Japanese exports in 1953, in return for the implementation of greater austerity measures by the Japanese government. The reduction of average tariffs on Japanese imports from 26 to 12 percent boosted Japanese exports which rose by $400 million in 1955 (Borden, 1984: 171, 180–2, 189). Additionally, to continue funneling dollars to Japan even after the cessation of armed hostilities in Korea, the Mutual Defense Assistance Agreement of 1954 providing for the stationing of US troops in Japan ensured a steady inflow of dollars. Special US military procurements between 1952 and 1956 from Japan alone amounted to $3.4 billion and accounted for almost 30 percent of the value of Japanese commodity imports for the period (Allen, 1981a: 21, 160; Allen, 1981b: 189–90; Borden, 1984: 167–76). Thus was inaugurated a relationship of mutual addiction – of Japanese addiction to high-income American markets and a parallel US addiction to cheap imports that was to have enormous consequences, to briefly anticipate the discussion in Chapter 4.

For our present purposes, it suffices to highlight a crucial difference in programs for postwar reconstruction in Western Europe and East Asia. Whereas European recovery was predicated on a revival of domestic demand through infusions of US capital and the integration of jurisdictionally-segmented markets which facilitated the transplant of the American model of industrial relations to the core states of Europe, the reindustrialization of Japan was almost singularly focused on production for exports. As Japanese workers 'tended to be viewed largely as cost-factors rather than potential consumers . . . this put a greater premium on keeping wage bills as low as possible so Japanese exports could underprice competitors' (McCormick, 1989: 89). The downward pressure on wages and the resulting low levels of purchasing power in Japan meant that it was an unattractive site for US FDI in manufacturing. This very reason, however, made it attractive to US retailers as a source for labor-intensive products as the greater maturity of Japanese industry meant that products of a higher quality could be sourced from Japan than from other low- and middle-income economies. Hence, major retailers in the garment industry – notably Regal Accessories, Republic Cellini, Marlene, Spartan Mayro, and CBS, or the 'big five' – began to source low-end products for the US domestic market from Japan by the mid-1950s. What was particularly noteworthy about this was that instead of pricing goods according to their costs of production, retailers initially priced them according to what the US market would bear, or as a Los Angeles member of the 'big five' was later to tell researchers:

> The role of the United States was mainly that it was just a willing market, willing to pay obscene prices for the work they had done in Asia. We didn't think they were obscene because they were four or five times lower than U.S. prices, but relative to the local standard of living they were. We paid 25 cents to put a flap on a pocket, and 25 cents to sew on a collar. And 50 cents was a day's wage there! We didn't make the correlation. It would be like someone coming to America to buy Fords, and paying $100,000 a car. It provided so much excess capital that they could go into anything.
>
> (quoted in Bonacich and Waller, 1994: 82)

Quite plausibly, a similar logic underpinned the large volumes of US military procurements from Japan and other East Asian client states. Thus, though US retailers (and the military?) obtained products of adequate *quality* more cheaply, the prices they were willing to pay provided substantial windfall profits to their suppliers in Japan. This pattern was later repeated sequentially in Hong Kong, South Korea, Taiwan, and Singapore though procurement costs spiraled downwards as retailers gained better knowledge of production conditions.

Strategic considerations also led to prodigious flows of US aid to Taiwan and South Korea even after the end of the Korean War. Between 1951 and 1965 when US aid to Taiwan was terminated, annual non-military aid deliveries averaged over $80 million a year, or a per capita annual average of $10 over the fifteen-year period, and totaled approximately $1.5 billion (Jacoby, 1966: 38; Ho, 1978: 111; Borden, 1984: 174; Simon, 1988a: 148).[6] South Korea received even more – $6 billion in American economic grants and loans between 1946 and 1978. In comparison, all of Africa received only $6.89 billion and Latin America $14.8 billion. Only India, with a population seventeen times larger than that of South Korea, received a larger amount of US aid, $9.6 billion. After the Korean War, approximately $9.06 billion in US military aid was given to South Korea and Taiwan between 1955 and 1978 when all Latin American and African states collectively obtained only $3.2 billion in military deliveries (Cumings, 1987: 67; Koo, 1987: 167–8; Woo, 1991: 45). When South Korea's receipts of US economic and military aid are taken together, a cumulative total of $12.6 billion between 1946 and 1976, it was larger than US assistance to any other country except South Vietnam and Israel (Mason *et al.*, 1980: 165). Put differently, US aid financed 95 percent of Taiwan's trade deficit in the 1950s, and 80 percent of South Korea's imports (Bello and Rosenfeld, 1990: 4; Amsden, 1989: 39).[7] US military procurements from Japan had accounted for $7.2 billion by 1964, or an annual average of $500 million over 20 years, and by 1970 continued military spending had raised the cumulative figure to nearly $10 billion (Borden, 1984: 220).

More importantly, containment of Soviet expansionism in Asia dovetailed neatly with US domestic economic considerations. The frenetic dislocations caused by the Second World War had temporarily relieved the chronic and recurring overproduction problems confronting American agriculture by transforming the United States into the granary of the Allied war effort. Since US support for European reconstruction – with agricultural assistance comprising almost a third of Marshall Plan deliveries – led to a reconstitution of European agriculture and reduced import demand for American wheat, the overproduction problem that had plagued US agriculture for decades resurfaced with greater intensity. New Deal legislation placing a floor below which prices for agricultural commodities could not fall, in the context of continuing technological improvements resulting from the industrialization of American agriculture, had led to mounting surpluses – with accumulated stocks amounting to an entire year's supply by 1954 when European production had recovered, and costing the US Treasury approximately $1 billion per year to maintain (Buttel, 1989: 49–50; Friedmann, 1982: S258–62; Friedmann, 1993: 33–4).

Given the repeated failure of legislation to limit production by restricting acreage, and the political unfeasibility of abrogating price supports, the passage of the Agricultural Trade Development and Assistance Act of 1954 – Public Law 480, or PL 480, as it is better known – provided an elegant resolution to the problem of chronic oversupply of agricultural production in the United States in conditions of a world-wide liquidity shortage by linking food exports to US foreign policy aims. By making US agricultural exports payable on concessionary terms in the currency of recipient states, PL 480 opened the way to channel the mounting US surpluses to states with the greatest need for food imports but lacking the foreign currency reserves for commercial purchases. While PL 480 was specifically targeted to the poorer states, the Mutual Security Act of 1954 provided US agricultural surpluses to Japan on identical terms, with US troops stationed in Japan being paid partly in yen obtained as payments for imported US agricultural surpluses. The balances in nonconvertible currencies accruing to the United States government could be used to acquire strategic raw materials – with $304 million worth of PL 480 currencies used for this purpose in 1955–56, the first full year of the act's implementation – and to finance military expenditures and more modest economic assistance to foreign countries without Congressional authorization (Friedmann, 1982: S262–3; Kobayhashi Chutaro, 1987: 32).

The largest recipients of PL 480 deliveries were all in Asia – India, Pakistan, South Korea, and Taiwan. The consequences of US food aid on peripheral states in Asia, however, was very different from its impact on

European core states. Whereas the US had helped in the recovery of European agriculture, disposal of American wheat surpluses in PL 480 recipient states 'was entirely directed toward feeding potential wage workers during industrialization' (Friedmann, 1982: S263). While the ample availability of cheap foodgrains with minimal drain on foreign exchange reserves relieved the need for states seeking to industrialize to make painful choices – investments to raise agricultural productivity would use up scarce capital and lead to growing rural unemployment; higher food prices would raise wage bills; and food imports would restrict the import of capital goods – the dumping of US agricultural products depressed farming conditions and transformed countries with agricultural surpluses into net importers. In contrast to European reconstruction where rapidly increasing industrial wages decreased the importance of the trade-off between high food prices for farmers and low food prices for industrial employers, the dumping of US agricultural surpluses enabled employers in Asia – particularly those in South Korea and Taiwan, the two largest per capita recipients of US aid – to embark on a program of industrialization based on low wages, since PL 480 deliveries kept reproduction costs down and low prices for farm products led to a steady supply of job seekers eager to leave the even poorer conditions in rural areas (Friedmann, 1982: S259, S268; Friedmann and McMichael, 1989: 104; McMichael, 1993; McMichael and Kim, 1994: 32; Chung, 1990: 147–8). Thus, reflecting the low levels of industrialization in Asia before the Second World War, and the large resource endowments of several states, in the 1950s the thrust of industrialization strategies everywhere in the continent except Japan was toward import-substitution rather than oriented toward exports based on their low labor costs.

The very magnitude of PL 480 deliveries – US food aid comprised 31.8 percent of total wheat exports for all countries between 1956 and 1960, and 35.6 percent between 1961 and 1965 (Friedmann, 1982: S271) – restructured global patterns of trade as the United States replaced Europe as the fulcrum of world trade. The bilateral nature of these deliveries – explicitly designed to further US foreign policy goals and restricted to 'friendly countries' – and the growing dependence of several states in Southeast Asia on US food aid enabled the United States to partially circumvent nationalist objections in these states toward a greater integration with Japan by tying US balances in nonconvertible currencies to purchases from Japan and by 1960 approximately 10 percent of Japan's exports to the area was financed by US aid. However, opposition from Congress to US aid subsidizing Japanese competition limited such financing and hence regional integration (Borden, 1984: 189–90, 202). The predominant pattern in trans-Pacific trade therefore remained bilateral linkages between the United States and its allies in Asia throughout the 1950s.

To recapitulate, the reconstruction of the world market under US auspices led to very different outcomes in Western Europe, East Asia, and in the United States itself. In Western Europe, the transnational expansion of multi-unit, vertically integrated US enterprises promoted regional integration of many small, fragmented national markets and served to enmesh West Germany in a densely knit filigree of interconnected networks to the United States and its European allies. If the new organizational armature of industrial production undermined the power of craft unions and shifted control to managements, the accompanying pay explosion led to a rapid increase in living standards and to a decline in inequalities of wealth and income. Just as industrial structures in Western Europe were being remade in the American model, military Keynesianism and nuclear confrontation between the United States and the Soviet Union was transforming industrial geographies within the hegemonic power. While the removal of wartime restrictions on consumer durables had revitalized industrial production in the northeastern and midwestern states, strategic requirements of nuclear confrontation were changing the competitive terrain. Predicated on small-batch production, experimental fabrication of parts and materials, and an emphasis on performance rather than costs, the strategic imperatives of nuclear deterrence led to the creation of a new organizational network that was to prove decisive after postwar economic reconstruction was complete and competitive pressures increased. Finally, across the Pacific, widespread poverty and lack of stable markers implied that there was no parallel to the trans-Atlantic expansion of US corporate networks. Instead, seeking to contain alleged Soviet expansionism, the US funneled large doses of capital to its client states, either directly through economic and food aid or indirectly through military procurements, while also providing them with the technical assistance to rebuild their industries with the newest technologies available. Low wages in East Asian states – kept in check by US-sponsored anti-communist offensives – also enabled them to expand their exports to the US. Thus, while economic reconstruction after the Second World War was based on a revival of domestic demand in West European states, it was based on low wages in Japan and other US client states in East Asia. Though the strategies and structures of accumulation installed by US hegemony provided the institutional scaffolding for the reconstruction of capitalist economies along Asia's Pacific coasts, their reconstruction was also determined by the dialectic between state, class, and capital in each location – issues we examine sequentially in the following chapters.

2 Strong states, weak societies

State and class in the Asian rimlands

[Materialist dialectics] holds that external causes are the condition of change and internal causes are the basis of change, and that external causes become operative through internal causes. In a suitable temperature an egg changes into a chicken, but no temperature can change a stone into a chicken, because each has a different basis.

Mao Zedong, *On Contradiction*

Surveying the economic meltdown spreading across Asia's Pacific Rim, Alan Greenspan, the Chairman of the US Federal Reserve, prophesied in January 1998 the coming triumph of 'the Western form of free market capitalism' (quoted in Hamilton, 1999: 46). Seizing the opportunity to exploit the leverage presented by cascading declines in values of East and Southeast Asian currencies since 1997 and to remake them in the Anglo-Saxon image, mainstream economists sought to retrospectively indict administratively guided industrial strategies by attributing the economic malaise to 'crony capitalism.' Viewed through this orthodox lens, 'crony capitalism' had two connotations – as collusion between governments and businesses, and as cartel-like networks based on interpersonal associations – both of which undermined, subverted or otherwise distorted market forces. Caught flat-footed by the velocity and intensity of the crisis, like an earlier generation of apostates who had recanted that their 'god had failed,' a new generation of apostates in the region also ruefully concluded that 'Asian capitalism' had merely been a footnote in the history of capitalist development, 'a temporal detour in the longer historical evolution of capitalism' (Chung In Moon and Sang-young Rhyu, 2000: 98).

In both cases, the common assumption was that there was an 'East Asian model' of capitalism counterposed to a 'Western' model of free markets. If one had failed, only the other could provide succor to economies devastated by capital outflows and insolvencies, was the unwavering message from Western capitals and the International Monetary Fund (IMF). Leaving aside the issue of an ideal-typical 'Western' model, though proponents of 'Asian miracles' had attributed the success of these economies to a common model, the differential impact of the crisis on these several economies suggests grounds for skepticism. Derived from studies of national-economy making, notions of an 'East Asian model' were typically extrapolations from the experience of a single state to the region as a whole and tended to homogenize different patterns of resistance and accommodation. Without high levels of corporate debt, Robert Wade and Frank Veneroso (1998a) have argued, the South Korean *chaebol* (conglomerates) would never have been able to scale the peaks of industrial production and emerge as formidable competitors in the most technologically-exacting markets in so short a time. Yet, while corporations in Thailand and in other ailing economies also incurred high levels of debt, they functioned in an entirely different context and to generalize from the South Korean experience is to obscure the fundamental importance of national economic planning. Indeed, as we shall see in a subsequent chapter, as South Korean economic growth made national economic planning increasingly anachronistic, continued reliance of high debt–equity ratios without corresponding checks led to overproduction.

Nevertheless, the development of regionally-integrated production and procurement networks, and the concentration of sustained economic growth along the Pacific perimeters of Asia suggest the need to examine the systematic integration of these countries with each other and of the region with the world 'at large.' Central to this project is the reconstruction of state–society relations in Japan and the 'Four Dragons' after the Second World War, a reconstruction conditioned by the strategic imperatives of the Cold War. The relative autonomy of states taken by theorists of the developmental state to be crucial to the spectacular economic successes registered by the Asian 'miracle' economies was a feature shared by the state apparatuses of these five jurisdictions. Although the 'mini-dragons' of Indonesia, Malaysia, and Thailand may have formally constituted similar institutional mechanisms to provide 'administrative guidance' for national economic planning, none of their pilot economic agencies had the autonomy enjoyed by elite planning agencies in Japan, Singapore, South Korea, and Taiwan – Hong Kong being a partial exception to this blanket characterization as we shall see shortly (see Henderson, 1999). Moreover, the expansion of corporate production and procurement networks based in Japan and the 'Four Dragons' was the fundamental ingredient in regional integration across the Asian rimlands. Hence our focus here is on the similarities and differences underpinning the constitution of the 'bureaucratic-authoritarian industrializing regimes,' to use Bruce Cumings' marvelously adequate phrase, in Japan and the Four Dragons.

Postwar reconstruction was perhaps the most significant climacteric in state–society relations in East and Southeast Asia since the incorporation of these territories into the capitalist world-economy. The American occupation of Japan and South Korea, civil war and revolution in Korea, Vietnam, and China, the establishment of an ethnically-bifurcated state in

Taiwan, decolonization of European empires, and the marginalization of elites in several key locations, led to an unprecedented concentration and centralization of power in state apparatuses in these locations. Since our focus is on the local processing of larger global forces of transformation, we will begin by examining how the strategic political and military arrangements of US hegemony that conditioned postwar rehabilitation and reconstruction of its client states along Asia's Pacific Rim were extended, deflected, or otherwise modified by internal constellations of power in each of these states, as well as by their prior experiences of social transformation and their varied cultural heritages. Hence, we sequentially examine changes in the relations between governing elites and domestic classes in each of the five jurisdictions in the immediate aftermath of the Second World War.

Recasting state–society relations

Just as the foundations of dynastic empires in Central and Eastern Europe were eroded at the end of the First World War by a resurgence of radical national movements, Japanese defeat destabilized the political order all across the Pacific coasts of Asia. When military defeat, economic devastation, and US occupation irrevocably tarnished the legitimacy of the Japanese ruling elite and divested them of the material bases of their power, the liberation of territories occupied by Japan had unleashed a wave of nationalist movements that undermined the foundations of European colonial empires. Meanwhile, rampant corruption and intense exploitation of the peasantry during decades of civil war combined with external aggression had discredited Guomingdang (GMD) rule in China. Where disruptions of rural institutions, social relationships, and agricultural routines had been the most intense either through war, as in China and Vietnam, or through forced industrialization since the 1930s as in Korea (Cumings, 1981: 54), nationalist movements were also accompanied by demands for the radical redistribution of land. Everywhere, runaway rates of inflation in the immediate postwar years made urban insurrection an almost inevitable accompaniment of agrarian revolt.

   If unsuccessful attempts to restore the antebellum status quo in French Indochina and the Dutch East Indies demonstrated how thoroughly Japanese occupation and wartime destruction had destabilized colonial structures of control, the restoration of Chinese sovereignty over Taiwan was tantamount to a process of recolonization as the mainlanders had no historical or social links with its native inhabitants. While nationalist forces ousted their colonizers in Indonesia and Indochina, and the GMD consolidated its power in Taiwan by marginalizing the indigenous elite, the presence of Soviet troops on the Korean peninsula and the revolutionary redistribution of land by 'people's committees' changed the equation in the US occupied zone south of the 38th parallel. Here, within three months of the Japanese surrender, in a dress-rehearsal of what was to become US policy in the Cold War, the American Military Government (AMG) revived colonial structures of control and rehabilitated the Koreans who had collaborated in the Japanese colonial enterprise. Finally, predicated on the assumption that Japanese militarism was an aberration stemming from anachronistic 'feudal' survivals, American plans to reconstruct Japan on a democratic and demilitarized basis entailed policy measures to fundamentally restructure power relations through land reforms, to promote the rights of labor, and to dismantle industrial–financial monopolies (see Schonberger, 1989: 3–4, 90–110).

Based on coercion rather than consent, the occupation regimes in Japan, Taiwan, and South Korea represented genuinely new constellations of power not only because prewar elites had been sidelined, but also because social and economic dislocations caused by war, revolution, and civil strife necessitated a complete overhaul of the foundations of rule. As the marginalization of prewar elites in Japan, South Korea, and Taiwan conferred unprecedented autonomy on their reconstituted state apparatuses, the demolition of the ideological bases of *Ancien Regimes*, symbolized by the Japanese emperor's renunciation of his divinity, made it incumbent on politicians and bureaucrats to seek new bases of legitimacy. Simultaneously, massive devastation caused by allied bombing, the dismantling of its colonial empire and the consequent loss of sources of raw materials and markets had aggravated the task of economic reconstruction in Japan. Three years after surrender, Japanese economic output was only at one-third its level in the mid-1930s (Pempel, 1998: 83). A large influx of refugees – with an estimated 1.7 million fleeing from the Soviet-occupied zone to South Korea, and the inflows of the defeated remnants of the GMD army and their supporters accounting for the sharp rise in the population of Taiwan from less than 6 million in 1944 to more than 8 million in 1950 (Kuznets, 1977: 31; Hamilton and Biggart, 1989: S54) – similarly exacerbated processes of reconstruction in the two former Japanese colonies.

Reverting to their status as British colonies after wartime occupation by the Japanese, colonial administrators in Singapore and Hong Kong faced different, though no less compelling, pressures as their reconstitution as entrepôts was undermined by social upheavals in their respective hinterlands – the Chinese Revolution and the anticolonial insurgency in Malaya. The staggering influx of refugees from war and revolution in China, for instance, almost quadrupled Hong Kong's population – which rose from 600,000 to 2,360,000 – between 1945 and 1951 (Castells *et al.*, 1990: 15; Cheng and Gereffi, 1994: 200), and compounded the effects of the loss of production facilities and markets in the People's Republic. On the heels of this disruption of commercial and social networks, the imposition of a United Nations embargo on the export of strategic goods to China in 1951 fatally undermined Hong Kong's entrepôt role, as China had accounted for 36.2 percent of its imports (Haggard, 1990: 120–1). These adverse consequences were partly offset by inflows of capital from China –

estimated to be around HK$300 to 600 million each year between 1948 and 1950 – as wealthy entrepreneurs repatriated their assets just before and soon after the Communist takeover (Choi, 1994: 43).

Just as revolution in its hinterland thwarted Hong Kong's reconstitution as an entrepôt, the postwar reorganization of British colonial possessions in Southeast Asia jeopardized Singapore's restitution as the pre-eminent entrepôt in the area. Reflecting both the geostrategic importance of Singapore to Britain and Malay apprehensions of the challenge to their political ascendancy posed by the island's dominant Chinese community, Britain consolidated its colonies in the area – the Malay states, the Straits Settlements, and the Borneo territories – into a Malay Union in 1946, renamed the Federation of Malaya in 1948. Simultaneously, to assuage Malay nationalism, Singapore was separated from the Union and declared a Crown Colony – 'a sort of District of Columbia,' the seat of the British governor-general for Southeast Asia (Turnbull, 1989: 219; Rodan, 1989: 53–4). By thus placating Malay nationalists, these political arrangements undermined Singapore's entrepôt function by severing the city-state from its hinterland (Rodan, 1989: 87).

Neither Washington nor Whitehall could countenance continuing instability along the Asian rimlands. If the specter of communism haunted US officials, natural resources from its Southeast Asian colonies were vital for Britain's precarious balance of payments situation.[1] Given the magnitude of wartime destruction of manufacturing facilities, disruption of production and procurement networks, and socio-political changes in the aftermath of Allied victory, it quickly became evident to policy makers in the United States and Britain that the stability of postwar administrations in the Asian rimlands could only be ensured by a wholesale restructuring of the relations between state and civil society in each location.

What was peculiar to the postwar reconstitution of Japan, South Korea, Singapore, and Taiwan and the characteristic that separated them from all other state apparatuses outside the centrally-planned economies was their relative autonomy from domestic constellations of power and class interests. Perched precariously along the ideological faultlines of the Cold War, even as American occupation authorities and their local collaborators in Japan and South Korea and the GMD regime in Taiwan waged an unrelenting offensive against militant labor movements, this offensive was tinged with the realization that their subject populations could be inoculated against the appeals of revolutionary socialism only if the regimes could plausibly promise to raise living standards (Johnson, 1982; Johnson, 1987; Amsden, 1989; Wade, 1990; Appelbaum and Henderson, 1992). This was achieved both by extensive land redistribution schemes and by substantial infusions of economic assistance and food aid from the hegemonic power. Pressures to seek new bases of legitimacy through economic growth also assumed a more pronounced urgency as the US ended its occupation of South Korea and Japan and as the GMD administration in

Taiwan grudgingly acknowledged that the prospects of their victorious return to the Chinese mainland were becoming increasingly remote.

The imperative to promote material prosperity was no less compelling for the colonial administration in Hong Kong both because a cash-strapped British government insisted that the colony be financially self-supporting and because the imposition of the United Nations embargo on the exports of strategic goods to China led to a dramatic decline in its export earnings (Haggard, 1990: 103–10, 120–1; Castells *et al.*, 1990: 190–1). Singapore alone was a partial exception to these pressures in the early 1950s, because even though it was jurisdictionally divorced from its hinterland, it continued to be substantively integrated with the Federation of Malaya as both remained British colonies. It was only when peoples of both these territories began inching toward political independence from the mid-1950s that the adverse consequences of an entrepôt set adrift from its hinterland became a pressing concern for the presumptive ruling elite of the future city-state.

Widespread acknowledgment that the greater relative autonomy of state apparatuses and their propensity to intervene in the economic realm were common denominators shared by the new regimes in Japan and the 'Dragons' must be qualified by the diversity of their internal structuring and their varied insertions within larger political and economic networks. Ranging from Hong Kong, which does not even have a central bank, to South Korea where Syngman Rhee's government controlled over 90 percent of all industrial establishments when it took over from the AMG, the nature of their internal structures of power and class interests represented significant differences. These differences were heightened by the modalities of their political alliances and economic linkages with external powers – most notably with the United States and Britain. Patterns of state intervention, contoured by domestic constellations of power and privilege and resource endowments, will be examined in detail in the next chapter. Here we focus on how the post-Second World War dispensation reshaped domestic class alliances and how these refracted the strategic imperatives of the Cold War in each jurisdiction.

Land reforms and the elimination of landlords

As the legitimacy of established elites unraveled under the impact of political upheavals, social dislocations, and economic devastation, the United States sponsored land redistributions in Japan, South Korea, and Taiwan to diffuse the destabilizing consequences of the Japanese defeat. Land reforms assumed central importance in all three US client states, not only because there were 'few assets besides land left to redistribute,' as Susan Greenhalgh (1988: 92) observed of Taiwan, but also because it was the most effective strategy to transform the countryside from a fertile ground for agrarian revolt into a largely conservative base. Thorough-going agrarian reform, widely considered to have been the most successful in the capitalist world (Tuma, 1965; Ladejinsky, 1977), undermined the foundations of class privilege in all three states and led to a remarkable decline in the inequalities of income and wealth. But even as far-reaching changes in patterns of land ownership were implemented in the three client states, their modalities and outcomes were strikingly different.

Among the 'basic concepts' that General Douglas MacArthur and the occupation forces under his command sought to instill in the Japanese were the values of 'Jacksonian democracy' – a smallholding peasantry, small-scale manufacturing entailing the dissolution of the *zaibatsu* monopolies, and a greater recognition of the rights of labor. Within this trinity, land reform was accorded primacy because it was thought that the landlords were the backbone of Japan's 'feudal' structure, the ones who had derailed the locomotive of Japanese modernization. The implementation of land reforms between 1946 and 1950 led to over 90 percent of all cultivated land being in the hands of owners by 1950 and to the virtual extirpation of tenancy (Schonberger, 1989: 52–3, 65). Spiraling rates of inflation in the first two years of the Occupation, which pushed prices to ninety times their level at the end of the war, rendered the compensation paid to landlords almost worthless as it was based on 1945 land prices.[2]

Ironically, the chief beneficiary of the US-sponsored land reform was the state bureaucracy, not only because the reforms eliminated agrarian magnates as a social class, but also because the occupation forces could not conduct land surveys or registrations without bureaucratic assistance. Consequently, despite three waves of purges ordered by the occupation authorities, these were much less pervasive in Japan than in the US-occupied zone in Germany. Whereas the number of people purged accounted for 2.5 percent of the population in the latter, the corresponding figure in Japan was only 0.29 percent, and 80 percent of the 210,000 Japanese who were eventually purged and barred from holding public office were military officers. The bureaucracy, in fact, emerged stronger than it had ever been since the purge of military officers and the imposition of the famous 'no-war' clause in the 'MacArthur Constitution' removed the military as a force in Japanese politics (Schonberger, 1989: 61, 66, 115, 163; Toshihiko Kawagoe, 1993: 370; McMichael and Kim, 1994: 30; Pempel, 1998: 85).

Accompanying the land reforms, the government sought to integrate the agricultural cooperatives that had sprouted across the country – growing from less than 900 at the beginning of 1948 to almost 28,000 by the end of that year. This was achieved by sponsoring the National Association of Agricultural Cooperatives – better known by its Japanese acronym, Nōkyō – as an umbrella organization to integrate farm families. Organized in national, prefectural, and at local levels, the cooperatives provided a comprehensive array of facilities to farmers covering virtually all aspects of farm operations. Apart from purchasing and marketing facilities, they also provided credit, banking services, insurance and even instituted driving schools and mail-order bride arrangements. Since the government also provided subsidies and loans through the cooperatives, there were powerful incentives for farm families to join cooperatives and this provided conservative politicians with an important tool for voter mobilization. Though opposition parties had some small rural organizations, none could compare with Nōkyō in the size and range of their activities (Donnelly, 1984; Pempel, 1998: 73, 96–7; Eccleston, 1989: 130).

The United States government, through the Sino-American Joint Commission on Rural Reconstruction, also encouraged the GMD to implement land reforms in Taiwan. A redistribution of land was attractive to Chiang Kai-shek's administration because it not only did not have a vested interest in land in the island but also because agrarian reform enabled the regime to eradicate the last vestiges of power not yet under its effective control. The Japanese had nationalized the industrial assets of the native Taiwanese elite during the war and those that had not been destroyed were transferred to the GMD government. The financial assets of the local elite had largely been eliminated by the massive postwar inflation.[3] Land reforms – implemented in two stages with the placing of a ceiling on maximum rents at 37.5 percent of the annual yield of the main crop in 1949, and the Land-to-the-Tiller Act of 1953 – led to the redistribution of some 70 percent of eligible land, with a ceiling of three hectares on individual holdings (Gold, 1986: 66; for a marginally different estimate, see Ho, 1978: 355). Landowners were compensated with land bonds for 70 percent of the value of their lands and shares in four state corporations – often hastily cobbled together by merging expropriated Japanese firms – for the remaining 30 percent. Low interest rates on land bonds triggered panic selling which further lowered their values, while many landowners unused to the separation of ownership from control also quickly divested themselves of their shares in the corporations.[4] Only a select few – such as C. F. Koo (Taiwan Cement), T. T. Caho (petrochemicals, plastics), and Hsieh Ch'eng-yuan (Taiwan Pineapple) – used their land bonds to build successful industrial concerns in the ensuing favorable environment for manufacturers (Yang, 1970: 157; Ho, 1978: 160–7; Koo, 1987: 170; Greenhalgh, 1988: 92; Barrett, 1988: 134; Gold, 1986: 64–6, 71; Gold, 1988b: 188–9; Simon, 1988a: 140–1, 147–8; Haggard, 1990: 82–3).

The GMD party-state consolidated its control over the countryside by merging the various credit cooperatives, and community and peasants' organizations into some 340 Farmers' Associations. While these associations displaced rural moneylenders, they were also instrumental in the subordination of agriculture to the requirements of an industrialization drive as the regime instituted a rice-fertilizer barter system and a compulsory program of rice sales at prices that were 25–30 percent below the wholesale market price (Ho, 1978: 181–2). A government monopoly over the production and import of fertilizers enabled it to manipulate the terms of trade and in the 1950s and 1960s, the price paid by cultivators in Taiwan for ammonium sulfate – the most widely used fertilizer – was 50 percent more than the price paid by Japanese farmers and more than double the price in Pakistan, Sri Lanka, and Thailand. Declining conditions in the countryside, in turn, provided a cheap labor force as an estimated 1 million people migrated from rural areas to the cities between 1950 and 1965, and a further 860,000 between 1965 and 1982 – though these rates of rural–urban migration were lower than in Japan and South Korea for reasons discussed below. Additionally, the government's Food Bureau was empowered to collect taxes and rents in rice on publicly-held lands, and half of this intake was rationed to military personnel, civil servants, and other government employees (Ho, 1978: 179–84; Gold, 1986: 66–7; Haggard, 1990: 82–3; Bello and Rosenfeld, 1990: 184–6).

Land reforms in South Korea were an altogether different proposition. The stronger nationalist impulse in colonial Korea and peasant opposition toward the *yangban* who collaborated with the colonizers had resulted in a groundswell of support for independence and radical land reform through popular committees that sprang up in the countryside. Korea was also the only place in Asia where the military forces of the United States and the Soviet Union directly confronted one another. Stumbling upon domestic social upheaval, revolutionary land redistributions, and the presence of Soviet troops, the AMG established south of the 38th parallel in Korea *strengthened* the colonial state by reviving and even expanding the colonial Government-General bureaucracy and police forces and by reinforcing the power of the *yangban* elite that had been irretrievably tarnished through their collaboration with the Japanese. In contrast, the US occupation authorities had *weakened* the Japanese state, at least before the 'reverse course' was inaugurated in 1948. Within three months of the Japanese defeat, Korea in fact became the testing ground for strategies that would assume center-stage in Cold War US foreign policy: containment of the Soviet Union and the neutralization of labor movements. Yet, however much class and bureaucratic privilege were reinforced in South Korea, neither the AMG nor the Syngman Rhee regime it sponsored could ignore the tidal wave of popular demand for land reforms. As continuing rural unrest also made it amply evident that the thirst for land would not be quenched merely by the sale of confiscated Japanese properties to tenants, the government reluctantly enacted land reforms which, as in the case of Japan and Taiwan, placed a ceiling of three hectares on individual land holdings. However, not a single hectare was redistributed until the outbreak of the Korean War when the conquering North Korean forces dispossessed landlords everywhere outside the Pusan perimeter (Cumings, 1981; Koo, 1987: 167, 170–1; Haggard, 1990: 55; Bello and Rosenfeld, 1990: 78–9; Choi, 1993: 15–20; Cumings, 1989: 12).

The more authoritarian nature of the regime was also illustrated by the contrast between the Japanese agricultural cooperatives which remained far more democratic institutions even as they eventually came to organize the rural vote for the Liberal Democratic Party and the South Korean

NONGHYUP which, like the Taiwanese Farmers' Associations, was a parastatal organ designed to impose government policies in the countryside. Differences in the implementation of land reforms were heightened by the different cultural milieux of the three states. Whereas land was *equally* divided between all male heirs in Taiwan, the eldest son in South Korea inherited *most* of the land, while *all* the land went to a single heir in Japan. Consequently, farm population in Taiwan increased from almost 3.5 million in 1946 to 6.15 million in 1969 before declining slowly. In contrast, farm households declined by 3.5 percent between 1950 and 1980 in South Korea, even though the rural population as a whole declined by over 50 percent, and by a whopping 24.5 percent in Japan in the same period (Ho, 1978: 150–1; McMichael, 1993: 104–5; McMichael and Kim, 1994: 27, 30–1; Greenhalgh, 1994: 756–7).

Notwithstanding such differences, the elimination of landlords as a class removed a potential source of resistance to the subordination of agriculture to the industrialization drive in all three states. The requirement that new landowners reimburse the government in crops over a 15- to 30-year period – in conjunction with inflows of PL 480 deliveries to Taiwan and South Korea, and imports of cheap wheat from the United States to Japan – kept a lid on food prices, fostered the subsequent development of an import-substituting industrialization strategy in Taiwan and South Korea, and facilitated the expansion of cheap manufactured exports from Japan (Kobayhashi Chutaro, 1987: 32; McMichael, 1993: 105; McMichael and Kim, 1994: 32). The imposition of rigid limits on individual land holdings – which remained in place in Japan until 1962, in Taiwan until the mid-1980s, and in South Korea until 1991 – is also held to have created remarkably egalitarian social structures in rural areas, especially since financial assets had largely been wiped out with the runaway inflation of the early postwar years.[5]

Perhaps most importantly, by conceding the demand for land, the elimination of agrarian magnates and land redistribution to small peasants and tenant farmers created a large constituency of support for the new regimes and enabled administrations in the US client states to rollback urban insurgency. A quiescent countryside, then, was a necessary condition for the emergence of a state-led industrialization drive based on cheap labor.

Coercion, cooptation, and corruption in labor subordination

Virtually no one doubts that the emergence of Japan and the other East Asian 'miracle' economies as exporters of manufactured goods was based on low wages and labor peace. Yet, there is considerable disagreement on the well-springs of cheap labor and non-conflictual industrial relations in the Asian rimlands. On the one hand, conservative scholars are liable to stress the unique cultural legacies of a shared Confucian tradition of harmony, achieved through a symbiosis between a paternalistic concern for subordinates and loyalty toward superiors, and a mutually satisfactory consensus between political and business leaders and workers to subordinate their sectarian interests to the wider national good (Morishima, 1982; Berger and Hsiao, 1988). Indeed, Chie Nakane (1970) has even argued that Japan was, and remains, a homogenous society that is not riven by class divisions. More generally, in a survey of patterns of women workers in Asian industries, Aihwa Ong (1991: 280) argues that

> workers' struggles and resistances are often not based upon class interests or class solidarity, but comprise individual and even covert acts against various forms of control. The interest defended, or the solidarity built through such acts are more often linked to kinship and gender than to class.

Such timeless and ahistorical essentializations not only obscures the complex, conflict-ridden evolution of capital–labor relations (see Gordon, 1985; Garon, 1994; Deyo, 1989) but also virtually biologizes culture and ignores that cultural forms and genres are the symbolic resolutions to historically contingent political and social contradictions. On the other hand, more discerning analysts emphasize structural aspects of labor subordination in postwar industrialization – notably the repression of workers by American occupation forces, authoritarian client regimes, and managements; high turnover rates in labor-intensive, low-skilled work that discourage collective action; and 'nonproletarian' labor systems enmeshed in communal paternalism (Deyo, 1989; Bello and Rosenfeld, 1990; Hart-Landsberg, 1993; Seiyama, 1989).

As already indicated by the discussion on rural restructuring, similar outcomes in the three US client states were achieved by significantly different means and labor subordination in the Asian 'miracles' cannot be understood merely as the product of cultural traditions or repression: labor peace was achieved by coercion, cooptation, and corruption. While anti-communist drives in the early years of the Cold War in Japan and under authoritarian governments all through the 1980s elsewhere led to the repression of militant labor movements, this was tinged by the coopting of privileged sections of the working class through the revival of patriarchal familial rhetoric which preserved their status. The strategic imperatives of the Cold War also corrupted union movements by compelling governments to lower the cost of basic wage goods, provide low-cost housing of relatively good quality, and to ensure steady improvements in material conditions. In every case, the specific mixture of these strategies was determined by the complex interplay between the nature and strength of the different regimes, the size and organizational strength of the labor movement in each location, and the activities of agencies external to the region, most obviously the United States occupation forces but also the Chinese Communist Party and, in the cases of the two Crown Colonies, the British government and its colonial satraps.

In Japan, where the numerical strength and organizational maturity of the working class was most advanced despite repression since the 1930s, one of the earliest initiatives of the occupation authorities was to issue a civil liberties directive, SCAPIN-93 in October 1945, rescind anti-union laws, and force the Japanese parliament to enact the Labor Union Law by December of the same year (Yonekura, 1993: 223–5). These measures led to a spectacular rise in trade union membership – from 5,000 when SCAPIN-93 was passed to almost 5 million or 40 percent of all adult wage earners by December 1946 (Schonberger, 1989: 115; Itoh, 1990: 147; Gordon, 1996a: 17–18; Pempel, 1998: 88). Political liberalization combined with harsh economic conditions due to the devastation caused by allied bombing, disruption of production and procurement networks, and rampant inflation – according to the occupation authorities themselves, ¥509 per month was required to support a worker and three dependents in January 1946 when the average monthly wages of a 40-year-old male worker was only ¥213 – led to a wave of militant action and to a leftward drift that soon alarmed MacArthur. Where a strong and independent trade union movement had initially been seen as a check on the untrammeled power of conservative Japanese politicians and business monopolies, the growing incidence of strikes was increasingly viewed as representing a setback to economic recovery. Along with the 'red scare' associated with the 'manufacture' of the Cold War, the austerity measures of the Dodge Plan were designed to rein in the labor movement: enabling the government to retrench the more active militants, remove the right of government employees and employees of public corporations to strike or engage in collective bargaining, sponsor right-wing unions, and purge unions suspected of affiliation to the Communist Party. Despite these measures, real wages grew three-fold between 1947 and 1951 due to increased militancy, and labor peace was achieved only with the tremendous spurt given to the economy by the Korean War (Allen, 1981a: 136–7, 141; Schonberger, 1989: 6–7, 62–4, 82–3, 114–33; Cusumano, 1985: 137–56; Itoh, 1990: 147).

For the long-term evolution of relations between capital and labor, American occupation was far more significant in setting parameters of permissible protests. As it was evident to radical factions that the occupation authorities would not tolerate a revolutionary overthrow of the system, militant actions took the unique form of 'production control' strikes whereby the management was locked out by workers who took over plants in increasing numbers. Since the occupation authorities controlled access to raw materials and capital, these plant occupations quickly fizzled out but their real significance lies elsewhere. In the unsettled and uncertain conditions of the early phases of the Occupation, when unemployment soared and food was scarce, the workplace offered the best means of economic survival for those employees who had not forsaken the towns for the countryside. As plans for war reparations, break-up of *zaibatsus*, and purges of the business elite inhibited production operations, in order to retain a core of experienced and skilled workers, firms were content to let them use their facilities to produce goods for barter – extracting salt by boiling sea water in giant kettles in steel mills, or growing crops on unused company land, or even trading company supplies for food (Gordon, 1996a: 36–8). While anxieties regarding their own futures and uncertainties about the occupation authorities' intentions made managements concede workers' demands for marriage, birth, and funeral arrangements, and for a veto over production decisions and hiring practices, these measures also reinforced workers' conceptions of the workplace as a community. At least as important, economic deprivation led to a widespread consensus that workers and managements were in the same predicament of subordination to the Occupation and fostered what has been called an 'enterprise society.' Differently put, if economic sustenance derived from the workplace where workers had significant veto rights over production and personnel decisions at least in early phases of the Occupation, membership in the workplace took precedence over membership in the class. Indicative of this sense of workplace-as-community were the bitter struggles over status – in prewar Japan, supervisory staff wore special uniforms to denote their superior status and had separate facilities from workers – and the success of workers' demands that status distinctions between them and supervisory staff be abolished. However, a corollary to this was that Japanese enterprise unions included not only blue-collar workers, but also white-collar workers and even the management (with the exception of the firm's president) and were confined to a single shop. Consequently, the new organizational structure of labor unions tended to limit working class power and foster intra-plant cooperation (Schonberger, 1989: 299, n. 6) and laid the basis for the cooperative labor–management relations – or 'coercive consensus' in Norma Field's (1991: 29) nice phrase. Perceptions among workers that the workplace was their primary source of identity and locus of community, rather than class or neighborhood, was also to have more wide-ranging resonances when industries migrated off-shore in increasing numbers, as we shall see in subsequent chapters.

Though the Korean War provided the Japanese economy with a considerable boost since it was cheaper for US forces to obtain goods of the requisite quality from Japan than from elsewhere, Japanese corporations were apprehensive that the boom may not last very long. Hence rather than incurring heavy capital expenditures by building new plants that may soon be under-utilized and avoiding unneccessary increases in their labor forces, they sought to use idle productive capacities of parts manufacturers by creating a wide variety of subcontracting arrangements, as we shall see in Chapter 3 (Smitka, 1991: 6–10, 53–78; Eccleston, 1989: 31). For our present purposes, it is important to note that multi-layered subcontracting arrangements permitted Japanese manufacturers to contain labor conflicts by maintaining relatively homogenized wages within the corporation

Table 2.1 Wage disparities between manufacturing enterprises of different sizes in Japan (average wages of employees in enterprises with 500 or more employees = 100)

Year	Enterprise size (no. of employees)			
	Over 500	100–499	30–99	5–29
1960	100	73.6	65.8	54.2
1965	100	83.7	78.3	72.6
1970	100	83.4	76.2	71.4
1975	100	85.7	75.8	70.3
1980	100	81.9	70.5	67.6
1985	100	79.4	68.7	64.7

Source: Itoh (1992b: 122, table 5.3).

through the contracting out of lower-skilled labor processes to a variety of ancillary firms. The wage disparities between large and small enterprises were even greater than indicated by the data presented in Table 2.1 since employees in medium and small enterprises received fewer fringe benefits (such as the annual bonuses which typically amounted to two months' salary and welfare plans administered by company unions).[6] They were also not entitled to a continuous escalation of wages based on seniority and to a lifetime of guaranteed employment (Itoh, 1992: 123). It was hence a strategy for preserving homogeneity in wages in a heterogeneous labor market (Smitka, 1991: 89–114; Hill, 1989: 467; Morales, 1994; Shapira, 1993).

At the other end of the spectrum was South Korea. Far from supporting the rights of labor and instilling the values of 'Jacksonian democracy' here, the AMG was centrally concerned with suppressing the 'people's committees' and excluding the left from political power. By the end of 1946, after the autumn harvest uprising had been brutally cauterized, revolutionary popular organizations in the countryside were dismembered, and the National Council of Korean Trade Unions – which represented almost the entire non-agricultural workforce, with almost a half a million members at the end of 1945 – decapitated and banned. It was replaced by the Federation of Korean Trade Unions which was officially an organ of Rhee's Liberal Party and had only 40,000 members. Laws protecting new unions from challenging the incumbent union gave the ruling party's union a legal monopoly. Even if collective bargaining was permitted, an elaborate mediation mechanism severely curbed the possibility of strike action (Cumings, 1981; Deyo, 1989: 118–21; Bello and Rosenfeld, 1990: 30; Choi, 1993: 18; Koo, 2001: 25–6).

The success of these repressive measures derived not only from the greater force deployed against South Korean workers, but also because industrialization under Japanese colonial rule had been disproportionately skewed in favor of the zone under Soviet control after the war and because of the demolition of war-related industries below the 38th parallel (Koo, 1996: 56, n. 8). Despite extensive industrialization under colonial occupation (Mason *et al.*, 1980: 78–9; Cumings, 1981: 26–30; Cumings, 1987: 56), partition and the demolition of war-related industries led to a dissipation of the working class.[7] Casualties during the Korean War, estimated to be almost 1.3 million civilians and armed forces personnel including some 98,000 who were executed (Kuznets, 1977: 37), further decimated the working class. This, perhaps more than any other factor, explains the relative quiescence of workers newly recruited to factories during the 1950s and early 1960s in spite of almost tyrannous conditions of life and work. Unlike their Japanese counterparts, the new working class emerging in South Korea after the end of hostilities were first-generation workers, alienated by urban life and unused to the rigors of industrial discipline.

If revolution and war decimated the working class in South Korea, the establishment of an ethnically-bifurcated conquest state undermined the strength of the working class in Taiwan. Reverting to GMD control after Japanese defeat, mass uprisings on the island in February 1947 against the corrupt and authoritarian provincial governor, Chen Yi, triggered a crackdown on labor which is variously estimated to have claimed between 10,000 and 12,000 victims (Gold, 1986: 49–54). The declaration of martial law and the transfer of Chiang's administration to the island in 1949 sealed the exclusion of labor from power and even led to a ban on the formation of political parties. To further consolidate the GMD's power, legislation also prohibited the unionization of workers in government employment, in educational institutions, and in military-related establishments. Strikes were virtually banned as they could not legally be called prior to mediation, and the decisions of tripartite arbitration boards were binding on all parties. Most damaging to the union movement was the provision that they could not 'demand an increase in wages to the extent of exceeding the standard wage' (quoted in Deyo, 1989: 115–16), a provision so ambiguous that it gave the government wide latitude to declare almost any wage demand 'excessive' and therefore illegal. The effects of these restrictions can be easily gauged from the fact that there was not a single major recorded strike in Taiwan from 1949 to 1987 when martial law was finally lifted, though there were many localized work stoppages (Deyo, 1989: 3, 58–9; Lee, 1995).

Since the GMD was a cadre-based party organized on Leninist lines, its organizational reach penetrated more deeply into the social fabric of the island than that of Rhee's Liberal Party. Reflecting this greater reach, it was able to foster what has been called 'exclusionary corporatism'; only a single union was permitted at an enterprise and all enterprise unions were linked through a provincial federation which, in turn, was linked to the island-wide Chinese Federation of Labor. Structured thus, the organized labor movement was prevented from developing horizontal links across enterprises, industries, and administrative units. More importantly, as unions were forbidden in enterprises with fewer than 30 workers, the bulk of employees were excluded from collective bargaining since the overwhelming majority of industrial enterprises in the island were small-scale units as we shall see. Finally, the provision that unions could be formed at the enterprise level only with the approval of both the local labor department and the local GMD committee tightened the party's grip over the union movement (Bello and Rosenfeld, 1990: 221–2; Deyo, 1989: 115–18; Haggard, 1990: 80–1).

While a rural elite had never been prominent in the social topography of the lilliputian city-states of Hong Kong and Singapore, labor subordination was at least as much a foundation of their emergence as low-cost manufacturers as it was in the cases of the larger Asian 'miracles.' Following the extreme repression of labor in Hong Kong during its occupation by the Japanese, there was a wave of labor militancy which peaked in 1948 as the pulse of the Chinese Revolution reverberated through the colony. Though the colonial government legalized trade union activity that year, the Illegal Strikes and Lockouts Ordinance of the following year banned strikes of government employees and those which would 'inflict social hardship on the community.' Even though the Trade Union Registration Act of 1961 recognized the right to strike and to picket peacefully, by permitting the registration of unions with as few as seven members and by prohibiting unionization across industries, trades, and occupations, other provisions of the same law severely diluted the bargaining power of labor (Deyo, 1989: 131). The ability of the colonial administration to harness the labor movement was largely due to changes in Chinese policy. Just as the Chinese Communist Party (CCP) had encouraged strikes against the colonial government and GMD supporters in the immediate aftermath of the Second World War, it discouraged further disruptions after 1948 as its victory over the GMD became assured since a politically stable Hong Kong provided a window to gather political and commercial intelligence and a vital source of foreign exchange, providing almost 40 percent of China's import bill before the reforms of Deng Xiaoping (Miners, 1993: 105–6; Haggard, 1990: 118; Castells *et al.*, 1990: 81–2). Simultaneously, a persistent split between the GMD-affiliated Chinese Labor Union and the CCP-affiliated Federation of Trade Unions weakened the organizational basis of the union movement. Not only was the labor movement split between these two opposing factions, but ethnic and dialect differences spawned a multiplicity of parochial and narrowly specialized unions (Lethbridge and Ng Sek-Hong, 1993: 86). Thus in 1961, of the 366 registered unions, 298 had a membership of less than 1,000 each, though they collectively represented only 20 percent of the total union membership (England and Rear, 1975: 83–5, 279; Selden, 1983; Deyo, 1989: 112–14).

Compounding the fragmentation of the working class by these divisions, the existence of a three-tier employment structure in many Chinese firms distinguished primarily by job security, skill differentials, and distribution of fringe benefits – with the 'long-term or permanent worker' or *cheung-kung* receiving bonuses, subsidized meals, and transport allowances, the 'casual or temporary worker' or *saan-kung* being hired on a daily basis and ineligible for these benefits, and the 'long-term casual worker' or *cheung-saan-kung* being eligible for some benefits – was also inimical to the creation of a strong and cohesive union movement. Finally, and perhaps uniquely among colonial administrations, the political thrust of the labor movement was blunted because British rule was universally seen as the only realistic alternative to Hong Kong's absorption into the People's Republic of China. The government of Hong Kong was, therefore, insulated from an anticolonial insurgency (England and Rear, 1975: 4–5; Lethbridge and Ng Sek-Hong, 1993: 80–6, 95; Miners, 1993: 108–9; Levin and Ng Sek-Hong, 1995).

No such inoculation was available to the British Military Administration in Singapore, where both middle class professionals and a working class dominated by the communist-affiliated Singapore Federation of Trade Unions intensified their anticolonial agitation after the war. Even as the colonial government's ferocious military assault on the Malayan Communist Party indicated the strategic importance of the area to Britain, and the Western alliance more generally, the same magnitude of repressive force could not be deployed against the skilled and unskilled workers in Singapore without destroying the economic interests Britain sought to preserve (Tremewan, 1994: 16). Though a broad spectrum of civil liberties was suspended in the Crown Colony under 'emergency' regulations, and the anti-colonial movement restricted to a narrow range of permitted trade union activity, the Left in Singapore was provided with a vital political space. The People's Action Party (PAP), founded in 1954, represented a mutually convenient alliance between middle class professionals and the Left. Given the close political, economic, and cultural affinities between the colony's small commercial and industrial bourgeoisie and British colonial administrators and business interests, middle class professionals seeking decolonization lacked a social base of any real consequence. The Left provided the missing mass base among the Chinese working class for the independence movement in return for a veneer of 'respectability' and political security that accrued from an association with middle class professionals (Rodan, 1989: 54, 57, 83). However, strains in this alliance became increasingly evident as the draconian emergency laws were gradually rescinded after the defeat of the Malayan Communist Party in 1953 and elections to the Singapore Legislative Council in 1955. If the more liberal atmosphere after the elections enabled the left wing of the PAP to gain strength, the detention of a swathe of activists in 1956 aborted its attempt to capture the party leadership. Thereafter, Lee Kuan Yew moved quickly to consolidate his position by restructuring the party organization and restricting the right to elect members of its Central Executive Committee (CEC) to 'cadre' members who themselves had to be approved by the

CEC: '[t]he new structure simply amounted to the existing leadership selecting an elite band of cadres who in turn elected the leadership' (Rodan, 1989: 60; see also Tremewan, 1994: 21–3).

Despite these measures, and the PAP's victory in the elections of 1959 when Singapore became self-governing, the left wing continued to broaden its base of support, and when thirteen members of the PAP resigned in 1961 to form the *Barisan Socialis* (Socialist Front) over the issue of merger with Malaysia, they took with them between 60 and 80 percent of the party's membership (Rodan, 1989: 68–9; Tremewan, 1994: 27). If defections reduced the PAP to a shell of its former self, it also clearly identified the regime's opponents against whom the full weight of the security apparatus could be brought to bear. Since an erosion of its mass base did not immediately jeopardize the PAP's legislative majority, Lee Kuan Yew sought to shore up his support both by persecuting his opponents and by creating a new social base for his regime. Thus, the government launched a systematic campaign to harass its opposition and deregister their grass roots organizations, accompanied by a propaganda barrage against communism (Rodan, 1989: 68–71; Tremewan, 1994: 26). Simultaneously, by touting the potential economic benefits of a merger with Malaysia and by undertaking a massive developmental program – between 1961 and 1963 the state Housing Development Board (HDB) constructed 22,336 new apartments to house almost 100,000 people and by 1963 increased expenditure on education meant that there was a place for every child in the primary schools (Rodan, 1989: 73) – it sought to foster greater public support for itself. Perhaps most importantly, as the formation of the *Barisan Socialis* had left the rump PAP with virtually no grass roots organization, the government built a network of community organizations, chiefly the Citizens' Consultative Committees and the Street Committees, to deliver both welfare services and government propaganda. As in the case of the GMD in Taiwan, this symbolized the systematic merger of the PAP with the state (Rodan, 1989: 73–4; Castells *et al.*, 1990: 193).

Finally, the Indonesian government's '*Confrontasi*' (confrontation) policy provided the pretext for the administration to decapitate the opposition leadership through a round-up of over 100 leading activists in a February 1963 police raid, aptly named 'Operation Cold Store' since some of those arrested were incarcerated for almost twenty years. The eruption of ethnic riots in Singapore in 1964, stemming from the resentment of Malays who had been resettled from their kampongs to pave the way for the HDB flats, and the expulsion of the island from the Malay Federation in 1965 also contributed to the heightened sense of insecurity among the Chinese population. By skillfully exploiting the acute sense of isolation among the island's dominant Chinese population, and casting itself as a government not beholden to any interest group, the PAP was to subordinate labor more thoroughly. Stressing the importance of industrial peace for national survival, it was able to justify the wholesale deregistration of opposition unions immediately following the ethnic riots. Further restrictions were placed on industrial action in the following three years, banning sympathy strikes and strikes in essential services altogether; lengthening the working day and fortifying management prerogatives by excluding promotions, dismissals, and work assignments from the purview of union negotiations; and establishing arbitration procedures that effect-ively foreclosed the possibility of legal strike actions except with the consent of the government. The impact of these measures, perhaps the most restrictive legislations on worker organization anywhere outside the centrally-planned economies, is evident from the number of recorded work stoppages which declined from 116 and 88 in 1961 and 1962 to five in 1970 and to none at all between 1978 and 1986 (Bello and Rosenfeld, 1990: 303–5; Castells *et al.*, 1990: 170; Deyo, 1989: 62–3, 121–30; Rodan, 1989: 91–2; Tremewan, 1994: 28; Haggard, 1990: 103–7).

Fortuitously for the PAP government, its expulsion from the Malaysian Federation coincided with the search for cheap, low-skilled assembly opera-tions in the electronics industry by US corporations due to an intensifica-tion of competitive pressures caused by the reconstruction of the West European and Japanese economies (Pang Eng Fong and Lim, 1977). The requirements of US manufacturers in the semiconductor and electronics industries for cheap labor dovetailed nicely with the PAP government's strategy to buy labor peace by providing laborers with employment and material benefits (Bello and Rosenfeld, 1990: 304). Consequently, through its expenditures in public housing as well as in infrastructural development discussed later in more detail, the government created conditions con-ducive to investments by transnational corporations – and between 1968, when National Semiconductors established its first plant in Singapore, and 1972, industrial production, employment, and exports all increased at an annual average rate of 23 percent (Castells *et al.*, 1990: 194).

Hence, while labor subordination was a common characteristic shared by all the Asian 'miracles,' the modalites of subordination were strikingly different. If American occupation was conducive to political liberalization in Japan, it also facilitated the creation of more cooperative relations between management and labor. Moreover, the rhetoric of paternalism, in the more democratic conditions of Japan with the presence of a numer-ically large and well-organized industrial labor force, was not all one way, even if it was skewed toward the management. Thus, to take one instance, workers at the Kawasaki steel mills couched their demands for a 200 percent wage hike in 1946 by arguing that it was their 'burning love for the company' that lay behind their demands, since without protecting their livelihoods they could not 'revive Japan from this tragic condition' (quoted in Gordon, 1996a: 40). Whereas the deployment of corporation-as-family rhetoric served to create a labor aristocracy in Japan, the evolu-tion of hierarchical, multi-layered subcontracting systems fragmented the working class.

Unlike in Japan, in both South Korea and Taiwan their strategic location along the ideological fault lines of the Cold War was used as a justification for the retention of more authoritarian structures of control and for the virtual ban of public dissent. As containment of 'communism' in East Asia conveniently dovetailed with domestic farm policy in the hegemonic power, the United States underwrote the costs of industrialization in both countries by disposing of surplus farm products through the PL 480 aid program. The ample availability of cheap foodgrains not only lowered wage costs – directly by reducing reproduction costs, and indirectly by exerting a downward pressure on urban wage rates by providing a steady stream of migrants seeking to escape even poorer material conditions in the countryside – but also did not threaten to unravel the alliance between the regimes and the peasantry because of the lack of substitutability between rice and feed grains. The bifurcation between national production of food and the international sourcing of feed grains enabled these states, and Japan, to increase price support on rice while simultaneously importing feed grains without protection. In all three US client states, labor quiescence was hence also purchased by lowering wages through the disposal of American farm surpluses which did not threaten political alliances and processes of reconstruction in the countryside, unlike in the case of Europe where there was no bifurcation between national and international food sectors since food grains such as wheat and rye were perfectly substitutable for feed grains (Hayami, 1988; Friedmann, 1982; Friedmann, 1993; Friedmann and McMichael, 1989; McMichael, 1993; McMichael and Kim, 1994; Tubiana, 1989).

As British colonies, neither Hong Kong nor Singapore were recipients of American food aid. If the subordination of labor did not carry a high price in Hong Kong – both because of divisions within the working class and because colonial political control was not challenged either by the subject population or by the Chinese government – no such luxury was afforded to the PAP government in Singapore. Moreover, while the Chinese government's need for a 'window on the world' led it to conclude agreements to provide 80 percent of Hong Kong's food requirements since the early 1950s at prices favorable to the colonial government, Singapore could rely on no similar arrangements from its neighbors. However, by portraying the island as a Chinese enclave in a sea of Malays, the government played on the apprehensions of the Chinese majority to win support for its rule while provisions of better housing and job opportunities served as additional incentives in the subordination of labor.

In sum, the reconstitution of Japan, South Korea, and Taiwan as US client states in the context of the Cold War entailed a fundamental restructuring of social relations. The elimination of agrarian magnates and the redistribution of land not only created some of the most equitable distributions of income and wealth in the world but also guaranteed social peace in the countryside. By securing the countryside, governments were free to launch 'anti-communist' offensives against organized labor in the cities, though the strength and maturity of the Japanese working class enabled them to wrest some limited though significant concessions. While fragmentation of labor organizations and a recognition that British rule was the only viable alternative to Hong Kong's absorption to China curbed labor militancy in the Crown Colony, state repression was necessary in Singapore to subordinate its working class. Despite political quiescence in the countryside and labor subordination in the cities, it was widely recognized that the newly reconstituted regimes could only be secure by increasing the material prosperity of their subject populations. Yet, domestic bourgeoisies in each of these jurisdictions were too weak or non-existent. This prompted, as we shall see in the next section, symbiotic alliances between state and capital along the Asian rimlands.

Dependent bourgeoisies

Notwithstanding pressures on the reconstituted regimes to vigorously promote the material welfare of their subject populations to legitimize their rule and the ensuing congruity of interests between political elites and 'captains of industry,' the postwar reordering of the political order along the Asian rimlands intensified the dependence of bourgeoisies on their state apparatuses in all five future Asian 'miracles.' The convergence of interests was based on the removal of impediments to a more expeditious transfer of surplus from agriculture to industry through land reforms and the elimination of landlords in the three US client states, and the corralling of trade union movements and the creation of more optimum conditions for capital accumulation in all five jurisdictions. The destruction of production facilities and the disruption of prewar procurement and production networks, however, rendered bourgeoisies dependent on their respective state apparatuses for capital and protection. Indeed, in South Korea and Taiwan, the new regimes even had to incubate bourgeoisies to create domestic constituencies of support. The very weakness of the domestic bourgeoisie in Singapore and the small size of its domestic markets and low endowments of natural resources foreclosed even this possibility. The PAP government was compelled, therefore, to create structural conditions to attract transnational corporations (TNCs) to relieve chronic unemployment and thereby stabilize political conditions in the city-state. The large diversified commercial and financial bourgeoisie in Hong Kong may not have relied on the colonial state for capital infusions and protection. However, the Chinese Revolution undermined Hong Kong's entrepôt role and they depended on the government to provide the infrastructural underpinnings in the colony's transition to an export-oriented industrial platform.

Broadly speaking, relationships between political and business elites in each location were conditioned by the nature and structure of state power and the organizational strength and technological maturity of the bourgeoisie, by the size of their domestic markets and their varied endowments of natural resources, by the extent of the dislocations of their prewar production and sales networks and by the patterns of political and economic linkages in which they were enmeshed. Additionally, as the consequences of wartime destruction were overcome, as postwar reconstruction changed patterns of economic and political linkages with the wider world, and as the organizational capacity of enterprises expanded with the establishment of new production and procurement networks and the saturation of domestic markets, the dynamism of these relationships caused further variations as these changes impacted differently on enterprise and regime structures in each location.

While landlords were being eliminated and the labor movement tamed in Japan, the decision of the US occupation forces to exercise indirect rather than direct rule conferred immense leverage on the revived bureaucracy to subvert or even to ignore the reform program concerning the financial-industrial conglomerates. For instance, the reluctance of the ultra-conservative Japanese cabinet headed by Yoshida Shigeru, which took office after the first elections based on universal adult suffrage in 1946, to rein in inflationary tendencies made a mockery of the punitive levies and indemnities imposed on the *zaibatsu* as the enterprises merely paid these fines in the devalued yen. The penalties were, in fact, effectively funded by the public exchequer since the Japanese government continued to pay for military contracts, indemnities for factories converted to munition facilities under wartime regulations, and war production loans and guarantees until June 1946 – in the first three months of the Occupation alone, disbursements to the *zaibatsu* under wartime ordinances and rules totalled ¥26.6 billion, or almost a third of the total Japanese military expenditures between September 1937 and August 1945. Even after the occupation authorities compelled the Japanese government to terminate these payments, the creation of the Reconstruction Finance Committee in January 1947 allowed the government to continue pumping money to the conglomerates in the guise of low-interest loans until the promulgation of the Dodge Line in 1949 (Johnson, 1982: 43, 178–9; Schonberger, 1989: 99, 102–3).

The *zaibatsu* were, however, subject to the highest-ever levels of government control during the Occupation. Unlike the bureaucracy, the rentier class which controlled the *zaibatsu* through family holding companies was not spared from the purges despite the premature termination of the program of *zaibatsu* dissolution. Though the purges were much less pervasive in Japan than in postwar West Germany, some 2,100 top executives from 632 firms were barred from office (Johnson, 1982: 25, 41–2, 44, 70–2, 174–88; Aoki, 1987: 268–9; Yonekura, 1993: 214–20).

In the immediate aftermath of defeat, the destruction wrought by war was so massive that the occupation authorities permitted the government to set up fifteen *kōdan* or public corporations for rationing materials and products, and authorized the enactment of the Temporary Materials

Supply and Demand Control Law of 1946 which empowered the government to control all commodities through the *kōdan* and other public institutions – notably the Coal Agency and the Economic Stabilization Board. By purchasing all major products from the manufacturers at high prices and selling them to consumers at low prices, the government effectively subsidized economic recovery.

Control over foreign exchange and trade, including statutory powers to regulate the import of technology, gave the government considerable leverage in targeting specific industries for accelerated growth. Reinforcing this leverage, the onset of the Korean War led to a loosening of monetary controls to ensure that adequate investment capital was available to industries to meet the rapid expansion of US military procurements – for munitions, uniforms, trucks, and other war-related items – which accounted for 37 percent of all Japanese foreign exchange receipts in 1952–53 (Johnson, 1982: 200). To meet these requirements, the government increased its loans to the 'city banks' or the twelve national banks, enabling them to extend loans much larger than the net worth of individual firms, as well as setting up a string of government-owned banks, most notably the Japan Development Bank and the Export-Import Bank. As the ultimate guarantor of loans, the Bank of Japan and the Ministry of Finance acquired comprehensive control over the lending policies of banks while the availability of ample low-interest loans reduced the dependence of industrial corporations on equity capital. The policy of 'overloaning' not only enabled Japanese companies to raise money more cheaply – since interests on loans were tax-deductible while dividends on profits were not – but also freed them to concentrate on long-term product development rather than short-term profits. At the same time, the policy enabled the government to easily use monetary controls to modulate the rhythm of economic activity and target particular sectors with precision (Johnson, 1982: 194, 203–4, 302, 313; Yoshino and Lifson, 1986: 32; Eccleston, 1989: 31–3, 48).

Indicative of the extraordinary concentration of power in the Ministry of Commerce and Industry, the precursor to the Ministry of International Trade and Industry (MITI), was its control of the third largest share of the general account budget after the Prime Minister's office and the Ministry of Finance by 1948–49 when the Dodge Plan was implemented. Perhaps an even more telling indication of the depth and range of government control over economic activities during the Occupation is that when MITI was created in 1949 it employed 21,199 persons, while in 1974 it had only 13,891 employees even though the Japanese economy had become infinitely more complex. In this context, the institutionalization of the practice of *amakudari* (literally 'descent from heaven'), or the reemployment of retired bureaucrats on the boards of industries, provided them with preferential access to the government while cementing the alliance between the government and private industry.

Despite the devastation of their physical plants through Allied bombing and disruptions to their supply and distribution networks, the big Japanese industrial bourgeoisie was highly cohesive and class conscious. The day after the surrender documents had been signed, top industrial and financial leaders met at the home of the Minister of Commerce and Industry, Nakajima Chikuhei, to forge a united strategy to revitalize their enterprises. To coordinate these efforts, they launched the Federation of Economic Organizations, or *Keidanren*, composed of the 100 top trade and industrial organizations and some 750 of the largest individual firms. Notably, unlike industrial and trade associations elsewhere in the world, Keidanren explicitly excluded small and medium-scale industries from its membership: it was the apex coordinating body of big business (Eccleston, 1989: 117–18; Pempel, 1998: 94–5).

Divisiveness among small and medium-size firms implied that though they accounted for some 99.7 percent of all firms in the country – and were grouped into some 50,000 organizations – they did not have the influence enjoyed by large firms. One chairman of the Keidanren, Ishikaza Taizo, even commented that organizing small and medium firms was akin to making rice balls with imported rice! Nevertheless, recognizing the electoral importance of these small and medium sized firms which employed 82.9 percent of the total national labor force in the mid-1950s, the government allowed small businesses to create cartels to harmonize production, marketing, and investment in selected sectors in 1952. Eventually, the creation of *Sōrengō* or the General Federation of Small and Medium Enterprise Organizations, institutionalized support from these firms to the government in return for subsidies. In tandem with these national measures, large firms began organizing their own suppliers and thus created further bonds between small and large firms (Pempel, 1998: 95–8)

If American occupation and its policies conferred enormous powers on the Japanese government to intervene in the economic arena, the dependence of the bourgeoisie on the state was even greater in South Korea and Taiwan than in Japan due to the virtual absence of the set of political and economic institutions which could be rebuilt through additional doses of capital and technology. Despite the location of industries and the creation of an industrial proletariat in colonial Taiwan and Korea,[8] there was no corresponding development of an indigenous bourgeoisie or a technocratic strata in either colony.[9] With the virtual absence of a bourgeoisie and institutional infrastructures essential for capitalist development, the political dependence of the Chiang and Rhee regimes on the United States in the context of the political ecology of superpower rivalry conditioned the postwar rehabilitation of both former colonies.

While both post-colonial regimes nationalized Japanese assets, the greater leverage exercised by the AMG on the Rhee administration compelled it to rapidly privatize state-owned enterprises and the South Korean–American agreement of 1954 led to the sale of 50 major industrial enterprises. In contrast, American ambivalence toward the GMD in the immediate aftermath of the Second World War meant that there were no corresponding pressures on Chiang's regime in Taiwan to privatize the economy. Indeed, concluding that the island's survival as an independent state was unviable, the Truman administration had even cut off all assistance to Taiwan in 1949. At the same time, unlike most other post-colonial states, the GMD regime not only had a large cadre of technocrats with extensive experience in industrial production and economic planning on the Chinese mainland but the establishment of a conquest state over indigenous islanders also rendered the party hierarchy very resistant to the idea of granting economic power to a relatively hostile subject population. Hence, the GMD party-state's domination of the economy in Taiwan was staggering especially since virtually no leading Chinese entrepreneur followed Chiang to the island.

State enterprises in Taiwan accounted for almost 57 percent of industrial production in the early 1950s and though the growth of private industries in the ensuing decades diluted this overwhelming dominance, the state sector still accounted for about 20 percent of industrial production in the early 1970s. Some ministries even established separate commercial ventures – as, for instance, the Ministry of Communications and the Ministry of Economic Affairs, both of which had their own 'private' engineering companies. The military's holding company – the Vocational Assistance Commission for Retired Servicemen – was perhaps the largest conglomerate in the island, with businesses spanning a wide spectrum of activities from restaurants, orchards, and dairy farms to trucking, construction, manufacturing, and foreign trade. Finally, quite apart from government enterprises, the ruling GMD itself controlled a network of some 50 corporations spanning a wide array of sectors including communications (Central News Agency), petrochemicals (Orient Union Chemical Corporation), finance (Central Investment and Trust Corporation), and transportation. The *Asian Wall Street Journal Weekly* estimated that approximately half of Taiwan's corporate assets were directly or indirectly controlled by the government or the GMD in 1989, a share higher than almost anywhere outside the centrally-planned economies and sub-Saharan Africa (Gold, 1986: 70; Wade, 1990: 176, 266, 273–4; Bello and Rosenfeld, 1990: 232–3). Moreover, since US assistance, channeled through the government, accounted for almost 40 percent of annual gross domestic capital formation in the island between 1951 and 1965 (Simon, 1988a: 149–50), business success or failure was unusually dependent on the GMD's favor.

Privatization of nationalized industrial assets was, however, a mixed blessing for Syngman Rhee. Though it deprived him of the institutional mechanisms of control available to Chiang, as he had no significant bases of support in Korea, the giveaway of confiscated Japanese assets to ex-managers and supporters of the regime at below-market prices enabled him to create a powerful constituency based on patronage (see Woo, 1991: 67).

South Korea's strategic location in the geopolitical calculus of the Cold War also more than compensated for the enforced privatization of expropriated Japanese assets. In the first instance, though the Korean War catapulted Taiwan to the front line of the US attempt to 'contain communism' and led to the resumption of economic and military assistance to shore up Chiang's regime and to dissuade it from attempting an invasion of the mainland – a venture that would have inevitably led to the commitment of significant numbers of US troops (Gold, 1986: 69; Wade, 1990: 82, 246) – South Korea received far larger infusions of overseas aid, as already indicated in Chapter 1. Apart from US economic and military disbursements of $12.6 billion between 1946 and 1976, South Korea received an additional $1 billion from Japan and some $1.9 billion from international financial institutions. Taking the South Korean population in 1960, the mid-point of these three decades, this total of over $15 billion amounted to a per capita figure of $600 in comparison to a per capita figure of $425 for Taiwan, or a total of $5.6 billion (Mason *et al.*, 1980: 165, 185; Krueger, 1979).

Despite Rhee's greater dependence on US aid, he was less vulnerable to American pressures to implement wide-ranging social and economic reforms than Chiang because the presence of large numbers of American troops on South Korean soil and the country's precarious political and military location along the geopolitical fault lines of the Cold War enabled him – like Ngo Dinh Diem in South Vietnam – to play off security interests against aid officials (Barrett, 1988: 126–7, 133–5). Hence, frustrating American designs to re-create an East Asian trading bloc centered on Japan, Rhee resisted pressures to normalize diplomatic relations with Japan and pursued a vigorous import-substituting industrialization (ISI) program with US aid funds which resulted in the manufacturing sector registering an annual average growth rate of 10.8 percent during the 1950s compared with 2.5 percent for the primary sector and 3.9 percent for services (Haggard, 1990: 59; see Amsden, 1989: 40–1). Of course, the pursuit of an ISI program was also facilitated by the military volatility, political instability and the sheer poverty of the country which made it an unappealing market for US corporations, especially when much richer pickings were to be had in Western Europe, Australia, and Argentina. Similarly, parlaying the regime's political and military vulnerability, Rhee was able to thwart American pressures to devalue the currency after 1955, since an overvalued exchange-rate lowered the cost of imported capital and intermediate goods necessary for an ISI strategy while increasing the real value of inflows of foreign aid. At the same time, the maintenance of multiple exchange-rates – lowering exchange-rates for particular export items and destinations – eliminated some of the more egregious effects of an overvalued currency (Krueger, 1979: 61–5; Woo, 1991: 53–65).

Conversely, notwithstanding smaller inflows of American economic and military assistance, the GMD party-state's domination of the 'commanding heights of the economy' – including aluminum, fertilizers, heavy machinery, petrochemicals and petroleum refining, shipbuilding, steel, sugar, and synthetics – rendered the regime more vulnerable to American pressures to promote private enterprise, particularly in the context of the progressive bureaucratization of US aid disbursements. The greater vulnerability of the regime in Taiwan to US influence was vividly illustrated by the creation of two supra-ministerial agencies in 1953, the Economic Stabilization Board (ESB) and the Council on US Aid (CUSA), the meetings of both of which were routinely conducted in English to accommodate American advisers (Jacoby, 1966; Gold, 1986: 67–9; Haggard, 1990: 86–7; Wade, 1990: 82, 199).

In both cases, the political subordination of the bourgeoisie was further cemented by their reliance on the state for finance and tariff protection. In Taiwan, the GMD party-state not only monopolized the banking sector through its ownership of the banks that migrated from China and its confiscation of majority shares from Japanese partners of private banks on the island, but measures taken to curb hyperinflation in early 1950 to soak up excess money supply – chiefly raising nominal interest rates to 7 percent per month, or a real annual rate ranging from 28 to 82 percent – increased its control over domestic savings as well. Even if these interest rates quickly proved to be unsustainable and were cut to a monthly rate of 3 percent, the rate was high enough to ensure that time and savings deposits in banks accounted for some 56 percent of the money supply by late 1952 (Gold, 1986: 108; Wade, 1990: 58). Though nominal interest rates were lowered further as prices stabilized, these still averaged about 9 percent per year between 1955 and 1965 while nominal rates on unsecured loans in the 'unregulated' market averaged around 40.7 percent (Wade, 1990: 58–9).

Moreover, apart from the retention of strict controls over foreign exchange, import restrictions, bank credit, and industrial licensing, government control over the economy was cemented by the mandatory requirement that industrial associations be formed in any sector with more than five firms. As the GMD appointed the secretaries of the major associations, and monitored and controlled elections to their boards of directors, these functioned not as autonomous bodies representing the interests of their members but as conduits to gather information and convey government directives (Wade, 1990: 271–2).

Once again, even if US pressure compelled the Rhee administration to sell the commercial banks and grant autonomy to the country's central bank in 1957, as American interference in the management of aid funds was less intrusive than in Taiwan, the South Korean government could reward its supporters more freely than its GMD counterpart. Moreover, since large doses of US assistance – estimated to account for over 80 percent of the country's foreign exchange earnings between 1953 and 1958 (Koo, 1987: 167; Amsden, 1989: 39) – were funneled through the government, Rhee was able to use aid disbursements to provide windfall profits for his cronies: tolerating them reselling their allocation of scarce imported raw materials and countenancing their refusal to repay the 'loans' they received (Amsden, 1989: 39; see also Haggard, 1990: 54–61).

Indeed, beneficiaries of undervalued state assets in South Korea never lost their early lead and when commercial banks were sold in 1957, these were largely acquired by the favored industrialists. While access to political patronage gave these 'entrepreneurs' import permits and preferential rates of foreign exchange, they found it more lucrative to sell foreign exchange and lease their import permits rather than increase their productive capacity, as the regime had no mechanism to specify the use of these scarce resources (Cheng, 1990: 147–51). Finally, while Chiang's regime included a large cadre of economic managers, Rhee's Liberal Party, dominated by exiled nationalists and remnants of the Korean aristocracy, and collaborators in the Japanese colonial enterprise had no comparable cadre (Kuznets, 1977: 32–5; Cheng, 1990: 146–7; Wade, 1990: 246–7).

At first sight, the economic and political dependence of the bourgeoisie on their respective state apparatuses in South Korea and Taiwan stands in sharp contrast to Hong Kong. With a flat-rate income tax of 15 percent, no tax on capital gains, no restrictions on the movement of capital and commodities, no mandatory minimum wage, unemployment insurance or retirement pensions, minimal regulations on working conditions, generally balanced budgets, extremely low public debt, and with not even a central bank[10], the Crown Colony presents an almost textbook example of a *laissez faire* economy. The dominance of the commercial and financial sectors in the colony's entrepôt economy also meant that government policy was set firmly against infant industry protection or subsidies to help manufacturers.

Yet, in 1949, even as its governor, Alexander Grantham, was proclaiming that 'he was proud to be the "Governor of a Colony of shopkeepers"' (Choi, 1999: 143), fundamental changes were transforming Hong Kong from an entrepôt to a locus of low-cost manufactures. In the first instance, Hong Kong was not only the recipient of a large influx of refugees in the late 1940s but also of a large inflow of capital from China as many firms from Shanghai transferred their assets to the Crown Colony – as much as US$50 million in 1947 alone according to a *Fortune* magazine estimate (England and Rear, 1975: 25) – and the number of industrial establishments increased from 972 in March 1947 to 1,788 four years later (Choi, 1994: 43–4).

If the commercial and financial bourgeoisie was initially reluctant to support policies conducive to the growth of manufacturing, the loss of markets and production facilities in China especially after the United States placed a virtual embargo on China in December 1950 due to the Korean War, provided an impetus for Hong Kong's large and diversified trading companies to establish closer ties with manufacturing establishments (Haggard, 1990: 121). With exports from the colony falling from HK$4.4 billion in 1951 to HK$2.5 billion in 1955 as a result of the loss of its entrepôt function, the colonial government began to respond to manufacturers' concerns that the hilly nature of the urban area limited the supply of land for industry. Land development for industrial use did not represent a significant departure from laissez faire principles, as Stephen Chiu (1996) has argued, since it 'was similar to other kinds of logistic support that the colonial state offered to private enterprise.' Government ownership of land also meant that lands could simply be transferred from the Government Lands Department to the Housing Authority and thus the estates, storage facilities, and industrial workshops could all be constructed at relatively low cost.

Moreover, soon after a devastating fire on Christmas Eve 1953 in the Shep Kip Mei squatter settlement in North Kowloon had made over 50,000 people homeless and spurred the government to embark on a massive housing policy, the Housing Authority soon realized the enormous commercial potential presented by the housing estates both as a means to provide profit-making facilities to residents of these estates and for the Authority itself. Public ownership of all land in the colony implied that the government's land policy was a redistributive tool as the large- and medium-scale businesses were charged high real estate prices which provided the government with the revenues required to construct the industrial infrastructure without incurring large debts and to subsidize low-cost housing for the poor. By 1981, the Housing Authority had leased space to some 5,000 private factories located in multistorey buildings and cottages, as well as to 13,750 shops, banks, and restaurants (Castells *et al.*, 1990: 18, 33, 43–4, 95–7).

With the chronic inadequacy of domestic supplies of food and the large influx of refugees, cheap sources of basic wage goods were vital for the colony's transition from a commercial entrepôt to a low-cost manufacturer of industrial goods, especially since food expenditures accounted for approximately 55 percent of the incomes of all households in the early 1960s and 1970s, and was considerably higher for blue-collar households (Schiffer, 1991: 183). Apart from importing food from China, the Hong Kong administration also adopted a 'Rice Control Scheme' in 1955 and established a distribution network to deliver rice, vegetables, and fish at controlled prices. In conjunction with price controls on public transport and utilities, it has been estimated that government subsidies amounted to 50.2 percent of the average wage of a blue-collar household as late as 1973–74 (Castells *et al.*, 1990: 79–80; Schiffer, 1991: 184–6).

Recognizing that export-oriented manufacturing could also provide large profits from foreign exchange services, some of the large expatriate-owned trading firms or *hongs* also diversified their operations and moved into manufacturing: Jardines into textiles, for instance, and Wheelock Marden into textiles and toys (Choi, 1999: 152–3). However, periodic bouts of political uncertainty – fear that strategic concerns during the Korean and Indochina Wars could outweigh economic advantages China derived from Hong Kong, that the Cultural Revolution would submerge the colony – meant that industrialists were as reluctant to invest in projects with long gestation periods as banks were to lend money for them. This implied that entrepreneurs in Hong Kong pursued what Kim-Ming Lee (1999) calls a 'guerilla strategy': they were 'committed to making money, not to making goods for sale' (England and Rear, 1975: 34; see also Choi, 1999: 145).

The colonial government's role in developing Hong Kong's infrastructure and in subsidizing wage-goods was crucial in the transformation of the colony from an entrepôt to a locus of low-cost manufacture. However, internal divisions among its industrial bourgeoisie enabled the colonial state to manipulate these ruptures for its own ends. Though the Chinese Manufacturers' Association (CMA), representing the interests of industrialists, consistently demanded protectionist measures and greater state intervention in the economy, the colonial state instigated and subsidized the creation of a rival organization, the Hong Kong Federation of Industries, controlled by Shanghainese industrialists rather than the Cantonese who dominated the CMA. By thus blunting the influence of the industrial bourgeoisie – and mobilizing its largest stratum behind itself – the colonial government insulated itself against the demands of small manufacturers (Choi, 1999: 154–5). Nevertheless, even though large-scale government intervention belied Hong Kong's laissez faire pretensions and fundamentally conditioned structures of accumulation, the large financial and commercial bourgeoisie had a great deal of influence on state policy – to a degree unmatched elsewhere along the rimlands. Hence, they prevented the emergence of selective state assistance for industrial development since greater public expenditure would result in higher taxes (Chiu, 1996: 243–4).

Singapore's expulsion from the Malaysian Federation was perhaps even more cathartic than Hong Kong's loss of its Chinese hinterland, because the collapse of the merger completely undermined the government's strategy to transform the island from an entrepôt to an industrial center. Based on a blueprint formulated by a United Nations Industrial Survey Mission headed by Albert Winsemius, the rapid increase in manufacturing investment, especially since mid-1963,[11] had been predicated on a common market arrangement with Malaysia. Though anti-Chinese pogroms in Indonesia in the 1950s had triggered a flight of capital to Singapore, it did not lead to a spurt of manufacturing activity as Sino-Indonesians were from the commercial rather than the industrial strata (Haggard and Cheng, 1987: 89). Acknowledging the inadequacy of commercial activities and financial services to generate sufficient employment opportunities and the weakness of domestic capital, the government's economic policy had revolved around attracting foreign capital by the provision of a low-wage, docile labor force, tax incentives, well-developed infrastructural facilities including the construction of industrial estates, and the free remittance of capital – in short, state support for private capital. In the context of the trade embargo imposed by Indonesia, the failure of the merger with Malaysia not only dealt a fatal blow to the PAP's development project but it also threatened the party's grip on power. On the heels of its expulsion from the Malaysian Federation, the beleagured Singapore government was additionally confronted by Britain's decision to close its military installations – which had directly or indirectly accounted for almost 24 percent of the island's GNP in 1967 and employed about 20 percent of the workforce the year the decision was announced (Rodan, 1989: 87; Castells *et al.*, 1990: 190–1; Cheng and Gereffi, 1994: 203) – by 1971.

The PAP government's strategy to attract foreign investments was underpinned by a massive construction scheme – funded by compulsory contributions to a government-organized social security scheme, the Central Provident Fund (CPF) – the creation of several major public sector undertakings, and by a concerted ideological campaign of 'social engineering.' Soon after Lee Kuan Yew's election victory in 1959, the government had begun one of the most successful public housing programs in the world, building some half a million units in 25 years and 15 fully-equipped satellite towns to house 85 percent of the population. The provision of relatively high quality housing for workers at low rents and prices along with a bundle of facilities in education, health, recreation, and other community services, eased pressures on wages without reducing the quality of labor. Additionally, public housing construction was also a device to curb unemployment rates, particularly in the late 1960s when it was feared that almost 100,000 jobs would be lost due to the closure of British military installations. The determined enforcement of the state's right of eminent domain and the enforcement of mandatory land-acquisition policies checked land speculation during a phase of rapid economic expansion, lowered project development costs, and facilitated not only the development of housing estates but also satellite towns and large industrial estates. In addition, by restricting the withdrawal of funds from the CPF almost exclusively for public housing, the government was able to effectively control the demand and supply of money. Finally, linking CPF rates to wage increases provided another string to the state's anti-inflationary bow (Castells *et al.*, 1990: 191, 193, 267, 304–6). Cumulatively, these measures closed the wage gap between Singapore and its three main rivals in the region – Hong Kong, South Korea, and Taiwan (Rodan, 1989: 105).

In tandem with the construction of public housing, the PAP government also launched a major drive to improve infrastructural facilities to attract foreign investors. Following recommendations of the Winsemius Report, 58 percent of the M$871 allocated for public sector investments in the State Development Plan 1961–64 was earmarked for these programs. The largest single allocation was to the newly-created Economic Development Board (EDB), the pilot agency designed to lower the establishment and operating costs of manufacturing concerns by underwriting the issue of stocks and bonds, guaranteeing loans, developing industrial estates, and providing technical assistance (Rodan, 1989: 64–5). Despite the provision of attractive terms for foreign investors, Singapore's relatively higher wage levels meant that the bulk of overseas investments were in the capital intensive sectors. Hence, though investments in the manufacturing sector had increased by 3.69 percent in 1964 (in 1968 prices) and 13.44 percent in 1965, industrial employment had risen only by 3,120 in 1964 and 5,820 in 1965 (Rodan, 1989: 81–2). The realization that industrial peace alone was not sufficient to ensure large infusions of foreign investments galvanized the Singapore government to grant overseas investors greater fiscal incentives while simultaneously expanding efforts to upgrade the island's infrastructure. Consequently, since Singapore's transformation to a low-cost, labor-intensive manufacturing base for export to high-income markets in North America and Western Europe brought it into direct competition with other sites pursuing similar strategies, most notably Hong Kong and Taiwan, the PAP administration slashed taxes on profits on exports of manufactured goods to one-tenth of the normal corporate tax rate – to an effective rate of only 4 percent – besides allowing unrestricted duty-free imports of capital goods and raw materials intended for exports and accelerated depreciation rates (Haggard, 1990: 111; Rodan, 1989: 87–8). Not content to wait for foreign investments, several public sector undertakings were also established – for instance, the Sembawang Shipyard to take over the Royal Naval Dockyard, the Singapore Electronic and Engineering Pte. Ltd (Rodan, 1989: 95–6).

Reinforcing these incentives, government expenditures on development projects almost doubled, rising from S$184.4 million in 1965 to S$332.8 million in 1969–70. Underlining the increased scale and range of development projects, several specialized agencies were created in the late 1960s to relieve the EDB of the more complex and specialized functions: the Development Bank of Singapore to provide long-term finance at low rates of interest; the International Trading Company to facilitate market penetration for Singapore's exports and to source cheaper sources of raw material imports; the wholly government owned Neptune Orient Lines to reduce reliance on foreign shipping lines and to ease trade with centrally-planned economies; and the Jurong Town Corporation with oversight responsibility for all industrial estates (Rodan, 1989: 93–5). The EDB, then, like the Taiwanese ESB, the South Korean Economic Planning Board (EPB), and the Japanese MITI became a general staff of macro-economic planning, overseeing and coordinating the work of these specialized agencies and public enterprises, formulating long-range plans, and setting targets.

Summary

To recapitulate, however much the post-Second World War regimes may have been bathed in the alpenglow of the old order, be it of the Meiji state or the Yi dynasty, there was nothing 'traditional' about the new order along the Asian rimlands. Colonialism, war, internecine conflict and revolution, and military defeat and US occupation had fundamentally restructured state–society relationships in the future Asian 'miracle' economies. Though these regimes originated in very different circumstances, and operated under different socio-economic and political constraints, it was the relative autonomy that their state apparatuses enjoyed which distinguished them from other 'newly industrializing economies' such as those in Latin America, and other US client states like the Philippines and South Vietnam, where landed oligarchies remained firmly entrenched.

The breakout of massive strike waves in Japan and civil war in China and Korea created the conditions for a thoroughgoing restructuring of state–society relations. It prompted the United States occupation forces in Japan to implement far-reaching institutional changes to diffuse socio-political dislocations, and to pressure US client states in South Korea and Taiwan to implement similar changes. Attempts to ameliorate the destabilizing effects of Japanese defeat, particularly since these coincided with heightening tensions between the United States and the Soviet Union, revolved around strengthening state apparatuses in all three jurisdictions, though these were differently accentuated in each case. In Japan, measures instituted by the US occupation forces to divest the elite of its control over the economy strengthened the autonomy of the state bureaucracy while the increasing concern with containing 'communism' emasculated the newly enfranchised trade unions. If the AMG in South Korea initially collaborated with the discredited Korean landlords in resisting land reforms, strong US pressure prevented the Rhee administration from reversing the reforms implemented by the North Korean forces during their occupation of most of the peninsula during the civil war, while martial law imposed in Taiwan was emblematic of the institution of a conquest state. The autonomy of state apparatuses in all three cases was additionally bolstered by large infusions of American aid and military procurements.

As British outposts, Hong Kong and Singapore were not beneficiaries of large infusions of American aid, while Britain itself had few resources to offer. Though the adverse conditions caused by the loss of its hinterland was exacerbated in Singapore by the unrelenting hostility of the Malaysian and Indonesian governments toward their Chinese minorities, these circumstances provided the pretext for the Singapore government to invoke emergency powers and propelled it to enact a battery of interventionist measures as its historically small bourgeoisie was hesitant to expand investments when short-run prospects looked so uncertain. Unlike Singapore, the colonial administration in Hong Kong faced neither a strong external threat nor demands for greater political rights or for independence. However, the imposition of a United Nations embargo on the export of strategic goods to China undermined Hong Kong's entrepôt role and compelled the colonial administration, acting in concert with major commercial interests, to gradually take measures to transform the economy from a trading center to a locus of low-cost manufactures for export to high-income countries in North America and Western Europe. The continuing strength of financial and commercial interests ensured that state intervention in Hong Kong meant in essence lowering costs for all manufacturers regardless of size, ownership, or sector (Chiu, 1996: 231).

Though the reconstitution of the future 'miracle' economies along the Asian rimlands shared several characteristics and they all adopted a broadly similar strategy of subordinating agriculture to state-directed industrialization drives, their internal balance of class forces and domestic resource endowments conditioned different patterns of accommodation. The democratic structure of the post-bellum Japanese polity and the greater maturity of its bourgeoisie and its proletariat led conservative politicians and bureaucrats to create institutional structures to integrate farm families, small and medium enterprises as well as big businesses in a coalition that underpinned the long electoral dominance of the Liberal Democratic Party. Conversely, by fragmenting the labor movement through a variety of measures, the conservative alliance severely handicapped the electoral prospects of the Japanese Socialist Party. Though the commercial and financial bourgeoisie in Hong Kong were highly class-conscious and formed a cohesive bloc, severance of their supply and marketing networks in China mitigated their strong laissez faire stance. Acting in concert with the commercial and financial bourgeoisie, the colonial government provided the infrastructural underpinnings for Hong Kong's transition from an entrepôt to a low-cost export-oriented manufacturing platform – though this did not involve subsidies, loans, protective tariffs, or other instruments deployed by the more interventionist states.

In the two former Japanese colonies of South Korea and Taiwan, the government had to virtually incubate a bourgeoisie. In the latter, the establishment of an ethnically-bifurcated state and the hostility of Mainland émigrées toward native islanders led to the state domination of the commanding heights of the economy. Pressure from US aid officials, however, compelled the regime to permit native islanders to develop small-scale industries, which relied largely on kinship networks as nationalized banks continued to discriminate against them. In South Korea, though the presence of US troops across the demilitarized zone enabled Rhee to play off strategic interests against aid officials, the lack of a cadre-based mass party restricted his ability to intervene deeply in the economy. By privatizing nationalized Japanese colonial assets, he created a domestic constituency for his regime but was unable to jump-start the economy. It was only after General Park Chung Hee's coup d'état in 1961 that the state's institutional capacity to pilot economic growth became entrenched, as we shall see in the next chapter. Finally, in Singapore, the weakness of the domestic bourgeoisie compelled the regime to create conditions conducive for foreign capital after the labor movement was knee-capped in the early 1960s.

3   The making of industrial behemoths

Patterns of state intervention and industrial organization

Presciently anticipating theorists of the 'developmental state,' Friedrich List had argued in 1885 that in 'less advanced nations...a perfectly developed manufacturing industry, an important mercantile marine, and foreign trade on a really large scale, can only be attained by means of the interposition of the power of the State' (quoted in Leftwich, 1995: 401). Similarly, Alexander Gerschenkron (1962) concluded from a study of patterns of 'late industrialization' that state intervention in 'relatively backward' countries was especially important because the average size of plants needed to be larger precisely when capital was scare. Building on his analysis, Ellen Kay Trimberger's (1978: 4) comparative study of Egypt, Japan, Peru, and Turkey indicated that states were able to be effective in economic development when the

> bureaucratic state apparatus achieved relative autonomy when, first, those holding high civil and military office were not drawn from dominant landed, commercial, or industrial classes; and, second, where they did not immediately form close relations with these classes after achieving power.

While a recognition of the significance of the relative autonomy of the state and the vital importance of government intervention in the economy for late-industrializers thus has a long and distinguished pedigree, the onset of the irreversible decline of centrally-planned economies since the late 1970s led to a neoclassical resurgence. It was argued that state intervention had 'generated inefficient industries requiring permanent subsidization for their survival' and that it also tended to foster 'rent-seeking' and thereby detracted 'the attention of economic agents from productive activities into lobbying for increased allocations of government subsidies and protection' (Onis, 1991: 109). The clearest empirical refutation against this revival of neoclassical orthodoxy emerged from the Asian rimlands.

By the early 1980s, the sustained rates of economic growth registered by these states led to a reassessment of the role of *dirigisme* in economic development. Characterizing Japan as a 'developmental state,' Chalmers Johnson (1982: 18–20) distinguished it from both the 'market rational' orientation of other core economies and the 'plan ideological' orientation of centrally-planned economies. Unlike 'market rational' states like the United States which were concerned with the rules and procedures of economic competition rather than with the type of industries that were needed, the 'plan rational' orientation of the Japanese government emphasized substantive economic issues. Conversely, unlike the centrally-planned economies, that he charged were primarily concerned with the state ownership of the means of production rather than developmental goals, the Japanese state emphasized economic development as its preeminent goal. Key elements of a 'developmental state' included an elite economic bureaucracy insulated from routine political pressures and endowed with the autonomy to pursue development goals and the 'perfection of market conforming methods of state intervention in the economy' (Johnson, 1982: 317). These methods centered on specifying a set of goals and comparing the performance of firms with a set of external reference economies. Expanding the application of the concept of 'developmental state' to South Korea and Taiwan, Alice Amsden (1989) and Robert Wade (1990) explored the complexities of strategic industrial policies. Similarly, several authors have underlined the critical importance of state intervention in the emergence of Hong Kong and Singapore as off-shore manufacturing platforms (Castells *et al.*, 1990; Appelbaum and Henderson, 1992; Bello and Rosenfeld, 1990; Schiffer, 1991; Rodan, 1989; Henderson, 1993).

If these accounts successfully dethroned the neoclassical orthodoxy, their tendency to view the state apparatus as a narrowly defined decision-making body 'rather than as a set of complex and highly contested social relations' (Choi, 1998: 51) tended to reify the state. Moreover, their exclusive focus on the administrative apparatus precluded a recognition of the wider political context of industrial planning and, at least implicitly, suggested that the installation of similar technocratic methods of industrial guidance will lead to a replication of East and Southeast Asian trajectories of growth in other low- and middle-income states (Friedman, 1988: 5, 30).

Additionally, though advocates of the developmental state were clear in distinguishing the relatively autonomous state structures along the Asian rimlands from other 'newly-industrializing countries,' once developmental state apparatuses had been installed, they tended to view these as perpetual growth machines. In particular, there was no recognition that rapid economic growth could tilt the balance of power from elite bureaucratic agencies toward other social actors as working classes became more class conscious and as corporations outgrew the need for subsidies and protection. Most notably, as Ziya Onis (1991: 122) forewarned, the 'inability of the state elites to discipline private business in exchange for subsidies may lead to a situation where selective subsidies can easily degenerate into a major instrument of rent seeking by individual groups.'

Despite these reservations, there is widespread acknowledgment of the fundamental importance of state intervention. Strategies of intervention and the institutional structures of capital accumulation in each of these jurisdictions were, however, shaped by different configurations of relations between state bureaucracies, social classes, and multinational capital within the wider political and trading arrangements of US hegemony. The scope of *dirigisme* was also determined by their different endowments of land and natural resources, the maturity and technical sophistication of their domestic bourgeoisies, the competence and technical expertise of their pilot economic agencies, and the size of their domestic markets. The three US client states were able to embark on a strategy of state-led industrialization with large infusions of aid from the hegemonic power and American military procurements from Japan. Hong Kong and Singapore had neither the land, natural resource endowments nor domestic markets comparable to South Korea or Taiwan, not to speak of Japan, to embark on an ISI strategy. As British colonies, the two city-states were also not recipients of large doses of American aid. At the same time, while political conditions led to the creation of a vast state sector in Taiwan which was supported by a large number of small- and medium-scale enterprises, the Rhee administration sought to create a domestic constituency of support by fostering the emergence of a class of big capitalists. If the creation of gigantic industrial conglomerates in South Korea bore some resemblance to the revival of monopoly capital in Japan, organizational immaturity and technical inexperience characterized the former. Once again, the two city-states faced different constraints. The transformation of Hong Kong from an entrepôt to an industrial and financial center occurred under the auspices of a colonial administration that acted in many ways as the executive committee of large business interests. The small size of domestic capital in Singapore compelled the Lee administration to create favorable conditions to attract foreign investments, and auspiciously for the host government the timing could not have been better as an increase in competitive pressures in the core disposed TNCs to relocate the lower end of their manufacturing operations to off-shore locations to cut labor costs precisely when Singapore was expelled from the Malaysian Federation.

The combination of these divergences imply that though the reconstitution of postwar regimes in the US client states and in the two city-states strung along Asia's Pacific coasts were marked by the propensity of their administrations to intervene in economic affairs to a degree unparalleled outside the centrally-planned economies, the patterns of state intervention and institutional structures of capital accumulation were strikingly different in each jurisdiction. Consequently, rather than trace similarities in these patterns, this chapter will chart the confluence of the varied trajectories of class forces, external influences, political exigencies, and internal constraints on their respective patterns of state intervention and dominant forms of industrial organization.

In the context of the geopolitical ecology of the post-Second World War reconstitution of the world market under US tutelage, the timing of the adoption of an industrialization drive in each jurisdiction also had important consequences. While the Korean War provided a spur for the reconstruction of the Japanese economy, it led to the initiation of a strategy for economic development in Taiwan and reoriented developmental strategies in Hong Kong. If the war finally led to agrarian change in South Korea and laid the political conditions for its future development, the material and human devastation caused by the hostilities had consequential consequences for class formation. What the Korean War did for the rehabilitation of the Japanese economy, the Vietnam War did for the economies of Singapore, South Korea and Taiwan. Singapore, which gained independence more than a decade after the decolonization of Korea and Taiwan, confronted an entirely different set of problems and constraints – narrow domestic markets, low natural resource endowments, and a small national bourgeoisie. Daunting as these conditions were, deepening US involvement in Vietnam boosted demand for petrochemicals and other supplies from Singapore while Taiwan and South Korea became suppliers of a variety of labor-intensive products for the US military. The coincidence of increasing welfare benefits in the 1960s with the sharp rise in military expenditures occasioned by the war in Vietnam led to a pressing need for the US government to economize in the procurement of supplies – and it was cheaper to obtain supplies of requisite quality from Japan and the future 'dragons' than from within the United States or elsewhere (Arrighi, 1994: 341). Successive US administrations therefore tolerated the closure of markets along the Asian rimlands to American products while allowing enterprises in these economies relatively free access to US markets – a privilege not accorded to American allies elsewhere.

Most importantly, the different patterns of state intervention and industrial organization conditioned the emergence of networks of regional integration charted in subsequent chapters and were themselves reshaped in turn. The singular characteristic of the outward expansion of Japanese capital in the 1960s – being spearheaded by small- and medium-scale enterprises – was possible only due to the hierarchical structure of subcontracting networks and the organizational armature of the general trading companies. If the widespread filigree of small- and medium-scale enterprises in Taiwan could readily accommodate this transfer of less-skilled manufacturing processes from Japan, the large South Korean *chaebol* could more easily accommodate the transfer of heavy and chemical industries in the 1970s. At the same time, the practice of channeling huge loans to the *chaebol*, necessary to finance large undertakings, created a culture of high debt–equity ratios, the adverse consequences of which were brutally exposed during the economic meltdown of 1997–98. Discrimination by nationalized banks against native islanders in Taiwan fostered no similar culture of debt-financed industrialization. The greater weight of state-owned enterprises in Taiwan and Singapore, as we shall see in Chapter 6, enabled their governments to deploy macroeconomic controls more effectively even when the transborder expansion of corporate networks had rendered national industrial policies increasingly anachronistic in Japan and South Korea.

Politics in command?

If Albert Hirschman (1958: 5) was right in arguing that economic development 'depends not so much on finding optimal combinations for given resources and factors of production as on calling forth and enlisting for development purposes resources and abilities that are hidden, scattered, or badly utilised,' then in low- and middle-income countries, the state was best placed to formulate long-term developmental plans. Private investors in these economies, as advocates of Big Push developmental strategies had argued, were hesitant to make new investments because they were unsure whether other complementary investments necessary to sustain their investments would occur. Japan and the Four Dragons were especially well-placed to coordinate national industrial plans because they were relatively free from populist pressures.

This was most clearly evident in the case of South Korea, where rapid economic growth was initiated only after General Park's coup d'état of 1961. If Singapore was spared a military coup, repressive measures implemented by the Lee Kuan Yew administration virtually emasculated political opposition to the PAP – not a single opposition candidate won an election to parliament between 1965 and 1981. Authoritarianism in Taiwan lasted until the lifting of martial law in 1987 while elections based on adult franchise were instituted in Hong Kong only in 1991, a few years before the British transfer of sovereignty to China (see So and May, 1993). Even in Japan, where democratic norms were observed, the iron grip of the LDP was loosened only in 1993, and for almost 40 years it was effectively a one-party state. Differences in power structures and in their relationships to state bureaucracies and social classes were important determinants of the patterns of state intervention and institutional structures of capital accumulation adopted in each jurisdiction.

In all three US client states, though land reform was a key element in the subordination of agriculture to a state-directed industrialization drive, the dynamics of agrarian change were conditioned by the relative potency of rural insurrection and by the specific institutional patterns of state power in each jurisdiction. Similar considerations also determined the corralling of labor movements in these states as well as in Hong Kong and Singapore. Finally, though domestic bourgeoisies in all five future 'miracle' economies were dependent on the state apparatus, the degrees of dependence varied considerably. If industrialists in Japan and Hong Kong were 'mature' and able to work in partnership with state bureaucrats and had a significant input into policy formation, the budding industrialists in South Korea and Taiwan were considerably more subordinate to political authority and the small commercial bourgeoisie in Singapore so insignificant that they were bypassed by the state altogether.

Japan

Spared from the 'winnowing hand' of the Supreme Commander Allied Powers (SCAP), the civil service had a virtual monopoly on governmental expertise, representing as they did almost all of Japan's remaining 'political grownups' (Pempel, 1998: 85). Indeed, far from being decimated, in the first three years of the Occupation, the civil service had grown by 84 percent over its highest wartime strength (Johnson, 1982: 44). A widespread consensus among the elite that the bureaucracy was vital to postwar recovery was encapsulated in a lead editorial in *Chūō kōron* in August 1947:

> under the present circumstances of defeat, it is impossible to return to a laissez-faire economy, and ... every aspect of economic life necessarily requires an expansion of planning and control, the functions and significance of the bureaucracy are expanding with each passing day. It is not possible to imagine the dissolution of the bureaucracy in the same sense as the dissolution of the military or the zaibatsu, since the bureaucracy as a concentration of technical expertise must grow as the administrative sector broadens and becomes more complex.
>
> (quoted in Johnson, 1982: 44)

This consensus reflected the close cooperation between the bureaucracy and the *Keidanren*.

The three main instruments for state intervention included control over foreign exchange and the ability to strategically target industries for development; provision of loans at preferential rates of interest, and tax concessions to lower production costs in chosen sectors; and the power to order the creation of industrial cartels and bank-based industrial groups (Johnson, 1982: 199). Control over foreign exchange, initially vested in the Foreign Exchange Control Board – and transferred in 1952 after the peace treaty, to MITI – lasted until the liberalization of trade in 1964. The establishment of a Foreign Investment Committee with oversight over all contracts involving foreign investments, acquisition of licenses and patents, conferred enormous statutory power on the ministry to regulate the import of foreign technology that lasted until the laws were rescinded in November 1979, almost thirty years after the law was approved as a temporary measure by the US occupation authorities (Johnson, 1982: 194, 217, 302; Morris-Suzuki, 1994: 168).

The imperative to ensure that adequate investment capital was available to meet the rapid expansion of US procurements occasioned by the Korean War led to a loosening of monetary controls as the Japanese government set up several banks to provide low-interest loans to industry. From the very beginnings, it was clear that the policy of 'overloaning' alone could not solve the capital shortage and ensure the industrial reconstruction of Japan. Since the Dodge Plan mandated balanced budgets, the Japanese government sought to overcome capital scarcity through the creation of new government-owned banks and the expansion of existing ones. The two major sources of funds for these financial institutions initially came from the US 'counterpart funds' – or the revenues in yen obtained from the sale of US aid that were held in a special account – and from the government-operated postal savings accounts. Once the Occupation had ended, the government empowered the Japan Development Bank to raise capital by issuing its own bonds, and sought to ensure the growth of deposits in the postal savings accounts by exempting the interest on the first ¥3 million of each account from taxes. As individuals could open accounts in multiple post offices, each of which was tax-exempt up to this ceiling, these accounts grew exponentially. Simultaneously, the government consolidated the postal savings accounts into a large investment account – the Fiscal Investment and Loan Plan (FILP) – which became, since 1953, the single most important source of finance for development, ranging from one-third to one-half of the general budget and not subject to legislative scrutiny until 1973 (Johnson, 1982: 207–8, 210; Eccleston, 1989: 49; Pempel, 1998: 67).

Between 1953 and 1961, over and above indirect support to industry through government loan guarantees, the government supplied between 19 and 38 percent of all capital. This support was especially critical in regards to strategic industries – electricity generation and power supply, ships and shipbuilding, coal, and steel – which accounted for 83 percent of disbursements by the Japan Development Bank. The elimination of risk in designated growth sectors by government guaranteed loans was reinforced by the tight controls exercised by the Finance Ministry over all interest rates, bank operations, and dividend rates. Since even permission to open new branches had to be obtained from the ministry, bank managers had to concentrate only on expanding the bank's share of loans and deposits (Johnson, 1982: 206–11).

Perhaps the most important consequence of the policy of overloaning was the creation of bank-led *keiretsu* (industrial conglomerates) in place of the *zaibatsu* based on family-owned holding companies. Capital shortages had encouraged each enterprise to establish close ties with a particular bank because even if it did not necessarily get all the money it needed or preferential terms from its primary bank . . . it did get one thing it could not do without – access to capital in the first place because it was an established customer. The banks in turn became dependent upon the financial health of their heavily indebted priority industries and therefore took responsibility for them.

(Johnson, 1982: 205)

Apart from banks, industrial firms also re-established ties in the 1950s to the old *zaibatsu* trading companies that had been broken up by the occupation forces. With the end of the Occupation in 1952, the government repealed antimonopoly laws over the protests of small- and medium-scale businesses, and MITI actively encouraged the recomposition of prewar industrial conglomerates on a new foundation. The ministry's policy of '*keiretsu*-ization' even led its Industrial Rationalization Council to assign industrial enterprises to a trading company (*sogo shosha*) if an alliance had not already been established. The ministry also used its licensing powers and control over preferential financing to reduce the numbers of trading companies from 2,800 at the end of the occupation to about 20 massive ones, each associated either with a bank-led *keiretsu* or a constellation of smaller firms (Johnson, 1982: 205–6; Borden, 1984: 164).

Crucially, the creation of cartels and bank-led industrial groups led to the mobilization of capital on a scale adequate to create competitive enterprises in the more technologically-sophisticated sectors. The pace of consolidation in the 1960s and 1970s was so extensive that by 1974 'five corporations or fewer controlled 90 percent or more of the markets in the steel, beer, nylon, acrylic, aluminum ore, automobile, and pane glass industries' (Pempel, 1998: 94).

The combination of the policies of overloaning to strategic sectors and government facilitation of alliances between large banks, industrial firms, and trading companies led to the creation of what is often called 'one set-ism,' or the formation of a full complement of designated growth industries within each *keiretsu* group to prevent being excluded from virtually risk-free sectors. Each of the six main banks – Dai Ichi Kangyo, Fuji, Mitsubishi, Mitsui, Sanwa, and Sumitomo – for instance, established ties with a major automobile company: Isuzu, Nissan, Mitsubishi, Toyota, Daihatsu, and Mazda respectively. This led to fierce competition and to inevitable overproduction as each group sought to maximize its share of government-guaranteed loans (Johnson, 1982: 206–8; Yoshino and Lifson, 1986: 33; Morales, 1994: 100–1; Gerlach, 1989; Hamilton and Biggart, 1989: S57–8; Yonekura, 1993: 211–13).

In short, the Japanese bureaucracy and big business forged an alliance to resuscitate the economy after its wartime devastation. The bureaucracy's control over vital foreign exchange and the mobilization of domestic savings through FLIP enabled MITI and the Ministry of Finance to strategically target specific sectors for accelerated growth by providing loans at preferential rates. If capital shortages fostered close coordination between enterprises, the bureaucracy used its financial leverage to reinforce these tendencies and create large units that could reap the economies of scale.

South Korea and Taiwan

Despite their shared heritage of Japanese colonial occupation, postwar regimes in South Korea and Taiwan were reconstituted on very different foundations, though both had very narrow bases of support and were almost entirely reliant on their bureaucracies and their coercive forces. Since the American occupation forces chose to work with the Korean Democratic Party (KDP), the most conservative faction, it provided an avenue for the privileged landed aristocracy, the *yangban*, to reemerge as the elite of the new order in South Korea (Cumings, 1981: 97; Amsden, 1989: 36–7). If this provided continuity in government personnel, the reconstituted Korean colonial bureaucracy was ill-equipped to promote economic development because the Rhee government lacked both the technical expertise for guided industrialization and a mass mobilizational party to establish its domination over civil society.

In contrast, as the GMD was staffed by a large cadre of experts with considerable expertise in industrial production and economic planning on the Chinese mainland, the regime's higher degree of autonomy from domestic classes in its island redoubt reinforced the strength of the state apparatus. If the GMD party-state thus had more policy instruments and options to pursue a *dirigiste* policy than most other states, Chiang's preoccupation with returning to the Chinese mainland meant that economic growth was assigned a low priority. Hence, though the Taiwan Production Board was established in May 1949 to stabilize the chaotic conditions following his retreat to the island, and its functions expanded early the following year with the creation of an Industrial and Financial Committee, there were no serious attempts to address the issue of economic growth before the Korean War.

When Chiang's fiction of maintaining that the GMD was the legitimate government of all of China and the consequent duplication of ministries at the 'national' and 'provincial' levels blurred lines of responsibility, the creation of two supra-ministerial agencies and the parallel bureaucratization of US aid disbursements shaped a distinctive political economy of development in Taiwan. These agencies – the Economic Stabilization Board (ESB) and Council on US Aid (CUSA) – chaired by the prime minister and composed of the key ministries and departments, provided a platform for technocrats to operate unimpeded by inter-departmental struggles for control of policy. Vested with a formidable array of powers – control over industrial development, monetary and banking policies, foreign trade and the allocation of foreign exchange, military spending, budget and taxation, agriculture and price stabilization, and utilization of US aid – the ESB was far more capable of monitoring the pulse of the economy and selectively targeting specific sectors than any comparable regulatory body in the Rhee administration. Indeed, precisely because state assets in South Korea had been sold at heavily discounted prices to political supporters of the regime, no elite bureaucratic organ was created to oversee the economic performance of firms. Hence even as 'entre-preneurs' were abjectly dependent on state patronage for access to aid allocations and privileged exchange and interest rates, the South Korean regime was quite unable to monitor their performance, as indicated by the widespread practice of 'entrepreneurs' selling their foreign currency allocations and industrial licenses to the highest bidder.

The ESB in Taiwan also emerged as the arena to reconcile differences between hardline conservative elements in the GMD hierarchy who remained hostile to the development of a powerful bourgeoisie among the indigenous islanders and US aid officials advocating the creation of a strong private sector. At the same time, as hopes for a triumphant return to the mainland receded by the end of the Korean War, Chiang's adminis-tration recognized that economic growth was a better guarantee for its long-term survival since it could dilute indigenous islanders' resentment of their political and economic domination by mainland émigrées. Given these considerations, the regime and its US advisors sought to channel funds toward the promotion of agriculture and the creation of infrastruc-tural projects that would encourage the broadest possible expansion of industrial production as long as the units of capital accumulation remained 'small and until the point where its transactions involve the external world' (Wade, 1990: 268).

The promotion of rural development assumed cardinal importance not only because the party hierarchy attributed their humiliating defeat on the Chinese mainland to the exploitation of the peasantry by the land-lords with whom the party was closely identified (Gold, 1986: 68; Wade, 1990: 82, 246–8, 260), but also because technocrats could siphon agricul-tural surplus toward industrial development by manipulating the terms of trade against agriculture. Greater support for agriculture – the rural sector received 21.5 percent of all US aid as opposed to 15 percent for industry (Jacoby, 1966: 50–1; Cheng, 1990: 45) – consolidated the GMD party-state's hold on the small peasantry while ensuring that the native Taiwanese did not pose a credible threat to the economic dominance of the émigrées. Support of the farm sector also satisfied the demands of US advisors that aid disbursements be more equitably shared while manipula-tion of the terms of trade was tantamount to a recycling of these funds to industry (Ho, 1978; Simon, 1988a: 148; Wade, 1990: 82–4).

In these conditions, the shift to project-specific grants which gave Agency for International Development (AID) officials greater control over their disbursements strengthened the tendency toward a relatively even regional distribution of funds within the island. Thus, almost two-thirds of all non-military assistance were allocated to the development of infrastructural projects – in power generation, transportation, communications, and education – which generated substantial external economies and provided the framework for the emergence of a broad base of consumer goods industries in the private sector, especially in such key sectors as plastics, rayon, glass, soda ash, and hardboard. American prodding also led the government to establish the Industrial Development and Investment Center and the China Productivity Center in 1960 to promote the growth of the private sector, convert the system of multiple exchange-rates to a single rate, and ease restrictions on foreign trade to encourage foreign private investments (Jacoby, 1966: 134–8; Ho, 1978: 195–7; Gold, 1986: 69, 76–8; Koo, 1987: 168; Haggard and Cheng, 1987: 115; Simon, 1988a: 148–50; Wade, 1990: 52–3, 202; Bello and Rosenfeld, 1990: 238).

Whereas only a few indigenous Taiwanese entrepreneurs – like the journalist Wu San-lien, who fronted the Tainan Textile Corporation for several business men from Tainan, or the five largest former landlord families who controlled the Taiwan Cement Corporation – had benefitted because of their ties to the GMD before economic conditions had stabilized in the island in the mid-1950s, these measures led to the emergence of a new breed of entrepreneurs among the indigenous islanders by the end of the decade. This was not, however, indicative of a loosening of state controls over the economy. In the first instance, though some of these entrepreneurs – such as Wang Yung-ch'ing and Lin Tin-sheng – were to become major players in their own right, public enterprises still received the bulk of aid allocations: 67 percent of the assistance to the industrial sector as a whole, as opposed to 27 percent for mixed enterprises and only 6 percent to private firms (Gold, 1986: 71–3, 82; Gold, 1988b: 189; Wade, 1990: 91; Bello and Rosenfeld, 1990: 237–40). In the second instance, government control over the banking sector ensured the party-state's control over credit allocations as well as enhancing its ability to channel domestic savings toward priority sectors, especially to enterprises controlled by the GMD. Finally, the extent of state control over domestic sources of finance did not end with government ownership of the banking sector as firms required prior approval from the Securities and Exchange Commission, an agency with wide discretionary powers, to raise capital by issuing shares.

The difference between the broad-based and increasingly autonomous and self-generating development in Taiwan, and the comparatively narrow-based and heavily aid-dependent South Korean trajectory was manifestly evident by the end of the 1950s. Within five years of the end of the Korean War, US aid officials were confident enough of the reconstruction of the Taiwanese economy to begin a gradual phase out of assistance. Despite exceptionally high rates of growth, there was no such complacency regarding South Korea. Given the generalized venality of state and

business elites in South Korea, the tapering off of American assistance –
after peaking at $383 million in 1957, US economic aid fell to $321
million in 1958 and to $222 million in 1959 (Woo, 1991: 46, table 3.1, 72)
– precipitated a sharp decline in growth rates as it undermined the provision of subsidized credit to industry. By another measure, per capita
income in South Korea in 1960 was only $62 – the same as in Japan in
1868 (in 1960 prices) – and lower than in Ghana, Senegal, Liberia,
Zambia, Honduras, Nicaragua, El Salvador, and Peru (Hart-Landsberg,
1993: 26; Mason *et al.*, 1980: 181; Cumings, 1987; Amsden, 1989: 41; cf.
Wade, 1992: 277, n. 21).

Growing economic pressures added fuel to the fire of a student-led
opposition to the authoritarian Rhee government, leading ultimately to
the military coup on May 16, 1961. If issues of political stability and
national unification had dominated the agenda of the Rhee administration, rapid economic growth dominated the agenda of the military junta,
particularly since students and the urban middle-class had spearheaded
the ouster of the former regime and the countryside had remained quiescent (Koo, 1987: 169). Or as Alice Amsden (1989: 49) pithily puts it: 'If
the lesson that the United States learned from the Korean upheavals was
the need for stability before growth, then the military learned that causal-
ity ran in the opposite direction, from growth to stability.'

The changed priorities of the new regime entailed a restructuring of
government organization and the institutional conditions for capital accumulation more generally. Within five months of the coup, the military
government established comprehensive controls over the financial infrastructure and capital flows by re-nationalizing commercial banks, subordinating the Bank of Korea to the Ministry of Finance, and forming two new
state-owned financial institutions, the Medium Industry Bank and the
National Agricultural Cooperatives Federation. In addition, the functions
of the Korean Development Bank were enlarged to enable it to borrow
from overseas sources and to underwrite foreign loans of domestic enterprises (Kuznets, 1977: 78; Amsden, 1989: 16, 72–3; Woo, 1991: 51–2, 84).
As a result, by 1970, the government controlled an astonishing 96.4
percent of the country's financial assets (Bello and Rosenfeld, 1990: 51).

While these changes had some similarities with Taiwan, there were also
marked contrasts reflecting differences in the balance of class forces in
the two jurisdictions and in the nature of their regimes. The most notable
feature of the reconstitution of political power in South Korea after the
coup was a greater centralization and concentration of power in the executive. As in Taiwan, the regime created a pilot agency, the Economic Planning Board (EPB), which controlled the national budget, foreign
investments, and government guarantees of overseas loans. Its mandatory
powers were augmented by the fact that its chief chaired the Council of
Economic Ministers and since 1963 was also designated deputy prime
minister. However, the creation of two secretariats in the Blue House – the

presidential mansion – and of a Board of Audit and Inspection which reported directly to the president provided independent checks on the EPB. These measures were accompanied by a reorganization of government ministries, with the Ministry of Trade and Industry being charged with the promotion of exports and controls on imports, plans for industrial development, industrial licensing, approval of applications for investments and the designation of strategic projects and firms; the Ministry of Finance with the regulation of all financial institutions, tax assessment and collection, and foreign exchange; and the Ministry of Construction with infrastructural development (Cumings, 1987: 72; Johnson, 1987: 154; Haggard, 1990: 64–5; Hart-Landsberg, 1993: 48–50, 54).

If this reorganization of the government apparatus enabled the new regime to monitor economic activities on an almost daily basis, the creation of watchdog agencies that bypassed the elite bureaucracy underlined President Park's inability to create a mobilizational party modeled on the GMD. When the failure of his Democratic Republican Party to become a mass-based party became evident in the elections of 1963, which Park won only narrowly, organs of the state began to function as substitutes for front organizations of a mass party. Among these, the most prominent was the Korean Central Intelligence Agency which combined internal and external information-gathering capacities and vastly augmented the surveillance capabilities of the state. Similarly, the new government's decision to directly appoint all the staff of local agricultural cooperatives, who had previously been elected by members, reflected an attempt to strengthen control over rural areas since fertilizers and government credit were solely distributed through the cooperatives.

Paralleling this move, the government made it mandatory for all incorporated businesses to join one of 62 producer associations which functioned as intermediaries between the Ministry of Trade and Industry and individual firms, and acted as conduits for information. Through these associations, the government was able to negotiate price controls on strategic goods and services, grant industrial licenses, and promote targeted sectors. The new government also reorganized and strengthened the powers of the Korean Foreign Traders' Association, which had powers to arbitrate international trade disputes, grant import and export licenses, and monitor individual firms' compliance with government trade regulations and targets. Finally, the military disbanded all labor unions and created the state-sponsored Federation of Korean Trade Unions in which all candidates for offices required government approval (Amsden, 1989: 16–18; Haggard, 1990: 62–3; Hart-Landsberg, 1993: 51–3).

Though these measures to reinforce the regulatory capabilities of the state bore striking resemblances to the measures implemented in Taiwan, differences between the two regimes were equally striking. For one thing, the uneven economic record of South Korea made it increasingly vulnerable to American pressure. When Park's freedom to maneuver had been constrained by bad harvests and high domestic inflation, increased pressures from US aid officials compelled a reluctant regime to devalue the currency in 1964, raise domestic interest rates in 1965, and normalize diplomatic relations with Japan the same year. In these conditions, the Park administration sought to reduce its reliance on American aid by vastly expanding overseas borrowing. In contrast, rather than resorting to increased overseas borrowing when US economic aid to Taiwan was being phased out in the late 1950s and early 1960s, and ceased completely in 1965, the GMD regime eased restrictions on foreign investments, which rose from 1.7 percent of gross domestic capital formation between 1952 and 1960 to 6.9 percent between 1969 and 1974 (Simon, 1988a: 149–50).

Paradoxically, a major impetus to increased overseas borrowing by the South Korean government and enterprises was the insistence by US aid officials and International Monetary Fund advisors that domestic interest rates be raised to mobilize private savings and lessen dependence on foreign borrowing. This advice was, in turn, based on the experience of Taiwan where high interest rates had led to a rise in domestic savings from approximately 5 percent of national income in the early 1950s to more than 30 percent in the late 1970s.[1] However, in South Korea, a virtual doubling of domestic interest rates in 1965 rendered the cost of domestic borrowing more expensive than borrowing from overseas and reinforced the dominant position of the government, as it had amended to the Foreign Capital Inducement Law in 1962 to guarantee foreign loans and thereby eliminate the risk of default and exchange-rate depreciation. The shift to overseas borrowing was so pronounced that net indebtedness rose from $301 million in 1965 to $2.57 billion in 1970, with two-thirds of the loans in the late 1960s being from private sources, and the debt-equity ratio of manufacturing firms increased from 1:2 in 1966 to 3:9 in 1971. Put another way, by one estimate, without this tremendous inflow of foreign capital, South Korean production in 1971 would have been smaller by a third (Kuznets, 1977: 78–80; Jones and Il SaKong, 1980: 101; Frieden, 1987: 149; Amsden, 1989: 73; Cheng, 1990: 157; Hart-Landsberg, 1993: 58–9; Koo and Kim, 1992: 127–8).

The obverse side of the increasing resort to overseas borrowing in South Korea was an extremely restrictive foreign investment policy. Though the exhaustion of the ISI phase led the Park administration to slightly ease restrictions on foreign investments after 1962, such investments continued to be prohibited in many sectors and even in those sectors that were legally open to outside investors, government regulators routinely rejected applications not deemed to be in the 'national interest.' In practice, then, majority equity participation by foreign owned firms was seldom approved unless they were entirely export-oriented and the preferred option was to permit joint ventures with a local partner to transfer technology. As a result of these measures, FDI accounted for only 3.7 percent of net capital transfers to South Korea between 1967 and 1971 while the equivalent figure for Mexico was 36.6 percent, for Brazil 33.8 percent, and for Thailand 26.1 percent (Evans, 1987: 207; Amsden, 1989: 74–7; Bello and Rosenfeld, 1990: 54–5; Hart-Landsberg, 1993: 86–90).

Complementing these restrictive policies on overseas investments were stiff import tariffs which were retained even after the exhaustion of the ISI strategy. Though quantitative controls on imports were gradually eliminated, the imposition of special tariffs since 1961 to absorb the differential between domestic prices and landed cost of imports implied a steep increase in the average legal tariff. Similarly, the shift from a positive list system whereby listed goods could not be imported without explicit government permission to a negative list system when listed goods were automatically approved for import in 1967 masked a variety of practices which sharply restricted the range and volume of imports – and the share of freely importable goods in total imports declined from 55.6 percent in 1968 to 46.7 percent in 1974 and to 38.8 percent in 1978. By another measure, it has been estimated that, even as late as 1990, less than 3 percent of imports could be classified as luxury goods (Kuznets, 1977: 153–4; Krueger, 1979: 89–92; Mason *et al.*, 1980: 128–32; Bello and Rosenfeld, 1990: 52–3; Hart-Landsberg, 1993: 37, 78–81; Haggard and Moon, 1993: 72–3).

The choice of foreign investments over increased overseas borrowing in Taiwan and the opposite in South Korea reflected fundamental differences between the two regimes. The failure of the military regime to institutionalize itself through the creation of a mass mobilizational party on the lines of the GMD led President Park to attempt to substitute economic performance for organizational capacity as the basis for political legitimacy (Cheng, 1990: 159). Once economic growth assumed priority, it was imperative that an alliance be established with the largest firms since 'the only viable economic force happened to be the target group of leading entrepreneurial talents with their singular advantage of organization, personnel, facilities and capital resources' (Kyoung-dong Kim quoted in Haggard and Cheng, 1987: 111).

The emerging 'sword-*won*' alliance between the junta and leading industrialists in South Korea was, however, based on an entirely different foundation from the alliance instituted under the Rhee regime. By virtue of its stranglehold over the financial infrastructure, the government was able to shape the direction of industrial production through the allocation of subsidized capital, credit guarantees, and favorable – even negative – interest rates to targeted firms and industries.[2] As a result, the debt–equity ratio of firms in South Korea averaged between 300 and 400 percent in the 1970s when compared with 100 to 200 percent for Brazilian and Mexican firms or 160 to 200 percent for firms in Taiwan. Moreover, by 1981, over 200 types of policy loans – targeted for specific industries at rates lower than the already highly discounted rates, and over which the banks had no control – had evolved to further promote specific types of manufacturing activity (Woo, 1991: 12). By virtue of its control over industrial licensing, the government could also reward firms entering sectors with long-fruition lags or high risks with licenses in the more lucrative sectors. Due to the higher technical requirements of targeted sectors, and the emphasis on increased exports, the regime tended to favor larger firms often controlled by political supporters: the Ssangyong group in cement rather than the more established Tongyang Corporation, for example, or the state-owned Pohang Iron and Steel Company, or the Hyundai group in shipbuilding, or the trio of Hyundai, Samsung, and Daewoo in the machine building sector (Amsden, 1989: 14–18, 73).

However, in return for privileged access to capital and industrial licenses, the government imposed stern discipline, most often related to export targets. Export-related criteria assumed preeminence in assessing enterprise performance both because continued improvement in exports provided a reliable indicator of efficiency and because tight control over the allocation of industrial licenses and cheap credit and high debt to equity ratios rendered financial indicators a poor guide. To increase market share overseas, firms were not only provided with a variety of subsidies – including lower taxes on export earnings, accelerated depreciation allowances, and duty-free imports of selected capital and intermediate goods – but were also allowed to sell products at inflated prices in domestic markets to partially off-set the costs of dumping products abroad. At the same time, the government imposed restraints on the market power of large conglomerates by negotiating price controls annually, and as late as 1986 some 110 commodities ranging from flour and sugar to automobiles and chemicals were subject to such controls (Kuznets, 1977: 156–62; Krueger, 1979: 92–9; Amsden, 1989: 17. 144–51; Bello and Rosenfeld, 1990: 52–3).

If secure access to cheap credit and a battery of incentives encouraged *chaebol* to pursue expansion into areas with long-fruition lags and high risks, it heightened their dependence on the government and the regime did not hesitate to dismember firms that failed to fulfill their export targets or other performance criteria without plausible excuses. Even the very largest conglomerates were not immune to such sanctions, as indicated by the experience, for instance, of the Shinjin company which had a larger share of the domestic automobile market than Hyundai in the 1960s. However, as Shinjin could not survive the oil crisis of the early 1970s and competition from Hyundai's 'Pony,' its credit lines were cut and the government, in its role as banker, transferred the company's assets to Daewoo Motors (Amsden, 1989: 15; Bello and Rosenfeld, 1990: 70–1; Hart-Landsberg, 1993: 69–70; see also Cumings, 1987: 74). In this context, it is significant that though the government imposed strict discipline on the *chaebol* and had no hesitation in dismembering and cannibalizing poor performers, business failure did not lead to unemployment as assets were simply transferred to other politically better connected conglomerates (Amsden, 1989: 15, 139–55; Eckert, 1993: 102–4).

With the rapid increase in exports and the emergence of successful entrepreneurial groups there was both a greater stratification of wealth in Taiwan and the emergence of wealthy indigenous islanders. By 1983 seven of the leading ten leading business groups were led by native Taiwanese (Bello and Rosenfeld, 1990: 238–9). Equally importantly, the predominance of small- and medium-scale firms and their spatial dispersal across the island,[3] provided a relatively even regional development of industrialization on the island, with the obvious exception of the EPZs. The percentage of industrial employment in the five big cities, for instance, declined from 36.8 percent in 1966 to 22.8 percent in 1986, while it rose correspondingly in the four suburban regions from 31.9 percent to 45.8 percent. The increasing dispersal of industrial production was reflected in the decline of their unit size. While the average size of industrial plants in the five big cities declined from 26.9 employees in 1966 to 21.6 employees in 1986, it remained relatively stable in the four metropolitan regions, falling from 25.8 in 1966 to 25 in 1986, and rose from 13.5 to 21.8 in the twelve rural regions (Deyo, 1989: 20–1, 41; Amsden, 1991: table 6; see also Cheng and Gereffi, 1994: 210).

In sharp contrast, one important consequence of the strategy of 'betting on the strong' firms in South Korea was the progressive growth of regional imbalances. Ironically, reflecting their rural background, the military junta had initially attacked the illicit accumulation of wealth under the First Republic, and demonstrated a marked bias toward agriculture. Almost immediately after the seizure of power, they liquidated most of the farm debt and shifted the terms of trade in favor of farm produce so that rural and urban incomes were on par by 1965. However, once emphasis shifted toward rapid industrialization, the centralization and consolidation of political power in the executive and the concentration of economic power in the *chaebol* meant that despite Seoul's proximity to one of the most volatile political frontiers of the Cold War, urban and industrial growth was skewed toward the capital city where more than 96 percent of all firms were headquartered. Another pole of industrial concentration, reflecting the high dependence on imports and exports and the need to lower transportation costs, has been the Pusan–Kyongsang corridor on the southeastern coast. The polarization toward these two nodes is indicated by decline of population in the Cholla provinces on the southwest seaboard, falling from some 25 percent of the population in 1949 to 12 percent in 1983, and its share of manufacturing employment showed similar decline, falling from 13.1 percent in 1958 to 5.4 percent in 1983. In contrast, the population of the Kyongsang provinces rose from 28 percent of the total in 1949 to 30 percent in 1983 and its share of manufacturing employment from 28.6 percent in 1958 to 40.1 percent in 1983 (Chon, 1992; Douglass, 1993b).

Clearly, the polarization of industrial production toward these two industrial nodes was a result of the greater emphasis placed on industrial production at the expense of the rural sector. Due to the concentration of investments in these growth poles and the predominance of large-scale industries, employment opportunities were not only disproportionately greater in Seoul and the Pusan–Kyongsang corridor, but the pattern of investments had the effect of precluding the development of small- and medium-scale industries in the rural areas. Moreover, for those without land, re-entry to the farming sector was difficult (Cheng, 1990: 160–1; Deyo, 1990: 195).

Regional imbalances, however, reflected more than merely the subordi-nation of agriculture to the state-led industrialization drive. The Kyongsang provinces provided the political base of the military junta and 32 percent of government officials from 1961 to 1986 were recruited from these provinces. Similarly, the founders of nine of the top 20 *chaebols* also came from these provinces. Conversely, as the Cholla provinces, the richest agricultural zone in the country, declined in relative terms, it became the center of resistance to the military (Chon, 1992).

Briefly put, however much Taiwan and South Korea may have inherited a shared legacy of Japanese colonialism, differences in the constitution of their postwar regimes, and the adoption of different patterns and tools of state intervention led to sharp divergences in their economic structure:

> The logic of the Korean approach – hierarchical, unbalanced, and command-oriented – calls for the intensive use of resources to foster a highly select and obedient business sector to carry the specific tasks the leadership may assign. The logic of the Taiwan approach – hori-zontal, balanced, and incentive-oriented – implies the extensive use of resources to allow a more pluralistic economy within the broad para-meters delimited by the state.
>
> (Cheng, 1990: 142)

These differences in industrial structures were to have consequential consequences over time. The greater addiction of South Korean *chaebol* to high debt–equity ratios and debt-financed expansion made them household names the world over as they trespassed with impunity into technologically-sophisticated sectors but made them vulnerable to the vicissitudes of short-term capital markets, as amply evident by their expo-sure to the economic crisis that began to unravel their corporate struc-tures in 1997. If the smaller size of Taiwanese enterprises meant that they did not enjoy the same brand name recognition, their smaller exposure to foreign loans largely insulated them from the financial crisis that engulfed the *chaebol*, as we shall see in Chapter 5. Conversely, the spatial concentra-tion of industrial production endowed workers in South Korea with much greater political power than their Taiwanese counterparts.

Hong Kong and Singapore

Dirigisme in the two city-states was based on an entirely different set of conditions. The loss of their hinterlands meant that their entrepôt role was fatally compromised and their small markets, poor endowment of natural resources, and the absence of large infusions of US aid ruled out the incubation of a domestic bourgeoisie. If Hong Kong's large expatriate industrial bourgeoisie and the migration of Chinese manufacturers from Shanghai partly ameliorated its conditions, no such relief was available to the Singaporean government. Not only did they have to confront and corral a strong left-wing movement which had no counterpart in Hong Kong, but the British naval withdrawal further exacerbated Singapore's economic plight. Governments of both city-states were therefore compelled to intervene in a manner designed to transform their territories from entrepôts to off-shore manufacturing platforms and to provide conducive conditions for foreign investments.

In Hong Kong, there was a great degree of cohesion between government and business elites as evidenced by the fact that all major legislation was circulated in draft form to the main employers associations – the Federation of Hong Kong Industries, the Chinese Manufacturers' Association, the Hong Kong General Chamber of Commerce, and the Employers' Federation of Hong Kong. While the General Chamber, dominated by the big British 'hongs,' even nominated one of the members to the Legislative Council, similar privileges were not accorded to the labor unions that were not represented on the Council. However, employers' associations rarely acted in concert. The sheer numbers of small firms – there were 141,708 establishments in 1981, of which 47,996 were in manufacturing – made consensus difficult while the political weakness and fragmentation of labor meant that there was little incentive to close ranks. Besides, close interrelationships between major firms and their informal ties to the colonial administration made it possible for them to safeguard their interests without recourse to the larger associations (Deyo, 1989: 14, 43–5; England and Rear, 1975: 12; Lethbridge and Ng Sek-Hong, 1993: 92–5).

While the British government appointed the governor and all senior officials in the Crown Colony, and nominated all official and unofficial members of its Executive and Legislative Councils and had the power to override local laws, local officials had almost complete autonomy in practice and the last time the parliament at Westminster overruled local laws in Hong Kong was in 1913. Apart from foreign affairs, citizenship, and landing rights for aircraft (which enabled British airlines to negotiate reciprocal rights with airlines in East and Southeast Asia), laws were enacted entirely by local officials, even though the Governor was theoretically vested with almost unlimited powers – subject only to the stipulation that he consult with the Executive Council composed of six senior officials and eleven nominated unofficial members. In practice, laws were passed by the

Legislative Council. Close links between the officials, who often serve a longer term than the governor's five-year stint, and directors of major corporations led to a great deal of social cohesion among the government and business elites, as indicated by the appointment of top government officials, after their retirement from the civil service, to key executive positions in employers' associations.

By shouldering the costs of infrastructural development and subsidizing wage-goods, the colonial government provided conditions conducive to an expansion of low-cost manufacturing activities. The very success of these policies led to greater state involvement in the economic arena as the rapid rise of cheap exports from Hong Kong led to the imposition of quotas on their exports by the governments of the United Kingdom, the United States, and other high-income states from the late 1950s. Beginning with the textile industry, and subsequently expanding to an increasing number of sectors, the impositions of quotas prompted the colonial administration's Industry Department to set quotas for individual firms to ensure that Hong Kong's global quotas would be equitably shared between the major firms. However, though the government had initially allocated quotas on the basis of installed capacity, the quotas soon became tradable commodities between textile mills and garment manufacturers (Lau and Chan, 1994: 116; Miners, 1993: 110–11; Castells *et al.*, 1990: 90–1, 119–21; Yeung, 2000: 144).

Despite protestations of non-interference in the economy, the precariousness of the small-scale industries on which its export production was based encouraged the colonial administration to provide a variety of services to these firms that they could not otherwise obtain for themselves. Thus, beginning in the mid-1960s, as other low- and middle-income states began to attract foreign investments and to abandon ISI policies for reasons more fully explored in the next chapter, the Hong Kong government established a number of public agencies – most notably, the Hong Kong Tourist Association, the Hong Kong Trade Development Council, the Hong Kong Export Credit Insurance Corporation, and the Hong Kong Productivity Council – to provide commercial intelligence, personnel training, legal and technological assistance, and insurance for high-risk ventures for small- and medium-scale enterprises. Collectively, these measures amounted to an ad hoc industrial policy until 1979 when the government formulated an explicit industrial strategy to upgrade the technological level of industries as well as to transform Hong Kong into a financial service center (Castells *et al.*, 1990: 90–1).

The absence of a strong domestic bourgeoisie imbued *dirigisme* in Singapore in shades of a very different color. Rather than seeking to incubate or revive a home-grown class of entrepreneurs, government policies were fashioned to attract foreign investments to transform the island-state into an offshore manufacturing platform. Such investments also served to preclude the emergence of domestic Chinese capital as an alternate base of power as well as ensuring that Western powers had a stake in Singapore's survival. Once the militancy of labor had been curbed and steps taken to reduce the costs of reproduction through public housing schemes, the government moved to create an institutional framework to entice foreign investors. Toward this end, and given Singapore's relatively high wage structure, the government offered foreign investors a raft of incentives: reduction of taxes on the profits of exports of manufactured goods to one-tenth of the standard corporate rate; exemption of machinery, equipment, and raw materials required for industrial production from all import duties; unrestricted repatriation of profits; and generous depreciation allowances (Rodan, 1989: 87; Bello and Rosenfeld, 1990: 291–3; Haggard, 1990: 111).

As in other developmental states, the EDB determined industrial policy and aimed to target sectors of increasing technological sophistication for accelerated growth. However, rather than nurturing domestic industries, the EDB assessed applications for 'pioneer industry status' which enabled designated sectors to receive low-interest loans, tax holidays, and other special privileges (Haggard, 1990: 113). The institutional scaffolding for the more efficient implementation of these policies was provided by a range of specialized agencies: the Jurong Town Corporation created in June 1968 to oversee the development of industrial estates and lands; the Development Bank of Singapore (DBS) in July 1968 to provide long-term finance at low-interest rates; the International Trading Company (Intraco) in November the same year to lower procurement costs of raw materials by buying in bulk and to expand overseas markets; and the Neptune Orient Lines in January 1969 to reduce dependence on foreign shipping. Finally, not content to rely solely on private capital, the government also established 13 new public manufacturing enterprises in 1968 and eight more the following year (Rodan, 1989: 94–5).

The focus on attracting foreign investments inevitably meant that the government neglected to nurture domestic entrepreneurs and this had become starkly evident by 1976 when locally-based capital in manufacturing declined from S\$123.1 million or 42.2 percent of all manufacturing investments in 1974 to S\$42.8 million or 42.1 percent in 1976. Consequently, the government launched the Small Industries Finance Scheme in 1976 to advance low-interest loans for the establishment of small industries and for the diversification of existing ones. However, since protectionist measures would contravene the primary strategy of attracting large foreign investments, the intent behind small industry promotion was to create synergies between local industries and the TNCs to create fully integrated industrial sectors, especially in the electronics industry. The expansion of Japanese subcontracting networks in the 1970s limited the success of this strategy since low-cost suppliers were emerging in neighboring locations as limitations of narrow domestic markets in Malaysia and Thailand, ethnic conflicts in Malaysia, and the oil boom in Indonesia led to an opening of these economies at the same time. As these tendencies led to a less than expected degree of integration in the manufacturing sector, the Singaporean government introduced the Product Development Assistance Scheme in 1978 to boost research and development capabilities of local firms (Rodan, 1989: 124–5).

Just as different socio-political constitutions led regimes in South Korea and Taiwan to shape distinct political economies on their shared legacy of Japanese colonialism, so too did the governments of Hong Kong and Singapore shape distinct political economies on their shared legacy of British colonialism. Despite their differences though, the reintegration of these economies into the post-Second World War world market exhibits some striking parallels. The fallout of the Chinese Revolution prompted the GMD regime in Taiwan and the British colonial administration in Hong Kong to promote or subsidize small-scale manufacturing to accommodate refugees from China, as well as to broaden the regime's constituency among the indigenous islanders in Taiwan and to compensate for the Crown Colony's loss of its hinterland. A different dynamic shaped the political economy of South Korea and Singapore. Confronted by the need to quickly incubate a domestic bourgeoisie and also to bolster its support base, the Rhee administration sold off expropriated Japanese assets to its supporters. Reckoning that reliance on the big conglomerates will yield quicker results, the Park regime continued to support them even in the face of opposition from US aid officials. Without the influx of manufacturers that conditioned Hong Kong's transformation into a locus of low-cost manufacturing, the Lee administration in Singapore sought to entice large foreign investments as manufacturers in Western Europe and North America faced increasing competitive pressures in their home bases. Finally, while the resuscitation of the Japanese economy also led to the revival of large-scale enterprises, these were tied in a symbiotic relationship to small- and medium-sized enterprises, as we shall see in the next section.

Patterns of industrial organization

By the early 1980s, when economies strung along the Asian rimlands registered the fastest rates of growth, several analysts attributed these high growth rates to the 'Confucian family values' they shared, including the subordination of sectoral interests to the larger national interest, the respect for education, and the predilection for hard work. The spectacular rise of Japan was said to spring from the three 'sacred pillars' of its dominant pattern of employment relations – lifetime employment, seniority wage system, and enterprise unionism. It was suggested that stability of employment provided the basis for cooperative relations between workers and management while seniority wages replicated family hierarchies and by providing an array of benefits (from housing to holiday travel), enterprise-based unions reinforced the image of company-as-family. However, closer examination revealed that Japanese corporations provided long-run employment rather than lifetime employment and that this was also the case with large, well-managed corporations elsewhere. Small enterprises, which constitute the overwhelming majority of firms in Japan and elsewhere, were never able to provide similar conditions of employment nor were they able to provide welfare benefits on the scale of enterprise unions of large corporations (Aoki, 1987).

Nevertheless, industrial structures and employment relations in these economies evolved along lines markedly different from the normative Euro–North American patterns. Unlike in the United States, for instance, where hiring can take place at any time during an individual's career trajectory and is done in a decentralized manner, Japanese firms tend to hire at graduation through a centralized personnel department. However, while Japanese workers can more easily change jobs within the firm once they are hired, US workers tend to get locked into specific job categories. Finally, while US workers tend to be paid by skill and job classification and only secondarily by seniority, workers in major Japanese corporations tend to be paid according to seniority rather than by job classification, but seniority was never a sacrosanct principle in Japan when layoffs were concerned (Morales, 1994: 54). Yet, as briefly alluded to in Chapter 2, rather than being traditional, these employment practices were the outcome of management strategies to improve labor productivity and union attempts to improve the status of industrial workers and their working conditions in the 1950s (Gordon, 1985; Shapira, 1993: 242).

The greater job security enjoyed by workers in major Japanese corporations was also due to the maturity of the working class. Elsewhere along the rimlands, where industrial working classes were constituted after the Second World War, the ideological offensive against 'communism' generated by the wars in Korea and Vietnam and the very different institutional structures of accumulation conditioned employment conditions. Though workers in colonial Korea had a tradition of militancy, war and partition had so decimated the old working class that workers in the postwar era were recruited from the countryside and virtually none of them had prior experience in wage-employment (Koo, 2001). In Taiwan and Hong Kong, on the other hand, the predominance of small-scale industries led to a reconstitution of patriarchal, family-based workshops that often generated a new gender politics articulated in the idiom of familial values (Greenhalgh, 1994). While a full discussion of these patterns of employment relations and the forms of resistance they generated is outside the purview of this chapter, we seek to sketch dominant patterns of industrial organization in which workers were embedded in Japan, South Korea and Taiwan, and Hong Kong and Singapore. Complementarities and differences between industrial structures in these jurisdictions conditioned the emergence of regional networks of trade, production, and investment charted in the next two chapters. Thus, this integration of studies on their varied characteristics provides an essential background to our analysis.

Japan

When the Japanese government after the Meiji Restoration in 1868 embarked on a crash program of industrialization, they created several key institutional innovations, perhaps the most notable of which was the *sogo shosha* or general trading company. These were diversified enterprises with interests ranging from procurement, financing and transportation of capital goods and raw materials to the distribution and sale of finished goods. With their vast network of agencies, the *sogo shosha* established alliances with the *zaibatsu*, serving as their primary if not exclusive distributors, and fledgling industrial ventures to reap economies of scale in the purchase of raw materials. The *sogo shosha*'s large network of procurement agencies and distribution outlets provided critical market intelligence and freed their client firms from bearing the costs associated with maintaining such systems of their own. Even after the US occupation forces began dismantling monopoly houses – including the two largest *sogo shosha*, the Mitsui Bussan and the Mitsubishi Shoji – senior executives of the former companies were aware of the benefits that would accrue from pooling their resources and as soon as the Occupation ended, the Japanese government facilitated the reconsolidation of the *sogo shosha*. By virtue of its diversified activities a *sogo shosha* could spread costs over a number of transactions and thereby lower unit costs for its member firms. Its ready access to raw materials, markets, and information could reduce risks and monitor price movements far better than any one of its client firms, no matter how large, could do by themselves. Banks also preferred lending directly to *sogo shosha* as it freed them from processing a large number of small loans while a *sogo shosha*'s intimate knowledge of market conditions and a firm's creditworthiness reduced risks of default (Yoshino and Lifson, 1986). Yet, since the client firms were independent entities, they were not necessarily tied to one *sogo shosha* and may indeed sell their products to outside firms or to clients of rival *sogo shosha*.[4] At the same time, each *sogo shosha* often included rival firms who competed with each other. Hence, as Michael Yoshino and Thomas Lifson (1986: 47) note, a *sogo shosha* product system 'is best understood not as a rigid body whose constituent units are mechanically linked into a tightly balanced system but as a constellation of firms active at various stages of a complex production process.' Nevertheless, the *sogo shosha* represented an enormous concentration of economic power with the top ten controlling between 50 and 60 percent of Japanese foreign trade and some 20 percent of its domestic wholesale trade in the 1960s (Pempel, 1998: 70).

After the premature termination of the program for *zaibatsu* dissolution, postwar restructuring of industrial organization in Japan was marked by two distinct forms of industrial conglomerates – the intermarket groups or *kigyo shudan* (for example, Dai Ichi Kangyo, Fuyo, Mitsubishi, Mitsui, Sanwa, and Sumitomo) and independent industrial groups or *kaisha* (for example, Hitachi, Industrial Bank of Japan, Matsushita, Nippon Steel, Nissan, Tokai Bank, Tokyu, Toshiba-IHI, Toyota, and Seibu). As the name suggests, intermarket groups were horizontal coalitions of firms built around financial institutions and *sogo shoshas*, while the independent industrial and financial groups represented vertically integrated firms in one or more sectors built around a large parent company. In both cases, control over affiliated firms was established through interlocking stock ownership, though the degree of control exerted tended to be stronger among intermarket groups than among firms within the independent groups. Though the six major horizontal *keiretsu* represented only 0.1 percent of all the companies in Japan, they accounted for almost 25 percent of the total value of shares in the Tokyo Stock Exchange (Eccleston, 1989: 40–1; Hamilton and Biggart, 1989: S57–9; Glasmeier and Sugiura, 1991: 399–401; Pempel, 1998: 70).

Even if horizontal linkages between financial institutions, industrial firms, and commercial organizations through interlocking shareholding, lender–borrower, buyer–seller, and director relationships provided the institutional base for the reconstruction of the Japanese economy, the scalar magnitude of US military procurements at the start of the Korean war was so extensive that major firms sought to utilize idle productive capacities of parts manufacturers by sourcing out components (Smitka, 1991: 6–10, 53–78; Eccleston, 1989: 35; Glasmeier and Sugiura, 1991: 399). As wage workers constituted only 39.3 percent of the working population at the onset of the Korean War (Itoh, 1990: 145), this strategy was seen as a temporary expedient especially since the length of the war-induced boom was uncertain. Large firms, however, soon abandoned their efforts to recreate their prewar structure of vertically integrated production systems as the advantages offered by stable subcontracting arrangements rapidly became evident.

From these beginnings, as several theorists associated with such ungainly coinages as 'Fujitsuism,' 'Toyotism,' and 'global Japanization' have underscored, subcontracting arrangements in Japan evolved in a manner that contrasts sharply with similar practices elsewhere. First, as indicated by Table 3.1, though small- and medium-scale firms as a percentage of all manufacturing enterprises in Japan are approximately the same as in other core states, they account for a much higher percentage of employment, shipments, and value added to production. Correspondingly, small and medium scale enterprises in Japan were highly dependent on a few large firms and in the early 1980s over 90 percent of all subcontractors in the textile sector were found to have sold the bulk of their output to three firms or less (Eccleston, 1989: 30–1; Glasmeier and Sugiura, 1991: 401; Pempel, 1998: 71).

Table 3.1 Significance of small- and medium-sized corporations in selected core
states[a]

	Japan[b] (1986)	Japan[c] (1988)	USA[c] (1982)	FRG[d] (1988)	UK[c] (1988)
Percent of total	99.4	99.1	96.3	90.8	97.0
Percent of employment	80.6	72.9	46.9	38.3	39.2
Percent of shipment	n.a.	52.4	38.2	32.1[e]	n.a.
Percentage value-added	n.a.	55.5	38.4	n.a.	33.3

Source: Arrighi *et al.* (1993: 50, table 3.3).

Notes
a Japan: fewer than 300 employees; USA: fewer than 250; Germany: fewer than 300; UK:
  fewer than 200.
b Nonprimary sector. The size of small and medium-scale corporations are: fewer than 300
  employees for manufacturing; fewer than 100 for wholesale, and fewer than 50 for retail
  and service sectors.
c Manufacturing sector.
d Manufacturing sector, excluding hand manufacturing.
e Total sales.

Second, though Japanese manufacturers may depend on fewer primary
subcontractors than vertically-integrated corporations in other high-income
states, subcontracting networks are more extensive in Japan due to the
highly stratified nature of these networks. Thus, whereas a typical Japanese
automotive maker has 170 primary subcontracting (*ichiji shitauke*) firms
(producing machinery such as robots, jigs, and large body panels; subassem-
blies like engines and seats; and major body parts such as brakes), the latter
depend on 4,700 secondary (*niji shitauke*) subcontractors (supplying dies,
metal work, small body parts, and such single components as brake linings)
who, in turn, depend on 31,600 tertiary subcontractors (*sanji shitauke*).
Below this layer are the large numbers of households where women fabricate minor parts – metal stampings of brand names, tiny electronic components, etc. (Sheard, 1983: 56; Cusumano, 1985: 250–3; Hill, 1989: 464–6;
Fujita and Hill, 1993: 180–2; Morales, 1994: 108–9; Arrighi *et al.*, 1993: 51).
A government survey on the state of industry in 1976 revealed that more
than 90 percent of firms employing 50 workers or more, and more than 75
percent of firms with 10 to 40 workers farmed out work to subcontractors.
What was still more remarkable was that almost 50 percent of firms employing four to nine workers and one-sixth of firms with one to three workers
issued subcontracting work (Sheard, 1983: 60; Cusumano, 1985: 192;
Kenney and Florida, 1988: 136).

Third, instead of purchasing components under short-term contracts
from a large number of suppliers, as was the norm for vertically-integrated
US corporations until recently, Japanese firms built long-term relationships with a small number of primary suppliers (Smitka, 1991: 4–10,
58–88, 175–89). The continuity of these affiliative relationships enabled

major Japanese manufacturers to circumvent the high transaction costs, irregular deliveries, and poor quality of parts that plague outsourcing arrangements in other core states, and in pre-Second World War Japan itself (Morris-Suzuki, 1994: 154–5; Glasmeier and Sugiura, 1991: 399). This was very different from the arm's-length, market-based, short-term contracts with independent companies that was the norm in the United States and Western Europe.

By farming out production to a large number of suppliers who have no direct relationship with each other, mass manufacturers in the United States were often confronted with incompatible parts. In contrast, by relying on a smaller number of primary subcontractors, Japanese manufacturers tended to merely specify performance requirements and leave engineering decisions to their first-tier suppliers who were responsible for an entire component (Womack *et al.*, 1990: 60–1, 142, 146–7).

This crucial difference between cooperative subcontracting relationships constructed by major Japanese manufacturers in the 1950s and 1960s, often idealized as a familial relationship in contrast to the fundamentally antagonistic buyer–seller relationships in arm's-length arrangements, enabled major manufacturers to reduce transaction costs, lower inventories through the vaunted *kanban* ('just-in-time') system, and monitor quality control. Originated by Toyota, but soon pervasive throughout corporate Japan, *kanban* denotes a card attached to each batch of parts supplied by a subcontractor to a firm higher up the production chain.[5] When the first part is taken from the consignment by an assembly worker, the card signals that it is time for the subcontractor to prepare another consignment. Due to the close coordination that resulted from frequent deliveries of small consignments, the 'parent' firm regulated the production rhythms in subcontracting firms and effectively transformed them to spatial extensions of the assembly line. The delivery of components in small batches also facilitated continuous and multiple improvements in product design, component quality, and to the production process itself. Since continuous adjustment of deliveries was crucial to the smooth operation of the system, subcontracting firms tended to be located in close proximity to the 'parent' firm – and in some cases, as when suppliers were located within the premises of the larger firm, the distinction between firms itself became tenuous – and this led to further reductions in transaction costs and minimized possible disruptions and delays of deliveries. In contrast, since mass-manufacturing corporations in the United States sourced components from parts manufacturers on the basis of cost, their suppliers were dispersed much further afield. Consequently, to avoid possible disruptions of supply, they were forced to stockpile parts and bear much higher overheads. Larger stockpiles in the 'just-in-case' system also made it unfeasible to make continuous design modifications (Sheard, 1983: 53–4, 61–3; Hill, 1989: 469–70; Eccleston, 1989: 36; Gwynne, 1991: 63; Fujita and Hill, 1993: 183–4).

First-tier subcontractors, in turn, were themselves large firms and their size and technological sophistication implied that, despite their close relations with major manufacturers, they were not totally dependent on the 'parent' enterprise. Though Toyota holds about 22 percent of shares in Nippon Denso, its supplier of electrical products, for example, the company also supplies parts to some of Toyota's competitors, while a large number of the 203 first-layer suppliers for Subaru were also major subcontractors to Nissan. By virtue of its size, Nippon Denso was also able to implement new innovations and Toyota's first quality-control system was, in fact, modeled on the one pioneered by its electrical parts supplier (Sheard, 1983: 56–9; Cusumano, 1985: 250–3; Kenney and Florida, 1988: 136–7; Womack *et al.*, 1990: 61).

Extensive inter-group shareholding between firms in the multi-layered subcontracting chain – the share of cross-ownership in 1974 ranged from about 30 percent in Mitsubishi (30.6 percent) and Sumitomo (27.9 percent) to less than 20 percent in Mitsui (17.4 percent), Fuyo (17.4 percent) and Dai Ichi Kangyo (16 percent) – insulated their managements from unwelcome takeover bids, and thus encouraged them to focus on long-term performance rather than short-term profits (Kenney and Florida, 1988: 153, n. 78; Eccleston, 1989: 31–3; Womack *et al.*, 1990: 61). Employees of the smaller firms sometimes labor alongside workers in the 'parent' firms, and even take responsibility for complete sections. Primary subcontractors similarly transfer equipment at nominal cost and provide worker training and financial assistance to secondary subcontractors, who in turn replicate these patterns right down to the level of the household. To share ideas and promote greater cooperation, subcontractors of major firms are also organized into *kyoryokukai*, or associations (Cusumano, 1985: 252; Kenney and Florida, 1988: 137; Odaka Konosuke *et al.*, 1988; Womack *et al.*, 1990: 153; Morales, 1994: 101).

Correspondingly, the evolution of a complex, hierarchically integrated network of subcontracting arrangements meant that major Japanese manufacturers were not burdened with the rigidity of long-term, large-scale fixed capital investments. Whereas large investments in standardized, mass-production techniques predisposed both American enterprises and their suppliers against basic design changes, the lower investments entailed by flexible small batch production processes in the *kanban* system enabled Japanese manufacturers to market a greater diversity of models and thereby create and dominate several market niches (Friedman, 1983: 361).

Extensive government support underpinned the evolution of this pervasive network of subcontracting arrangements. In the early 1950s, MITI set up an office of Small and Medium Enterprises and the Japan Small Enterprises Corporation to coordinate a nation-wide policy of support to these firms and to assist them to upgrade their technology, to help establish alliances with larger firms, to provide market intelligence and to provide low-interest loans. Additionally, in each prefecture a bank was designated to assess the requirements of small businesses and to help them develop business plans. These regional banks were also instrumental in creating non-profit associations called *shokotai* to provide training in business administration, tax planning, and labor relations for small enterprises. The difference in the level of government support to small enterprises in Japan and in the United States is vividly illustrated by the fact that the Japanese government had $66 billion in outstanding loans to the these firms in 1982 compared with the $3.8 billion that the US Small Business Administration loaned out, despite the American population being twice as large (Glasmeier and Sugiura, 1991: 406–7; Fujita and Hill, 1993).

Compared with the replication of the technostructures of US corporations in post-Second World War Europe discussed in Chapter 1, the mode of corporate governance in Japan was strikingly different. The more flexible contractual arrangements between 'parent' firms and their suppliers, organized in a multi-layered subcontracting network, enabled major Japanese manufacturers to drastically reduce the huge corporate bureaucracies associated with multi-unit technostructures of US corporations. In contrast to vertically-intergrated production structures, where the size and complexity of administrative hierarchies compromised effectiveness, the looser coordination of production processes by the *sogo shoshas* reduced uncertainty for its client firms without burdening them with an increasingly cumbersome bureaucratic structure (Yoshino and Lifson, 1986: 39–47). 'Just-in-time' production processes enabled Japanese firms to lower inventories, implement better quality controls and faster and continuous design improvements, and provide a greater diversity of products at lower cost. Subcontracting work arrangements also enabled manufacturers to segment the workforce and thereby undermine the unity of the labor movement and sap its strength.

South Korea and Taiwan

Despite the expropriation of Japanese corporate assets within their jurisdictions by postcolonial regimes in South Korea and Taiwan, differences in socio-political conditions meant that the corporate structures that evolved from these shared foundations were strikingly different. Though in their size and in the diversity of their product range, the South Korean *chaebol* bore more than a passing resemblance to the Japanese *keiretsu*, the former were invariably family-held enterprises. Whereas family ownership of firms in other countries was diluted due to the need to raise capital for growth, the ready availability of credit guarantees and subsidies from the South Korean government enabled the *chaebol* to preserve their family ownership structure (Amsden, 1989: 128; Mason *et al.*, 1980: 276–7). Consequently, decision-making tended to be highly centralized within these

Table 3.2 Combined sales of top ten *chaebol* as percentage of GNP, 1974–84

Chaebol	1974	1975	1976	1977	1978	1979	1980	1981	1982	1983	1984
1	4.9	4.3	4.7	7.9	6.9	8.3	8.3	10.5	10.4	11.8	12.0
2	7.2	7.5	8.1	12.5	12.9	12.8	16.3	19.1	19.0	21.2	24.0
3	9.0	9.8	11.3	16.0	16.9	17.6	23.9	27.6	27.4	30.5	35.8
4	10.3	11.4	12.9	18.2	20.7	22.1	30.1	35.2	35.6	38.7	44.3
5	11.6	12.8	14.5	19.8	22.9	24.6	35.0	41.3	42.2	46.7	52.4
6	2.7	14.1	16.1	21.3	24.7	26.6	38.2	44.9	46.0	51.0	56.2
7	13.5	15.3	17.5	22.8	26.4	28.5	41.0	48.0	49.2	54.2	59.4
8	14.3	16.2	18.4	24.0	27.7	30.3	43.6	50.9	52.2	57.1	62.1
9	14.7	16.7	19.3	25.2	28.9	31.6	46.0	53.5	55.1	59.8	64.8
10	15.1	17.1	19.8	26.0	30.1	32.8	48.1	55.7	57.6	62.4	67.4

Source: From *Asia's Next Giant: South Korea and Late Industrialization* by Alice H. Amsden, copyright – 1989 by Oxford University Press, Inc. Used by permission of Oxford University Press, Inc.

enterprise structures and the major subsidiaries and many minor ones were headed by family members (Amsden, 1989: 151–5; Whitley, 1990: 57–8; Orru *et al.*, 1991; Hamilton and Biggart, 1989: S58–9).

The *chaebol* also represented a marked concentration of economic power, virtually unparalleled elsewhere, as indicated by Table 3.2. In comparative terms, the largest 100 manufacturing firms in South Korea accounted for 40.6 percent of all manufacturing sales in 1970, 43.6 percent in 1972, 44.9 percent in 1977 and 46.9 percent in 1982. Corresponding figures for the top 100 manufacturing firms in Japan were 28.4 percent in 1975 and 27.3 percent in 1980 (Koo, 1987: 176; Amsden, 1989: 115–37; Gereffi, 1990: 95–7; Bello and Rosenfeld, 1990: 63–75; Koo and Kim, 1992: 136–7; Douglass, 1993b: 158; Hart-Landsberg, 1993: 63–5; Eckert, 1993: 122).

The product range of these *chaebol* was equally remarkable. Though like industrial conglomerates elsewhere the *chaebol* initially diversified into related businesses either because of the advantages of scope provided by a multi-divisional enterprise structure, or because local suppliers were unavailable, or because a market of sufficient size had not developed to permit specialization, very quickly the *chaebol* diversified into several unconnected businesses. The Lucky-Goldstar group, for example, diversified from consumer electronics to petrochemicals while Hyundai was prominent in the automobile and shipbuilding sectors. In contrast to the experience in the United States and other core states where diversification into unrelated fields occurred during periods of industrial decline or market saturation (Chandler, 1977: 481), diversification in South Korea occurred during phases of high-speed economic growth perhaps because of the *chaebol*'s 'relative lack of technical expertise to build upon in related products or in higher quality product niches. Their widely diversified structures complemented their strategy to compete at the bottom end of many markets' (Amsden, 1989: 151).

Given that the wellsprings for the remarkable concentration of economic power were government patronage and the immaturity of technical development, unlike the Japanese *keiretsu*, the *chaebol* did not develop an extensive subcontracting network. The increasing scale of industrial production is vividly illustrated by the growth of large manufacturing establishments: whereas firms with more than four and less than 20 employees had accounted for 29 percent of total employment and 19 percent of the value added in manufacturing in 1963, their share had dropped to 16 percent of employment and 7 percent of value-added in 1972. Correspondingly the share of establishments with over 200 employees had risen from 34 percent of employment and 47 percent of value-added in 1963 to 55 percent and 72 percent respectively in 1972 (Kuznets, 1977: 165).

The socio-political basis of the GMD party-state – particularly its links with small farmers, labor, and small industrialists – precluded a similar alliance between state and big capital. In particular, as the land reform legislation imposed rigid ceilings on land ownership, increases in farm incomes were invariably channeled into the manufacturing sector, especially since high positions in government or in enterprises run by the GMD were effectively closed to the native Taiwanese in an ethnically-bifurcated society (Greenhalgh, 1994: 766). This is indicated, among other things, by the decline in the percentage of full-time farming in rural households from 47.6 percent in 1960 to 31.9 percent five years later (Cheng and Gereffi, 1994: 209, n. 29). At the same time, since credit allocations from nationalized banks tended to discriminate against indigenous islanders in favor of mainland émigrées and GMD-controlled enterprises, native Taiwanese entrepreneurs were compelled to rely on kin and community networks to mobilize capital and labor and it has been estimated that by the early 1970s over 82 percent of the capital raised by small and medium entrepreneurs came from the informal money market (Bello and Rosenfeld, 1990: 242). Typical of the emergent pattern of industrial organization was, hence, a bifurcated structure with a few relatively large firms dominated by the mainland émigrées at the top and a large network of family firms (*jiazquqiye*) and business groups (*jituanqiye*) at the bottom, as indicated by Table 3.3.

The rapid proliferation of these small industries – Ramon Myers (1984: 516) reports, for instance, that Wang's success in establishing Formosa Plastics led to such an extraordinary spurt of imitators that the plastics industry grew at an annual rate of 45 percent between 1957 and 1971 and while only 100 small firms processed products supplied by Formosa Plastics in 1957, over 1,300 small units bought from plastic suppliers in 1970 – led to a saturation of Taiwan's narrow domestic markets in small consumer goods, precisely when US aid was tapering out. This situation was exacerbated by prevalent inheritance patterns which led to a division of land between all male heirs who often set up small manufacturing operations to compensate for their smaller land holdings. In these conditions, a

Table 3.3 Industrial employment in Taiwan

Year		No. of employees (%)					Total
		1–19	20–99	100–499	500–999	1000+	
1961	Number		99.2			0.8	
	Employees		61.2			38.8	
	Production		35.5			64.5	
1966	Number	85.6	11.7	2.3		0.5	27,709
	Employees	21.4	21.4	22.5		34.8	589,660
	Production	19.3	15.2	19.9		45.6	85,085
1971	Number	81.9	13.5	3.8		0.8	42,636
	Employees	15.7	19.9	28.2		36.1	1,201,539
	Production	11.5	14.8	26.0		47.3	242,940
1976	Number	81.0	14.3	4.1	0.3	0.3	69,517
	Employees	16.4	22.2	30.2	9.7	21.5	1,907,581
	Production	10.4	16.9	29.2	11.2	32.3	819.452
1981	Number	82.1	13.8	3.5	0.4	0.2	91,510
	Employees	17.4	24.1	28.8	10.3	19.6	2,201,470
	Production	8.9	17.6	26.0	10.6	36.8	2,067,430

Source: Wade (1990: 67, table 3.6).

Note
Number refers to number of enterprises; production refers to gross production, not value-added, and is in millions of NT$.

liberalization of controls over foreign trade and encouraging foreign investments through tax incentives – most notably the 1962 Statute for the Encouragement of Technical Cooperation and the creation of the Kaohsiung Export Processing Zone in 1965, the year US economic assistance ended – was an attempt to break out of the economic bottleneck through increasing exports.

Though the initial response from overseas investors was relatively luke-warm, as indicated by Figure 3.1, once General Instruments established a bonded electronics factory near Taipei in 1964 foreign investments soared rapidly, rising from US$18 million in 1963 to $248.8 million in 1973 (Gold, 1988b: table 9.5). Underlying this impressive rise in overseas investments was the search by American enterprises for low-cost labor – the wages of a skilled worker in Taiwan in 1972 were $73 a month when they were $102 in South Korea, $122 in Hong Kong, $183 in Singapore, and $272 in Japan – to reverse the inroads being made into their domestic markets by cheap Japanese imports at a time when peripheral and semiperipheral states in Latin America and elsewhere were beginning to impose restrictions on the operations of TNCs. At the same time, Japanese corporations also increased their investments to recapture their market shares in the United States being lost to off-shore plants of US enterprises, as well as to evade quota restrictions being placed on Japanese exports to core states. Prior colonial ties further predisposed Japanese enterprises to

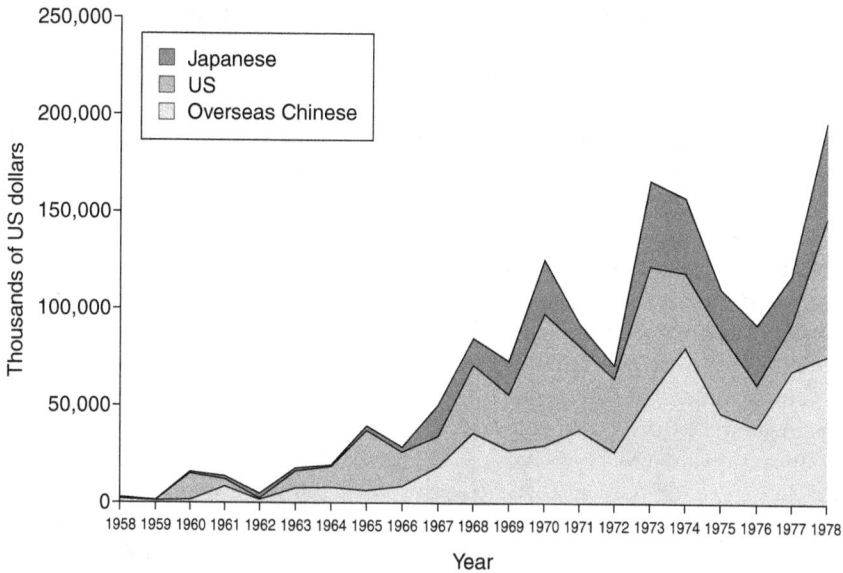

Figure 3.1 Foreign direct investment approvals in Taiwan, 1958–78.

Source: Adapted from Gold (1988b, table 9.5).

locate a disproportionate percentage of their offshore investments in Taiwan. Finally, persecution in Malaysia and Indonesia and additional incentives offered to overseas Chinese entrepreneurs by Chiang's administration as a part of its ideological claim to represent the legitimate government of China was responsible for the rise in investments by Chinese émigrées (Gold, 1986: 79–81; Gold, 1988b: 190–8; Bello and Rosenfeld, 1990: 245).

Apart from the availability of a literate, docile and low-wage workforce, the absence of irksome health and safety regulations, and the provision of a raft of tax incentives, the existence of a dense network of family-based small enterprises also provided a conducive environment for foreign investments. This was particularly true in the case of the small- and medium-scale enterprises which spearheaded Japanese investments as they not only lacked the resources to make large investments but also because the history of Japanese colonialism made it politically expedient to establish joint ventures with a local partner. Hence, the average size of the 349 cases of Japanese investments in Taiwan between 1964 and 1970 was $235,000 compared with an average of $1.6 million for the 123 cases of US investments during the same period and $230,000 for the 587 cases of investments by overseas Chinese investments. Even though the larger size of American investments indicated that US corporations tended to set up wholly-owned operations to export products back to their domestic markets, they often contracted out the production of intermediate components to the small family firms to further hold down production costs. Consequently, while the number of manufacturing firms in Taiwan increased by 250 percent between 1966 and 1976, the number of employees per firm increased by only 29 percent. In contrast, during the same period the number of manufacturing establishments in South Korea increased by only 10 percent, though the number of employees per firm doubled (Wade, 1990: 67).

Since holding companies are legally prohibited in Taiwan, these figures may underestimate the size of enterprises as census data do not include business groups. Nevertheless, they clearly indicate that increased foreign investments were compatible with Taiwan's bifurcated industrial structure. Encouragement of foreign investments did not amount to a reversal of an ISI strategy, as the government in its role as gatekeeper for the national economy evaluated proposals in terms of their ability to open up new markets, create new exports, transfer technology, and deepen internal economic relationships between component suppliers and final assemblers. The government also sought to safeguard local producers by insisting on foreign investors exporting their products and not competing with local enterprises in the domestic market. The power to restrict or expand imports gave the government a powerful leverage against domestic producers and overseas companies (Gold, 1986: 85; Wade, 1990: 150–1; Hart-Landsberg, 1993: 41–2).

The general protection extended to local producers not only safeguarded the GMD party-state's domination of the commanding heights of the economy but also vastly expanded the range of opportunities for the *jiazquqiye* and the *jituanqiye*. The combination of deliberate denial of access to credit to these firms with the provision of attractive tax incentives for exporters actively encouraged the creation of OEM (original equipment manufacturer) arrangements with Japanese and American TNCs (Hart-Landsberg, 1993: 41). Cheap products by small- and medium-scale Taiwanese firms, marketed under such well-known brand-names as Sears, J. C. Penny, Hewlett-Packard, IBM, Sony, Sharp, Mitsubishi, National, Westinghouse, Wilson Sporting Goods, and Schwinn Bicycles, were so pervasive that the executive of an American transplant operation told researchers that 'You really can't consider Taiwan an exporting nation. Taiwan is simply a collection of international subcontractors for the American market' (quoted in Bello and Rosenfeld, 1990: 243).

A telling testimony to the sheer pervasiveness of subcontracting relationships is provided by the lack of brand name recognition for Taiwanese products, despite the fact that on a per capita basis Taiwan's trade surplus in 1984 was twice that of Japan (Hamilton and Biggart, 1989: S54; Cheng and Gereffi, 1994: 211, n. 35). If OEM arrangements meant that more small enterprises participated in export trade in Taiwan than in other states – between 1978 and 1985 it was estimated that small- and medium-scale firms were responsible for over 60 percent of exports from Taiwan (Wade, 1990: 70; Cheng and Gereffi, 1994: 209) – these arrangements also ensured that the benefits accruing to these firms from increased exports were disproportionately small. According to one estimate, Japanese *sogo shosha* control some 50 to 70 percent of Taiwan's exports to the United States. By another reckoning, the export price of many commodities from Taiwan is said to be only 10 to 20 percent of their retail price in the United States (Bello and Rosenfeld, 1990: 243–4).

As might be expected, relations between local firms and their overseas partners exhibited considerable variation, though in most cases there was a distinct asymmetry in these relationships that worked against the former. In fields such as textiles and food processing where local firms dominated, they relied on the TNCs for access to export markets. In petrochemicals and microelectronics when the local collaborator was typically a GMD-controlled enterprise, TNCs supplied technology and capital while the local firm contributed capital and its downstream plants purchased the output. In other sectors, especially in consumer electronics, the relationship was far more complex since partnership arrangements with Japanese investors routinely tied the Taiwanese firms in a web of contractual obligations which compelled them to purchase raw materials from, and sell the completed products to, their Japanese partner (Gold, 1986: 82–3; Gold, 1988b: 189–90). If the government proved relatively ineffective in preventing Japanese firms from implementing very restrictive subcontracting arrangements on Taiwanese firms, it also turned a blind eye on local firms counterfeiting foreign labels and manufacturing substandard items (Simon, 1988b: 216; Wade, 1990: 268)!

The minimal vigilance the government exercised over small companies was also indicative of the much lower capacities of the government to monitor economic activities when compared with South Korea. As many analysts have noted, while the government formulated economic plans it had few procedures to monitor their implementation and one study found that there were an estimated 480,000 peddlers in 1984, with some 20,000 in Taipei alone, and that two-thirds of them were unregulated. Another study indicated that only 2,687 of the 16,000 construction firms were legally registered in 1984 (Cheng and Gereffi, 1994: 210). In fact, the government's most potent instrument – its control over industrial licensing – was effective only on the larger companies. Similarly, Robert Wade (1990: 162–4) argued that Taiwan's equivalent of the subsidy in South Korea was the postdated check – when a loan is negotiated the borrower gives the lender a postdated check covering the principal and interest – which was a poor substitute as far as monitoring economic performance is concerned.

Compelled to rely on kin and community networks, the dominant characteristic of small manufacturing and service firms in Taiwan was that each enterprise was owned by a single proprietor or family and functionally linked together in a system of satellite factories or *weixing gongchang* to produce a single product. These inter-enterprise networks, sometimes between members of the same family who owned separate firms and sometimes between unrelated proprietors, based on noncontractual agreements regarding quantity and price of their products, were the foundation stones of the structure of industrial and service organizations in Taiwan. Precisely because small family firms – merely extended households in many cases – had neither access to large resources nor the ability to forecast conditions in export markets, to diversify risks successful businesses tended to expand horizontally rather than to integrate vertically in interrelated businesses (Hamilton and Biggart, 1989: S66–7; Cheng and Gereffi, 1994: 209–10).

Unlike the unified management structure of South Korean *chaebol*, Taiwanese *jituanqiye* or business groups tended to be associations of single-unit enterprises managed by close relatives and the owners often held several managerial positions in different firms within the group. A detailed survey of the 96 largest *jituanqiye* in 1985 indicated that 59 percent were owned and controlled by family groups and a further 38 percent represented partnerships between unrelated individuals which could be expected to become family-based organizations in the next generation (Hamilton and Biggart, 1989: S66–7).

In short, though industrialization in both South Korea and Taiwan had been initiated by Japanese colonial authorities in the early twentieth century, the political economy of their post-colonial reconstitution led to the installation of very distinct structures of accumulation in these two jurisdictions. In South Korea, recognizing that only economic growth could guarantee political stability, the Park regime funneled enormous resources to the *chaebol* and used government control over finances to discipline the conglomerates. Different political conditions in Taiwan dictated a different strategy: a more decentralized and dispersed pattern of manufacturing based on small- and medium-sized enterprises with the government retaining control over the commanding heights of the economy. Similarly, though the two city-states of Hong Kong and Singapore had functioned as entrepôts in the British Empire, their transformation into off-shore manufacturing platforms in the 1950s and 1960s entailed very different patterns of industrial organization.

Hong Kong and Singapore

Hong Kong's economy was dominated by large expatriate holding companies, often associated with the old trading companies of the nineteenth century – Butterfield & Swire; Jardine, Matheson & Co. Ltd; Hong Kong & Whampoa Dock Ltd; Wheelock Marden Co. Ltd; Hutchison International Ltd; and China Light & Power Co. Ltd, among others. Not only were they the largest employers in the colony in the immediate aftermath of the Second World War, but through a system of interlocking directorships, they formed a powerful political bloc and were well represented in the Executive and Legislative Councils. When the loss of the Chinese hinterland deprived them of their markets and sources of supply, they shifted their activities toward manufacturing even though they continued to maintain their traditional interests in shipping, shipbuilding, public utilities, and trade. The Chinese Revolution also led to an exodus of manufacturers from Shanghai to Hong Kong, as we have already seen, and they were central to the transformation of Hong Kong from a colonial entrepôt to an export-oriented industrial platform. They dominated the textiles sector but by the 1960s had also diversified into garments, plastics, knitware, and enamelware. The overwhelming majority of workers in the manufacturing sector, however, continued to be employed by the Cantonese firms. Though many of them were established only after the Second World War, they had spread to all branches of industry. Finally, the development of Hong Kong as an export-oriented industrial platform also led to the establishment of large US manufacturing concerns, chiefly in the electronics sector. Factories established by US corporations tended to be larger in scale than those established by expatriate British firms or by Shanghainese or Cantonese firms. Though wages in US-owned electronic assembly firms tended to be higher than similar operations in other export-oriented Asian locations, their wage levels were lower than in the plastics, garments, and wig industries in Hong Kong and accordingly suffered from high labor turnover (England, 1971: 224–30).

Hong Kong's small domestic market and the lack of protection to industries had three major consequences for its economic structure. First, growing competitive pressures in labor-intensive industries encouraged a slash-and-burn attitude as entrepreneurs sought to reap quick profits. In his survey of industrial relations, Joe England (1971: 216–17) observed that in the 1960s, the large note-issuing banks who provided the bulk of funds for industries expected their loans to turn over within five years, and hence most investors did not plan beyond this term. As a result, bank credit to the manufacturing sector in Hong Kong consistently remained much lower than in the other dragon economies and even declined as it increased in the others (Yeung, 2000: 137). Second, as other low-cost sites of export-oriented industrialization serially emerged they exerted a corresponding pressure on wages and hence wage levels in low-skilled, labor-intensive manufacturing sectors were determined more by the productivity of firms than by the bargaining power of labor. This was reflected by the higher average hours worked per loom: 8,160 hours per year in Hong Kong in 1965 compared with 6,401 hours in South Korea, 4,864 in Taiwan, 4,786 in Japan, and 4,149 in Thailand (England, 1971: 212; Owen, 1971: 148, table 4.5). Third, the continuing domination of the commercial and financial factions of capital meant that services contributed over 60 percent of the colony's GDP as early as 1970 (Yeung, 2000: 126).

In manufacturing, extensive government subsidies of basic wage goods and the massive public housing program, in the context of the influx of refugees – the 1981 census indicated, for instance, that net immigration accounted for 58 percent of the population increase between 1976 and 1981 (Cheng and Gereffi, 1994: 201) – created propitious conditions for the development of an extensive network of subcontracting arrangements, especially since the colonial administration routinely ignored violations of environmental and safety regulations in the housing estates. Thus, as indicated by Table 3.4, the average number of employees per industrial estab-

Table 3.4 Distribution of manufacturing establishments and employment in Hong Kong

Persons employed[a]	Total no. (1981)	Percent of total				
		1951	1971	1977	1978	1981
Manufacturing establishments						
1 to 9	30,272		51.9	66.9	61.6	62.6
10 to 19	7,732	57.0[b]	19.1	14.9	16.9	16.0
20 to 49	6,271	26.7	15.5	11.1	12.2	13.0
SIE (total)	44,275	26.7	86.5	92.9	90.7	91.6
50 to 99	2,235				5.2	4.8
100 to 199	1,048				2.5	2.2
200 to 499	497				1.2	1.0
MIE (total)	3,780	19.0	12.6	7.5	8.9	8.0
500 to 999	119				0.4	0.2
≥ 1,000	49				0.1	0.1
LIE (total)	168	1.4	0.7	0.3	0.5	0.3
Total (no.)	48,223	1,778	17,115	37,568	44,903	48,324
Manufacturing employment						
1 to 9	115,273		6.0	6.9	11.0	11.6
10 to 19	101,759	10.5[b]	8.4	7.5	9.7	10.2
20 to 49	186,129	15.7	15.1	14.0	15.8	18.7
SIE (total)	403,161	15.7	29.5	28.4	36.5	40.5
50 to 99	154,357				15.2	15.5
100 to 199	138,424				14.3	13.9
200 to 499	138,097				14.7	13.9
MIE (total)	430,878	47.3	47.4	47.5	44.2	43.3
500 to 999	81,273				10.1	8.2
≥ 1,000	80,819				9.3	8.1
LIE (total)	162,092	26.7	22.9	24.2	19.4	16.3
Total (no.)	996,131	93,837	118,568	593,494	863,334	996,121

Source: Castells *et al.* (1990: 66, table 3.5).

Notes
a SIE, MIE, LIE small, medium large industrial establishments.
b Refers to establishments employing less than 20 workers.

lishment declined from 52.5 in 1951 to 20.0 in 1981. By another measure, while the bulk of manufactures from Hong Kong were exported, only 11.1 percent of manufacturing establishments received orders directly from overseas and import-export houses were responsible for almost 57 percent of overseas orders in the mid-1970s. Moreover, some 75 percent of these import–export houses were themselves small-scale firms (Sit *et al.*, 1979).

Unlike in the case of Japan, however, small firms in Hong Kong were generally not exclusively tied to a single large manufacturer or trading company and according to one study only 14.7 percent of small enterprises considered themselves to be satellites of larger firms (Sit *et al.*, 1979). Instead, the main commercial intermediaries – except in the case of the electronics sector where production and procurement were more tightly organized by the TNCs – placed orders with smaller firms, based on their assessment of market demands in high-income states. The latter firms, in turn, subcontracted out part-processes to still smaller firms on the basis of personal and family connections. The smaller firms were responsible for the purchase of their raw materials and components directly from wholesalers, and often the subcontracting processes took place within the premises of a larger firm as when, for instance, the ironing of garments were subcontracted to an individual or a family unit who performed the operations in the larger firm on piece rates. Similarly, it was not unusual for a group of workers of an enterprise to try and outbid their own firm for an order by undertaking to provide it at a lower cost. While the lack of hierarchical relationships organized by large enterprise groups as in Japan may make the subcontracting networks more flexible, it also led to greater insecurity. Although no systematic data on business failures exist, a study in 1984 found that 57.1 percent of the firms surveyed had been in existence for less than four years and that only 22 percent of the firms had been in operation for longer than 10 years (Castells *et al.*, 1990: 66–74; see also England, 1971: 212).

Given the precariousness of small enterprises in Hong Kong, most of which were family-owned and managed, it was not uncommon for them to produce goods in high demand – such as toys and other plastics, gloves, and garments – to order as subcontractors and then invest in an entirely different line of production according to new orders from larger firms. The inherent instability of small firms meant that though a hard core of technicians was essential, other workers tended to be treated as casual labor. Correspondingly, workers had little loyalty to any firm or industry and changed jobs frequently (England, 1971: 223–4).

The prevalence of widespread subcontracting arrangements and the proliferation of small workshops in Hong Kong stood in sharp contrast to Singapore where, reflecting the government's strategy of relying on TNCs for investment, subcontracting arrangements with locally-owned firms were minimal. Though the electronics industry, to take one instance, was estimated to have created over 80,000 new jobs between 1968 and 1981 and sourced over 50 percent of its material inputs locally, it signally failed to generate backward linkages with Singaporean-owned firms. Since the smaller scale and telescoped industrial experience of Singaporean manufacturers meant that they were generally not competitive in the early years of industrialization in price, product range, technological sophistication, and time-critical delivery schedules, locally-sourced inputs were routinely procured from foreign-owned subsidiaries in the island state. Additionally, as only industrial ventures with over $1 million in investments were eligible for tax breaks conferred on 'pioneer industries,' small domestic entrepreneurs were ineligible for most of the incentives offered to the TNCs. The absence of protectionist measures also meant that Singaporean firms had virtually no insulation against adverse market conditions and some 38 percent of all wholly-owned Singaporean firms established since 1961 had declared bankruptcy by 1978 (Lim and Pang Eng Fong, 1986: 54–5, 92; Bello and Rosenfeld, 1990: 294–5).

Conversely, the stock of foreign equity investment grew by almost ten times in the eleven years between 1970 to 1981 – from $1.7 billion to $16.8 billion. While inflows of foreign investment to the island state began in earnest only after the failure of its merger with Malaysia in 1965, within four years foreign investment represented 54.2 percent of all fixed assets in manufacturing. This increase in foreign investments was reflected in a sharp rise in the value of exports from $349.2 million in 1965 to $1265.3 million by 1969, or a rise of 262 percent. At the same time, Malaysia's share of Singapore's manufactured exports fell from 53.7 percent to 15.4 percent. However, this also led to a dramatic falling off of Japanese investments – except in the shipbuilding and repair sectors – as these ventures had been designed to penetrate Southeast Asian markets rather than to export to Western Europe and North America (Bello and Rosenfeld, 1990: 293; Rodan, 1989: 99–103).

United States-based capital swiftly replaced the Japanese as leading investors in Singapore's manufacturing sector, with US investments rising from $27 million in 1967 to $131 million in 1969. Japanese investment, in contrast, grew by just $9 million between 1965 and 1969. US firms also tended to be much larger in size, with an average employment size in 1981 of 363 workers per establishment compared with 243 for Japanese firms, 226 for Swiss firms, and 164 for firms owned by Hong Kong based capital. Between 1965 and 1969, US companies were followed by British- and Dutch-based capital as leading investors, though these investments were primarily directed toward the petroleum sector (Rodan, 1989: 103; Lim and Pang Eng Fong, 1986: 54–8).

The magnitude of foreign investment in Singapore meant that it dominated all sectors of industry, unlike the case with Hong Kong and Taiwan where foreign investments were concentrated in specific sectors. This is indicated by Table 3.5 which depicts how foreign capital, which had been relatively insignificant in 1959, had come to dominate Singapore's economy by 1973 (Haggard and Cheng, 1987: 98–9).

Table 3.5 The role of foreign paid-up capital in Singapore's industry, 1959 and
1973

	Sectoral share of total paid-up capital (%)		Foreign proportion (%)	
	1959	*1973*	*1959*	*1973*
Food	32	15	13	52
Textiles	1	11	53	89
Chemicals	3	9	19	84
Petroleum and products	0	19	0	100
Metals	11	9	54	51
Machinery	5	10	43	49
Electrical products	3	8	95	74
Scientific and photographic equipment	1	4	62	94
Others	44	15	11	83
Total	100	100	21	76

Source: Haggard and Chang (1987: 99, table 8).

The dominance of foreign firms continued unabated over the next decade as the Singaporean government sought to increase the quality of labor to counteract competition for overseas investments from other low-wage economies. Though low wages initially attracted US corporations, the rapid growth of industrial production virtually eliminated unemployment in the island by 1970. As this coincided with the opening up of Malaysia – where wage levels were lower – to foreign investments, the Singapore government sought to upgrade its nascent industrial structure. It withdrew 'pioneer industry' status from pure assembly operations in the electronics industry in 1970 and centralized wage determination in a tripartite National Wages Council (NWC), created in 1972. The following year, the NWC tried to force firms to adopt more capital- and technology-intensive processes by raising wage levels. These steps not only discouraged further inflows of foreign capital to labor-intensive sectors especially but also continued to undermine the Singaporean bourgeoisie unable to enter into higher value-added production. By the mid-1980s, transnational corporations accounted for over 70 percent of Singapore's industrial production, 50 percent of employment and 82 percent of exports (Rodan, 1989: 103–9, 124; Haggard and Cheng, 1987: 119; Bello and Rosenfeld, 1990: 293).

To recapitulate, though the dislocations caused by the Second World War and the Japanese defeat, the Korean War, the marginalization of prewar elites, and bipolar rivalry between the United States and the Soviet Union combined to confer greater relative autonomy on governments along Asia's rimlands, it also made it incumbent on them to seek new bases of legitimacy. Seeking to inoculate their subject populations from the appeals of revolutionary socialism by increasing their material prosperity, these governments adopted a variety of strategies – shaped by their domestic political coalitions, external alliances, resource endowments, size and maturity of their domestic bourgeoisie, and the organizational capabilities of their bureaucratic apparatus. In Japan, the largest and most powerful of these states, the bureaucracy – which did not suffer a debilitating purge – emerged as a key actor and established an alliance with the big bourgeoisie to strategically target sectors of increasing technological sophistication for accelerated development by providing loans at preferential rates of interest, tax concessions, and the creation of bank-led industrial conglomerates and cartels to reap economies of scale. The establishment of a conquest state in Taiwan as the GMD suppressed the indigenous islanders meant that no similar alliance between the bureaucracy and big business could be established in the island state. The greater organizational capabilities of the GMD state, and the provision of substantial assistance from the United States in pursuit of its Cold War aims, led to the creation of a massive state sector. Dependence on US aid, however, meant that American pressure led to the provision of assistance for the development of a broad-based, small-scale consumer goods industry in the private sector. Without a comparable cadre of bureaucrats with planning and technical expertise and a mass party, Syngman Rhee's inability to promote broad-based economic development ultimately led to General Park's coup d'état in 1961. Recognizing that only economic growth could guarantee political stability, the military junta established an alliance with the big bourgeoisie and established comprehensive controls over the financial sector by re-nationalizing all commercial banks. Simultaneously, attempting to lessen the regime's dependence on the US for aid, the government vastly expanded its borrowings overseas, thereby laying the foundations both for the spectacular growth of South Korean corporations and for their equally spectacular meltdown during the economic crisis of 1997–98, as we shall see in Chapter 5. When Hong Kong was confronted with the loss of its hinterland, the great degree of cohesion between government and business elites led to the government shouldering the costs of infrastructural development and subsidizing basic wage goods in the colony's transition from an entrepôt to an low-wage manufacturing platform. Finally, the absence of a strong domestic industrial bourgeoisie in Singapore led the government to develop the island state's infrastructure and offer foreign investors a variety of incentives as well as to create a significant public sector.

These strategies of government intervention, in turn, shaped patterns of industrial organization and employment relations. The premature termination of the *zaibatsu* dissolution program and vast increases in American procurements led to significant transformations in Japanese industrial organization and labor relations. Unsure of how long the Korean War-led boom would last, major Japanese corporations farmed out work to a variety of subcontractors. This was eventually institutionalized as a hierarchically organized, multi-layered subcontracting network which enabled corporate Japan to respond quickly to market changes and make incremental quality improvements during the production process, as well as to divide the labor market into segments with differential pay and benefit rates. The *sogo shosha* provided an organizational umbrella, more-over, to coordinate the activities of many small- and medium-sized firms within these networks.

If the size of the South Korean *chaebol* invited comparisons with the Japanese *keiretsu*, the former tended to be family-held enterprises and did not initially resort to extensive outsourcing of components. In contrast, the marginalization of native islanders in Taiwan and obstacles to them accessing capital from the nationalized banking structure led to the emer-gence of a large network of small enterprises based on relations of kinship and neighborhood. While the large, expatriate business houses domin-ated Hong Kong's economy, the influx of refugees from China and exten-sive government subsidies of basic wage goods and a massive public housing program led to the development of a dense network of small, family-based enterprises. Unlike in Japan, however, they were not organ-ized within hierarchical, multi-layered subcontracting networks and were hence more precarious. Finally, the Singapore government's strategy of betting on foreign investments meant that linkages between large, vertically-integrated enterprises and domestic firms were minimal.

These complementary industrial structures led to the greater regional integration of production along the Asian rimlands. As production costs rose in Japan, the *sogo sosha* enabled small- and medium-scale enterprises engaged in low-skilled production processes to transfer their operations to neighboring locations – especially to Taiwan and Hong Kong where the emerging network of small-scale units provided a propitious environment. The imposition of export quotas on textiles and other commodities from Japan, and later from the other 'dragon' economies, by high-income states in North America and Western Europe also triggered a trans-border expansion of production networks as firms sought alternate sites of pro-duction. Greater Japanese concern with dependence on imported raw materials and environmental pollution and the consequent move to cleaner, higher value-added industries led to the progressive transfer of heavy and chemical industries to South Korea, where access to large amounts of overseas capital enabled the *chaebol* to enter these fields. Singa-pore, meanwhile, continued to be a recipient of large doses of foreign investments. We turn to these issues in the next chapter.

4   Crisis of US hegemony and the growth of regional economic integration in Pacific-Asia

Each time decentering occurs, a recentering takes place.

Fernand Braudel

By almost every conceivable yardstick, the 23 years from the beginning of the Korean War in 1950 was an exceptional period of material expansion – 'the golden age of capitalism' as Stephen Marglin and Juliet Schor (1991) among others have called it. The installation of state-centered strategies of development under the Bretton Woods system heralded a sustained burst of economic growth not only in the reconstructed economies of Western Europe and Japan, but also in the 'people's democracies' of Eastern Europe, in the USSR, in Latin America, and in the newly-independent states of Asia and Africa:

> the quarter century following post-World War II reconstruction was a period of unprecedented prosperity and expansion of the world economy. Between 1950 and 1975 income per person in the developing countries increased on average by 3 per cent p.a., accelerating from 2 per cent in the 1950s to 3.4 per cent in the 1960s. This rate of growth was historically unprecedented for these countries and in excess of that achieved by the developed countries in their period of industrialization. . . . In the developed countries themselves . . . GDP and GDP per head grew almost twice as fast as in any previous period since 1820. Labour productivity grew twice as fast as ever before, and there was a massive acceleration in the rate of growth of the capital stock. The increase in capital stock represented an investment boom of historically unprecedented length and vigour.
>
> (Glyn et al., 1991: 41–2)

The remarkable expansion of material production occasioned by the reconstitution of the world market under US tutelage led not only to the emergence of a mass market for consumer durables – most notably the automobile – in Western Europe, Japan, and Australasia, but also to the rapid industrialization of many former European colonies, and across the ideological divide, in the Soviet Union and other centrally-planned economies. The pursuit of multiple, parallel strategies of industrialization, however, eventually increased competitive pressures that led to a whole-sale restructuring of the structural and institutional scaffolding of the world economy provided by the Bretton Woods agreements. In these conditions, attempts by Japanese corporations to relieve the adverse impact of growing competitive pressures, and limits imposed by narrow domestic markets in neighboring locations, led to greater regional integration along the Pacific coasts of Asia. This enabled these economies not only to withstand the collapse of most other low- and middle-income states during the debt crisis of the 1980s but also to post spectacularly high rates of economic growth, earning them the sobriquet of 'Asian miracles.'

The reconstruction of high-income West European states in America's image by the mid-1960s and the rebuilding of Japan as a low-cost exporter, as the first section shows, increased competitive pressures in the world market and led to a decline in the US current account surplus. In smaller low- and middle-income states, import-substituting policies came up against the limitations of narrow domestic markets just as centrally-planned economies in Eastern Europe came up against the limitations of extensive models of economic growth. In short, constraints on capital accumulation appeared almost everywhere, in the core and in the periphery, in the West and in the 'socialist' bloc, though given socio-historical differences between states, there were considerable variations in the magnitude, nature, and timing of the impact of these constraints. These conditions led to a remapping of the geography of manufacturing. To counter increased wage pressures in their home bases, US and West European corporations recruited newer migrants. In the United States there was also a shift in manufacturing to the southern and western states. More importantly, since capital flows toward Europe represented the most substantial outflow of resources from the United States, the US government sought to curb these outflows. In contrast, since lower wages in East Asia could cheapen costs and hence lower welfare and military expenditures, successive US administrations encouraged capital outflows across the Pacific. As this coincided with an expansion of Japanese investments overseas due to rising labor costs, it heralded a new phase of regional integration along Asia's Pacific coasts. These shifts in patterns of cross-border corporate investments were lubricated by a vast increase in the liquidity of major financial institutions due to the emergence of a supranational money market created through the hoarding of the profits of TNCs in specially denominated bank accounts.

The relentless transnational expansion of US capital contributed to American deficits and the worsening US balance of payments led to a growing contradiction between the interests of the increasingly global US corporations and those of the US government. Unable to stem its persistent balance of payments deficit, the Nixon Administration revoked the US dollar's convertibility into gold and sought to shift competitive pressures onto enterprises in Western Europe and Japan, as demonstrated in the next section. The massive increase in global liquidity that followed loose US monetary policies led to a rapid expansion of public debt in many low- and middle-income states as they sought to construct multiple, parallel, state-centered industrial sectors. Far from heralding a 'new international division of labor,' this debt-led industrialization drive came undone when the United States government reversed its loose monetary policies as the ensuing world inflation threatened the role of the greenback as world money. It was now that the significance of regional economic integration along the Pacific coasts of Asia under the aegis of Japanese corporate networks became evident. Rather than constructing parallel and competing industrial structures, the creation of complementary industrial structures along capitalist Asia's Pacific coasts enabled these economies to withstand the debt crisis of the early 1980s.

The serial transfer of declining industries from Japan to neighboring locations in Asia – celebrated as the 'flying geese' model – provided a framework for regional economic integration and laid the foundations for rapid rates of growth not only in the 'Four Dragons' but also in Indonesia, Malaysia, and Thailand in the 1980s. The transfer of declining industries from Japan was especially smooth since Japanese corporations did not insist on majority equity participation, preferring to rely on non-equity forms of control. Along the Asian rimlands, inflows of foreign capital provided regional elites with the means to stabilize their rule. Even though they created agencies formally similar to pilot economic agencies in Japan, Singapore, South Korea, and Taiwan, these agencies never had the autonomy of the former as we shall see in the third section. Finally, we shall examine the implications of these developments for the next phase of industrial expansion and the changing dialectics of business–government relations in Pacific-Asia within the context of a world-wide process of capitalist restructuring in the 1980s and 1990s. Most notably, rapid structural transformation unraveled the domestic coalitions that had made the developmental state possible, an issue discussed at length in the following chapter.

The gathering storm

Though the reconstitution of the world market under US hegemony in the context of the bipolar rivalry between the United States and the Soviet Union led to a remarkable expansion of material production, it contained the seeds to constrain the possibilities for continued expansion and to unravel the bipolar partitioning of the world instituted by the Cold War, and eventually undermined the foundations of US hegemony itself. The soil in which these seeds germinated was fertilized by several elements: the growing incompatibility between the interests of increasingly global US corporate capital and the interests of the American government, an intensification in competitive pressures caused by the implementation of multiple state-centered strategies of economic growth and the increasing 'workplace bargaining power of labor,' the spatial relocation of manufacturing operations facilitated by constraints imposed by relatively narrow domestic markets in many low- and middle-income states, and the onset of structural limits to extensive economic growth in the centrally-planned economies.

Reintegration of the world market under US auspices had, as we saw in Chapter 1, led to the spread of multi-unit vertically-integrated enterprises to Western Europe. As reconstruction proceeded apace, European enterprises had begun to trespass on each others' market niches as well as those of US enterprises. While the resulting fall in US merchandise surpluses and the related growth of a supranational currency market hampered the geo-political strategies of the US government, it encouraged the flow of investments to East Asia to compensate for the decline in official aid to 'friendly' states. Meanwhile, increasing labor costs in Japan triggered a smaller outward expansion of Japanese production networks to select locations in East and Southeast Asia which was facilitated by internal developments in these locations. This new phase of regional integration in the Pacific-Asian region, as we shall see, was paralleled by shifts in the geography of manufacture in the United States and the greater recruitment of new migrants by American and West European industrial enterprises. Meanwhile, the limitations of extensive economic growth in Eastern Europe was also eroding the geopolitical partitioning of the globe between the United States and the Soviet Union that had enabled the reconstitution of the world market after the Second World War, as we also saw in Chapter 1.

In the first instance, the rebuilding of core states in Western Europe through massive flows of military assistance and the transnational expansion of US corporate capital transformed the world-wide liquidity shortage into a dollar glut by 1960. One indicator of the extent of American investments in Western Europe, especially after the formation of a Common Market and the restoration of currency convertibility in 1958, is provided by the fact that between 1957 and 1966, the number of American subsidiaries in Europe more than tripled to nearly 9,000 (Glyn *et al.*, 1991: 99; calculated from Wilkins, 1974: 330).

The relentless transnational expansion of US corporate capital, particularly the high levels of FDI in manufacturing in Western Europe, enabled these economies to chip away at the impressive lead in industrial production that had been established by the United States during the Second World War, and the expansion of output produced abroad was also accompanied by a steep decline in US export earnings. By one reckoning, in the ten years after the creation of the European Common Market, a third of all US investments in transportation equipment, a quarter of all investments in chemicals, and a fifth in machinery were located abroad, mainly in Europe (Bluestone and Harrison, 1982: 42, 113; calculated from Wilkins, 1974: 331).[1] The US share of world-wide exports of manufactured goods, for instance, fell from 28.7 percent in 1957 to 23 percent in 1962 and to 16.1 percent in 1970, while the West German share rose from 16.7 to 19.5 percent and to 16.8 percent (van der Wee, 1986: 262–77; Itoh, 1990: 48). The presence of US transplants in Europe was so prominent that when Servan-Schreiber raised the prospect of an 'American challenge' in 1968, his main concern was that, 'Fifteen years from now it is quite possible that the world's third great industrial power, just after the United States and Russia, will not be Europe but American industry in Europe' (quoted in Chandler, 1990: 615)! As a consequence, from an average annual trade surplus of $5.41 billion between 1961 and 1965, the US trade account sharply declined to a deficit of $2.7 billion in 1971 (Glyn *et al.*, 1991: 98; Parboni, 1981: 48; Itoh, 1990: 48; van der Wee, 1986: 450–3).

Since the US merchandise surplus had helped finance unilateral transfers of capital in the form of aid and military assistance to American allies and 'friendly' states, a decline in its current account surpluses increasingly hampered the power pursuits of the US government and weakened the complementarity of interests between it and the increasingly global US corporations. Additionally, the steady growth of dollar surpluses, and *ipso facto* foreign claims on income produced in the United States – which rose from nearly half the size of US gold reserves in 1959 to one and a half times larger than these reserves by 1967 (Glyn *et al.*, 1991: 98) – undermined the ability of the US government to freely convert dollars to gold at $35 per ounce and its commitment to maintain free capital markets (Itoh, 1990: 48–9; van der Wee, 1986: 458). Simply put, the continually deteriorating balance of payments situation progressively eroded both the position of the dollar as world money and the national foundations of American power.

The growing fiscal crisis of the US government was compounded by the increased commitments to social welfare made by the Johnson administration. When government expenditure had grown by only $50 billion in the decade between 1955 and 1965, the 'Great Society' project led to an increase in budget expenditure of $75 billion between the fourth quarter of 1965 and the first quarter of 1969. Even more important than the magnitude of this increase was the inflexibility of new expenditures on welfare programs and public services – rising from 25.1 percent of total federal expenditures in 1965 to 46.5 percent in 1975, while the share of military expenditures fell from 40.8 percent in 1965 to 25.6 percent in 1975 (Aglietta, 1987: 239–40).

To counteract the aggravating fiscal crisis, the United States government adopted very different policies regarding capital flows to Western

Europe and East Asia. As outflows to Western Europe represented the greatest drain on US resources, even before its merchandise trade registered a deficit, the Kennedy administration sought to extend its jurisdiction over foreign subsidiaries of US corporations by subjecting them to American trade laws and imposed controls on outflows of capital to the region (van der Wee, 1986: 470). However, as successive American administrations sought to monitor and restrict investments and lending abroad, US transplants with the connivance and collaboration of West European governments, began to develop a dynamic of their own that could not be controlled by the US government.

The creation of a supranational money market provided American transnational corporations (TNCs) with the means to evade US government controls. The unique status conferred on the dollar as the principal reserve currency and the medium for the settlement of international balances of payments by the Bretton Woods agreement enabled non-US banks to legally accumulate dollars. Though these funds were initially redeposited in US banks, European banks quickly recognized the advantages of holding funds in currencies outside the country of their issue. While the creation of Eurodollars – or, more broadly, supranational currencies – were initiated by dollar deposits of the USSR and its allies in specially denominated accounts in European banks to evade seizure by the US government, these were rapidly overshadowed by deposits of American-based TNCs seeking to evade US tax laws. As these deposits grew, American banks entered the market by establishing offshore branches and, by 1961, they controlled approximately 50 percent of the dollar deposits in Europe (Arrighi, 1994: 301–2). In the context of the growth of a supranational currency market, the Kennedy administration's attempt to stem the outflow of dollars by restricting foreign investments and lending merely shifted the center of financing dollar loans to London and hence outside the jurisdictional reach of US authorities. The emergence of a financial network parallel to, and outside the purview of, the Bretton Woods system initially buttressed the role of the dollar as world money and facilitated the further transnational expansion of US capital by enabling corporations to borrow in Europe. Thus, the growth of Eurodollars expanded exponentially after 1968 when the US trade account began a steady slide into deficit (Arrighi, 1994: 302–3; van der Wee, 1986: 469–72).

Meanwhile, the reconstruction of West European economies and the continuing flow of US investments had increased competitive pressures and constrained the further expansion of US capital in the region. Equally significantly, the growth in employment led to militant wage demands. While tight labor markets significantly diminished the threat of dismissals, workers evolved a series of strategies – lightning strikes, 'go slows,' rolling strikes, 'confetti strikes' (when different groups of workers struck for specified periods determined by the color or last digit of their registration cards) – to cause the greatest disruption with the least cost to themselves, and reaped rich rewards in the form of higher wages, reduction of wage differentials, greater shopfloor representation in bargaining, and increased workplace control (Armstrong *et al.*, 1984: 236–46, 271–82; Silver, 1997).

In marked contrast to its attempts to curb capital outflows to Western Europe, the United States government encouraged an increase in US corporate investments to its allies and other 'friendly' states in Asia. This was done, in the first instance, to ensure the viability of a non-Communist model of development, especially in Taiwan, as American aid was being phased out. Transnational expansion to East and Southeast Asia also provided US corporations with a means to relieve increasing competitive measures as opportunities for further expansion in Europe declined. Additionally, relocation of manufacturing operations to East Asia enabled US-based TNCs – and less significantly, those based in Europe – to recapture market shares in their home bases which were being lost to cheap Japanese imports (Gold, 1988b: 195).

Unlike the case of India, Brazil, or other large low- and middle-income states, the smaller governments and businesses in several locations in East and Southeast Asia were more favorably inclined to foreign investments as limitations placed on the continued pursuit of ISI strategies by their narrow domestic markets and relatively poor resource endowments became evident by the mid-1960s. Thus, when the larger low- and middle-income states were beginning to impose restrictions on TNCs, Taiwan and South Korea were courting foreign investments by establishing the Kaohsiung Export Processing Zone (KEPZ) in 1965 and the Masan Export Processing Zone in 1970 respectively. Even earlier in Thailand, after Field Marshal Sarit Thanarat's take-over of power in 1958, the government had abandoned its dirigiste policy, privatized many state enterprises and, on the advice of a World Bank team, invited foreign investments. However, a symbiosis between bankers and industrialists frustrated demands by traders and consumers for a more liberal trading system until excess capacity in the domestic consumer goods sector became acute by the early 1970s when the government began to shift to an export-oriented industrialization strategy (Hewison, 1987: 56–8). In Indonesia, soon after his brutal overthrow of President Sukarno in 1965, General Suharto sought to regain the confidence of foreign investors as the old regime had largely nationalized foreign assets in 1957–58 (Winters, 1996: 50–76). And in Malaysia, the Malay-dominated state also began to be more receptive to overseas investors – permitting the establishment of free trade zones and severely curtailing the rights of labor – after the ethnic conflicts of 1969, as domestic industry was dominated by the Chinese minority (Rasiah, 1993; Jomo *et al.*, 1997: 98).

Equally importantly, given the presence of large pools of cheap labor in East and Southeast Asia, the development of the region as a low-cost

exporter to the United States enabled 'the US government to *cheapen* supplies essential to its power pursuits, both at home and abroad' (Arrighi,
1994: 341, emphasis in the original). Indeed, in the absence of the
tremendous escalation of cheap imports from East and Southeast Asia –
with US imports from Japan alone increasing more than three-fold, transforming an American trade surplus with Japan of $130 million in 1964 to a
deficit of $1.4 billion in 1970 (Calleo and Rowland, 1973: 209) – the crisis
of what James O'Connor (1973) calls the US 'welfare-warfare state' would
have been far more acute than it already was by the end of the 1960s.

The constraints of narrow domestic markets on ISI strategies in East
and Southeast Asia, the increasing substitution of corporate investments
for US aid, and the development of several locations in the region as low-
cost exporters to the United States in the mid-1960s led to a fundamental
transformation in the patterns of US investments in Asia. Whereas these
had been predominantly concentrated in India, Japan, and the Philippines until 1966, they became far more diversified with a quadrupling of
US FDI in Asia (excluding Japan) between 1966 and 1977. Hong Kong
and Indonesia accounted for two-fifths of the cumulative value of US
investments in low- and middle-income Asian states by 1977, and Singapore, Malaysia, South Korea, Taiwan, and Thailand had also emerged as
important new sites for American investments (Encarnation, 1992: 153,
158–9).

Though natural resources – especially petroleum in Indonesia –
continued to attract the largest sectoral share of US investments, a considerable portion of new investments were directed toward offshore manufacturing, most notably in textiles and electronics. Unlike earlier US
investments in manufacturing which had been oriented to supplying local
markets in host countries, new investments were principally designed for
export back to the United States.[2] Nevertheless, US investments in Asia
remained relatively small – the book value of its FDI in manufacturing in
Asia was only 4.7 percent of total US overseas investments in the sector in
1970, compared with 42.5 percent for the UK and the EEC, 31.2 percent
for Canada, and 14.3 percent for Latin America (calculated from Wilkins,
1974: 331). Finally, deepening US military involvement in Indochina also
fostered economic growth in neighboring countries. By locating strategic
military bases in remote areas of Thailand and constructing highways, for
instance, these areas were opened up for production for the world market
and were central to the emergence of Thailand as an exporter of agricultural products (Phongpaichit and Baker, 1998: 22–3).

The surge in the expansion of US corporate capital to Asia was
accompanied by a parallel, though smaller, outward expansion to the
region by Japanese capital since the mid-1960s. The rapid expansion of
industrial production in Japan during the preceding decade had led to a
tightening of the labor market and raised wages by the early 1960s
(Ozawa, 1979: 14, 78–80).[3] The coincidence of labor shortages at home,

and the opening of new opportunities abroad – with the conclusion of a peace treaty with South Korea in 1965, the establishment of the KEPZ in Taiwan, Singapore's expulsion from the Malaysian Federation and the ouster of the Sukarno government by Suharto's right-wing regime in Indonesia the same year – provided a favorable climate for the transborder expansion of Japanese capital. An additional impetus derived from the weakness of Japanese corporate and government structures and their greater dependence on American markets that made them far more susceptible to US pressure than enterprises and governments across the Atlantic. As domestic US manufacturers of relatively unskilled, labor-intensive, low-technology products began to lobby against the large volume of cheap imports flooding the American market, beginning with a five-year agreement with Japan on cotton textiles in 1957, the US entered into a series of bilateral agreements with its trade partners in East Asia requiring them to 'voluntarily' limit their exports to the United States in specified categories, and until 1971 over 34 percent of Japan's exports to the United States were covered by these voluntary restrictions (Calleo and Rowland, 1973: 210). The imposition of quota restrictions inaugurated a process of regional integration along the Asian seaboard of the Pacific as Japanese producers – 'quota refugees,' as Rosalinda Ofreneo (1994) so aptly calls them – sought to circumvent quotas on exports to the US by setting up offshore manufacturing facilities. Tightening restrictions of the Multifibre Agreements subsequently led textile manufacturers based in Hong Kong, South Korea, and Taiwan also follow the Japanese lead in setting up off-shore production facilities in Pacific-Asia.

Consequently, while Japanese manufacturing investments in East and Southeast Asia had been limited to only nine cases before 1960 – four in Thailand, three in Taiwan, and one each in Hong Kong and Singapore – these numbers rose significantly after 1966, as indicated by Table 4.1. Despite this rise, overseas investments in manufacturing continued to be overshadowed by Japanese investments in resource extraction throughout the 1960s and the share of manufacturing in total Japanese FDI, measured in dollar terms, actually fell from 27.4 percent in 1960 to 20 percent in 1970 (Dicken, 1991: 19; Tokunaga, 1992). However, a more accurate indicator of the importance of Japanese overseas manufacturing investments is provided by the number of projects than by their value.

Unlike the transnational expansion of US capital which was spearheaded by large, vertically integrated TNCs, and directed toward the manufacture of relatively sophisticated products, small- and medium-scale firms specializing in labor-intensive, low-skilled, low-technology sectors were the primary agents for the transborder expansion of Japanese capital (Ozawa, 1979: 25–30; Ozawa, 1985: 166–7; Steven, 1990: 14). These small firms had neither the resources to construct large production facilities nor access to advanced technologies that would give them enough leverage with host governments to insist on retaining majority control over their

Table 4.1 Number of Japanese overseas investments in East and Southeast Asia approved by the Ministry of Finance until 1973

Year	Hong Kong	Indonesia	Philippines	Singapore	South Korea	Taiwan	Thailand
Pre-1960	1	0	0	1	0	3	4
1960	1	0	0	0	0	4	4
1961	4	0	0	1	0	2	2
1962	1	0	0	0	0	9	6
1963	7	0	0	8	0	8	5
1964	4	0	0	0	0	0	14
1965	3	0	0	3	0	9	10
1966	10	0	0	4	0	24	9
1967	2	0	5	4	3	46	6
1968	1	1	2	3	8	80	8
1969	6	8	2	10	15	73	17
1970	5	19	2	7	58	50	15
1971	10	18	5	14	51	16	14
1972	16	13	6	26	113	13	17
1973	19	33	15	38	290	68	30

Source: Adapted from Yoshihara (1978: 18, 65).

subsidiaries. Abiding resentments against the Japanese for their colonial occupation of Taiwan and South Korea and their wartime atrocities against peoples of Southeast Asia made it strategically prudent for Japanese investors not to insist on majority equity participation in their joint ventures. Thus, the average size of Japanese manufacturing investments in the region was far smaller than the average size of US or European investments. In Taiwan, for instance, Japanese investments in the electronics and electric machinery sectors averaged $339,000 at the end of 1970, and $417,575 in chemicals as opposed to average US investments of $3,975,676 and $2,344,478 respectively (Ozawa, 1979: 88; Denker, 1994: 55).

Small- and medium-scale firms were able to establish beachheads for Japanese capital on the Asian perimeters of the Pacific only because the *sogo shosha* could provide the infrastructural support necessary for foreign investments that none of them could have borne individually. Despite the panoply of services provided by the *sogo shosha* – arranging finances, identifying local partners, providing market information and other consultancy services, organizing imports of components from Japan – the crux of their leverage over Japanese transplants lay in their control over local and global distribution networks (Yoshihara, 1978: 126; Steven, 1990: 70).

The transborder extension of hierarchically-linked Japanese subcontracting networks, and of the operations of TNCs more generally, to the 'Four Dragons' was eased by the absence of a landed aristocracy and the political subordination and structural dependence of their indigenous bourgeoisies on their respective state machineries. At the same time, repressive legislation and the lack of political representation for labor in dominant one-party or colonial regimes licensed managements to treat workers with impunity – ignoring protective legislation, dismissing activists, and even delaying payment of wages (Deyo, 1989; Bello and Rosenfeld, 1990; Koo, 1990; Koo, 1993). In the initial phase of export-oriented, light industrial production, the recruitment of large numbers of previously unwaged workers into factories, and the high levels of unemployment and underemployment further undermined the bargaining position of labor. Small- and medium-sized Japanese firms found Taiwan an especially hospitable environment because familiarity with Japanese business practices among the older Taiwanese eased small-time Japanese entrepreneurs' problems in 'suddenly going global.' Finally, high levels of job turnover and attempts by managements to atomize workers – the practice of some South Korean textile companies to frequently rotate shifts to prevent the development of social bonds, for example – created further obstacles to collective action (Deyo, 1989; Bello and Rosenfeld, 1990; Gold, 1988b: 196).

As low wages were a primary consideration in the transborder expansion of Japanese capital, they were concentrated in Taiwan and South Korea rather than in the two city-states where wages were much higher (see Tables 4.2a and b). In contrast, given the wide differences in wage

Table 4.2a Comparative average daily industrial wages (including fringe benefits in US dollars)

Location	1964	1965	1966	1967	1968	1969	1970	1964–69 average annual growth rate (%)
South Korea	0.48	0.56	0.65	0.80	1.00	1.24	1.51	20.80
Taiwan	1.10	1.20	1.27	1.44	1.61	1.67	n.a.	8.70
Hong Kong	1.72	1.93	2.05	2.19	2.17	2.39	2.80	6.80
Singapore	2.48	2.48	2.40	2.56	2.53	2.53	n.a.	0.40

Source: Yoshihara (1978: 26).

Table 4.2b Comparative average monthly wage rates, 1972 (US dollars)

Job category	Taiwan	South Korea	Singapore	Hong Kong
Engineers	200	213	762	451
Craftsmen	99	96	133	142
Skilled workers	73	102	183	122
Semi-skilled workers	73	66	87	84
Unskilled workers	45	88	60	82
Electrical and electronic assemblers	25	n.a.	39	72

Source: Yoshihara (1978: 26).

scales between the region and their home bases, US corporations were more concerned with tax incentives, government regulations (or lack thereof), and labor laws than with wage differentials within East and Southeast Asia. Consequently, American investments tended to be disproportionately sited in Hong Kong and Singapore. Finally, since Japanese overseas manufacturing investments were concentrated at the lower end of the technological scale, a far greater share of their sales was directed toward local markets in host countries and neighboring jurisdictions than was the case with US investments (Yoshihara, 1978: 30–46; Ozawa, 1979: 83–94; Gold, 1988b: 195–7; Steven, 1990: 70–1).

A third, and smaller, strand of transborder investments came from Overseas Chinese, who invested mainly in Taiwan until China began to solicit their investments in the early 1980s by creating Special Economic Zones and offering them other benefits. When there was considerable anti-Chinese animosity in Indonesia and Malaysia, many Sino-Indonesians and Sino-Malays invested in Taiwan, which offered them greater stability and a more skilled workforce. Though they constituted 50 percent of foreign investments in Taiwan by 1985, they accounted for only 23 percent of the capital invested. Most of these investments were small, averaging US$672,285 in 1985 and almost three-quarters of them were joint ventures. Thomas Gold (1988b: 197–8) reports that many of these

Overseas Chinese were really 'front men for local businessmen' since Overseas Chinese received preferential treatment from officials, and these arrangements also provided Taiwanese businessmen with a convenient way to transfer capital to more secure locations abroad. Unlike small-scale Japanese businesses, since the Overseas Chinese came from places that were less technologically developed than Taiwan, these investments generally did not lead to technology transfers.

Notwithstanding differences between these strands of investments, they all promoted regional integration in East and Southeast Asia – the goal that had eluded American policy makers in the 1950s – and fostered the growth of economic linkages between the Pacific coasts of North America and Asia. Unlike the case in Western Europe though, where regional integration was a *precondition* to postwar reconstruction, it was the *outcome* of economic reconstruction in East Asia. Further, rather than attempting to reconstruct East and Southeast Asian economies in the American image, the purpose of these investments in the 1960s (and later) was to enable the US government to economize in its power pursuits at home and abroad while relieving the competitive pressures on Japanese and American enterprises caused by rising wages in their home bases.

In tandem with the flows of manufacturing investments to select low- and middle-income states, located mainly in East and Southeast Asia, major firms in the United States and Western Europe adopted two strategies to undermine the bargaining power of labor and to lower wages in their home bases: increased recruitment of previously unwaged workers and a further round of industrial decentralization. The recruitment of a fresh wave of migrants to the industrial labor force in the United States was facilitated by the elimination of immigration restrictions that had discriminated against migrants from Asia and Latin America, while core states in Europe encouraged migrations from their former colonies or, in the case of West Germany, from the outer fringes of Western Europe – Greece, Turkey, and Yugoslavia. Though these newly proletarianized migrants were less prone to militant wage bargaining, in the heightened conditions of labor militancy, the gains accruing to firms were not as significant as those resulting from industrial decentralization (van der Wee, 1986: 236–9).

With the growing capital-intensity of production that placed a greater premium on space, industrial relocation toward the suburbs and rural areas was a pronounced tendency during the 1960s in the United States and the core states of Europe. During the decade, the 15 largest conurbations in America lost almost a million jobs while the suburbs gained an additional three million and the percentage of the American population living in such locations rose from 25 percent in 1950 to nearly 40 percent in 1970 (Lash and Urry, 1987: 115–16). This spatial transformation of industrial production in the United States was heavily skewed toward the southern and western states of the 'Sunbelt' – which accounted for 86 percent of all new manufacturing jobs. During this period, metropolitan areas in the Northeast registered a net *decline* of 600,000 jobs in manufacturing (Davis, 1986: 130; Lash and Urry, 1987: 121–3; Kasarda, 1988: 218–19).

Moreover, though western states gained more jobs in the 1960s than the corroding industrial heartland, the southern states surpassed them in total employment gains during the decade (Kasarda, 1988: 218). Most impressively, by 1970 the thirteen southern states attracted almost half the annual inflow of foreign investments in manufacturing to the United States (Cobb, 1984: 58). This shift of manufacturing to the southern states is attributable to lower wages, taxes, energy costs, and land prices; improved accessibility to major markets through the construction of the interstate highway system and airport expansions; an abundance of local and state subsidies; a massive expansion in public schools systems and universities to offer a skilled laborforce; and perhaps most importantly, anti-union legislation. Along with spatial relocation, the size of manufacturing plants declined – while, for instance, the number of establishments in the United States with over one thousand employees remained stable between 1967 and 1977, the number of plants with less than 250 employees increased by more than 15 percent (calculated from Lash and Urry, 1987: 115). The magnitude of these changes in industrial structure within the United States partly accounts for the marked decline in the American share of total FDI between 1967 and 1974 (see Dunning, 1988: 91).

Finally, across the ideological divide in Eastern Europe and the Soviet Union, parallel tendencies were operating to irrevocably breach the hitherto impenetrable walls between the US- and Soviet-led blocs, though even a cursory examination of these trends falls outside the purview of the present analysis. Suffice it to note that the exceptionally high rates of material expansion registered in the region after the end of the Second World War – rates so remarkable that British Prime Minister Harold Macmillan could tell President John Kennedy in the early 1960s that the 'buoyant economy [of the USSR] would soon outmatch capitalist society in the race for material wealth' (quoted in Hobsbawm, 1994: 9) – were abruptly coming to an end by the late 1960s as additional inputs of labor and material resources yielded progressively diminishing returns (Brus, 1973: 34; Brus, 1975: 163–4; Sik, 1976: 54, 93–4). Simultaneously, the notorious inefficiency of its agriculture and the determination of the Brezhnev administration to increase animal proteins in Soviet diets increased pressures on the USSR to import feed grains for its growing herds of livestock (Morgan, 1980: 192–214). The final breach was sealed by the massive grain deal concluded between the United States and the Soviet Union in 1972, a deal that accounted for fully three-quarters of all commercially traded grain in the world market in the 1972–73 crop year (Friedmann, 1993: 40). Though grain sales to the USSR and the concomitant shift in US policy from food aid to commercial exports also provided the declining hegemonic power with a badly needed influx of foreign exchange, it was entirely inadequate to help redress its worsening balance of payments deficits.

Briefly put, by the mid to late 1960s, massive flows of US aid and the prodigious transnational expansion of US corporate capital along with an escalation of domestic social expenditures in the hegemonic power, and the creation and rapid growth of supranational currencies eroded the industrial and financial lead built by the United States before and during the Second World War over other core states. The exacerbating fiscal crisis confronting the US government led successive American administrations to encourage greater outflows of investments to East Asia to substitute for declining levels of US aid to 'frontline' states in the bipolar rivalry with the USSR and to economize in the means necessary for its power pursuits at home and abroad. This policy stood in sharp contrast to the unsuccessful attempts by the US government to curb capital outflows to Western Europe and signaled the beginnings of regional integration along the Asian perimeters of the Pacific as rising wages and the imposition of quotas on Japanese imports to the United States stimulated a corresponding, though smaller, outward expansion of Japanese investments to the region. The expansion of US and Japanese investments in manufacturing to Hong Kong, Singapore, South Korea, and Taiwan were facilitated by the appearance of the limitations of narrow domestic markets on the continued pursuit of ISI strategies in these territories, particularly in the two larger jurisdictions. Similarly, in a bid to lower production costs within the United States, there was a parallel shift of manufacturing from the industrial heartland of the northeastern and midwestern states to the western and, especially, to the southern states. While these processes laid the foundations for the emergence of a nexus of densely interconnected networks along the North American and East Asian coastlines of the Pacific, and across the ocean, these territories continued to be overshadowed by the concentration of industrial, commercial, and financial power in the eastern United States and in Western Europe throughout the 1960s and 1970s.

Nevertheless, as we will see in the next section, since these measures did not address the problem of ballooning US balance of payments deficits, it led the Nixon administration to revoke the dollar's convertibility to gold. This shifted competitive pressures onto enterprises in Western Europe and Japan. Combined with a rapid upsurge in world liquidity, this fueled a further and more intense transfer of manufacturing operations to low- and middle-income economies. While industrial upgrading in Japan and the transfer of both low-skilled and heavy industries from Japan was responsible for high rates of growth along the Asian coasts of the Pacific, as we shall also see, these rates were by no means exceptional. The recycling of increased revenues of members of the Organization of Petroleum Exporting Countries (OPEC) through European and American banks had led to the adoption of debt-led strategies of industrialization in several middle-income economies in Latin America and Eastern Europe which were more impressive. However, the transborder expansion of Japanese corporate networks further consolidated an emerging regional integration of production networks along Asia's Pacific shores.

Riding the dollar juggernaut

Despite attempts to alleviate the intensification of competitive pressures and the resulting overaccumulation crisis, none of the measures sketched above proved sufficient to the task and the persistence of the US balance of payments deficits compelled the Nixon administration to formally suspend the convertibility of the dollar to gold. Once the fixed dollar–gold standard was abandoned in 1971, as there was no viable alternative to the dollar as reserve currency and international medium of settlement, the US government was freed from the need to control its balance of payments deficits since

> it was now possible to release unlimited quantities of non-convertible dollars into international circulation. Therefore, while continuing to depreciate the dollar in an attempt to recover competitivity in the pro-duction of goods, the United States was no longer saddled with the problem of generating a current account surplus with which to finance its capital account deficit. ... In practical terms, the problem of the settlement of the American balance of payments simply disap-peared.
>
> (Parboni, 1981: 89–90; see also Itoh, 1990: 49–50)

Loose monetary policies, in fact, bestowed two substantive competitive advantages on US firms. First, by causing a steady depreciation of the dollar, it increased the competitiveness of US goods in foreign markets while simultaneously reducing American imports by making foreign goods more expensive. Second, after the sharp escalation of oil prices in 1972, the liberal release of dollars served to divert oil supplies to the United States. The imposition of a ceiling on the price of oil extracted from domestic wells in operation before 1972 also meant that oil prices in the US were approximately 40 percent below the world market price (Parboni, 1981: 34–5, 53–4; Arrighi, 1994: 309). Lower American energy costs served to further intensify competitive pressures on West European and Japanese enterprises. Additionally, the autocentric nature of the US economy and the role of the dollar as the international reserve currency and medium of exchange meant that the United States was relatively less constrained by balance of payments deficits than the more extroverted economies of Western Europe and Japan. Hence, the crisis of the 1970s was more properly a Euro-Japanese crisis, and the consequent narrowing of the gap in rates of growth between the United States and core states in Europe and Japan resulted in the US economy being stronger at the end of the 1970s than it had been at the beginning of the decade (Parboni, 1981: 99–113).

Though the impact of a liberal expansion of US money supply was less severe on Japanese enterprises than on those in the core states of Europe, the end of the regime of fixed exchange-rates led to a considerable appreciation of the yen – rising by almost 12 percent against the dollar in 1972 over the previous year, and by 40 percent between 1969 and 1979 (calculated from Parboni, 1981: 126). This rendered Japanese exports increasingly less competitive relative to exports from neighboring territories along Asia's Pacific perimeters which began pursuing aggressive export promotion policies at precisely the same time. Compounding the pressures on the Japanese economy were rising wage rates due to low levels of unemployment, and the country's abject dependence on imported raw materials and energy supplies when the composite index of raw materials prices increased by 300 percent between 1970 and 1973 (Parboni, 1981: 110). Caught between the twin pincers of rising import bills and declining exports – with net profit share of its domestic manufacturing sector falling by over 60 percent between 1970 and 1975 (Itoh, 1990: 165; Leyshon, 1994: 124) – Japanese manufacturers, under MITI's direction, developed a coordinated strategy for industrial restructuring which led to a consolidation of regional integration along Asia's Pacific perimeters.[4] This hinged on upgrading domestic industrial structure by transferring both light and heavy industries to low-wage locations while retaining as much of the value-added segments of production processes within Japan as possible to enhance the export competitiveness of their products and reduce dependence on raw material imports. As the oil price hikes had demonstrated that unpredictable political events could hold the Japanese economy to ransom, the government even granted 100 percent tax remissions for offshore investments in resource extraction and processing in a bid to diversify and expand supplies of vital raw materials by (Eccleston, 1989: 245; Steven, 1990: 74–85).

In the first instance, led by the electronics and textile industries, the flight of manufacturing investments was so extensive in 1972 – when it topped the $2 billion mark for the first time, and represented a 172.5 percent increase over the previous year as shown in Figure 4.1 – that the Japanese often refer to the year as the *gannen* (the very first year) of overseas direct investment (Yoshihara, 1978: 112–66; Ozawa, 1979: 94–110; Encarnation, 1992: 169). As the lower end of production processes was dominated by small- and medium-sized companies, it accounted for about one-half of all Japanese overseas manufacturing investments in the 1970s, and 90 percent of these investments were in neighboring locations along Asia's Pacific seaboard (Eccleston, 1989: 245–6; Ozawa, 1979: 94–103; Yoshihara, 1978; Steven, 1990: 136–44).

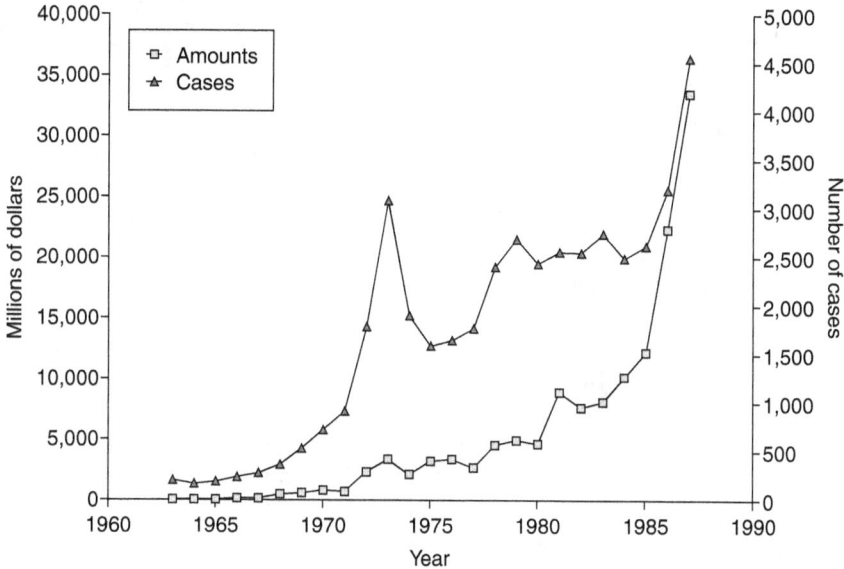

Figure 4.1 Japanese foreign direct investment in manufacturing.

Source: Adapted from Steven (1990: 67).

The transfer of labor-intensive, low-skilled production processes also represented an attempt by Japanese manufacturers to preserve their established market shares in East and Southeast Asia as many governments erected protective tarrifs on these sectors while offering inducements to foreign investors. In Indonesia, increasing popular discontent with foreign investments highlighted by the Malari riots of 1974 had led to a change of course. To counteract this discontent, and its coffers flush with the quadrupling of oil prices in 1972, the Suharto government revised foreign investment laws in 1974, mandating a transfer of majority ownership to Indonesians within ten years, requiring that all investments be joint ventures, and favoring the *pribumi* ('indigenous' Indonesians) – changes that were prompted by the displacement of domestic Indonesian industries by Japanese transplants.[5] To maintain their share of the large Indonesian domestic markets, and to circumvent quotas imposed by the Multifibre Agreements, Japanese investments in the textile industry expanded dramatically after 1967. By 1974 only South Korea had more Japanese investments than Indonesia in the sector (Steven, 1990: 210–13; Yoshihara, 1978: 65–7; Morris-Suzuki, 1991: 139).

Though the average size of Japanese investments in the original member-states of the Association of Southeast Asian Nations (ASEAN) – Brunei, Indonesia, Malaysia, the Philippines, Singapore, and Thailand – involved fewer than 200 employees in 1980, and 37.5 percent of the 2,406

Japanese manufacturing projects in the trading bloc had a paid-up capital of less than $5,000 (Saravanamuttu, 1988: 144), there were significant differences in their sectoral composition, structural characteristics, and locational patterns in the 1970s when compared with the earlier wave of outward expansion. Thus, while the number of overseas investments in textiles increased from 207 between 1951 and 1971 to 321 between 1972 and 1979, and of electronics from 175 to 557, as a proportion of total Japanese overseas manufacturing investments in Asia, the sectoral share of these sectors declined from 18.6 percent to 11.2 percent and 14.4 percent to 12.0 percent respectively, as indicated by Table 4.3. Moreover, while the average annual flows of investments in textiles and electronics between 1972 and 1979 were $35.7 million and $45.4 million respectively, these were overshadowed by investments in iron and non-ferrous metals and chemicals that averaged $76.9 million and $55 million respectively over the same years. Largely due to the large investments in resource extraction, Indonesia accounted for 70 percent of the cumulative value of Japanese investments to ASEAN states between 1951 and 1971, though only 8.8 percent of the total number of Japanese companies operating in the region were located in Indonesia. However, 69.4 percent of these ventures had a paid-up capital higher than $1 million. At the opposite end of the scale, though the Philippines accounted for the largest number of Japanese companies among the ASEAN states (30.7 percent of the total), 56.2 percent of these had a paid-up capital of less than $5,000 in 1980.

The small-scale and low skill- and capital-intensities of Japanese joint ventures in manufacturing did not undermine the salience of industrial policies in the several jurisdictions as the governments of Thailand, Malaysia, and Indonesia had also adopted some of the institutional accouterments of a 'developmental state' as they began to encourage foreign investments. However, their economic bureaucracies never achieved the autonomy and proficiency of their counterparts in Japan and the 'dragons' (Henderson, 1999). In Thailand, despite the creation of pilot agencies such as the National Economic and Social Development Board and Board of Investment in the 1960s, concern for macro-economic stability took precedence over industrialization because economic policy was dominated by the Bank of Thailand and the Ministry of Finance. Consequently, though the Sarit government had abandoned dirigisme in 1957, the chief beneficiaries tended to be capitalists closely associated with the military. The appointment of senior military figures to head state enterprises further constrained the powers of the economic agencies. Moreover, there was little coordination between economic agencies – in the 1970s, for instance, the Board of Investment, the Fiscal Policy Office (an interministerial committee to deal with individual petitions for protection), the Ministry of Commerce, and the Ministry of Industry all had authority to impose tariffs and often made mutually conflicting decisions (Hewison, 1987: 54–6; Phongpaichit and Baker, 1998: 20–2; Dixon, 1999: 103).

Table 4.3 Sectoral distribution of Japanese FDI in manufacturing

Year	Food		Textiles		Wood and pulp		Chemicals		Iron and non-ferrous metals		Machinery		Electronics		Transport equipment		Other		Total	
	Cases	Amt.	Cases	Amt.	Cases	Amt.	Cases	Amt.	Cases	Amt.	Cases	Amt.	Cases	Amt.	Cases	Amt.	Cases	Amt.	Cases	Amount (Number)/($ millions)
								(Percentages)												
1951–71	**4.3**	**6.3**	**18.6**	**36.0**	**3.0**	**4.3**	**13.3**	**7.2**	**7.3**	**8.8**	**9.2**	**4.5**	**15.8**	**14.4**	**2.0**	**4.4**	**26.6**	**15.8**	**915**	**320**
1972	6.7	3.2	12.9	47.7	6.7	5.1	5.6	3.2	13.5	11.2	6.5	3.6	24.2	13.0	2.5	6.9	21.3	6.1	356	277
1973	3.7	2.5	17.2	39.3	8.5	7.8	6.6	6.6	8.8	6.0	9.7	3.9	22.9	17.1	3.2	9.1	19.4	7.8	681	486
1974	6.3	5.9	12.6	33.0	10.4	6.4	14.8	9.5	11.3	10.6	7.1	5.0	11.8	8.4	4.1	5.3	21.4	15.9	364	358
1975	10.3	6.5	7.4	19.3	6.6	3.5	18.1	13.4	9.9	18.0	11.5	4.9	14.0	9.8	6.6	8.7	15.6	15.5	243	367
1976	10.5	2.5	7.3	16.5	4.6	2.1	14.6	15.4	11.9	23.5	14.2	4.2	17.4	15.4	6.4	2.8	13.2	17.9	219	285
1977	8.6	2.4	9.0	24.9	4.3	2.4	11.2	22.5	11.2	8.7	11.6	4.8	14.2	9.6	4.3	7.2	25.8	17.1	233	334
1978	7.1	1.6	6.9	4.1	2.5	0.2	8.8	22.0	11.3	45.3	17.0	7.5	26.1	10.8	4.4	5.0	15.9	3.3	364	858
1979	8.8	3.9	7.7	7.8	4.0	2.1	12.5	14.4	11.7	9.8	15.7	14.9	19.2	12.6	3.5	8.2	16.8	26.5	375	437
1972–79	**7.0**	**3.3**	**11.2**	**20.9**	**6.3**	**3.3**	**10.6**	**14.6**	**10.9**	**20.3**	**11.4**	**6.5**	**19.6**	**12.0**	**4.1**	**6.6**	**18.8**	**12.4**	**2,835**	**3,402**
1980	12.5	1.4	9.3	6.9	3.4	1.4	16.5	26.7	15.6	41.3	13.4	4.3	11.5	9.8	3.4	4.0	14.3	4.4	321	724
1981	7.9	2.8	12.7	6.1	2.3	1.5	18.9	19.8	11.0	45.3	13.6	6.1	13.6	8.3	3.7	5.7	16.4	4.5	354	688
1982	6.2	1.7	10.9	7.4	6.2	1.7	21.4	24.4	9.3	26.6	9.3	9.6	13.0	7.9	5.9	8.3	17.7	12.5	322	542
1983	9.5	2.6	6.9	17.9	5.2	2.3	19.1	28.0	8.4	8.5	9.8	10.0	15.3	6.1	6.4	16.7	19.4	8.0	346	738
1984	10.6	5.2	7.7	7.6	3.5	1.6	11.3	10.9	6.5	21.5	11.3	12.2	21.0	18.0	9.7	12.8	18.4	10.5	310	516
1985	13.0	7.4	6.8	1.7	2.2	0.9	13.0	8.5	7.1	7.8	12.1	16.5	14.6	11.1	8.4	32.8	22.7	13.0	322	460
1980–85	**9.9**	**3.2**	**9.1**	**8.5**	**3.8**	**1.6**	**16.8**	**20.8**	**9.7**	**26.3**	**11.6**	**9.2**	**17.1**	**9.8**	**6.2**	**12.1**	**18.1**	**8.3**	**1,975**	**3,668**
1986	10.8	3.5	3.9	2.6	2.8	1.1	9.3	5.8	6.9	7.6	11.3	11.8	24.0	32.6	7.8	16.2	23.2	18.7	462	804
1987	8.0	8.5	5.7	1.7	3.2	0.8	10.1	14.7	12.0	18.2	9.6	6.1	23.3	27.8	7.7	12.3	20.4	10.1	790	1,679
1988	8.3	3.8	11.3	6.3	5.7	7.5	9.4	8.4	10.9	8.6	12.6	10.9	17.5	35.9	3.7	6.5	20.4	12.0	935	2,370

Source: Adapted from Tokunaga (1992: 18, table 2).

In Malaysia, while the adoption of the 'New Economic Policy' in 1971 involved the creation of ministries and economic agencies modeled on those in Japan and the 'dragons' – the Ministry of Trade and Industry, the Malaysian Industrial Development Authority, the Economic Planning Unit, and state-holding companies – these were dominated not by a technocratic elite but by a political elite seeking to further their personal interests, both political and economic. The government's policy of ensuring *bumiputera* ('indigenous' Malay) ownership of 30 percent of the corporate sector led to the selective allocation of concessions, industrial licenses, low-interest loans and monopolies to companies owned or controlled by politicians, retired bureaucrats, and politically connected entrepreneurs – to 'crony capitalists' (Yoshihara, 1988: 3–4, 71; Gomez and Jomo, 1997: 25). Since the main beneficiaries of the New Economic Policy were those linked to the ruling party, *bumiputeras* came to view involvement in politics as a quick route to obtain profitable business opportunities and the creation of patronage networks as well as the establishment of a large number of public enterprises – growing from 23 in 1957 to 1,149 by 1992 – in virtually every economic sector as sinecures undermined the disciplinary functions of the economic bureaucracy. At the same time, the split between domestic capital dominated by the ethnic Chinese minority and foreign capital ensured that linkages between these fractions of capital remained weak and the economy did not benefit from synergies and spin-offs.[6]

Finally, in Indonesia, President Suharto also instituted an economic bureaucracy – creating a plethora of agencies such as the National Economic Planning Board, the Investment Coordinating Board, the State Logistics Boards, and the Technology Research and Development Board – under his direct control. If these organizations played key roles in the development and expansion of state-funded industrial projects, it was more in the interests of appropriating the benefits for the Sino-Indonesian and *pribumi* conglomerates and for the companies owned by the President's family and friends. Unlike the case in Malaysia, the lack of equity capital meant that *pribumi* investors were a much smaller component of Indonesia's domestic bourgeoisie and that even as late as the early 1990s, only four *pribumi*-owned conglomerates figured among the top twenty and two of these belonged to President Suharto's sons (Hill, 2000: 111–12; Berger, 1997; Robison, 1993: 48–9, 56; Wolf, 1992: 36). Crucially, the pervasive clientalism that characterized developmental strategies in Malaysia, Thailand, and Indonesia meant that economic bureaucracies did not have the autonomy to subject businesses to performance criteria or to deflect counter-productive investment flows (Henderson, 1999: 14–19).

With the greater diversification in the range of overseas investments, there was a corresponding increase in the importance of large manufacturing corporations in Japanese FDI. This is indicated by the fact that the average size of investments in the heavy and chemical industries – almost exclusively undertaken by large corporations such as Kawasaki Steel, Mitsubishi, Mitsui, Nippon Steel, and Sumitomo – were much larger than in the case of textile and electronics industries. Even in the electronics industry, where only Sony among the major manufacturing corporations had figured among the top ten overseas investors as late as 1974, other large manufacturers became increasingly prominent in offshore production as it became a vital element in their global strategies due to the appreciation of the yen and the imposition of quotas on exports from Japan by core states in Western Europe and North America. Similarly, the increased transfer of synthetic textile production to East and Southeast Asian locations can be calibrated by the growing prominence of large textile firms such as Kanebo, Teijin, Toray, Toyobo, and Unitika in Indonesia, the Philippines, Thailand, Malaysia, Hong Kong, and less significantly in South Korea, Taiwan, and Singapore (Yoshihara, 1978: 102–38; Steven, 1990: 71–3).

The greater importance of heavy and chemical industries in overseas investments also reflected a fundamental restructuring of Japanese domestic industries. By the mid-1970s, increasing concern over the social and environmental costs of an industrialization drive based on heavy and chemical industries, and the rising costs of commodity prices, led to the progressive transfer of primary, 'pollution-prone,' and 'resource-consuming' stages of processing raw materials to offshore locations. Taiwan and, more importantly, South Korea, where the average wage level was only one-seventh of the Japanese level between 1972 and 1974, were the major destinations for the transfer of Japanese heavy industries (Amsden, 1989: 296; Fujiwara, 1989: 189; Ozawa, 1979: 18–19; Steven, 1990: 77–8).

In keeping with their internal structures, Taiwan and South Korea accommodated declining Japanese heavy and chemical industries differently. Its security concerns heightened by the US rapprochement toward China, the Taiwanese government encouraged foreign investments, and by the late 1970s foreign investors accounted for 54.7 percent of production in the electronics sector, 35.5 percent in machinery and 17.9 percent in chemicals. At the same time, the state sector also grew absolutely in size, as favorable current account balances in the 1970s enabled the government to create new enterprises in the intermediate and capital goods sectors to upgrade Taiwan's industrial structure. After the oil price hikes compelled the government to scrap its Sixth Four-Year Plan, generous tax incentives were provided for local research and development to attract high-technology industries to Taiwan, and state enterprises formed joint ventures with foreign firms in selected sectors (Cheng, 1990: 162–70; Haggard, 1990: 141–2; Bello and Rosenfeld, 1990: 244–5).

The disproportionate share of investments in heavy and chemical industries flowing to South Korea was due to the determination of the Park government to upgrade the industrial structure in the country with the initiation of the Heavy and Chemical Industries Drive (HCI) by presidential decree in the early 1970s. The larger size of the *chaebol* enabled them to undertake expensive, large-scale projects albeit with ample assistance from the government (Amsden, 1989; Bello and Rosenfeld, 1990: 57–60). Resorting to low-interest loans as the chief instrument of industrial restructuring, the new strategy favored larger firms – and aimed to create 'national champions' in different sectors. South Korea's overseas debt grew from US$1.7 billion between 1966 and 1970 to $4.5 billion between 1971 and 1975 and $11.7 billion between 1976 and 1980. In the latter part of the 1970s, Hagen Koo and Eun Mee Kim (1992: 136) estimate that between 53 and 63 percent of all domestic loans in South Korea were distributed to the *chaebol* by the government as 'policy loans' at heavily discounted rates. Additionally, some 70 percent of all bank loans in the 1980s were channeled to the *chaebol* – the top five receiving 20.3 percent in 1980 – these highly leveraged conglomerates were able to capture market shares by initially absorbing huge losses (Bello and Rosenfeld, 1990: 66–7; Haggard, 1990: 131–2; Cheng, 1990: 162–8; Koo and Kim, 1992: 135, table 5.2).

In 1975, the government also created General Trading Companies modeled on the *sogo shosha* and 13 *chaebol* were given GTC licenses. This led to an even higher degree of centralization and concentration of capital.[7] While the *chaebol* had diversified into unrelated sectors like the Japanese *keiretsu*, they had not nurtured the vertical, inter-firm organization of the latter. One survey of 81 ancillary firms in the South Korean automobile sector in the mid-1970s indicated that 70 percent did not receive any form of assistance from the primary firm and that only a quarter of them received technical assistance. Typically, the *chaebol* not only did not provide financing or loan guarantees or arrange for the supply of raw materials but also maintained a competitive cost pricing relationship with their suppliers. Ancillary firms therefore had little incentive not to cut corners and a study conducted by the Korean Automobile Association in 1976 indicated that only 10 percent of 1,200 products met international standards, and 60 percent were significantly below par. To upgrade product quality necessary to be competitive in overseas markets, the state encouraged joint ventures and mergers by designating specific firms for low interest loans and tax incentives, and assisted with their acquisition of technical know-how, thus creating an autonomous supplier base (Chuk Kyo Kim and Chul Heui Lee, 1983: 314; Morales, 1994: 138–9).

Accompanying the transfer of heavy industries overseas, and in accordance with the MITI-directed strategy of retaining as much of the higher value-added segments of production processes within Japan as possible, there was a spectacular expansion of Japanese investments in resource extraction in the 1970s. The rise of commodity prices had underlined the dependence of the Japanese economy on imports of raw materials and shifted the relative balance of power to elites in resource-rich low- and middle-income states. Consequently, unlike the large, integrated US-based resource extracting and processing corporations which had insisted on majority ownership – and were thus vulnerable to the nationalization of their operations by peripheral states frustrated by the failure of foreign investments in the extractive sector to relieve chronic levels of unemployment and to transfer technology – Japanese investors sought access to resources through joint ventures with host governments. The most prominent destination for these investments in resource extraction was Indonesia, which by 1981 accounted for 15.1 percent of the cumulative value of Japanese FDI and emerged as the second largest locus of all Japanese investments after the United States (Saravanamuttu, 1988: 140; Shibusawa *et al.*, 1992: 20).

The massive level of these investments gave the Japanese government and businesses considerable leverage to insist that loans be tied to purchases of machinery and equipment from Japan and hence benefitted a wide range of Japanese enterprises including those not directly involved in resource extraction. This was most clearly evident in the increased activities of Japanese construction companies throughout Southeast Asia and further afield (Steven, 1990: 75; Edgington, 1991).

Rob Steven (1990: 78–81) has argued that a central reason for Japanese corporations to invest heavily in resource extraction and processing facilities in low- and middle-income countries in Asia and elsewhere was because governments in these countries had a typically cavalier disregard for the highly toxic and polluting effects of these projects on their peoples and the land. While this observation contains an important element of truth, for the purposes of this discussion the main significance of industrial restructuring in Japan through the transfer of light and heavy industries to neighboring locations along the Pacific perimeters of Asia was that it denoted a new phase of regional integration. The scale of outflows of capital from Japan to East and Southeast Asia was so extensive that by 1977 the cumulative value of Japanese FDI equaled the historically larger US investments in the region and by the end of the 1970s Japan was the largest foreign investor in Indonesia, Thailand, and South Korea, the second largest in the Philippines, Taiwan, Malaysia, and Hong Kong, and the fourth largest in Singapore (Encarnation, 1992: 154–64; Steven, 1996: 83; Shibusawa *et al.*, 1992).

The ordinal ranking of Japanese investments in East and Southeast Asia actually understate the extent of Japanese expansion in the region. As already indicated, the transborder expansion of Japanese capital took the form of joint ventures with low levels of equity participation by Japanese investors. In the ASEAN states, for instance, almost half (47.1 percent) of all Japanese manufacturing investments involved an equity participation of less than 10 percent in 1980 (Saravanamuttu, 1988: 156). As small- and medium-sized Japanese firms rarely controlled all aspects of the production process, rather than exporting finished products back to their home market, wherever practicable the trading companies imported Japanese components to East and Southeast Asian sites for processing and then exported them back to Japan for finishing – the intent being to retain as much of the value-added in Japan as possible and going overseas only to cut wages at particular stages of manufacture (Gold, 1988b: 195–7).

In contrast, the average size of US investments was considerably larger. Until 1985, for instance, though the number of US investments in Taiwan represented 14.5 percent of the total number of foreign investments, they accounted for 33 percent of foreign capital invested in the island and the average size of American investment was $3.39 million.[8] In the bulk of these cases, US corporations set up wholly-owned subsidiaries rather than joint ventures with local entrepreneurs. Moreover, until 1980, with only a few exceptions (producers of chemical products used for agriculture, the plastics industry, and intermediate components for other American subsidiaries on the island), most of the US plants exported finished products back to the United States rather than develop a market within Taiwan or elsewhere.

Apart from the transborder expansion of Japanese subcontracting networks, in response to rising wages in their home bases and to accommodate the declining industries being transferred from Japan, South Korean- and Taiwan-based capital began to extend its own subcontracting networks to Hong Kong, the Philippines, Indonesia, Malaysia, and Thailand through a transfer of labor-intensive, light industrial production (Eccleston, 1989: 245). Though many small- and medium-sized enterprises from Taiwan also began to invest in Southeast Asia, since they were not tied to *keiretsu*-like networks, they largely relied on kinship ties. A typical characteristic of this type of investment tended to be their clustering together to reduce transaction costs and to facilitate networking. However, these networks tended to be more fluid and open-ended than in the *keiretsu* structures. Conversely, South Korean investments were generally led by the *chaebol* (Jomo *et al.*, 1997: 49–51).

Despite the Hong Kong government's ideological commitment to laissez faire, as the political energies of the Cultural Revolution echoed across the colony in the 1960s and raised real apprehensions about its political future, the colonial administration was compelled to respond to changing conditions. The shift to export-oriented industrialization in neighboring jurisdictions had increased competitive pressures on Hong Kong's electronics and plastics industries while the Multifibre Agreements limiting the exports of textiles had a disproportionate impact on the colony. Though an Industrial Development Board was set up, it was headed by the Finance Secretary and was more involved in courting foreign investments and promoting closer institutional relations with large domestic firms than in providing low-interest loans and other incentives (Castells *et al.*, 1990: 59; Haggard and Cheng, 1987: 119–21).

Far more important in Hong Kong's emergence as a leading exporter in the 1970s and 1980s – rising from the 27th largest exporter in 1960 to the 10th largest by 1988 (Yeung, 2000: 128) – was a rapid expansion in government expenditure. In real terms, government expenditure rose by 26 times between 1949 and 1980 when real GDP grew only by 13 times (Sung, 1982: 48–9; Jao, 1993: 160). Even more tellingly, government expenditure on social services (education, health, social welfare, and housing) increased by 72 times during the same period, while public expenditure on transportation, land reclamation, and water services increased by 37 times, and the Royal Hong Kong Police Force grew to become larger than the New York City Police Department. 'In fact, Hong Kong has the highest proportion of social expenditures over government expenditures of any Asian country, including Japan' (Castells *et al.*, 1990: 88).

In the absence of high taxes, the Hong Kong administration financed the rapid expansion of public expenditures at a rate faster than the rate of growth of the colony's GDP without causing high rates of inflation by increasing its nontax revenues – the income from licences, fees, fines, public enterprises including the Mass Transit Railway system in the 1980s, and most importantly from the sale and lease of land – which consistently accounted for over one-third of all government receipts, and rose to 46 percent of total revenues by the late 1970s. However, because domestic research and development was weak and the colony lacked upstream industries, small contractors were vulnerable to pressure from foreign firms. This led to a reversal in the trend toward income inequality – the Gini coefficient that had declined from 0.487 in 1966 to 0.435 in 1976 rose to 0.481 by 1981. Additionally, rapid industrialization entailed longer working hours in conditions where health and safety regulations were poorly implemented (Castells *et al.*, 1990; Haggard, 1990: 152–3).

Conversely, in Singapore though the oil price hikes and the recession of the 1970s had forced a roll back of the high wage policy designed to promote higher value-added production, the government sought to assist small domestic entrepreneurs to upgrade their technologies so that there could be greater integration with international firms, especially in electronics. Thus, while the government had adopted a high-wage policy in 1973, the recession led to a loss of some 20,000 jobs between July 1974 and December 1975 with about two-thirds of the retrenchments coming from the electronics and electronic industry sectors. This was matched by a 61 percent drop in foreign investment commitments in 1975 as full employment had pushed labor costs in Singapore above prevalent levels in Hong Kong, Taiwan, and South Korea. As we have seen above, this compelled the government to revise wage levels downwards and introduce measures to assist small domestic entrepreneurs (Haggard, 1990: 146–7; Rodan, 1989: 113–28). The development of a large base on ancillary industries was a vital element in insulating Singapore from the more adverse effects of the economic crisis of 1997–98 as we shall see. Similarly, to foster OEM arrangements, for instance, the Taiwanese government not only provided tax incentives for exporters but as gatekeeper for the national economy it insisted that foreign investors not compete with local enterprises in the domestic market and included stringent domestic content requirements in approvals for foreign investments.

Meanwhile, reflecting the greater concentration of heavy industries in South Korea, investments by corporations based in that country in overseas resource extraction surged during the 1970s and early 1980s, with foreign investments in the mining sector – mainly in Indonesia, the Philippines, and Thailand – accounting for $172.7 million or 36.3 percent of South Korean FDI between 1968 and 1985 compared with $91.8 million in the manufacturing sector. In contrast, Taiwanese overseas investments in the manufacturing sector during the same period accounted for $183.2 million – more than twice the South Korean aggregate – or 85.3 percent of its FDI (calculated from Muraoka, 1991: 157).

The installation of manufacturing complexes in low- and middle-income states along the Pacific perimeters of Asia was also facilitated by the large-scale commercialization of agriculture. The globalization of the US agro-industrial complex through an expansion of contract farming and the implementation of new on-farm technologies and labor processes transformed family farms from being primarily concerned with local markets and household consumption to out-growers for large consolidated agro-marketing corporations, and converted growers into a 'self-employed proletariat' in low- and middle-income states. The expansion of contract farming in low- and middle-income states, which represented both a partial decomposition of plantation and estate agriculture and the integration of independent peasants and/or pioneer growers into corporate circuits of capital, resulted in widening disparities within rural areas, often culminating in the eviction of poor and highly indebted peasants, and in the conversion of acreage under food crops to export agriculture (see Watts, 1992; McMichael, 1993).

While the expropriation of subsistence farmers contributed to a massive emigration from rural areas, leading to historically unprecedented rates of urbanization, the mobilization of displaced farmers as an urban reserve army of labor was paralleled by an equally unprecedented recruitment of previously unwaged women in low-skilled, labor-intensive assembly processes as the impetus toward the installation of manufacturing complexes in low- and middle-incomes states by the TNCs stemmed from their search for a low-wage, submissive industrial workforce (Sassen, 1988: 18–19, 107–16). Hence, the expansion of manufacturing was accompanied by a major transformation in the sex composition of rural-to-urban migrations, and the overwhelming majority of such migrants were now women (Sassen, 1988: 110). At the same time, the cultural distancing of women employed in export-processing zones from their rural families, amidst increasing male unemployment, ruptured existing patternings of gender relations, and exacerbated social tensions (Ong, 1990; Wolf, 1992).

This massive expansion of multilateral subcontracting networks, which served to more tightly link low-waged peripheral producers in East and Southeast Asia to high-income consumers in the core through the mediation of corporations in Japan, South Korea, and Taiwan, was responsible for the high rates of industrialization registered by several states along the Asian perimeters of the Pacific. There was, however, nothing exceptional about these levels of industrialization. The unprecedented increase in global liquidity by the early 1970s through the creation of a large, supranational money market and the consequent availability of cheap credit spurred a wave of industrialization in several low- and middle-income states – most notably in Argentina, Brazil, and Mexico in the Americas, in Poland and other centrally planned economies in Eastern Europe, Italy and Spain in Southern Europe, and in Iran and some other oil-exporting states. The expansion of liquidity due to the loose monetary policies pursued by the US government and, more importantly, to the explosive growth of supranational currencies was so extensive that real long-term interest rates were *negative* between 1974 and 1979 – minus 1 percent in Western Europe, minus 0.2 percent in the United States, and minus 0.4 percent for the 'Group of Seven' (Canada, France, Italy, Japan, the US, the UK, and West Germany) as a whole (Itoh, 1990: 43).

The ample availability of cheap credit appeared to present a painless way to achieve economic growth, especially to leaders of one-party regimes and military dicatatorships. Since low-interest loans could finance the construction of industrial plants without resorting to higher taxation or other unpopular measures, it was thought that the incremental export earnings from higher industrial production could repay the loans. Thus, for instance, in Latin America, the share of private institutions in the net inflow of capital rose from 39.8 percent of a total capital inflow of $1.6 billion between 1961 and 1965 to 92.7 percent of a total *annual* inflow of $21.8 billion by 1978, while the share of public agencies fell from 60.2 percent to 7.3 percent. During this period, the share of FDI by the TNCs and their subsidiaries which had accounted for 25.2 percent of all capital inflows between 1961 and 1965, declined to 16 percent in 1978, while the share of private banks rose from 2.1 percent to 56.6 percent (Roddick, 1988: 26–8). Similarly, the magnitude of the flows of cheap credit to the People's Democracies of Eastern Europe is indicated by the rise in Poland's cumulative external debt from $1.2 billion in 1970 to $20.5 billion in 1979 (Nuti, 1981: 107; Damus, 1981: 105).

Viewed in the light of the vast expansion of industrial production in several low- and middle-income states in the 1970s, the rapid industrialization of what were to be subsequently called the 'Four Dragons' was hardly exceptional. The rates of industrialization registered by several Latin American states – particularly Brazil, which accounted for a population almost three times that of Hong Kong, Singapore, South Korea and Taiwan combined – appeared far more impressive to most contemporary observers, and it is often forgotten that it was Brazil and *not* any of the 'dragons' that was hailed as an economic 'miracle' in the 1970s. However, as illustrated by Table 4.4, despite rapid industrialization, differentials in GNPs per capita between these states and the organic core continued to widen in the 1970s – except for Brazil, which collapsed slightly later in the early 1980s. Though different national accounting procedures complicate similar comparisons with East European states, there is considerable evidence to suggest that their trajectories resembled those of the Latin American 'miracles' of the 1970s (Nuti, 1981; Marer, 1985). The only exception to this generalization were Italy and Spain, the two Southern European states integrated into the EEC.

Rather than heralding a phase of regional industrial expansion unprecedented elsewhere in the world, the real significance of the transborder expansion of production networks based in Japan – and less significantly in South Korea and Taiwan – under the pressure of currency appreciation, rising wages in their home bases, and raw materials constraints in the 1970s was that it denoted the consolidation of regional economic integration along the Asian perimeters of the Pacific. Although it was the unfavorable bargaining position of Japanese corporations and government in the context of rising energy and commodity prices and the growth of 'resource nationalism' in low- and middle-income states that led them into joint ventures with host governments, by the early 1980s it became apparent that minority participation in joint ventures better served their needs. This was because participation in such projects enabled Japanese investors to greatly diversify their sources of supply by shifting a sizable share of project development costs onto host governments rather than sinking their own capital into projects with long gestation periods. Loose monetary policies pursued by the US government and the recycling of petrodollars and the resultant expansion of world liquidity enabled several resource-rich low- and middle-income states to exploit their resource endowments through external borrowing and technological assistance from TNCs, especially those based in Japan. The pursuit of multiple, parallel paths of state-led resource extraction projects, however, significantly impaired the capacity of producers to affect prices by rapidly expanding supplies without corresponding increases in demand. In these conditions, the increased exposure of host governments to risk and external debt reduced their ability to regulate overseas investors (Bunker and O'Hearn, 1993: 93–100).

Simply put, just as revoking the convertibility of the US dollar to gold had freed the US government to issue unlimited dollars and depreciate its value, the recycling of petrodollars through European banks removed restrictions on spending for other governments as they could easily borrow from supranational currency markets. Along with high rates of

Table 4.4 Comparative economic performance (index of GNP per capita as percentage of organic core)

Region/economy	1938	1948	1960	1970	1980	1990	2000
Latin and Central America							
Argentina	45.0	32.1	32.7	27.0	21.3	11.5	25.6
Brazil	12.1	11.4	10.8	11.9	18.3	13.0	12.3
Mexico	14.0	10.8	17.4	21.7	18.6	13.0	17.5
Eastern Europe							
Poland	23.2	19.3		37.1	34.8	8.2	14.5
Hungary	40.4	16.6		42.4	37.3	13.5	16.3
Southern Europe							
Italy	32.2	22.9	35.4	53.0	57.8	81.7	68.9
Spain	41.9	18.5	17.6	29.4	48.2	53.5	51.5
Turkey and Egypt	14.9	13.0	8.4		9.4	5.5	7.9
East and South East Asia							
Japan	20.8	14.6	23.2	51.7	88.2	123.5	117.8
Hong Kong			18.8	23.9	37.8	55.8	89.3
Singapore			23.3	25.2	39.5	54.2	85.2
South Korea			8.1	7.2	13.6	26.2	30.7
Taiwan					19.2	35.4	
Malaysia			13.9	10.3	14.5	11.3	11.6
Thailand		8.2	5.2	5.6	6.0	6.9	6.9
Indonesia	5.3		4.1	2.1	3.8	2.8	2.0
Philippines	9.7	4.2	8.4	6.1	6.2	3.5	3.6
China	4.1		4.3	3.4	2.6	1.8	2.9
India	8.2	7.6	3.8		2.1	1.7	1.6

Sources: Calculated from W. S. Woytinsky and E. S. Woytinsky, *World Population and Production: Trends and Outlook* (New York: Twentieth Century Fund, 1953) for 1938 and 1948; United Nations, *Compendium of Social Statistics, 1977* (New York: United Nations, 1980) for 1960; World Bank, *World Tables, 1976* and *World Tables on Disk, 1992* (Washington, DC: World Bank) for 1970; World Bank, *World Development Report* (Washington, DC: World Bank, 1982, 1992, and 2000/2001) for 1980, 1990, and 1999; data for Taiwan was obtained from Republic of China, *Statistical Yearbook of the Republic of China* (Taipei, various years).

Notes
a The figures indicate the GNP per capita of each area or jurisdiction as a percentage of the organic core.
b The organic core refers to Austria, Belgium, Denmark, Finland, France, Luxembourg, the Netherlands, Norway, Sweden, Switzerland, the United Kingdom and the former West Germany in Europe; Canada and the United States; and Australia and New Zealand.

inflation in the US, the unchecked growth of world liquidity not only threatened the dollar's role as world money but also raised the possibility of a severe global financial crisis. In these conditions, as the US Federal Reserve tried to curb inflation by raising domestic interest rates above the world average, it led to a dramatic shift in capital flows – with the US emerging as a debtor nation in quick succession. Correspondingly, as the flow of cheap credit to the 'newly industrializing economies' of Latin

America and Eastern Europe was abruptly choked off, their industrialization programs came to a grinding stop and the debt crisis that followed virtually erased all the gains they had registered over the preceding thirty years or more. In contrast, since the transborder expansion of Japanese production networks, rather than debt-led strategies of autarkic national economy-making, underpinned industrialization along Asia's Pacific seaboard, there was no similar meltdown in these economies. However, if this gave cause for celebration, the benefits of industrial growth as we will see in the next section were very unevenly distributed.

Making the 'miracle' economies of the Pacific Rim

The exceptional nature of industrialization along Asia's Pacific seaboard became evident only in the late 1970s and the early 1980s, when most other low- and middle-income states posting high rates of growth slumped as rapidly as they had risen. The proximate causes for the collapse of these states were two-fold. First, the pursuit of multiple, parallel paths of industrialization had worsened the conditions for all by rapidly increasing supplies precisely when most high-income states, reeling under the effects of recession and growing rates of unemployment, were implementing protectionist measures to shield their domestic industries from further ravages. The rise of protectionism undermined a fundamental premise on which industrialization financed through borrowing from international private capital markets was based – that the loans could be repaid through incremental export earnings – especially when there was also a reduction in real wages in the core. Second, the reversal of loose monetary policies by the United States government and its aggressive competition for footloose capital from 1979 choked off the ample supplies of cheap credit that low- and middle-income states had enjoyed during much of the decade. This not only imperiled their industrialization strategies but also posed further complications as these states did not have the pecuniary or other resources to hedge against currency fluctuations created by floating exchange-rates.

Though loose monetary policies had enabled the United States government to shift competitive pressures to enterprises and governments in Western Europe and Japan, it proved to be only a temporary palliative for the US economy. The volatility of flexible exchange-rates had stimulated a further wave of transnationalization of US capital as corporations sought to hedge against variations in their cash-flows, sales, profits, and assets caused by currency fluctuations. These outflows were facilitated by the elimination of controls on capital outflows from the United States in 1974 – with the accumulated value of US FDI rising from $78 billion in 1970 to $168 billion in 1978 – which reversed the sharp decline in US overseas investments between 1969 and 1974 (Dunning, 1988: 91; Kirby, 1983: 40). While holdings in diverse currencies provided a long-term hedge against currency fluctuations, these provided no insurance at all against short-term variations. Consequently, major US and non-US enterprises engaged in short-term speculations in financial markets and thereby added to their volatility. Finally, the oil shock of 1972, which quadrupled the price of crude oil and the resultant problem of recycling petrodollars, led to a spectacular growth in international liquidity. As members of the Organization of Petroleum Exporting Countries (OPEC) channeled a major share of their earnings through European banks, the assets of these banks increased by 95 percent between 1976 and 1980 (Daly, 1987; Sassen, 1991: 66).

The consequent explosive growth of liquidity became the fount of a major destabilizing inflationary wave:

> Formerly, countries other than the United States had to keep their balance of payments in some sort of equilibrium. They had to 'earn' the money they wished to spend abroad. Now they could borrow it. With liquidity apparently capable of infinite expansion, countries deemed credit-worthy no longer had any external check on foreign spending. . . . Under such circumstances, a balance-of-payments deficit no longer provided, in itself, an automatic check to domestic inflation. Countries in deficit could borrow indefinitely from the magic liquidity machine. Many countries . . . thus joined the United States in avoiding any real adjustment to higher oil prices. Not surprisingly, world inflation continued accelerating throughout the decade, and fears of collapse in the private banking system grew increasingly vivid. More and more debts were 'rescheduled,' and a number of poor countries grew flagrantly insolvent.
>
> (Calleo, 1982: 137–8)

The uncontrolled creation of world liquidity and the equally unregulated competition between banks to recycle the growing volumes of supra-national currencies – especially in the context of a dramatic growth in off-shore banking made possible by advances in telecommunications, and the plethora of financial innovations – made the world financial system increasingly resemble a proverbial house of cards teetering on the brink of collapse. The collapse of the world market, and with it the US dollar as world money, in a catastrophic financial crisis was even more threatening to the smaller and more extroverted economies of Europe and Japan. Transnational corporations and the offshore banks that had vastly expanded their scale of operations were perhaps even more vulnerable to the threat of an imminent collapse. Consequently, starting with the appointment of Paul Volcker as Chairman of the US Federal Reserve in 1979, the United States government aimed to tighten its control over world liquidity by raising its interest rates above the rate of inflation. In lockstep with interest rate hikes, the US government also deregulated its banking and financial system, thereby offering banks all the advantages they could get in offshore locations plus the additional advantage that none of these offshore locations could offer – proximity to the most important center of world power (Arrighi, 1994: 309–18). These policies led to a sharp reduction in American and European FDI to low- and middle-income states. Thus, while peripheral and semiperipheral states had been the leading recipients of FDI in the 1970s, the deregulation of financial markets in the core led to a situation where intra-core flows have constituted the bulk of FDI since the 1980s.

The resulting recentralization of financial power in the United States and the drying up of the streams of cheap credit to low- and middle-income states led to a precipitous fall in commodity prices, the composite index of which declined by nearly 40 percent between 1980 and 1988 and of oil by 50 percent (United Nations, 1990). The rise in the London Inter-bank Offering Rate (LIBOR) from 11 percent in mid-1977 to over 20 percent in early 1981 caused by the interest rate hikes in the United States was particularly catastrophic for the Latin American economic 'miracles' of the 1970s as their debt service payments soared from less than a third of their export revenues in 1977 to almost two-thirds in 1982 (Frieden, 1987: 142–3; Arrighi, 1994: 323). Beginning with Poland in 1981, a debt crisis spread across the low- and middle-income states that had implemented debt-led strategies of industrialization in the 1970s. Between the Mexican debt crisis of 1982 and 1990, the restructuring of highly indebted low- and middle-income economies under joint World Bank and IMF supervision led to the debtor states collectively owing 61 percent more at the end of the period than they did at the beginning. While total resource flows – all bilateral and multilateral aid, grants by private charities, direct private investments, trade credits, and bank loans – to 'developing countries' amounted to $927 billion, these highly-indebted low- and middle-income states remitted $1,345 billion in debt service alone to the high-income states. To put this in perspective, if US Marshall Plan aid to Europe amounted to about $70 billion in 1991 dollars, in the eight years from 1982, the poorer countries have financed six Marshall Plans for the richer ones through debt service alone (George, 1992: xv–xvi)!

In this context, the ability of states along the Pacific perimeters of Asia, with the exception of the Philippines, to consistently post high rates of growth in the midst of this general collapse of peripheral and semiperiph-eral states was rooted in the unabated extension of subcontracting net-works based in Japan, South Korea, Taiwan, and Hong Kong (see Douglass, 1991: 16, table 1; Arrighi *et al.*, 1993; Palat, 1996; Palat, 1999). As export-oriented industrialization in much of East and Southeast Asia was based on the transfer to these jurisdictions of declining Japanese indus-tries – and attempts by firms based in Japan and the 'Four Dragons' to cir-cumvent quota restrictions – they were not predicated on large capital inflows. After all, the exports of textiles, toys, plastics, and small consumer electronics like transistor radios did not have the same capital requirements as the production of the fighter aircraft, automobiles, and large iron and steel plants that were the industrial flagships of the more illustrious Latin American 'miracles.' In fact of the five states – Mexico, Brazil, Venezuela, South Korea, and Algeria – which received the lion's share of the flows of cheap credit, about one-half of all publicly announced bank loans in Euro-dollars in the 1970s, only one was in East Asia (Frieden, 1987). South Korea was able to weather the debt-crisis because its industrialization strategy was coordinated within a broader regional strategy.

Conversely, Thailand was unable to withstand the collapse of low- and middle-income economies in the early 1980s precisely because it was less integrated within the evolving regional production network and domestic firms still dominated its economy (Anek Laothamatas, 1994: 203). US withdrawal from Vietnam and increased military procurements due to security concerns had led to a steep escalation in overseas borrowings, and debt servicing accounted for 20.5 percent of the GDP. Combined with the oil price hike of 1978, this contributed to a rising incidence of domestic bankruptcies: growing by 15 percent between 1978 and 1979, by 47 percent rise in 1980, and by 35 percent the following year. Even though rapid inflows of foreign investments had meant that the share of manufactured goods in Thai exports had increased from 15.4 percent in the early 1970s to 26.8 percent in 1980, the government had to approach international financial institutions for structural adjustment loans in 1982 and 1983. The conditions attached to these loans – reduction of government expenditures, elimination of subsidies, abolition of export restrictions and taxes, removal of protections for domestic industries, adoption of deflationary fiscal and monetary policies – virtually erased the success of the poverty alleviation measures of the previous ten years (Hewison, 1987: 60, 65–8; Phongpaichit and Baker, 1998: 75–7; Dixon, 1999: 114–16).

The serial transfer of low-skilled, labor-intensive Japanese industries also entailed the creation of a matrix of core–periphery relations, a new regional divisioning of labor, rather than the construction of parallel and competing national industrial structures as was the case with the contemporaneous patterns of debt-led industrialization in Latin America, Eastern Europe, and elsewhere. Hence, though industrialization in low-income states in East and Southeast Asia may have appeared to be more pedestrian than in the 'newly industrializing countries' of Latin America, the former were not competing with each other for export markets in high-income states but occupied distinct market niches. Better coordination of manufacturing investments, orchestrated by MITI, ensured the installation of complementary industrial structures in much of Pacific-Asia and these economies began to consistently register favorable trade balances with high-income economies in Western Europe and North America, though not with Japan.

Elite bureaucracies in both South Korea and Taiwan formulated national industrial policies to ensure that partnerships with Japanese and other foreign enterprises would generate optimal synergies through backward and forward linkages. The Chinese government's decision to undertake market-oriented reforms was especially fortuitous for Hong Kong as it restored its old entrepôt function to the colony precisely as lower-waged areas like Thailand, Malaysia, and Indonesia were being enmeshed within the technostructures of Japanese corporations. To counteract the more extensive incorporation of reservoirs of low-waged labor in these jurisdictions, Singapore's Economic Development Board (EDB) attempted to transform the island state into a base for higher value-added production by launching its 'Second Industrial Revolution' program in 1979.

Following Akamatsu Kaname's imagery of the 'flying geese,' economic development along Asia's Pacific coasts has been widely conceptualized as a regional phenomenon in which declining Japanese industries are transferred to less industrialized countries – first to the 'Four Dragons' and subsequently to Malaysia, Thailand, Indonesia, China, Vietnam, and other locations. In this conceptualization, the developmental experience of less industrialized states replicated those of the more advanced economies. At the level of industrial sectors this is analogous to Raymond Vernon's conception of product cycles formulated to explain the behavior of individual firms. He suggested that while product innovation occurs in high-income countries and innovative firms reap the benefits of oligopositic competion, as production processes become standardized and competition grows, costs of production gain greater salience and manufacturing operations are transferred to low-wage locations (Cumings, 1987; Kojima Kiyoshi, 1977).

While the regionally-integrated character of industrialization along Pacific-Asia is evident from our discussion above, as Mitchell Bernard and John Ravenhill (1995) suggest there are several reasons to be skeptical about this benign imagery of the Japanese goose leading the lesser geese toward development. In the first instance, the 'flying geese' model is based on the presumption that technological maturity will result in 'stable-state' technologies that less developed states can use, perhaps with the kind of shop-floor focus that Alice Amsden (1989; 2001) suggested was a characteristic of 'late-late industrializers.' However, the microelectronics revolution has not only speeded up technological change in every aspect of the production process but also raised the barriers to entry and made companies reluctant to transfer technology because production processes have become interrelated. Additionally, by facilitating an increasing fragmentation of production processes, the progressive automation, computerization, and robotization of production, the lowering of freight costs through containerization, and the development of satellite communication systems, has made the installation of backward and forward linkages with domestic industries far more tenuous (Palat, 1996; Palat, 1998). When computerization makes production processes more interrelated,

Bernard and Ravenhill (1995: 207) note, 'abandoning production of certain mature products carries the risk of losing know-how in manufacturing techniques or component manufacturing that might have been critical to seemingly nonrelated future production.' Thus, the transborder expansion of Japanese production networks have not been accompanied by the elimination of domestic production in Japan as predicted by the 'flying geese' model.

Rather, it has led to a regional hierarchy of production structures and, contrary to expectations that Japanese companies would serially exit from the production of consumer goods of lower technological sophistication, new innovations have led to the concentration of core technologies in product design and innovation in Japan. While small Taiwanese entrepreneurs initially welcomed collaboration with small Japanese firms, they soon found that they were bound in an intricate web of contractual agreements that even precluded them from handling their own procurement and marketing arrangements (Gold, 1988b: 190). In a typical instance, Jinbao Electronics – a Taiwanese firm that makes low-end calculators on an original equipment manufacturer (OEM) basis for Japanese firms such as Casio, Canon, and Sharp – set up a factory in Thailand in 1990 when rising Taiwanese wages made production in the island unprofitable. Nevertheless, all critical components in the Thai factory were imported from Japan while the Taipei office oversaw its administration and controlled all procurements; the labor alone was Thai (Bernard and Ravenhill, 1995: 186–7; see also Simon, 1988b: 210).

Due to the regionally integrated character of production networks and continuing product innovation at home, domestic production of consumer goods in Japan did not suffer the catastrophic declines that occurred in the United States in the 1980s. However, unlike the Japanese case, Taiwanese investments in electronics assembly in Southeast Asia led to precipitous declines in Taiwanese domestic output precisely because manufacturers had not institutionalized product innovation. The continuing deficits that Taiwan and South Korea register in their trade with Japan indeed underline their continued technological dependence on Japan especially since the greater deployment of microelectronics has made reverse engineering far more difficult if not impossible (Bernard and Ravenhill, 1995: 187–91). In Pacific-Asia, then, the transborder expansion of Japanese subcontracting networks 'produced a new regional division of labor that is based not on national economies but on regionalized networks of production' (Bernard and Ravenhill, 1995: 206). Hence, rather than signifying a progressive transfer of technology as suggested by the 'flying geese' analogy, the widespread dispersal of production operations led to a concentration of control in Japan.

Strangely enough, while proponents of the 'flying geese' model have underscored parallels between their conceptualization for whole economies with Vernon's 'product cycles' at the level of individual firms, they appear to gloss over the fact that the rewards at each stage are less than those reaped at earlier stages of the 'product cycle.' This is demonstrated, to take just one instance among many, by the Malaysian government's attempt in the early 1980s to mimic the South Korean shift to heavy and chemical industries which was not nearly as successful. Under the aegis of a new public sector enterprise – the Heavy Industries Corporation of Malaysia set up in 1980 – the government entered into joint ventures with foreign firms in automobiles, cement, iron and steel, and small internal combustion engines. However, sluggish demand in the world economy and the foreign debts incurred by the government in its heavy industry drive – total outstanding public debt including loans guaranteed by the federal government rose from M$11.9 billion to M$26.5 billion in 1980 and to M$57.8 billion in 1983 – led to a contraction of its economy and the Malay GDP fell by 1 percent in 1985 (Bowie, 1994: 175–8; Jomo, 1987: 125–30; Jomo *et al.*, 1997: 101–3). Moreover, as Beverly Silver argues, the monopolistic windfall profits that accrued to early innovators allowed them 'to finance a more generous and stable labor-capital accord' while

> lower profit levels associated with the intense competitive pressures towards the end of the life cycle (and the relative national poverty of the favored new sites of production) make such social contracts increasingly difficult to sustain economically.
>
> (Silver, 2003: 79)

This contrast creates additional pressures for economies accommodating declining industries at the mature stage of a product cycle, especially in heavy industries, since the installation of factory complexes also brings into being large well-organized labor forces. An increasingly mature industrial proletariat, concentrated in considerable numbers, can and would challenge the social coalitions that exclude them as we shall see in the next chapter.

Whereas a combination of substantial US military procurements, favorable trade balances, high rates of domestic savings, and large infusions of US aid financed industrial restructuring and growth in Japan, South Korea, and Taiwan, other economies in the region had to depend on inflows of foreign investments or loans. By reducing the scope of control that pilot economic agencies can exercise, reliance on foreign investments can produce mixed results, as indicated by the experience of Singapore's 'Second Industrial Revolution.' To transform the island into a base for higher value-added production, this strategy hinged on an over 40 percent increase in wage-rates, with a higher rate of increase at the lower wage scales, and a phase-out of migrant labor (Rodan, 1989: 145). Simultaneously, the government offered investors substantially increased incentives for research and development, and government funding of public research and development institutions rose from S$10 million in 1981 to S$50 million in 1982. Several other measures were also announced to help domestic firms upgrade their technologies and skills. While this led to the closure of many low-wage operations and to a fall in new investment commitments especially from Japanese enterprises, it was successful in attracting higher value-added production to the island, particularly computer disk drive manufacturers (Rodan, 1989: 174–80). However, despite increased incentives and greater government outlays, research and development continued to lag behind South Korea and Taiwan. Contrary to the goals of the 'Second Industrial Revolution' strategy, the manufacturing sector failed to become the motor force of economic expansion and its share of GDP (at 1968 prices) fell from 23.7 percent in 1979 to 20.6 percent in 1984. Instead of large-scale industrial upgrading, Singapore was progressively being transformed into a service sector as large TNCs began to locate their regional headquarters and service centers there to take advantage of its excellent communications and transport infrastructure and English-speaking workforce. Finally, for an extroverted economy, the combination of declining investment commitments and sluggish world demand led to a fall in GDP by almost 2 percent in 1985. This economic downturn prompted the imposition of a wage-freeze in 1986 and 1987 and the emphasis of government policy shifted from higher value-added production to hard labor (Rodan, 1989: 142–88; Bello and Rosenfeld, 1990: 297–300; Haggard, 1990: 146–7; Castells *et al.*, 1990: 195–6).

Reliance on overseas investments also made economies vulnerable to the vagaries of financial markets. Buoyed by increased oil revenues after the oil price hike of 1979, state corporations in Indonesia had embarked on major projects even as inflows of foreign investments were disappointing – between 1968 and 1985 only 45 percent of approved foreign investments were realized (Winters, 1996: 114).[9] This provided an engine for private sector projects in automobiles, beverages and foodstuffs, cement, engineering, metal fabrication, and tires. A sudden decline in oil prices in 1982, however, compelled the government to increase its borrowings and by 1983 it was forced to devalue the rupiah by 27.6 percent to boost non-oil exports – estimated to be the highest real effective devaluation among 'developing' countries by the Morgan Guaranty Bank (Robison, 1987: 18–19, 28–31; Winters, 1996: 107–32; Jomo *et al.*, 1997: 130–1; Berger, 1997: 343; Hill, 2000: 70–1, 158–9).

Overshadowed by the rapid debt-led industrialization of Argentina, Brazil, and Mexico in the 1970s, the exceptional nature of industrial transformation in several jurisdictions along Asia's Pacific coasts only became evident once the United States reversed its loose monetary policies. When the United States' Federal Reserve raised interest rates above the rate of inflation in tandem with the government deregulating the banking and financial systems, it pulled the carpet from under the more illustrious of the 'newly industrializing countries' as capital flows were channeled toward the United States. Precisely because industrialization in East and Southeast Asia was – with the exception of South Korea – based on less capital-intensive production processes, and integrated within the corporate technostructures of Japanese TNCs, they were not vulnerable to this quick about-turn of financial flows. Rather than creating parallel and competing industrial structures, the transfer of declining Japanese industries to neighboring locations led to the construction of complementary patterns of industrialization and to a greater regional economic integration. It was this increasingly densely-knit manufacturing network that led to spectacular growth rates in the 1980s and early 1990s.

Reprise and preview

The emergence of Hyundai Heavy Industries as the world's largest shipbuilder in 1984, just eleven years after it built its first ship, and amidst the collapse of large Latin American 'newly industrializing countries,' symbolized the rise of several small economies along Asia's Pacific coasts as major growth poles of the world economy in the 1980s and early 1990s. The rapid structural transformation of muddied paddy fields in Southeast and East Asia to grimy factory complexes and dark workhouses, we argue here, can be traced to US attempts to resurrect the Japanese economy by ensuring access to markets and raw materials for its light industries, and to attempts by major US and West European corporations to gain greater wage flexibility and control over job specifications by relocating their manufacturing plants to 'greenfield' sites within their own jurisdictions, as well as to off-shore locations. Imports embodying low-wage labor from East Asia by cheapening the cost of essential supplies revealed a complementarity of interests between the US government and firms and state structures in the region. Conversely, mounting US balance of payments deficits in the 1960s revealed the growing incompatibility between the interests of successive American adminstrations and US corporate transplants in Western Europe.

The coincidence of an increase in competitive pressures in the core with the exhaustion of ISI strategies in many small low- and middle-income states in the late 1960s stimulated a massive expansion of manufacturing operations by TNCs in search of low-wage, docile labor forces both within their home countries and in other states. Several small East and Southeast Asian states – most notably the 'Four Dragons' – were particularly well-sited to reap disproportionate benefits during this phase of the transborder expansion of low-skilled, labor-intensive production processes. After General Suharto's coup in Indonesia and the anti-Chinese riots in Malaysia, inflows of foreign investments were welcomed for domestic reasons. Though the Sarit Administration in Thailand had reversed the kingdom's *dirigiste* policies, it remained less open to foreign investments in the 1960s and early 1970s than its neighbors due to a powerful alliance established by its domestic bankers and industrialists. While large, vertically-integrated TNCs based in the US and Europe had the resources to disperse their manufacturing operations over a wide arena, the relative weakness and multilayered structure of major Japanese corporations restricted the transfer of the lower end of their production processes to neighboring locations on the Pacific seaboard of Asia. Additionally, the greater relative autonomy of the state in the 'Four Dragons' minimized local oppositions, while their repressive apparatuses ensured labor peace.

A second wave of transnational expansion of capital was triggered by the Nixon Administration's decision to rescind the convertibility of the US dollar to gold and by the oil price hikes of 1972. The resulting depreciation of the dollar increased competitive pressures on Japanese and West European enterprises. Confronted with rising import bills and falling exports, MITI adopted a strategy to transfer both light and heavy industries to neighboring locations while retaining as much of the value-added segments of manufacturing operations as possible within Japan. This led to a massive outward expansion of Japanese capital, primarily to small East and Southeast Asian economies, and by the end of the 1970s, Japan had surpassed the historically larger US investments in the region. As the rise in commodity prices underlined both Japan's dependence on imports of raw materials and a shift in the balance of power toward elites in resource-rich low- and middle-income states, Japanese investors sought access to these resources through joint venture projects. This strategy enabled Japanese investors to diversify their sources of supply while simultaneously impairing the capacity of peripheral producers to affect prices by rapidly expanding supplies without corresponding increases in demand. Thus, unlike in 1972, the oil price hike of 1978 was not accompanied by a general rise in commodity prices.

Despite all this, economic growth in Pacific-Asia was not exceptional and was dwarfed by the achievements of some much larger middle-income states in Eastern Europe, Latin America and elsewhere which pursued a strategy of debt-led industrialization in the 1970s. However, when the US responded by raising its domestic interest rates above the rate of inflation and by deregulating its banks and the financial sector, it reversed the flow of cheap credit to low- and middle-income states and undermined debt-led industrialization strategies. It was only then that the exceptionalism of economic growth in Pacific-Asia became evident. As the growth of manufacturing was based on a spatial extension of hierarchically-linked Japanese subcontracting networks, and was less capital-intensive than in Latin America and Eastern Europe, they were less vulnerable to the credit squeeze that so adversely affected other peripheral and semiperipheral states. Celebrations of the 'flying geese' model – replication of Japanese patterns of industrialization in neighboring locations on the Asian mainland – were however both premature and essentially unfounded.

Just as the transnational expansion of US enterprises led to a contradiction between their interests and the power pursuits of the US government, the transborder expansion of Japanese corporate technostructures undermined the coherence of regulatory mechanisms in Japan. The economic ascendance of Japanese corporations meant that they were no longer restricted to investments within the Pacific-Asian region. Moreover, their greater credit-worthiness meant that they were less reliant on the government for loans at preferential rates. If deregulation of financial markets and the appreciation of the yen triggered a further wave of Japanese overseas investments, they simultaneously began to hollow out industry in the Japanese home islands. Meanwhile, the wholesale structural transformation of low- and middle-income economies in East and Southeast Asia undermined the social coalitions on which the developmentalist states were based as an increasingly mature proletariat began to challenge the terms of their exclusion. Finally, greater deregulation of international financial markets encouraged adoption of debt-led strategies which, in the face of a progressive erosion of regulatory frameworks, led to overproduction and the financial meltdown of 1997–98, as we shall see in the next chapter.

5   Debts and delusions
Crumbling of a regional economy

Reflecting on the interest hikes he presided over in the late 1970s and early 1980s, Paul Volcker said that the inflows of foreign capital into the United States were 'far greater than [he] had thought possible' (quoted in Murphy, 1996: 148). Not only did these inflows – 'at one point at a greater rate than all the personal savings in the US' by his own estimation – exceed Volcker's expectations: they also fundamentally reshaped the geography of manufacturing on both sides of the Pacific. By raising real US interest rates from an average of -2 percent in 1979 to an average of 7.5 percent in 1982, the US Federal Reserve engineered an unprecedented reversal in the flows of capital – transforming the United States from the largest creditor nation to the largest debtor country in less than a decade. If this recentralized financial power in New York and Washington, the high dollar also undermined the competitiveness of American industry and facilitated the emergence of the Asian rimlands as the most dynamic industrial region in the world economy in the 1980s and early 1990s.

Manipulations of interest rates and realignments of currency values not only had a deep impact on patterns of industrial organization and relations between governments and businesses along Asia's Pacific coasts. Switches in investment flows triggered by changing relative prices also transformed social topographies to such an extent that the coalitional logic of the developmental state was rendered anachronistic, as we shall see in this chapter.

The first section locates these changes in the context of the developments that led upto the realignment of exchange-rates by the Plaza Accord of 1985 and the ensuing changes in patterns of investment flows. Though interest rate hikes in the US curbed inflation, by conferring a competitive advantage on Japanese and West European competitors, it eviscerated the US industrial sector despite a rise in Japanese manufacturing investments in North America. As the continued decline of American manufacturing was not politically sustainable, the Reagan Administration negotiated a depreciation of the dollar. Rather than signaling a revival of manufacturing in the hegemonic power, however, the Plaza Accord led to a massive increase in intra-regional investments along Asia's Pacific seaboard as manufacturers transferred production facilities to lower-waged locations. A higher yen also led Japanese manufacturers to invest in new capital investments in contrast to US manufacturers who had no incentive to upgrade their capital stock due to a prolonged wage compression.

Since the Plaza Accord not only failed to revive US manufacturing but also led to a drop in capital inflows to the United States, it threatened the stability of the world financial structure. Hence, to revive capital flows to the US, the Japanese and West German authorities lowered their domestic interest rates in 1987 and agreed to cooperate with their US counterparts in stabilizing the dollar. Lower interest rates, however, led to a tidal wave of speculation in Japan that jeopardized the Liberal Democratic Party's (LDP) hold on power. When the Bank of Japan, to stem the erosion of the ruling party's base of support, raised interest rates in 1990, it pricked the speculative bubble and saddled Japanese banks with huge losses. To recoup these losses, the banks loaned large sums to enterprises and financial institutions in East and Southeast Asia where interest rates were higher. The availability of large infusions of capital fueled a more intensive round of industrial restructuring along the Asian rimlands.

These changes in the patterns of investment flows eroded the foundations of the developmental state, by transforming patterns of industrial organization, by emancipating large enterprises from dependence on governments for finance and protection, and by changes in the social structure entailed by rapid industrialization, as we shall see in the second section. Unlike the transborder expansion of Japanese corporate networks in the 1960s and 1970s, the relocation of industrial production in the 1980s and 1990s did not complement industrial production in its home islands and hence began to unravel the alliance between big and small businesses. Even earlier, by reducing corporate demand for investment funds, the transfer of heavy and chemical industries from Japan in the 1970s had loosened links between major industrial corporations and 'lead' banks. Increased government expenditure to compensate for declining employment opportunities led to a further loosening of regulations over cross-border capital flows since banks could more easily underwrite government bonds by borrowing from international financial markets. Finally, as large Japanese corporations used their favorable cash-flow positions to enter new fields unrelated to their core businesses, and to forge strategic alliances with other TNCs, it loosened their ties with their subcontractors and the hierarchical subcontracting structure began to unravel.

Elsewhere in the region, rapid industrialization transformed social structures and undermined the coalitional logic of the developmental state. Installation of large factory complexes led to the growth of a powerful labor movement in South Korea that eventually led to the end of the military regime, while democracy movements elsewhere were led by the rising middle classes. Large infusions of cheap credit enabled governing elites in East and Southeast Asia – barring Japan, Taiwan, Singapore, and Hong Kong – to coopt rising middle classes and provincial elites and to subvert working class movements. This required a shift in macro-economic priorities from strategic economic planning to inflation control and led to the eclipse, even abolition, of pilot economic agencies. However, since corporations continued to focus on capturing market shares rather than on profit margins, in conditions of easy access to credit there was an expansion of capacity without parallel increases in demand.

The decline of developmental states indicated not only a weakening of the national foundations of accumulation but also the creation of several competing industrial structures. At the same time, as we shall see in the third section, a low dollar and the prior off-shedding of obsolete plant and equipment led to major capital investments in manufacturing in the United States. Tendencies toward overproduction were aggravated when the US agreed to appreciate the dollar against the yen in 1995, as a secular rise of the yen since 1990 made it increasingly difficult for Japanese investors to support US deficits. A fall in the value of the yen along with a prior devaluation of the reminbi greatly increased competitive pressures on the East and Southeast Asian states which had pegged their currencies to the dollar to encourage capital inflows. Confronted with collapsing prices, enterprises resorted to short-term borrowings in unhedged currencies to meet their debt burdens until the whole edifice came tumbling down when the spigot of low-interest loans was abruptly turned off.

In short, the sheer magnitude of the transborder expansion of corporate networks along Asia's Pacific coasts also serially impaired the oversight capabilities of the elite economic agencies that had orchestrated these expansions in the first place. The resulting incoherence of manufacturing investments undermined the regional divisioning of labor and led to problems of overproduction. Meanwhile, accompanying changes in social topographies fractured the social coalitions that had made the developmental state possible and though these fissures could be papered over during years of high-speed growth by giving concessions and subsidies to excluded sectors, once the economic downturn set in the collapse was mercurially swift.

Years of living dangerously

Full employment in Japan and growing protectionism in high-income states, as we saw in the last chapter, had led to a serial transfer of lower-cost, less capital-intensive manufacturing to lower-waged areas in the 1970s. The consequent reduction in the demand for investment funds by Japanese enterprises lessened their dependence on 'lead banks,' as we shall see below. When these banks, to safeguard their earnings, refused to let enterprises repay their loans ahead of schedule, they plowed their cash reserves into speculative activities, and to finance an expansion of their manufacturing facilities to high-income states which had threatened to raise protective tariffs against imports from Japan. A round of labor disciplining in North America, and less significantly in Western Europe, facilitated the transfer of Japanese and Taiwanese industries to these locations. Unlike the previous transborder expansion of Japanese capital led by small- and medium-sized enterprises, the emergence of TNCs as the primary agencies of Japanese corporate expansion progressively undermined national industrial policies in Japan. To counter falling employment opportunities domestically, the Japanese government launched a massive expansion of public expenditures which was lubricated by loosening controls over cross-border capital flows and regulations over financial institutions to enable Japanese banks to borrow from international capital markets. In turn, this further constrained macro-economic options for the government and undermined the institutional scaffolding of the developmental state.

First, the global economic recession of the early 1970s and the structural shift of the Japanese economy from heavy and chemical industries also reduced overall corporate demand for investment funds. Total corporate liabilities in Japan fell from ¥181.6 trillion in fiscal 1975 to ¥9.5 trillion in 1980 and to ¥8.3 trillion in 1985 (Palat, 1996: 326–37; Calder, 1997: 19–20; Pempel, 1997: 350).

The fall in demand for investment funds lessened corporate dependence on banks and gradually weakened relationships between enterprises and lead banks that had been central to Japanese enterprises rapidly becoming competitive in sectors of increasing technological sophistication and complexity. With declining requirements for investment funds, however, enterprises tried to reduce their interest charges by repaying their loans ahead of schedule. Since this adversely affected the banks, they refused faster loan repayments – a refusal that enterprises had to honor since they still relied on banks for finances in the 1970s. So they began to invest more heavily in short-term securities where annual rates of interest could be as high as 20 percent in the mid-1970s (Gao, 2001: 162–4; Hatch and Yamamura, 1996: 68). As a consequence, major manufacturing firms like Toyota Motors and Matsushita Electric accumulated such large surpluses that they had begun lending to other enterprises and by the mid-1980s, financial activities or *zaitech* (*zai* = finance) had become the most important source of profits for a whole spectrum of Japanese automotive, electronics, and precision machinery manufacturers (Calder, 1997: 19–20).[1]

Second, the adoption of high interest rates in the United States in 1979 accelerated the outflow of capital from Japan and the country became the biggest international creditor by the mid-1980s. Japanese investments overseas in long-term funds (most of it in US dollar-denominated assets) increased from $11 billion in 1980 to $23 billion in 1981 and had reached $130 billion by 1986 – over half the $220 billion US Federal deficit that year (Murphy, 1996: 147):

> One thus witnessed the extraordinary spectacle of Japanese financiers providing the credit required by the US government to finance its budget deficits in order to subsidize the continuing growth of Japanese exports. . . . It was difficult to determine who was more dependent upon whom – the US Treasury on Japanese lenders or Japanese manufacturers on US borrowers and their demand. What was clear, however, was the degree to which the two leading capitalist economies – and thus the world economy as a whole – were relying on the historically unprecedented growth of debt in the US and the willingness of the Japanese to help fund it.
>
> (Brenner, 2002: 54)

As investors in Japan sought higher returns abroad, a steep rise in demand for foreign currencies depressed the value of the yen in foreign exchange markets – falling by 23.6 percent against the greenback between the end of 1980 and the end of 1984 (Itoh, 1994: 38) – and conferred an additional competitive advantage on Japanese businesses. Conversely, while the sharp hike in interest rates in the United States rolled back inflation and bolstered the dollar as world money, it also delivered a devastating blow to US manufacturing: output fell by 10 percent between 1979 and 1982, manufacturing investment by 8 percent followed by an additional 15 percent in 1983, and employment in manufacturing by 13 percent. One measure of the extent of devastation wrought on US manufacturing by the high dollar policy was the dramatic transformation of its current account surpluses into progressively larger deficits – plunging from a surplus of $5 billion in 1981 to a deficit of $119 billion by 1985 – as cheap imports from Japan and the 'dragons' captured ever-larger shares of the US domestic market (Harrison and Bluestone, 1990: 28–38; Morales, 1994: 57; Brenner, 2002: 50–6).

When the Reagan Administration tried to blunt the impact of the penetration of the US market by imports from the Asian rimlands by imposing 'voluntary export restrictions' on a range of imports, especially automobiles, Japanese manufacturers began to set up shop in Western Europe, North America, and less significantly in Australasia to guarantee market access (Ozawa, 1985: 168; Wade, 1990: 156–7). Japanese investment in the United States was facilitated in particular by an intense round of labor disciplining – automation and robotization of production, deunionization, labor givebacks, and constraints on collective bargaining – since 1972 that had lowered wages substantially (Harrison, 1984; Davis, 1986: 138; Soja, 1989: 172, 186; Brenner, 2002: 51). As a consequence, the real weekly wage in the US manufacturing sector dropped by 4.3 percent between 1973 and 1985 and real family income by almost 5 percent (Morales, 1994: 14; Gordon, 1996b: 28). Additionally, the hours of work increased in the United States: from an annual average of paid employment of 1,786 hours per labor force participant in 1969 to 1,949 hours by 1987, or a 9 percent increase (Gordon, 1996b: 105).

If the corrosive spread of a rust belt fostered protectionist tendencies in the US, growing unemployment lowered the costs of production in the United States for Japanese manufacturers in addition to the tax and other benefits offered them by state and local governments hoping to lure or retain jobs in their jurisdictions. Moreover, as Japanese corporations began to set up manufacturing facilities in the United States, a bout of farm failures had rapidly expanded the pool of low-wage workers.[2] Seizing this opportunity, Japanese automobile factories in particular were located in small towns and rural areas, without a history of strong labor movements, in the so-called 'transplant corridor' stretching from southern Ontario to Tennessee, organized around several interstate highways through Illinois, Indiana, Ohio, and Kentucky (Dicken, 1992: 295; Morales, 1994: 83–4). From having no overseas manufacturing plants as late as 1982, at least 13 Japanese and South Korean auto assembly facilities were operating in the US and Canada by 1991, as were some 250 Japanese automobile suppliers. In the following year, Honda began importing cars produced by its American subsidiary to Japan (Morales, 1994: 68).

Since the European Community itself was relatively closed to foreign direct investment, Japanese corporations tended to use Britain as a back-door to enter the European market. When the European Community began to indirectly control Japanese imports in 1983, Japanese companies entered into joint venture projects with British manufacturers (Morales, 1994: 96). The installation of Japanese manufacturing facilities, in Western Europe and North America, was often accompanied by the adoption of Japanese styles of industrial relations – use of non-unionized labor, team concepts, 'just-in-time' delivery schedules – even by European and North American firms. Combined with the spread of the US manufacturing belt into Canada and especially to the *maquiladoras* in Mexico, there was greater segmentation in the labor market (Morales, 1994: 132).

Japanese investments in North America and Western Europe were accompanied by parallel, though smaller, investments by Taiwanese enterprises. Just as an increasingly diplomatically isolated Taiwan welcomed inflows of foreign investments so that Western powers would have a stake in its survival as an independent state, Taiwanese government- and GMD-owned enterprises invested overseas, especially in constituencies of key US senators and Congressional representatives. By 1982 Taiwanese investments in the United States overtook US investments in the island state (Segal, 1990: 3; Dicken, 1992: 84–5; Schive, 1995: 19). Like the pattern of Japanese investments, while the first wave of investments by Taiwanese enterprises had been in Southeast Asia, in the early 1980s the United States became the most favored destination – accounting for 72.6 percent of Taiwan's total overseas investments between 1980 and 1986. This outward flow of investments was overseen by the Ministry of Economic Affairs which ranked sites by the opportunities to lower production costs and to acquire new technology as well as by political considerations. Unlike the second wave of Japanese investments, though, most overseas ventures by Taiwanese corporations tended to be small – between US$1 and 2 million (Schive, 1995: 19; Wade, 1990: 156–7; Greenhalgh, 1988: 84).

This greater geographical dispersion of Japanese investments underlines a third consequence of the accumulation of investment funds. While small- and medium-sized enterprises had spearheaded the outward expansion of Japanese capital until the mid-1970s, now the TNCs emerged as the primary agencies for overseas investments. While 40 percent of Japanese direct foreign investments in manufacturing had been in Asia in the mid-1970s, cumulative investments in the region accounted for only 28 percent in 1988 (Eccleston, 1989: 249; Palat, 1996: 321–3; Daly, 1994: 173–4; Nakao, 1995: 44–6).

The progressive transnational expansion of their operations and their large cash surpluses sharply reduced the dependence of Japanese conglomerates on their government and gradually undermined the salience of national industrial policies. Thus, whereas the earlier wave of Japanese FDI had complemented domestic production, the massive transfer of manufacturing facilities overseas in the 1980s termed *endaka fukyō* or 'recession' led to declining employment opportunities, a wave of bankruptcies and involuntary closures of small- and medium-scale industries, and a greater coercion of labor (Palat, 1996: 325; Steven, 1996: 42)!

Finally, measures adopted by the Japanese government to cushion the impact of higher prices of commodities and the slower growth of employment opportunities in the immediate aftermath of the oil price hikes further eroded the regulatory mechanisms of the developmental state. When the government sought to alleviate the adverse impact of these economic pressures by increasing government expenditure – between 1973 and 1985, the total value of all outstanding Japanese national government bonds rose more than twelve times in nominal terms and five times in real terms – it recognized that Japanese banks could underwrite these bonds only by borrowing from international currency markets. Additional pressures to remove restrictions on foreign exchange transactions and on the operation of foreign banks in Japan came from the internationalization of Japanese industry: as Japanese banks sought to follow Japanese industry abroad, foreign governments used restrictions on foreign banks operating in Japan as a reason to prevent the entry of Japanese banks to their financial centers (Calder, 1997: 21–6; Itoh, 1990: 171; Leyshon, 1994: 124–7). By 1985, partly because the staggering debts accumulated by peripheral and semiperipheral states had undermined the position of US trans-national banks, and partly as a function of the revaluation of the yen, Tokyo had become the world's leading banking center in terms of accumulated assets. Prefiguring this rise, Japan had already become the major exporter of capital by 1982, and the United States the leading recipient of foreign capital (Sassen, 1991: 66, 175).

Deregulation over capital flows also freed major manufacturers from dependence on government sources of finance. While only Toyota Motors and Matsushita Electric had been cleared to issue unsecured convertible bonds as late as 1979, over the next ten years some 300 firms issued such shares. The magnitude of the shift from reliance on main banks to bonds can be gauged from the fact that Japanese industrial corporations had issued bonds worth ¥391 billion, all domestically, in 1965. In 1989, the corresponding figure was ¥9,284 billion domestically and ¥11,129 billion overseas (Pempel, 1998: 162).

Thus, the decision to hike US interest rates above the world average, by depreciating the value of the yen, conferred competitive advantages on Japanese manufacturers. When higher energy prices had led to a transfer of heavy and chemical industries from Japan and to a corresponding fall in demand for investment funds, higher US interest rates were an incentive for Japanese manufacturers to shift a larger share of their cash reserves to speculative activities. In turn, government attempts to compensate for the slowdown in employment growth in Japan by increasing public expenditures resulted in a loosening of regulations over the financial sector and over cross-border capital flows. This further reduced the dependence of industrial firms on both the government and the 'lead' banks – a trend that was to fundamentally reshape economic fortunes in the region as we shall see in the last section of this chapter. Simultaneously, growing protectionist sentiments in Western Europe and North America prompted Japanese and less significantly, Taiwanese, TNCs to draw on their large cash reserves to set up manufacturing facilities in these jurisdictions. However, this was not enough to offset the decline of manufacturing in the United States caused in large part by the high dollar.

Plaza Accord and the changing topography of manufacturing

The inexorable downward pressure on manufacturing profits in the United States led enterprises to dispose of older plants and machinery. However, due to the high dollar, they refrained from investing in new plants and equipment. Though Japanese trade surpluses were crucial in financing US budget deficits, the continuing decline of American manufacturing was not politically sustainable for long (Brenner, 2002: 57–9, 105–6). Eventually, at a meeting of the finance ministers and central bank governors of France, Japan, the United Kingdom, the United States, and

West Germany at New York's Plaza Hotel in September 1985, the Reagan Administration prevailed upon its main trade partners, especially Japan, to realign exchange-rates by appreciating their currencies against the green-back on pain of excluding their products from US markets. As a result of the Plaza Accord, the yen soared from ¥238 to ¥170 to the US dollar within seven months and reached ¥120 by early 1988. In practical terms, it meant that if Japanese firms were to sell a product at the same price of US$100 in the US market, in yen terms they would have to cut the price from ¥23,800 in 1985 to ¥12,000 in 1988 (Itoh, 1990: 176; Leyshon, 1994: 130; Gilpin, 2000: 118, 132, 230–1; Brenner, 2002: 60–1, 106–7).

Rather than reviving an increasingly moribund US manufacturing sector, though, a higher yen led to a through-going revamp of the Japan-ese industrial structure, and the transfer of low-skilled manufacturing processes offshore accompanied by technological upgrading in the home islands boosted the competitive strength of major Japanese manufactur-ers. The emphasis on cost-cutting prompted a reorientation of Japanese manufacturing investments from other high-income states toward low- and middle-income states in East and Southeast Asia, along with similar trends in investments from South Korea, Taiwan, and Singapore. Meanwhile, the implementation of market reforms in China restored Hong Kong to its former entrepôt role and firms began to increase their investments to Guangdong and other special economic zones in the People's Republic. Conversely, a prolonged decline in manufacturing continued to hold down wages in the United States and the dollar was not low enough to be an incentive for manufacturers to invest in technological upgrading or to attract overseas investments. Hence, contrary to expectations, the Plaza Accord resulted in a tapering off of capital inflows to the United States.

As this once again threatened to undermine the architecture of global finance, the West German and Japanese governments undertook in 1987 to lower their domestic rates of interest and to help US authorities stabi-lize the dollar. Lower domestic interest rates stimulated a further outward expansion of Japanese capital as well as a surge in speculative activities. Together, as we shall see, these two tendencies fractured the alliance between big and small businesses in Japan just as the dependence between manufacturing establishments and the 'lead' banks had been weakened in the 1970s. The steady erosion of the domestic constituencies on which high-speed economic growth had been predicated threatened the LDP's long grip on power and as it sought to reestablish this alliance by raising interest rates in 1990, it pricked the speculative bubble of the Japanese economy. This, in turn, led to a massive expansion of credit to enterprises and financial institutions in East and Southeast Asia as Japanese banks sought to recoup their losses. To these issues we now turn.

In the first instance, the swift appreciation of the yen changed the cal-culus of relative costs, especially since it came in the context of an intense disciplining of labor in the United States. In dollar terms and taking 1980 as the index year, the per unit labor cost in the United States was 109 when the Plaza Accord was negotiated, while it was 98 in Japan and 69 in West Germany. Two years later, while it had risen to 159 in Japan and 116 in West Germany, it was only 106 in the US and it is estimated that a fall in the value of the greenback accounted for 80 percent of this decline in American wages (Kiyonari, 1993; see also Brenner, 2002: 61, 64). Since the rise in the index of Japanese wages was due to exchange-rate changes, it did not connote an increase in purchasing power (Steven, 1990: 8).

Japanese manufacturers responded by focusing on cutting their production costs and on moving up the technological ladder. Between 1985 and 1991, gross capital stock increased at an average annual rate of 6.7 percent – three times the rate in the United States. In 1987, for instance, Nippon Steel's research and development expenditures were larger than the research expenditure of all US steel firms combined. The greater implementation of technological innovations such as industrial robots – with the Japanese share of the world's industrial robots hovering around the 60 percent mark in 1986 – was accompanied by a re-intensification of labor discipline through the zero defect movement and the induction of quality control circles. As the high yen made domestic steel production uneconomic, just as new steel plants were coming on line in South Korea and China, greater mechanization enabled Japanese companies like Nippon Steel to produce as much steel with half as many workers in the early 1990s as it did in the 1980s (Shapira, 1993: 237–9; Brenner, 2002: 108, 114; Itoh, 2000: 17; Gao, 2001: 196).

Conversely, when US wages were low, rather than invest in new technologies, employers in the United States tended to substitute labor for capital and reallocate funds to financial activities in the 1980s. Robert Pollin estimated that non-financial corporations spent an annual average of $184 billion on mergers and acquisitions in the United States between 1984 and 1989 compared with an annual average of $84 billion on non-residential fixed investment. Nevertheless, the introduction of 'lean production' systems, increasing resort to out-sourcing, greater intensification of work and the application of information technologies such as computer-aided design led to an annual average growth in labor productivity of 3.5 percent, the same as during the post-Second World War boom (Brenner, 2002: 67, 77–9, 81).

More importantly, since a high yen undermined the competitiveness of Japanese exports it encouraged corporations to more vigorously transfer manufacturing operations overseas, especially when credit was cheap. Japanese FDI doubled in 1986–87 over the previous year, and in the manufacturing sector more was invested overseas in the first half of 1987 than in the whole of the previous year. On an annual basis, Japanese FDI grew at an average rate of 62 percent between 1985 and 1989 (Leyshon, 1994: 130; Bernard and Ravenhill, 1995: 318; Bowles and MacLean, 1996: 159; Eccleston, 1989: 252; see also Sassen, 1991: 36–41). In comparative terms, the Japanese share of world FDI increased from 6 percent in 1970 to 20 percent by the late 1980s; of equities outflows from 2 percent in 1970 to 25 percent; of bond outflows from 15 percent to 55 percent; and of short-term bank loans from 12 percent to 50 percent (Pempel, 1999b: 67–8).

While overseas manufacturing had only accounted for 9 percent of Japanese domestic production in 1987, the explosive growth of foreign investments by major Japanese corporations led to a corresponding rise in the share of output produced by off-shore plants (Eccleston, 1989: 249, 252). As a result of the consequent *kudoka* or 'hollowing out' of Japanese industry, exports to the United States fell by 17.4 percent between April and September 1988. Overall, between 1985 and 1991, the average annual rate of growth of Japanese exports was only one-third as high as it was between 1979 and 1985 (Steven, 1990: 35–7; Brenner, 2002: 109).

However, while the Plaza Accord shifted competitive pressures onto Japanese capital, lower US interest rates also led to a diversion of capital flows away from the United States (Brenner, 2002: 84). Instead, the Asian region once again became a favored destination for Japanese investments. Though higher land and labor costs meant that investment volumes in North America were larger, Japanese manufacturing investments in Asia between 1986 and 1989 'exceeded the *cumulative* total for the whole of the 1951–85 period' (Bernard and Ravenhill, 1995: 181, emphasis in the original)!

By 1989, investments by Japanese firms in Taiwan were four times as much as before the Plaza Accord, in Malaysia and South Korea five times as much, in Singapore six times, in Hong Kong fifteen times, and in Thailand twenty-five times (Pempel, 1999b: 67; Rodan, 1989: 199–200). Thailand emerged as a particularly favored destination for Japanese investments because it had been subject to the IMF's structural adjustment program in 1982 when, like many economies in Latin America and Sub-Saharan Africa, it too had been burdened with unsustainable overseas debt once the US adopted monetarist policies. Forced to devalue the baht in November 1984 by 14.7 percent and 'export its way out of trouble,' Thailand registered annual export growth of 10 percent per year between 1985 and 1995, the fastest rate of growth in the world by World Bank estimates. In 1994, some 7 percent of workers in the Thai manufacturing sector were employed by Japanese firms while another estimate indicates that by the late 1980s Matsushita alone accounted for 5 percent of Malaysia's GNP (Hatch and Yamamura, 1996: 6)! Another indicator of the transformation of production structures engineered by these changes in investment patterns is provided by the share of manufactured goods as a percentage of Indonesia's exports, which rose from 3 percent in 1980 to 40 percent in 1991 (Berger, 1997: 346).

Conversely, with the appreciation of the yen, Japanese investments in the United States were increasingly in finance, insurance, and real estate. In 1986, only 17 percent of these investments were in manufacturing compared with 32.4 percent in finance and insurance and 17.9 percent in US real estate. Whereas cumulative Japanese investments in US real estate until 1985 were estimated to be between $2 and $3 billion, in 1986 alone some $5 to $6 billion were invested in the sector (Gao, 2001: 197). The magnitude of these investments implied that Japanese investors were very adversely affected by the fall in US real estate prices following the Wall Street crash of 1987.

Experiencing the effects of similar currency revaluations as indicated by Table 5.1, and corresponding increases in land and labor costs, firms based in South Korea, Taiwan, and Singapore also expanded their manufacturing operations to neighboring low-waged locations. South Korea and Taiwan became hosts to products requiring intermediate technology, such as video recorders and color TVs, while South Korean and Taiwanese corporations extended their own production and procurement networks to Southeast Asia and China (Daly, 1994: 174–5; Steven, 1996: 77–100).

The continued rise of wages due to labor militancy in South Korea in the 1980s led to an increase in unit labor costs in manufacturing by 46 percent between 1985 and 1996 compared with 25 percent for Taiwan and 4.4 percent for the United States (Butler, 1996). The *chaebol* adopted the time-honored strategy of the 'runaway shop' to counter labor militancy and their command over large resources meant that, unlike the smaller firms in the other 'dragons,' they were not restricted to contiguous locations in their investments. In 1989, new investments by South Korean firms in the ASEAN member-states reached $132 million when the cumulative total for such investments until 1985 had only been $42 million (Bernard and Ravenhill, 1995: 182). The following year, in 1990, South Korean investments abroad surpassed foreign investments in the country for the first time and then grew exponentially between 1991 and 1995 (Dicken, 1992: 83–4).

By the mid-1980s, when the average hourly wage of a textile worker in Taiwan was US$2.37 compared with 38 cents in Thailand, Taiwan's foreign investment according to official figures doubled each year from 1986 to 1990 – rising from $56.9 million to $1,552 million. Data from host countries indicate even higher levels of Taiwanese overseas investments. When currency appreciation raised labor costs in Taiwan, small- and medium-sized firms attempted to move up from their OEM status to original design manufacturing (Lin, 2002: 82–3). After the Chinese government decided to waive duties on imports from Taiwan in 1980, Taiwanese businesses also began investing heavily in China, especially since the Plaza and Louvre Accords led to a 40 percent increase in the value of the New Taiwan dollar and Taiwan's bilateral trade with China – not inclusive of the trade conducted through Hong Kong – more than doubled between 1985 and 1988, rising from $1.1 billion to $2.7 billion. By 1988, for the first time, Taiwan's overseas investments exceeded capital inflows to the

Table 5.1 Exchange-rates after the Plaza Accord

Year	Hong Kong HK$/US$	Singapore S$/US$	South Korea won/US$	Taiwan NT$/US$	Indonesia rupiah/US$	Malaysia ringgit/US$	Thailand baht/US$	China yuan/US$
1986	7.803	2.177	881.450	37.838	1,283	2.581	26.29	3.453
1987	7.798	2.106	822.570	31.740	1,644	2.520	25.72	3.722
1988	7.806	2.012	731.470	28.588	1,686	2.619	25.29	3.722
1989	7.800	1.950	671.460	26.407	1,770	2.709	25.70	3.765
1990	7.789	1.813	707.760	26.893	1,843	2.705	25.58	4.783
Percentage change on US dollar (1986–90)	0.18	16.72	19.71	28.93	−43.65	−4.78	2.70	−38.52
1991	7.771	1.728	733.350	26.815	1,950	2.750	25.51	5.323
1992	7.741	1.629	780.650	25.164	2,030	2.547	25.40	5.515
1993	7.736	1.616	802.670	26.387	2,087	2.574	25.31	5.762
1994	7.728	1.527	803.450	26.457	2,161	2.624	25.15	8.619
1995	7.736	1.417	771.270	26.486	2,249	2.504	24.91	8.351
1996	7.734	1.410	804.450	27.458	2,342	2.516	25.34	8.314
Percentage change on US dollar (1991–96)	0.48	18.40	−9.70	−2.40	−20.10	8.51	0.67	−56.19
1997	7.742	1.485	951.290	28.703	2,909	2.813	31.36	8.290
1998	7.745	1.674	1,401.440	33.456	10,014	3.924	41.35	8.279
Percentage change on US dollar (1996–98)	−0.14	−18.72	−74.21	−21.84	−327.58	−55.98	−63.18	0.42
Percentage change on US dollar (1986–98)	0.74	23.11	−58.99	11.58	−680.51	−52.02	−57.28	−139.76

Source: Asian Development Bank, Key Indicators of Developing Asian and Pacific Countries, 1999.

Note
Yearly averages, no adjustment for inflation.

island (Schive, 1995: 18–19; Wade, 1990: 156–7; You-tien Hsing, 1998; Hamilton, 1999: 56; Pempel, 1999b: 68–9).

Rapid expansion of investments overseas was reflected domestically in the increased size of enterprises in Taiwan – partly encouraged by government pressure to merge small- and medium-sized firms to increase their competitiveness – as indicated by Table 5.2. This table demonstrates that after the Plaza Accord, the share of GNP accounted for by the largest 100 business groups almost doubled from 28.7 percent in 1986 to 54 percent in 1998. In electronics, firms with less than 100 workers accounted for only 20 percent of output by 1999 while firms with more than 500 employees accounted for 60 percent. This was also because TNCs based in Japan and the United States began to withdraw from the logistical aspects of marketing to concentrate on cultivating brand loyalty and technical support services. As these TNCs sought to reduce their inventories, they required their Taiwanese suppliers to build and maintain warehouses at specified locations – in effect compelling the suppliers to move into marketing (Lin, 2002: 83).

Combined with Taiwan's large domestic savings, a rise in investments overseas also sparked an unchecked speculative boom between 1987 and 1990, when the stock market index rose from 1,000 to just below 12,500 and 10 percent of the population were estimated to be trading on a *daily* basis. Speculation was so rampant that on peak days the trading volume in the Taiwan Stock Exchange – 'an ungovernable man-eating casino,' Chiang Chi-cheng, the governor of the central bank called it – was greater than the combined turnovers of the New York and Tokyo markets. Capitalization of stocks in Taiwan approached the level of Germany before the crash began in February 1990, and within 10 months the stock market index bottomed out at 2,560. If Taiwan's large base of domestic savings cushioned the impact of so severe a stock market crash, it spurred a fresh wave of investments to China after the Tienanmen Square crackdown in 1989 had led to a temporary decline (Champion, 1997).

Rising wage bills in Singapore – unit labor costs increased by 40 percent between 1979 and 1984 – had weakened its competitive position relative to the other 'dragon' economies: by 15 percent against Taiwan, 35

Table 5.2 Taiwan's largest 100 business groups' sales as a percentage of GNP, 1979–98

	1979	1981	1983	1986	1988	1990	1992	1994	1996	1998
Sales of top 100 groups (A)	3,819	5,076	6,337	8,402	12,193	16,881	18,654	26,630	33,334	48,526
GNP (B)	11,962	17,642	21,032	29,257	36,115	44,119	54,598	65,571	77,671	89,867
Sales/GNP (A/B)	31.9	28.8	30.1	28.7	33.8	38.3	34.2	40.6	42.9	54.0

Source: Adapted from Amsden and Chu (2002, table 2-1).

percent against South Korea, and 50 percent against Hong Kong by Garry Rodan's (1989: 192) reckoning. By 1985, as a consequence of a recession in the world-economy and especially of Singapore's heavy reliance on exports to the United States, the economy contracted by 2 percent and the unemployment rate shot up to 6.2 percent despite the repatriation of some 60,000 guest workers (Rodan, 2001: 149). While the government moved to depress wages – by cutting employers' contributions to the Central Provident Fund and by imposing a two-year wage freeze – to restore competitiveness in the short-term, it also adopted a longer-term strategy of transforming Singapore into a regional service hub for business operations. Additionally, the government adopted a plan to integrate the Singaporean economy with neighboring economies – notably with the Malaysian state of Johor and the Riau islands of Indonesia – through an expansion of government-sponsored investments.

Though the Plaza Accord did not lead to a currency realignment for Hong Kong since its dollar was pegged to the greenback, the Sino-British Joint Declaration of December 1984 on the restoration of Chinese sovereignty in 1997 was a more important watershed. Additionally, wages had risen so significantly that there was an accelerated transfer of labor-intensive manufacturing activities to China's Pearl River Delta, where Victor Sit estimated that Hong Kong-based investors accounted for 3 million jobs by 1986 (You-tien Hsing, 1998: 184, n. 2). In Hong Kong itself, the number of industrial establishments fell from 50,606 in 1988 to 31,114 in 1995. Correspondingly, manufacturing employment in Hong Kong fell from 875,250 in 1987 to 386,106 in 1995 – with females, older, less educated and less skilled workers being most adversely affected (Lui and Chiu, 2001: 59). Just as enterprises in Singapore were extending their tentacles to neighboring locations in Malaysia and Indonesia, firms in Hong Kong were reaching out to Guangdong, while other 'growth triangles' were also emerging – Taiwan and China's Fujian province; Japan, South Korea, and Dalian province (Pempel, 1999b: 68–9). Finally, as sources of foreign investments diversified, Japan's share in total investment flows to Southeast and East Asia decreased.

The contradictions of the Plaza Accord – a low dollar and low interest rates causing inflows of capital to the United States to drop precipitously, even flowing out of the US on a net basis during much of 1987 – threatened to undermine the global financial structure. To reduce these pressures, the West German and especially the Japanese governments agreed at a G-7 summit at Louvre in 1987 to lower their domestic rates of interest, and financial authorities of both governments agreed to cooperate with US financial authorities in stabilizing the dollar within a certain band (Gilpin, 2000: 231; Brenner, 2002: 84–5). Far from lowering Japanese trade surpluses, however, a reduction of domestic interest rates fueled a surge in speculative activity as Japanese corporations launched a massive investment-led boom in which capital goods substituted for consumption goods and speculation in stocks and real estate substituted for export markets.

As a result, funds intermediated in Japan increased from an annual average of ¥58.6 trillion between 1975 and 1984 to an annual average of ¥122.9 trillion between 1985 and 1990. By another measure, the assets of Japan's largest twenty banks increased by 450 percent between 1980 and 1990, and by 1991 ten of the world's top twenty financial institutions and five of the top ten global firms measured by market value were Japanese (Leyshon, 1994: 132; Selden, 1997: 318). On average, money management accounted for 49 percent of the profits of the ten largest electrical goods exporters in 1987 (Eccleston, 1989: 234; see also Steven, 1990: 16).

Losses and steep declines in the profits of major industrial enterprises translated into even steeper declines for the small- and medium-scale firms. The tenacious existence of small- and medium-scale companies was also partly due to the preference of large firms to allow them to pioneer entirely new ventures in high technology fields like microelectronics as a means to shift the high rate of risk involved in such projects, and partly because the creation of small affiliated companies is one avenue to resolve promotion bottlenecks for middle-level managers in periods of declining output (Eccleston, 1989: 51; Friedman, 1988: 126–76). It is worth remembering that the relatively low rate of failure of minor enterprises in official statistics was also because many of them were too small to be counted (Eccleston, 1989: 241). Additionally, export-oriented small- and medium-scale firms tended to voluntarily disband themselves, especially if they owned valuable real estate. Thus, in 1987, for instance, there was a 190 percent increase in the voluntary closures of small firms (Steven, 1990: 39). In these conditions, pressure on small enterprises, particularly those unable to migrate offshore, was reflected in increased self-exploitation, long-term stabilization of piece-rates, tightened delivery schedules, and frequent changes of product specification. In short, whereas the earlier wave of the outward expansion of Japanese capital had complemented domestic production, the surge in Japanese overseas investments in the 1980s led to an estimated yearly loss of 0.7 million jobs (Eccleston, 1989: 252).

When *zaitech* activities and borrowings from international financial markets had loosened links between major corporations and large banks in Japan, smaller firms and less fiscally sound enterprises as well as organized crime syndicates began to account for a large and constantly increasing share of loans made by Japanese financial institutions (Pempel, 1997: 353; Gao, 2001: 183). While loans to small firms may have helped stave off bankruptcies, the massive expansion of credit spurred a wave of speculative investments within the country (Steven, 1990: 38). Speculation in stocks and real estate was so rampant that commentators had a field day estimating the value of land. The notional market value of land in the Greater Tokyo area exceeded that of all the property in the United States by the time the bubble burst in 1991, according to some. Others estimated that the notional book value of the five square kilometers surrounding the Imperial Palace in Tokyo was larger than the land value of the entire state of California and yet others that a 100 square meter plot of land in central Tokyo was worth as much as a European castle or a modest island in Australia or Canada (Pempel, 1998: 196; McCormack, 2001: 91; Gao, 2001: 156–7). By Gavan McCormack's (2001: 97) estimate, land constituted 65 percent of Japan's national wealth in the late 1980s, but only 25 percent for the United States and just 2.5 percent for the United Kingdom. Since Japanese banks assessed creditworthiness by the value of corporate land-holdings rather than cash-flows (Murphy, 2000: 37), skyrocketing real estate prices facilitated massive corporate investments overseas. And the Nikkei 225 stock index which had rung in 1980 at 6,556 had increased by almost six times when it peaked at 38,915.87 in December 1990: this was almost twice its level before the Louvre Accord (Morgenson, 1998).

The surge in speculative activities and the outflow of large volumes of capital overseas 'hollowed out' Japanese industries and savagely deepened social polarization as prices, especially of land, skyrocketed beyond the reach of most families. As far as labor was concerned, the increasing importance of offshore production led to a sharp decline in employment opportunities, more lay-offs, and a greater coercion of labor, which were not offset by reductions in the cost of living due to the strength of the yen. According to the Japanese Ministry of Labor, 577,000 jobs were lost in the manufacturing sector due to increased imports in 1986, and an additional 850,000 jobs due to declining exports (Steven, 1990: 48, table 2.5). Major corporations achieved further economies in labor costs by resorting to the employment of more part-time workers, particularly housewives (Itoh, 1992: 130; Douglass, 1993a: 103). Additionally, Japanese manufacturers sought to raise the intensity of work by sharply decreasing overtime and deregulating standard work procedures (Eccleston, 1989: 238; Steven, 1990: 56–62). By 1990, annual working hours for Japanese automobile workers averaged 2,275 compared with an average of 1,650–1,750 for French and German workers (McCormack, 2001: 80).

The widening gap between those with and those without assets threatened to unravel the domestic coalitions that had kept the Liberal Democratic Party in power since 1955, and prompted the Bank of Japan to raise interest rates. When the speculative boom and large capital outflows began to eviscerate the domestic coalitions underpinning the LDP, the Bank of Japan hiked interest rates to dampen speculation. However, this caused so precipitous a drop in land and stock values – between June and December 1990, land values in Tokyo declined by 50 percent and the Nikkei index by 40 percent – as well as of the yen in foreign currency markets, that Japanese banks were exposed to potentially devastating losses. The combined effect of sharp declines in bonds, stocks, and property values led to enormous losses for Japanese banks – with estimates of losses from imprudent loans running to ¥30 trillion. The full extent of their losses were, however, camouflaged by so-called *tobashi* accounts[3] and by shifting losses to off-shore banking centers like the Cayman Islands (Leyshon, 1994: 134–5).

In a bid to recoup these losses, Japanese banks increased their lending to corporations and financial institutions in East and Southeast Asia.[4] Since Japan accounted for fully one-third of world savings, bankers from overseas could borrow yen at less than 1 percent and then lend it to banks in economies along Asia's Pacific Rim and elsewhere at 2.5 to 3 percent. In turn, East and Southeast Asian banks charged their domestic investors 8 to 10 percent, and thus earned themselves a nice markup. Alternatively, investors from the region could bypass their domestic bankers and borrow directly from banks in Japan, the United States, or Western Europe – though interest rates on the US dollar were not as low as on the yen, at approximately 5 percent, it was still cheaper than loans in the rupiah, the baht, the peso, the ringgit, or the won. US investors even borrowed yen at low rates of interest, converted it into dollars, and lent it across the world. 'In fact,' Ron Bevacqua (1998: 415) notes, 'US investors borrowed, converted, and re-lent so much yen that the USA, though the world's largest debtor became a net lender of long-term capital in the mid-1990s.'

To put this in perspective, it should be recalled that private and public inflows of capital to 'newly industrializing countries' were relatively equal in 1984 – $35.6 billion and $33.4 billion respectively. Since then, the former increased at five times the rate of the latter. By 1995, private capital amounted to 75 percent of all investments in the 'developing world' and portfolio capital rose from 2 percent of total net capital inflows to these countries in 1987 to 50 percent in 1996. Put differently, private capital investments in 'developing countries' in 1996 and 1997 alone equaled the $300 billion in loans provided by the World Bank in the first 50 years of its existence for 6,000 projects spread across 140 countries (Winters, 2000: 36).

The Asian rimlands accounted for a disproportionate share of these capital inflows. Credit grew rapidly between 1990 and 1996: by 24 percent per annum in Thailand, by 16 percent in Malaysia, by 14 percent in Indonesia, by 10 percent in South Korea, and by an extraordinary 52 percent in 1996 alone in the Philippines (Jayanth, 1998; Fuerbringer, 1997; Uchitelle, 1997a; Uchitelle, 1997b; McDermott and Wessel, 1997). In absolute amounts, capital flows to South Korea, Indonesia, Malaysia, Thailand, and the Philippines grew from $47 billion in 1994 to $56 billion in 1996 (Wade, 1998a: 1539).

The 1980s thus witnessed considerable changes in the geography of manufacture. The decision by the US Federal Reserve to raise interest rates not only led to the collapse of debt-led strategies of industrialization in Eastern Europe and Latin America, but also to the liquidation of obsolete plant and equipment in the United States and to an intense downward pressure on US wages which discouraged new investments in capital goods. If a high dollar led to a secular decline in US manufacturing, high interest rates ensured that the ballooning Japanese trade surpluses were invested in dollar-denominated assets while growing US protectionism and low wages led to increasing flows of Japanese investments across the Pacific. As the continuing decline of US manufacturing became an increasingly politically contentious issue, pressure from the Reagan Administration forced a realignment of exchange-rates, raising the value of the yen. Higher production costs led to a redirection of Japanese investments in manufacturing towards the Asian rimlands and diverted capital flows from the United States. Since this threatened to destabilize the global financial flows, Japanese authorities lowered their domestic interest rates in 1987. This triggered speculation on so large a scale that it severely ruptured the social compact that had kept the LDP in power for so long, by rapidly widening gaps in income and wealth. When the Bank of Japan tried to ameliorate these conditions by raising the rate of interest, it not only dampened speculation but led to a steep fall in real estate and equity prices and saddled banks with heavy losses. In order to recoup these losses, Japanese banks massively expanded their loans to enterprises and financial institutions along the Asian rimlands. This rapid infusion of capital fundamentally ruptured regulatory mechanisms in these states and led to chronic overproduction, as we see in the next section.

A paradise of the blind

Two to three decades of sustained economic growth had so fundamentally transformed social topographies along the Asian rimlands that the coalitional logic of the developmental state was rendered increasingly precarious. Rising wage and other costs had led to a trans-border expansion of corporate production and procurement networks and lessened the dependence of enterprises on governments for protection and finance. Where large-scale factory complexes had been installed, as in South Korea and Indonesia, the growth of an industrial working class had made the exclusion of labor from power increasingly untenable. Economic growth had also tipped ethnic balances in multi-ethnic states and led to the rise of new factions demanding a proportionate share of the fruits of development. Rising incomes had gradually led to the emergence of strong middle class movements seeking a democratization of power in one-party dictatorships. In some states, where outflows of investments due to rising costs began to exceed capital inflows, 'administrative guidance' became increasingly ineffective. Singapore alone, as we shall see, was an exception to these trends since the government there had prevented the emergence of a large domestic bourgeoisie independent of the state while also closely controlling trade union activities.

Elsewhere, inflows of foreign investments allowed governing elites to counter the rising power of labor and to accommodate new factions into ruling coalitions. In Taiwan, leading native islanders were inducted into the governing elite. A strong working class in South Korea forced the military regime to hand over power by instituting an electoral democracy while South Korean industrialists sought to weaken the power of labor by investing more vigorously overseas. Taking advantage of movements toward economic liberalization, Sino-Indonesian entrepreneurs forged business alliances with President Suharto's children and cronies and transformed state enterprises into private monopolies.

To tap into cheap money from Japan, and international financial markets more generally, many East and Southeast Asian states offered off-the-book guarantees for loans incurred by their domestic industrial enterprises and financial institutions, pegged their currencies to the US dollar, deregulated cross-border flows of capital, and liberalized their financial sectors. This was tantamount to the wholesale liquidation of the apparatus of the developmental state as the liberalization of capital flows conferred greater priority on inflation control rather than on strategic economic planning while currency pegs constrained governments' options in macro-economic management. Nevertheless, unlike the case of low- and middle-income economies elsewhere in the world where highly-indebted governments were steamrollered into liberalizing their financial sectors by pressure from international financial institutions and core states, deregulation in East and Southeast Asia had the support of large domestic constituencies (Moran, 1991: 111).

However, as we shall see below, the erosion of the developmental state without associated changes in the operational practices of enterprises created the conditions for an economic meltdown. Whereas high debt–equity ratios had once allowed large industrial conglomerates to meet production standards set by elite economic bureaucracies, the dismantling of regulatory controls led to an uncoordinated expansion of production and further hollowed out industrial sectors in Japan and South Korea. Meanwhile the implementation of market reforms in China contributed to the decline of manufacturing sectors in Taiwan and Hong Kong.

In the first instance, the scale and velocity of manufacturing investments had transformed social structures all across the region. As the South Korean government initiated a heavy industrialization drive in the 1970s, the installation of huge factory complexes with a concentration of large numbers of workers had led to the emergence of a strong working class which spearheaded the successful drive against the dictatorship. The disproportionate concentration of large industries around Seoul and along the Pusan–Kyongsang corridor on the southeastern coast facilitated a more effective mobilization of grievances against a harsh and cruel regime of industrial relations – spectacularly manifested during the 1985–89 strike waves. The higher capital intensities and greater degrees of integration of production processes in large, vertically integrated industrial complexes (Douglass, 1993b; Koo, 2001: 41–4, 173–9) promoted the ability of a militant minority to disrupt the complex divisioning of labor within the corporation or, as Richard Edwards (1979: 128) nicely puts it, '[technical] control link[s] the entire plant's workforce, and when the line stop[s] every worker necessarily join[s] the strike.' The shift in the focus of workers' protests from intolerable working conditions to broader political conditions was inevitable given the structure of the military regime (Koo, 2001: 153–87). Unable to create a mass party with front organizations, the Park regime had created state organs as substitutes and directly intruded in industrial relations, as we saw in Chapter 3.

Similarly, high levels of labor militancy also characterized Indonesian export-oriented industrialization in the 1980s. The expansion of employment in the manufacturing sector from 2.7 million workers (6.5 percent of the total labor force) in 1971 to 4.4 million in 1980 (8.5 percent of labor force) and 8.2 million in 1990 (11.6 percent) – of whom 3 million were employed in medium- and large-scale units – was accompanied by a steady increase in the incidence of strikes. Moreover, almost 40 percent of all manufacturing employment in the archipelago were concentrated in two regions of Java – the Jakarta, Bogor, Tangerang, and Bekasi region in the west, and in Surabaya, Malang, Mojokerto, and Gresik in the east. The number of strikes, which had never been more than 35 a year between 1965 and the mid-1970s, rose to 72 in 1979, to more than 100 a year in 1980 and 1981, to over 200 in 1982, and to pre-1965 levels by 1990, according to official sources, and considerably more according to others including US embassy estimates (Hadiz, 1997: 208, n. 8). Most of these were concentrated in the export-oriented sectors – especially in the garments, textiles, and footwear industries – and primarily stemmed from the government's inability to ensure that employers followed regulations (Hadiz, 1997: 111–13; Berger, 1997: 350).

Despite the hollowing out of Japanese industry, high current account surpluses permitted corporations and enterprise-based unions to maintain their commitment to employment security until 1992. However, 'lifetime employment' did not imply employment in the same job. Since the larger conglomerates had operations in several sectors, workers could be assigned to different divisions, locations, and companies. Given the hierarchical nature of corporate subcontracting networks, employees approaching retirement age in 'parent' firms were sometimes seconded – or sent on *shukko* – to subcontractors or even to unrelated companies. In such arrangements the worker continued to receive his seniority wages and benefits – with the parent company picking up the difference between the rates paid by the subcontractor and those to which the employee was eligible if still working for the parent company. More importantly, shifting workers to other plants or job classifications prevented the type of worker–citizen alliances that became common as plants were closed in Western Europe and North America. Consequently, towns declined where shipyards, factories, and coal mines were closed (Shapira, 1993: 239–46).

The smaller size of industrial establishments in Taiwan and their more balanced regional distribution, as well as the GMD's corporatist incorporation of labor, was not conducive to militant workers' movements. However, as the GMD attempted to circumvent Taiwan's increasing diplomatic isolation since the 1970s by luring TNCs to the island, it paved the way for the rise of an indigenous bourgeoisie and undermined the dominance of mainland émigrées. Indeed, because Taiwan had large foreign exchange reserves, as Thomas Gold (1988b: 198) underscored, the choice to facilitate inflows of foreign investments rather than buying technology outright was to give the TNCs a stake in its continued survival. Inflows of foreign investments provided opportunities for the island's dense network of small firms – unable to scale the barriers to international trade by themselves – to act as original equipment manufacturers and subcontractors. Recognizing the shifting balance of ethnic forces, President Chiang Ching-kuo began to select his vice-presidents from the native islanders. Emboldened by support from the US House of Representatives which passed a resolution urging the GMD to allow rival political parties to function, by the People's Power movement in the Philippines, and the democratic movement in South Korea, some prominent native Taiwanese dissidents defied martial law to announce the formation of the Democratic Progressive Party (DPP) in September 1986. Despite the DPP's poor performance in the ensuing elections, the greater assertiveness of the native islanders combined with the lure of cheap labor in mainland China led the GMD regime to drop its Cold War policy of no cooperation with the People's Republic of China (Chun, 2000; Chu, 2000).

In contrast to the political upheavals in South Korea and Taiwan as a consequence of rapid economic growth, political quiescence in Singapore validates Barrington Moore's thesis: 'no bourgeoisie, no democracy.' The island-state's compact size and smaller population and its reliance on transnational corporations for investments and the scale of investments of its government-controlled companies implied that the ruling PAP did not face comparable challenges to its corporatist control. Singapore's political stability, excellent transport and communications infrastructure, and well-educated workforce made it a favored location for regional headquarters and service centers for transnational corporations and partly compensated for the decline in blue-collar employment. This was complemented by an expansion of profit-oriented statutory boards as white-collar workers approached one-fourth of the total labor force by the early 1990s (Rodan, 1997).

When the Sino-British agreement conditioned political activity in Hong Kong, the growing importance of the China trade had led to the eclipse of British *hongs* – by the mid-1980s, the Jardine group had been downsized while the Li Ka-shing and the Y. K. Pao families had acquired the Hutchison and Wheelock Marden groups. Hong Kong industrialists who exploited lucrative business opportunities in China formed an alliance with the Chinese state and were appointed as representatives of Hong Kong in the Chinese People's Political Consultative Conference and the National People's Congress (So, 2002).

When strong workers' movement stymied similar attempts at repression in South Korea, capital flight, decentralization of production, increased mechanization, and a better coordination of corporate strategies during wage negotiations through the National Association of Manufacturers (founded in 1989) and the Federation of Korean Industries enabled the *chaebol* to substantially claw back the gains won by workers by 1992 (Koo, 1990; Koo, 1993: 158–9; Koo, 2001: 189–93; Kwon and O'Donnell, 2001: 132–50). This is indicated by Figures 5.1 and 5.2. Figure 5.1 indicates that the percentage of the industrial labor force employed in units with less than 50 employees rose steadily while those in units with more than 500 employees declined equally steadily. At the same time, Figure 5.2 indicates that the wage-gap between employees in large firms and those in small firms grew especially rapidly after the strike waves of the mid-1980s.

Higher wages led to a massive transfer of manufacturing operations to neighboring locations in Asia, as well as to the United States and Europe – by one estimate, manufacturing wages in South Korea were 30 percent higher than in Britain (*The Economist*, 1997d). Unlike the outward investment of Japanese conglomerates in the 1980s, financed largely by profits generated by their *zaitech* activities, the overseas expansion of the *chaebol* was financed by borrowing on a large scale. Indeed, since the late 1980s,

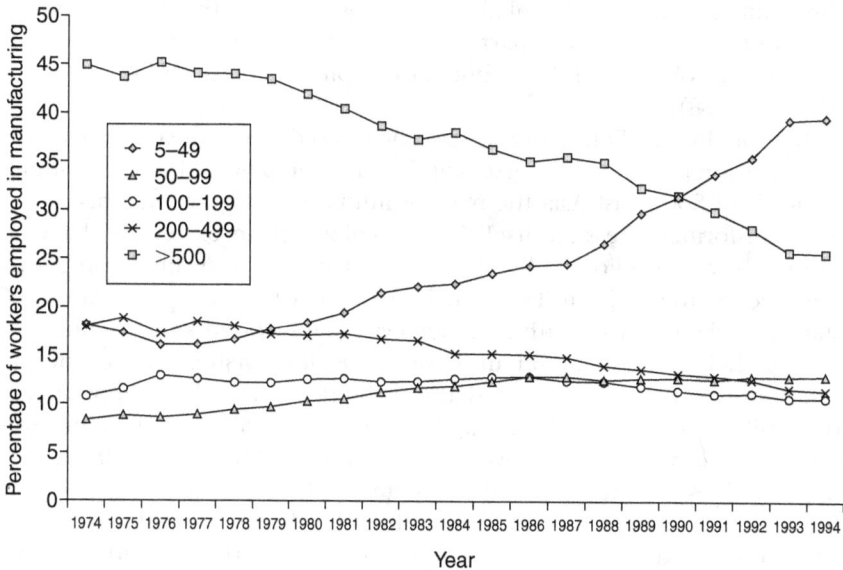

Figure 5.1 South Korea: Structure of industrial labor force by firm size.

Source: Korea Statistical Yearbook (various years).

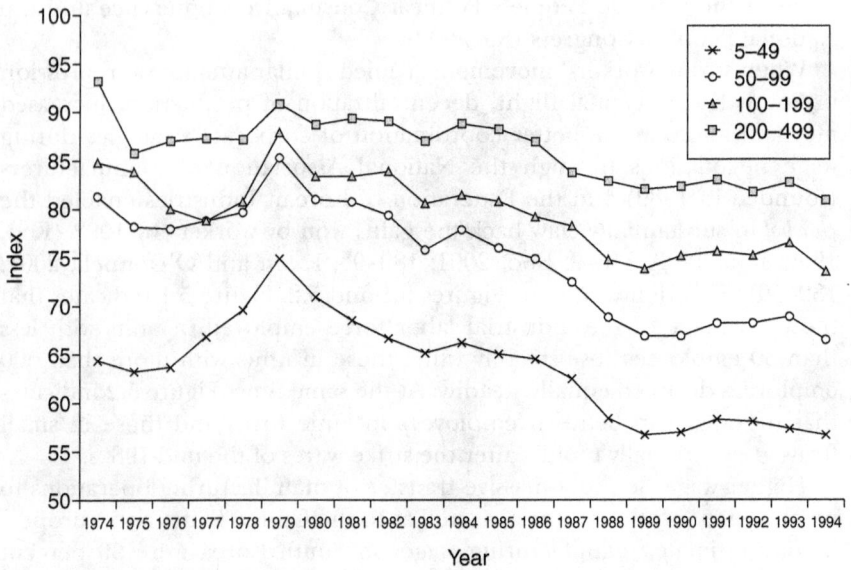

Figure 5.2 South Korea: Index of annual average wages in manufacturing.

Source: Korea Statistical Yearbook (various years).

the changing context of global capital flows also led the *Junkyungryun* – the South Korean counterpart of Japan's *Keidanren*, dominated by the *chaebol* – to lobby the EPB to liberalize capital markets (McMichael and Kim, 1994: 38).

If capitalists in South Korea saw cheap credit as a means to expand their corporate networks overseas and curtail the power of labor at home, in much of Southeast Asia the massive influx of foreign capital had virtually transformed the state itself into a 'colony of an extremely dynamic private sector' (Bello *et al.*, 1998: 14). Structural adjustment programs imposed by the IMF on Thailand in 1982 had led to a privatization of state-owned enterprises with a unique twist as it involved key generals converting their political power into corporate directorships and economic assets: one study even claimed that only 50 percent of the generals occupied military positions (Bernard, 1999: 187)! The subsequent twenty-five-fold increase in Japanese investments between 1985 and 1989 created opportunities for many provincial elites and for small Bangkok-based firms, as the old banking families who had thus far dominated Thai industry could not satisfy Japanese demands for local partners (Phongpaichit and Baker, 2000: 27; Hewison, 2000: 198). Resources of the old Sino-Thai elite had also been severely depleted by the economic downturn of the early 1980s that had hollowed out the financial sector while market saturation had burdened the large industrial houses with over-capacity. Without access to their own banks, the provincial elites who stepped into the breach pressed for financial liberalization as they could then bypass domestic banks and borrow from international money markets.

By the mid-1980s, a large Sino-Indonesian capitalist class with close ties to President Suharto's family and associates had taken advantage of a collapse in oil prices to successfully lobby for reforms that had opened potentially lucrative sectors – banking, television, transport and telecommunications, and electricity generation – that had hitherto been the exclusive preserve of state-owned corporations. Even though the share of private investment in total investment rose from 51 percent to almost 65 percent between 1980 and 1990 as a result of these measures, this did not necessarily signify greater competition. Rather, it symbolized the transformation of public monopoly to private monopoly dominated by the Suharto family and a coterie of Sino-Indonesian capitalists (Robison and Rosser, 2000: 175–6). Equally significantly, by the early 1990s, although Liem Sioe-Liong was one of the major beneficiaries of this system and a close business partner of President Suharto, more than half the earnings of his Salim Group were derived from holdings outside Indonesia (Tracy and Tracy, 1999: 7).

Across the Malacca Straits, falling commodity prices and rising public debt also promoted privatization in Malaysia. Again, rather than the dismantling and selling off of loss-making state enterprises, profitable state monopolies in energy and telecommunications tended to be privatized.[5] Entrepreneurs were also awarded contracts for large infrastructural projects, and hitherto closed fields such as health care and tertiary education were opened to them. Profitability in these sectors stemmed from government contracts and licenses – awarded to those with close links to the government – than from technological innovation or efficiency (Khoo Boo Teik, 2000: 218–19; Yoshihara, 1988; Gomez and Jomo, 1997: 79–116).

The Singapore government also divested its holdings from the late 1980s but as the government enjoyed an overall budget surplus, this did not indicate a decline in government intervention in the economy. Instead, proceeds from divestment were plowed back into further investments either in Singapore itself or overseas – between 1988 and 1990, 288 new government-linked companies (GLCs) were created. These GLCs either by themselves, or in joint-ventures, spearheaded a massive expansion of Singapore's overseas investments (Rodan, 2001). Finally, in the Philippines, President Fidel Ramos initiated a privatization program in 1992 (Hutchison, 2001: 60–2).

Governments that had begun to peg their currencies to the US dollar to encourage capital inflows after the Plaza Accord began to liberalize their financial sectors in the 1990s to facilitate the inflow of cheap money from Japan and elsewhere. As the shift to export-oriented industrialization in the 1990s gathered steam in Thailand, the Anand government largely dismantled controls over foreign exchange in 1992. The following year, the government established the Bangkok International Banking Facility (BIBF), seeking to turn Bangkok into a regional financial center by enabling local and foreign commercial banks to take deposits from overseas and to lend these funds to both local and foreign borrowers. As the entry of new firms to the banking sector remained tightly regulated, the liberalization of exchange controls licensed an unchecked expansion of finance companies which were not similarly constrained. Ninety-one of these companies accounted for 25 percent of total credit by 1996, when Thailand's external debt had climbed to 51 percent of GDP (MacIntyre, 1999: 149; Lauridsen, 1998: 138; Phongpaichit and Baker, 2000: 25).

Significantly, the liberalization of the financial sector and deregulation over capital flows coincided with a tapering-off of inflows of foreign direct investments to Thailand and of Japanese investments in particular.[6] However, by then a model of accumulation lubricated by foreign loans had taken hold and this was manifested by a shift in power from the old banking families to provincial capitalists aligned to foreign investors and to newer players in real estate, finance, and communications. Moreover, an expansion of electoral politics had led to closer collaboration between businesses and politicians and it is a testimony to the strength of this alliance that the military has refrained from intervening during the crisis of 1997–98 (Hewison, 2000; Phongpaichit and Baker, 1999; Bello *et al.*, 1998: 17–23).

In South Korea, though the Chun Doo Wan regime had privatized state-owned banks in the 1980s, the banks themselves had been tightly regulated until Kim Young Sam deregulated the financial sector as a part of his *segyehwa* ('globalization') strategy in 1994. Deregulation exposed the weaknesses of financial skills in the country as the Kim government granted banking licenses freely: nine in 1994 and 15 in 1996 when there had been only a total of six banks before 1994. The rapidity of financial deregulation meant that many of the new banks and financial institutions borrowing from off-shore sources were family enterprises without the skills and experience required to handle large volumes of capital and calculate exchange risks. Hence, the country's foreign debt almost trebled from $44 billion in 1993 to $120 billion in September 1997. Perhaps even more troubling was the fact that while 64 percent of overseas borrowings by these banks were short-term loans, over 85 percent of loans they dispersed were on a long-term basis and hence left them extremely vulnerable. It is also revealing that in the mid-1990s, FDI amounted to only 2.5 percent of South Korea's GDP while the corresponding figures for China was 20 percent and for Taiwan 7.4 percent (Chang Ha-Joon, 1998: 223, 226; Cumings, 1998: 50, 55; Wade, 1998a: 1539; Palat, 2001: 4478).

Financial deregulation did not proceed to a similar extent in Malaysia and Indonesia, as indicated by the higher exposure of South Korean and Thai banks and financial institutions to overseas loans in Table 5.3, while non-bank enterprises in Malaysia and Indonesia accounted for the bulk of their overseas loans. However, in 1993 Malaysia too established a mechanism to tap off-shore sources – the Lanuan International Offshore Financial Center – to access loans from 'debt-pushing' Japanese and continental European banks and the net foreign liabilities of commercial banks more than doubled from 10.3 billion ringgit at the end of 1995 to 25.2 billion ringgit in June 1997 while their net external reserves declined from −5.3 million ringgit to −17.7 billion ringgit over the same time-span (Jomo, 1998: 182–3). And in the Philippines where a favored few banks were the repositories of high-interest, low-risk treasury bills, the banks re-lent money they had borrowed from the government back to the government at much higher rates (Hutchcroft, 1998: 172–4, 193–5).

Close interpersonal relations between government and business elites meant that regimes routinely made off-the-book guarantees to underwrite loans to favored companies. Loans to private enterprises and financial institutions were hence assumed to be tantamount to sovereign debt and as governments in the region consistently produced surpluses, their ability to service debts was rarely questioned. In return for off-the-book guarantees by governments to underwrite borrowings by their domestic financial institutions, these institutions were routinely obliged to make loans to enterprises deemed to be in the 'national interest' and to those owned by people with the right political connections.

During the era of high-speed economic growth, these arrangements so admirably suited both banks and borrowers that financial institutions in the Asian 'miracles,' and those in South Korea and Thailand in particular, borrowed tens of billions of dollars overseas and agreed to repay the principal on a few months' notice to economize on interest expenses (Passell, 1998). This is indicated by Table 5.3, which reveals that short-term loans consistently overshadowed loans with longer maturities, except for Taiwan where cross-border interbank borrowing data largely reflects activities of off-shore banking units. While the data presented in this table reflects the activities of banks reporting to the Bank for International Settlements (various years) rather than total external indebtedness of various countries, it is indicative of the magnitude of short-term loans maturing in the 12 months or less to mid-1998.

Pegging currencies to the dollar and liberalization of cross-border capital flows transformed the competitive conditions that had facilitated the alliance between entrepreneurs and political leaders. Dependence on capital inflows conferred greater priority on inflation control than on strategic economic planning since a currency depreciation would escalate real debt burdens. Currency pegs, adopted to contain inflation, constrained governments' options in macro-economic management. Hence, accompanying the relaxation of controls on capital flows, governments first marginalized and then abolished elite economic bureaucracies. In South Korea, for instance, the Kim Young Sam government first subordinated

Table 5.3 Foreign debt of selected Asian economies

Positions vis-à-vis	Consolidated cross-border claims in all currencies and local claims in non-local currencies					
	Total (billions of US dollars)	Distribution by maturity		Distribution by sector		
		Up to and including one year	Over one year	Banks	Public sector	Non-bank private sector
	(percentage of total consolidated claims)					
South Korea						
end 1995	77.5	70.0	18.8	64.4	8.0	27.6
mid-1996	88.0	70.8	19.2	65.7	6.7	27.4
end 1996	100.0	67.5	20.0	65.9	5.7	28.3
mid-1997	104.2	68.0	19.7	65.3	4.2	30.4
end 1997	93.4	62.8	23.3	59.2	4.3	36.4
mid-1998	72.4	45.8	38.9	57.0	6.6	36.3
Thailand						
end 1995	62.8	69.4	27.3	41.0	3.6	55.2
mid-1996	69.4	68.9	27.4	40.3	3.1	56.4
end 1996	70.1	65.2	30.2	36.9	3.2	59.6
mid-1997	69.4	65.7	30.4	37.6	2.8	59.5
end 1997	58.5	65.8	30.7	29.9	3.1	66.9
mid-1998	46.8	59.3	36.5	26.1	4.2	69.6
Indonesia						
end 1995	44.5	61.9	34.8	20.1	15.1	64.7
mid-1996	49.3	60.0	35.8	20.5	13.3	66.2
end 1996	55.5	61.7	34.1	21.2	12.5	66.2
mid-1997	58.7	59.0	35.0	21.1	11.1	67.7
end 1997	58.2	60.6	36.1	19.9	11.8	68.3
mid-1998	50.3	55.0	41.7	14.2	15.1	70.6
Malaysia						
end 1995	16.8	47.2	40.9	26.4	12.4	60.4
mid-1996	20.1	49.7	41.1	28.1	11.4	60.5
end 1996	22.2	50.3	36.2	29.3	9.0	61.8
mid-1997	28.8	56.4	30.8	36.4	6.4	57.1
end 1997	27.3	52.7	37.8	35.3	6.4	58.2
mid-1998	23.0	48.6	41.6	31.2	6.6	62.1
Taiwan						
end 1995	22.5	87.2	11.8	63.7	1.7	34.6
mid-1996	22.5	86.4	12.7	57.7	2.5	39.8
end 1996	22.4	86.4	13.8	57.8	2.1	40.0
mid-1997	25.2	87.3	11.3	61.6	1.6	36.8
end 1997	26.0	81.6	15.4	55.2	1.6	42.5
mid-1998	23.2	80.1	16.6	56.4	1.5	41.5
Philippines						
end 1995						
mid-1996	10.8	55.1	39.3	32.0	25.4	42.6
end 1996	13.3	58.2	35.2	39.5	20.5	40.0
mid-1997	14.1	58.9	30.7	38.9	13.1	48.0
end 1997	19.7	60.4	34.0	45.2	12.2	42.6
mid-1998	17.8	56.7	37.1	45.5	12.4	41.6

Source: Bank for International Settlements, *Consolidated International Banking Statistics*, Basle: Bank for International Settlements (various years).

Note
Totals may not add up due to rounding and to the inclusion of unallocated amounts in country aggregates.

the EPB to the Ministry of Finance in 1993, and then abolished it altogether (Chang Ha-Joon, 1998: 227; Cumings, 1998: 54; Henderson, 1999: 346). Since the more sophisticated industries in Japan and South Korea had lobbied the government to dismantle tariffs and eliminate exchange controls, government intervention was no longer directed toward promoting technological sophistication and capture of export markets. Instead, it was focused on protecting inefficient industries with high employment like steel, shipping, and textiles in Japan (Pempel, 1998: 148).

If high debt to equity ratios had earlier enabled conglomerates to fulfill targets set by elite economic bureaucracies, the cross-border expansion of their corporate structures and deregulation of controls over capital flows in conditions of excess global liquidity led to a rapid expansion of manufacturing capacity along Asia's Pacific Rim. However, whereas previous waves of outward expansion of Japanese and South Korean capital had been coordinated by pilot economic bureaucracies, the erosion of regulatory mechanisms removed checks on predatory competition between *chaebol* for capturing and retaining market share by expanding output. Uncoordinated investments resulted in an over-expansion of manufacturing capacity and were linked to a hollowing out of domestic industries in Japan, Hong Kong, South Korea, and to a lesser extent, in Taiwan.

The relaxation of government controls and the easy availability of credit permitted heads of *chaebol* to compete against each other more vigorously by constructing bigger and more sophisticated plants over a wider range of industries. In particular, managements continued to elevate the capture of market share above all other considerations. Thus, although massive investments may have increased sales for the *chaebol* – rising at an annual rate of 8.2 percent between 1988 and 1992 compared with 3.7 percent for the United States and 2.6 percent for Germany – their profits continued to plummet. According to one World Bank study, as measured by real return on assets in the local currency, profitability in South Korea between 1988 and 1996 was 3.7 percent as opposed to 4.1 percent in Japan, 4.4 percent in Singapore, 4.6 percent in Hong Kong, 6.3 percent in Malaysia, 6.7 percent in Taiwan, 7.1 percent in Indonesia, 7.9 percent in the Philippines, and 9.8 percent in Thailand (Woo-Cumings, 1999: 122–3).

Even the unbridled expansion of production facilities was insufficient to accommodate the influx of capital and much of this excess capital was diverted into speculation in real estate. In South Korea, for instance, foreign portfolio investment inflows rose from $9 billion in 1990 to almost $121 billion in 1996, dwarfing FDI flows which merely increased from $7.2 billion to $19.5 billion over the same period. In conditions of rapid urban growth, this large influx of capital suggests speculation in real estate and infrastructure development (Henderson, 1999: 345). Similarly in Thailand, loans from financial institutions to property developers skyrocketed from a total of 264 billion baht in 1993 to 767 billion baht by March 1996, and by the following year residential vacancy rates in the country were estimated to be between 25 and 30 percent, and vacancy rates for offices in Bangkok were 14 percent (Lauridsen, 1998: 139; Bello *et al.*, 1998: 26–8). In the Philippines, financial deregulation, high interest rates, and stable exchange-rates led to inflows of some $19.4 billion net foreign portfolio investments between 1993 and 1997 while industrial growth dropped from a 17 percent annual rate in mid-1993 to −2.3 percent in mid-1997. In Malaysia, commercial bank lending to manufacturing, agriculture, and mining accounted for only about 25 percent of total bank lending and possibly less for foreign borrowings since these had to be backed by collateral in real estate or stocks (Jomo, 1998: 183). Finally, in Indonesia real estate loans accounted for about 25 percent of the total exposure of both banks and finance companies by 1997 (Bello, 1997).

Conversely, the two 'dragon' economies that fared the best in the crisis – Singapore and Taiwan – had mechanisms to moderate property market speculation. Though privately owned commercial banks were licensed from the late 1980s in Taiwan, the central bank mandated that their reserve requirements remain at 24 percent of their deposits. By contracting money supply, this requirement dampened speculative activity. Additionally, the government continued to regulate cross-border flows of capital. The Singapore Government also retained controls over the financial sector as well as restrictive trading regulations for the stock exchange. The requirement that all foreign stocks, excluding Malaysian ones, be denominated in foreign currencies shifted the exchange-rate risk onto would-be speculators and dampened their activities. Similarly, the state's central role in providing housing in Singapore, and the government enforced savings scheme, the Central Provident Fund, depressed speculation in real estate (Henderson, 1999: 359).

What was especially noteworthy was that despite high levels of borrowing, investment in research and development was insignificant. Though the government had stressed technological upgrading as a key policy objective, public spending on research and development amounted to only 0.4 percent of South Korea's GNP. In the early 1990s, IBM alone invested more in research and development than all South Korean corporations combined (Bello, 1998a; Lee, 1998).

Taiwan's large foreign exchange reserves meant that its government- and GMD-owned enterprises had little difficulties in acquiring technology through licensing agreements while small firms upgraded their technological levels through their OEM arrangements with foreign firms. Nevertheless, low government outlays on research and development meant that there was little attempt to adapt these technologies or for innovation. Since small firms depended more on kinship networks than on the government-owned banks for finances, they rarely had enough resources to institute product changes or process technology – with most firms spending only about 0.5 percent of their budgets in research and development in the mid-1980s. The one exception to this trend was in the electronics sector where the pace of change forced local firms to invest in research to keep up with their competitors (Simon, 1988b: 210–15).

Unsurprisingly, the situation was even worse in Hong Kong where a 1994 Federation of Hong Kong Industries study discovered that only 30 percent of its members carried out any research and development activities at all. On another measure, research and development expenditure as a percentage of GDP amounted to only 0.2 percent for Hong Kong in 1995 compared with 1.4 percent for Taiwan and 1.2 percent for Singapore. The adverse impact of low outlays on innovation was especially hard on the electronics sector where producers in Hong Kong were severely disadvantaged by competitors from lower-waged economies like Malaysia and Thailand (Yeung, 2000: 149; So, n.d.).

The rapid elimination of barriers to foreign investments exacerbated the problem of overproduction. Following the lead of Japanese transplant factories in North America, American and European firms also constructed factories in Asia and Latin America to circumvent real or imagined barriers and to exploit wage and cost differentials between and among different segments of the world market for labor and commodities. Consequently, though car exports from Japan fell from 8.6 million vehicles in 1986 to 2.9 million in 1995, only one Japanese car factory had been closed. Symbolically, 1995 was the first year when the value of Japanese off-shore manufacturing (¥41.2 trillion) surpassed the value of exports from the Japanese home islands (¥39.2 trillion) (Uchitelle, 1997b; *The Economist*, 1997c; Pempel, 1997: 350).

Accelerated transfers of labor-intensive manufacturing operations to areas with large reserves of docile, low-wage labor undermined the strategy of low-cost, export-oriented industrialization as it serially reduced benefits accruing to each state. Moreover, while manufacturing capacity was being expanded through debt-led industrialization strategies in East and Southeast Asia, real take-home hourly pay in the United States had dropped by 10.4 percent in 1994 from its postwar high in 1972 and manufacturing employment had fallen in the US by 14 percent between 1979 and 1994.[7] By 1994, US manufacturing wages were 25 percent lower than Japanese wages and about 14 percent lower than average European wages. At the very least, while production was increasing at a galloping pace, markets were not expanding proportionately and as William Grieder (1997: 221) pointedly observed:

> Shipping high-wage jobs to low-wage economies has obvious, immediate benefits. But roughly speaking, it also replaces high-wage consumers with low-wage ones. That exchange is debilitating the entire system.

The impact of the relocation of the manufacturing processes was very uneven. The smaller population base and size of firms in Taiwan and in the two city-states of Hong Kong and Singapore implied that enterprises based in these locations were more easily able to restructure their activities to more skill-intensive processes – sourcing production to affiliated factories overseas, product design, quality control, and marketing. Additionally, Hong Kong and Singapore were also able to transform themselves from offshore export-platforms to regional headquarters and financial centers and service hubs for large transnational corporations – though the Singapore government also provided a raft of direct and indirect subsidies to create a more capital- and technology-intensive industrial sector (Lim, 1999: 109). These were not viable options for states with much larger population bases since product design, quality control, and distribution were no substitutes for mass production.

Nowhere was the problem of over-production more evident than along Asia's Pacific shores. Between 1991 and 1996, manufacturing investment along the Asian rimlands was almost three times the level in Japan (Brenner, 2002: 117). Overall, investment in the 'dragons' and mini-dragons averaged about 35 percent of their gross domestic product in 1996, with Malaysia registering the highest rate of 43 percent (*The Economist*, 1997a; Ridding and Kynge, 1998). Nothing, it appeared to the region's boosters, could derail this pattern of relentless growth. An unchecked and uncoordinated increase in productive capacity was, however, to create its own problems as we see in the next section.

Things fall apart

Hypnotized by the rapid growth of manufacturing capacity all along Asia's Pacific coasts, observers seldom recognized that while the wholesale demolition of the foundations of the 'developmental state' emancipated enterprises from state-centric industrial policies, the easy availability of credit meant that there was no incentive for corporate leaders to change their operational procedures. If the single-minded pursuit of increasing their share of the world market in particular products had enabled many Japanese and South Korean corporations to leap-frog over well-established American and European competitors in some of the most technologically sophisticated sectors, this strategy had been predicated on national industrial plans which had serially targeted strategic sectors of increasing complexity.

The transnational expansion of corporate production and procurement networks had, however, also eroded the national foundations of accumulation. The rapid growth of Japanese investments overseas, as we shall see here, was accompanied by the creation of several competing transnational inter-enterprise alliances. As large Japanese corporations used their favorable cash-flow positions to enter into sectors unrelated to their main lines of business, it also loosened their ties with smaller subcontractors and rendered hierarchical subcontracting networks increasingly anachronistic. Elsewhere, the continued emphasis on capturing market share through debt-led patterns of industrial expansion without the administrative guidance provided by elite economic bureaucracies, led to rampant overproduction, often at the expense of technological innovation. While these problems were obscured by the rise of the yen in the early 1990s – due to Japanese investors repatriating their capital in the aftermath of the collapse of the speculative bubble – after 1995, a sharp appreciation of the US dollar to which currencies of highly-indebted East and Southeast Asian economies were pegged severely impaired the ability of companies to service their debts and the capacity of governments to underwrite loans incurred by private enterprises.

In the first instance, while structural transformations had fundamentally ruptured the foundations of ruling coalitions, rapid industrialization and current account surpluses had obscured deepening socio-economic fissures. The crisis thrust the growing tensions caused by the changing balance of class forces into the limelight just as policy options for governments became tightly constrained and the end of the Cold War meant that the United States had no incentive to prop up authoritarian regimes. When the rising middle classes and an increasingly militant proletariat were demanding political rights in South Korea and Taiwan in the 1980s, in Japan the social coalitions carefully crafted by the LDP had begun to unravel. T. J. Pempel has argued that the exceptional longevity of Japan's conservative regime – with the LDP or its predecessor parties enjoying an uninterrupted run of power from 1948 to 1993 – was based on a coalition between big and small businesses and agriculture, and the systematic exclusion of labor.[8] The adoption of an electoral system with multi-member constituencies also insulated the LDP from voter resentment since it enabled constituents to vote against incumbents without voting for opposition party candidates.[9]

Years of steady economic expansion had, however, whittled away at the logic of this coalitional politics. Growing urbanization cast into sharp relief the 4:1 rural bias of the electoral system while the decline of the farm population and the falling share of small businesses in total economic activity made their support less critical to electoral strategies. Though the LDP continued to mollycoddle rural supporters with new subsidies, virtually making rice farmers and agricultural cooperatives 'political wards of the state' as Michael Donnelly (1984: 336) once put it, this became increasingly difficult as international pressures mounted for agricultural liberalization and the Japanese bubble burst in 1990 (McCormack, 2001: 113–48).

Meanwhile, interests of big businesses had bifurcated as the more technologically-sophisticated sectors had outgrown the need for regulatory protections while declining industries sought the twin crutches of protection and profit guarantees. The increasing prominence of transnational inter-enterprise linkages between Japanese, European, and North American corporations – ranging from research and development to shared marketing networks and cross-shareholdings, in virtually every sector – corroded the coherence of national economic policies (Pempel, 1998: 147, 160–3; Harrison, 1994; Lash and Urry, 1987; Steven, 1990: 91–2, 120–1, 126–7, 219; Sassen, 1991: 25, 66, 188–91).

Large Japanese corporations also used their favorable cash-flows to enter into sectors unrelated to their main line of business: in the 1980s, Nippon Steel formed joint venture projects with Philips to develop functional ceramics, with the US-based GTX Corporation to create computer-aided design systems, with the Concurrent Computer Corporation to produce semiconductors, and the Calgene Corporation to genetically engineer crops. Diversification of large conglomerates into new sectors further eroded their ties with smaller subcontractors who in turn sought to diversify their own operations, supplying to rival companies, and even producing goods with their own brand labels. The resultant loosening of ties sometimes led to the dissolution of associations of subcontractors. Consequently, as some highly-specialized first-tier subcontractors developed their own expertise and began supplying different companies, small businesses began to form strategic alliances of their own. By developing their own expertise, first-tier suppliers began to be more involved in product development decisions of major companies (Kiyonari, 1993: 148–50; Morales, 1994: 111; Gao, 2001: 193).

One important consequence of this trend was a loosening of the internal cohesion within *keiretsu* groupings, with the percentage of relational cross share holdings falling from 72 percent of the capitalization of the Tokyo Stock Exchange in 1987 to 60 percent in 1996. Some of the subcontractors of the bigger Japanese firms also entered into alliances with European and North American firms and followed the larger manufacturers in setting up production facilities overseas. Finally, the progressive internationalization of large Japanese firms also led to the loss of over one million manufacturing jobs in Japan between 1992 and 1995 (Shapira, 1993: 240; Pempel, 1998: 162).

Despite downward pressure on wages, years of uninterrupted growth and commitment to low unemployment rates had de-radicalized labor politics. However, with the growth of unemployment in 1992, fissures in the post-Second World War arrangements between the state, business, and labor led to a major schism in the LDP in 1993. Though the party soon regained power, the socio-economic bloc that had hitherto kept it in power was increasingly divided over the entire gamut of policy issues: taxation, deregulation, fiscal incentives, exchange-rates, and welfare. Reflecting structural changes and population shifts, the electoral system was replaced in the early 1990s. In the new system, 300 single-member seats in the lower house were complemented by 200 members chosen from 11 electoral districts on the basis of party lists and proportional representation (Pempel, 1998: 65, 158, 163–7).

Meanwhile, the decade-long fall in corporate tax rates in the United States, low domestic interest rates, and a low dollar had led to a turn-around in the US manufacturing sector by the early 1990s. Under these propitious conditions rather than incurring debt to buy back their stock, major US manufacturers sold back their shares and invested in capital stock – the net manufacturing capital stock increasing at an annual average rate of 2.4 percent between 1993 and 1997. The earlier off-shedding of obsolete stock and the induction of new equipment and plants led to a substantial increase in productivity. Correspondingly exports of manufactures grew at an annual average rate of 11.2 percent during the same period (Brenner, 2002: 67–78).

In contrast, the excess factory capacity built in Japan in the early 1980s in expectation of a continued rise in demand that never materialized meant that it took a long time for Japan to absorb the overbuilt production capacity (Gao, 2001: 196). Hence, as Japanese investors began to liquidate the extraordinary swathe of US assets they had bought during the speculative boom the greater relative demand for yen led to a new round of currency appreciation – with the exchange-rate to the dollar jumping from ¥145 in 1990 to ¥79.75 by April 1995 (Wade, 1998b: 696; Itoh, 2000: 54; Murphy, 1996: 286–7; Brenner, 2002: 113).

Though US authorities viewed the continuing appreciation of the yen – reaching ¥79.95 to the dollar – with equanimity, it soon became clear that unless the rise of the yen was reversed it would undermine Japan's ability to prop up the US current account deficit as Japanese manufacturers could not even cover their variable costs. Without capital inflows from Japan – and with high capacity utilization rates precluding a swift increase in US output – the only way for the US to bridge its current account deficit would have been to sharply cut spending. This would have been politically very damaging for the Democrats, especially after the Republican capture of the House of Representatives in 1994, and would have jeopardized President William Jefferson Clinton's re-election bid. Hence, the Clinton Administration agreed to cooperate with Japanese and German authorities in 1995 in purchasing dollars while the Japanese lowered their domestic interest rates – from 1.75 percent to 1 percent in April 1995 and even lower to 0.5 percent in September – to depreciate the yen (Murphy, 2000: 41–2; Brenner, 2002: 130–2).

This 'Reverse Plaza Accord' led to a 60 percent depreciation of the Japanese yen against the dollar between April 1995 and April 1997 and once again transformed competitive conditions along Asia's Pacific coasts. Investments that had once seemed prudent now appeared 'excessive' (Johnson, 1998: 658; Wade, 1998b: 698). The rate of growth of exports from the East and Southeast Asian economies whose currencies were pegged to the dollar declined from 20 percent in 1994 and 1995 to a mere 5 percent in 1996. Compounding their problems, China had devalued the reminbi substantially in 1994.[10] Since the Chinese devaluation coincided with a capital flight from Latin America following the collapse of the Mexican peso in 1994, the *chaebol* responded by increasing their overseas borrowings to upgrade capital equipment to compensate for their rapidly declining ability to compete in labor-intensive segments of the manufacturing process. Consequently, South Korean investment rates soared in 1994 and 1995 by 56.4 and 43.5 percent respectively. New investments were also disproportionately allocated to the heavy and chemical industries sector, which grew by 43.1 percent between 1994 and 1996, while investments in light industries grew by only 15 percent (Haggard and Mo, 2000: 200). Simultaneously, a deceleration in the rate of growth in high-income economies in 1995 and early 1996 was not compensated for by a corresponding rise in intra-Asian trade, and hence further dampened the growth of exports (*The Economist,* 1997a). Responding to pressure from the *chaebol* on the high cost of doing business, and capitalizing on the popularity that accrued to him from cashiering two military dictators, President Kim Young Sam rammed through a law outlawing the independent Korean Council of Trade Unions in December 1996 and permitting firms to lay off workers and replace strikers with scabs. Angry resistance from hundreds of thousands of workers who occupied the streets of Seoul forced the president to rescind the law within a matter of weeks (Koo, 2001: 198–201).

In this new 'scissors crisis,' the smaller East and Southeast Asian economies were trapped in a pincer movement: the depreciation of the yen made it impossible for them to compete in upstream products embodying high-level technology while they could not match the labor cost advantages of China, Vietnam, and other low-income economies. By 1997, when Hong Kong reverted to China, firms based in the former British colony accounted for almost 30 percent of the FDI for all of China, and three-quarters of workers employed by Hong Kong-based firms were in China. By 1996, about one-third of Taiwan's annual foreign investment was directed toward China and the figure may well be double that if Taiwan capital based in Hong Kong is included (You-tien Hsing, 1998; Hamilton, 1999: 56; Pempel, 1999b: 68–9). Correspondingly, the Chinese share of regional exports rose from 6 percent in the mid-1980s to 26 percent in the mid-1990s, and in 1997 China replaced South Korea as the fourth largest exporter of electronics after the United States, Japan, and Germany (Cumings, 1998: 70).

Rather than scaling down their investments in manufacturing when export markets contracted, investors continued to rapidly increase productive capacity. This aggravated the problem of overproduction and increased the downward pressure on prices and profits. By early 1997, computer memory chips which comprised about 16 percent the value of South Korean exports fell to a fifth of their levels a year ago and firms like Samsung which had relied on these chips for about 90 percent of their profits in 1995 saw their earnings collapse (Pollack, 1997; *The Economist,*

1997a; Burton and Baker, 1998). To compensate for the sharp plunge in profits, the easy availability of credit and an entrenched corporate culture of competition between *chaebol* heads encouraged Samsung to enter an already saturated automobile market, and one in which one firm (Kia Motors) had already filed for bankruptcy and another (Ssangyong) had been sold!

This merely compounded the problem of growing mountains of debt denominated largely in unhedged foreign currencies for highly leveraged firms, especially since rates of domestic liquidity and inflation in the Asian 'miracles' was far in excess of those countries to which their currencies were pegged: by 1997, banks in Indonesia, Malaysia, the Philippines, Thailand, and Singapore had collectively run up debts of $73 billion, or about 13 percent of their joint domestic output (Bremner, 1997). Fears that enterprises would not be able to repay loans incurred in dollars or yen increased after the first of the bankruptcies that were to sweep the region occurred in January 1997 with the collapse of Hanbo Steel, the sixth-largest of the South Korean *chaebol* and a relatively minor Thai construction company, Somprasong Land (Hanke, 1997).

By February, investors started off-loading their holdings in Thai baht and as Thai interest rates soared, it pricked the bubble in the speculative real estate market where it was estimated that non-performing loans accounted for 25 percent of total loans and 33 percent of the country's GDP. In turn, the collapse of property prices undermined the asset base of the country's banking system and the country's central bank, the Bank of Thailand, was compelled to lend over $8 billion to financial institutions teetering on the verge of insolvency. In addition, the bank had committed so much of its foreign exchange reserves in forward contracts in a futile bid to defend the baht's peg to the dollar that by late June, its reserves amounted to just two days' imports. The relentless pressure finally compelled the Thai government not only to free the currency from its long-standing link to the US dollar but also to renege on its equally long-standing policy to prop up insolvent financial institutions (Bello, 1997; Bardacke, 1998; Hanke, 1997).

Once exchange stability had been compromised in Thailand, and leading financial institutions allowed to fail, it undermined the twin pillars of the regional financial system: the tying of the currencies of the Asian 'miracles' to the US dollar and the ability of their governments to under-write loans to private enterprises. The tight integration of structures of capital accumulation along the eastern shores of the ocean – by the early 1990s, trade within East and Southeast Asia had surpassed that across the Pacific (Islam and Chowdhury, 1997: 11–16; Katzenstein, 1997: 3–4; Kwan, 1994: 4–5, 11–12, 100–1, 106–9; Selden, 1997: 321–32) – led to fears that the contagion would spread to neighboring economies and investors stampeded to liquidate their holdings in these currencies, what Robert Wade (1998a) calls the 'gestalt effect.' As their currencies came under increasing pressure, news reports were punctuated by announcements that, one after the other, the 'miracle' economies had floated their currencies: Malaysia on July 14, 1997; Singapore on July 17; and Indonesia on August 14.

As the scope of the crisis was becoming evident, the creation of an Asian Monetary Fund (AMF) was floated at a meeting of the Association of Southeast Asian Nations (ASEAN) in August 1997 and strongly endorsed by the governments of Taiwan and Japan. The Japanese government proposed the creation of a regional multilateral financing facility with an initial capitalization of $100 billion at the annual meeting of the G-7 finance ministers in Hong Kong in 1997. Though there was little doubt that the creation of such a firewall would have prevented the contagion from spreading throughout the region, it was aborted due to strong opposition by the United States, other Western governments, and China. The United States government opposed the creation of a regional financial institution not only because it would decrease US influence over the liberalization of trade and finance but also because of fears that if regional central banks had financed the operations of an AMF through the sale of US Treasury instruments, it could precipitously raise long-term US interest rates (Johnson, 1998: 658; Nordhaug, 2002: 526).

Compounding the situation, when cross-national flows of capital were largely unregulated, many institutional investors are required to maintain portfolios only in investment-grade securities as they were not equipped to assess credit-worthiness of overseas borrowers. Hence, any downgrading of the sovereign credit-worthiness of states – especially by one of the two major credit-ratings agencies, Moody's Investors' Service and the Standard and Poor's Ratings Group – inevitably triggered an automatic outflow of money as foreign creditors called in their loans. The effects could be dramatic: when both Moody's and Standard and Poor downgraded South Korea's credit rating on October 24, 1997 just as the Hong Kong stock market had plunged, there was a massive run on the won. Despite the Bank of Korea using some $2 billion of its foreign exchange reserves to prop up the currency, the won nose-dived from 890 to the greenback in July 1997 to 1,200 in late November before the government requested IMF assistance.

Given the high debt–equity ratios of the *chaebol* discussed in Chapter 3, a depreciation of the won was disastrous to their balance sheets. Robert Wade and Frank Veneroso (1998a) demonstrate how the impact of a 50 percent devaluation is far more severe on an ideal-typical South Korean firm than on an ideal-typical Latin American enterprise. Table 5.4 assumes that both firms have the same rates of profit and the same percentage of dollar-denominated debt as a percentage of total corporate debt. However, as this illustration shows, because of the higher debt–equity ratio of the South Korean firm, a 50 percent devaluation would wipe out its equity while it would raise the Latin American firm's debt by only 20 percent.

Rather than stabilizing the currency, the government's acceptance of

Table 5.4 Consequences of different debt/equity ratios

	Typical 'Latin American' firm	Typical South Korean firm
Liabilities		
Equity	80 pesos	20 won
Debt	20 pesos	80 won
Debt/equity ratio	25%	400%
Rate of interest on debt	10%	10%
Gross return on assets	12%	12%
Gross profit	12 pesos	12 won
	(12% of 100 pesos)	(12% of 100 won)
Dollar-debt	25%	25%
	(5 pesos)	(20 won)
Domestic debt	15 pesos	60 won
50% devaluation	Dollar debt doubles to 10 pesos	Dollar debt doubles to 40 won
Total debt	25 pesos	100 won (wipes out company's equity)
Total interest cost	2.5 pesos	
Rise in interest rates on domestic debt	20%	20%
Increase in interest cost in pesos/won	1.5 pesos to 3 pesos (20% of 15 pesos)	6 won to 12 won (20% of 60 won)
Interest cost in dollars remains same	1 peso	4 won
Total interest cost	4.5 pesos	16 won
Fall in return of assets	8% or 8 pesos	8% or 8 won
Return minus interest	3.5 pesos	Minus 8 won

Source: Adapted from Wade and Veneroso (1998a: 10–11).

the conditions attached to the $57 billion rescue package led to an even more precipitous decline in the value of the won, as it plummeted to 1,962 by late December. Bad short-term loans were then estimated to amount to over $100 billion, and all types of non-performing loans were said to equal 51 percent of the South Korean GNP, before an advance of $10 billion in loans by thirteen high-income states and the IMF temporarily rallied markets. Nevertheless, between November 1997 and January 1998, South Korea slid from being the eleventh-largest economy to the seventeenth-largest – behind Mexico, India, and Russia – as its GNP dropped from $500 billion to $312 billion (*The Economist*, 1997f: 84–7; Cumings, 1998: 56–7).

Unable to defend their currencies, the governments of Thailand, Indonesia, the Philippines, and South Korea had reluctantly sought emergency assistance from the IMF. If other ailing economies were able to resist this humiliation, their currencies continued to plummet and sent debt repayments of their highly-leveraged companies skyrocketing. The sheer magnitude and brutality of currency depreciations hollowed out entire economies as buyers hesitated to place orders fearing that cash-starved firms would be unable to fill them, while firms hesitated to bid for business as volatile currency markets made it impossible to estimate costs. Finally, foreign banks, once so amenable to rolling over short-term loans, were now demanding quick repayment and cutting off lines of credit (Uchitelle, 1997c; Fuerbringer, 1997; Burton and Baker, 1998). Thus, as indicated by the figures presented in Table 5.5, the five ailing economies of Indonesia, Malaysia, the Philippines, South Korea, and Thailand suffered a net outflow of private capital to the tune of $12 billion in 1997 in contrast to a net inflow of $93 billion the previous year.

Most ominously, the worsening economic predicament along Asia's Pacific perimeters revealed the precarious position of Japanese banks. Renewed pressure from international organizations, Western governments, and international investors, led the Japanese banking industry to admit that potentially bad loans amounted to at least $600 billion, a sum larger than the entire Chinese economy, and possibly as much as $1 trillion. It was claimed, however, that only about $87 billion of this amount was fully unrecoverable (Tabb, 1995; *The Economist*, 1997e; WuDunn, 1998a; Tett and Wighton, 1998; Leyshon, 1994: 134–5; WuDunn, 1998b; WuDunn, 1998c; WuDunn, 1998d; Bremner, 1999; Nakamae, 1999). However, their exposure to bad loans in East and Southeast Asia was relatively modest – only about $93.3 billion of the total was lent to institutions in Thailand, South Korea, Indonesia, Malaysia, and the Philippines (Inter-

Table 5.5 External financing for the most afflicted Asian economies: South Korea, Indonesia, Malaysia, Thailand, and the Philippines (billions of dollars)

	1994	1995	1996	1997	1998e	1999f
Current account balance	−24.6	−41.0	−54.6	−26.3	11.6	43.2
External financing, net	47.4	81.5	100.6	28.8	−0.5	−1.2
Private flows, net	40.5	79.0	103.2	−1.1	−28.3	−4.8
Equity investment, net	12.2	15.9	19.7	3.6	8.5	18.7
Direct equity, net	4.7	4.9	5.8	6.8	6.4	14.2
Portfolio equity, net	7.6	11.0	13.9	−3.2	2.1	4.5
Private creditors, net	28.2	63.1	83.5	−4.7	−36.8	−23.4
Commercial banks, net	24.0	53.2	65.3	−25.6	−35.0	−18.8
Non-bank private creditors, net	4.2	9.9	18.2	21.0	−1.7	−4.6
Official flows, net	7.0	2.5	−2.6	29.9	27.8	3.5
International financial institutions	−0.4	−0.3	−2.0	22.1	21.6	−2.0
Bilateral creditors	7.4	2.9	−0.6	7.9	6.1	5.5
Resident lending/other, net	−17.5	−26.5	−26.8	−35.0	−16.9	−14.9
Reserves excl. gold (− = increase)	−5.4	−14.0	−19.3	32.5	−41.1	−27.0

Source: Institute of International Finance (1998).

Notes
e = estimate; f = forecast.

national Monetary Fund, 1997b: 1, table 2) – compared with the hundreds of billions of dollars in dubious loans in Japan itself, where property values had fallen by 80 percent between 1992 and 1998 (Bremner, 1998). By another estimate, all Japanese loans to East Asia excluding Hong Kong amounted to $119 billion, or just 3 percent of all outstanding Japanese bank loans. And 75 percent of these loans to Southeast Asia were to subsidiaries of major Japanese corporations (Strom, 1997).

The precarious position of Japanese banks was reflected in the sale of foreign bonds as cash-strapped banks traded in securities to raise funds and reversed the flow of capital. Prior to the current crisis, high domestic rates of savings and low interest rates had led Japan to become the largest exporter of capital, especially to the United States where private and public institutions were required to raise US$1.5 billion a day on average (Clairmont, 2003). The looming mountain of bad debts, however, led Japanese investors to sell a record net ¥3.5 trillion ($28.3 billion) in foreign bonds in December 1997. By the end of January 1998, British investors had overtaken the Japanese as the largest foreign holders of US government bonds, with $300.1 billion worth of Treasury bonds compared with $293.3 billion held by the Japanese (WuDunn and Kristoff, 1997; Coggan and Harris, 1998; Bloomberg News, 1998).

Put another way, the growing incoherence of national industrial policies along Asia's Pacific seaboard led to the creation of competitive rather than complementary structures of accumulation and eroded the emerging regional division of labor. This was, however, camouflaged by the growth of intra-regional trade in which trade in components replaced trade in finished goods, a trend indicative of the fact that the installation of factory complexes was not accompanied by forward and backward linkages. Additionally, the progressive expansion of the operations of large Japanese and South Korean conglomerates in North America, Western Europe, and elsewhere also meant that corporate strategies were less congruent with the interests of their respective national economies.

A change of skies

Almost twenty years after the US Federal Reserve raised interest rates and liberalized the American financial sector to contain domestic inflation in the United States the geography of manufacturing on both coasts of the Pacific and the flows of capital across the world were thoroughly reshaped. Whereas the concentration of industrial capacity in the United States at the end of the Second World War had slowed the pace of technological innovation in US industry while Japanese and European enterprises rebuilt their factories with state-of-the-art technologies, a high dollar led to the destruction of obsolete plant and equipment in the United States in the late 1970s and 1980s. Concomitantly, deepening industrialization along the Pacific coasts of Asia under the aegis of the Japanese state and conglomerates and growing Japanese surpluses helped finance the progressively larger US current account deficits generated by the decline of American manufacturing.

Spurred by the imposition of 'voluntary export restrictions' by the Reagan Administration, and lured by a new round of labor disciplining in the US, there was an inflow of manufacturing investments to 'greenfield' sites in the United States primarily by corporations based in Japan and Western Europe. Moreover, the emergence of TNCs as the primary agency for the outward expansion of Japanese capital meant that they had the resources to organize production facilities anywhere on a global scale and were not restricted to neighboring locations as the small- and medium-scale corporations had been during the late 1960s and 1970s.

One important consequence of the trans-border expansion of production and procurement networks was that it rendered national industrial policies anachronistic. If enterprises were dependent on state subsidies during post-Second World War reconstruction and into the 1970s, the very success of Japanese reconstruction weaned industrial houses from their dependence on the state after they acquired gilt-edged credit ratings. Since this coincided with the progressive deregulation of financial markets in Western Europe and North America, Japanese conglomerates and banks lobbied the government to liberalize controls over cross-border flows of capital in order to tap into the vast expansion of liquidity in world markets.

The break-neck pace of industrialization also eroded the social underpinnings of the developmental state all across East and Southeast Asia: in South Korea, the rise of a strong industrial proletariat successfully challenged the exclusion and marginalization of labor and toppled the military dictatorship. In Taiwan, demographic changes and the growing economic power of indigenous islanders transformed ethnic balances. Though the one-party regime in Indonesia remained in place until 1998, rapid industrialization in the 1980s led to a resurgence of working class movements. Singapore was a conspicuous exception precisely because its reliance on overseas corporations for investments had prevented the emergence of a domestic bourgeoisie capable of challenging the government.

However effective high interest rates may have been in curbing US inflation, the continued evisceration of American manufacturing led the US to demand that its chief trade partners appreciate their currencies against the greenback. Japanese manufacturers responded by increasing the organic composition of capital in their home bases, diversifying their range of activities, and by shifting manufacturing operations to neighboring locations in East and Southeast Asia. Substantial increases in capital inflows further transformed social balances in recipient areas. Small Bangkok-based traders and the provincial elite in Thailand began to emerge as partners in joint-venture projects with, and suppliers to, Japanese enterprises. Politically-connected entrepreneurs in Malaysia and

Indonesia who had benefitted from the privatization of state-owned enterprises also entered into contracts with TNCs and everywhere these local partners began lobbying for the deregulation of capital flows and the liberalization of the financial sectors.

Since low wages in the US provided employers with no incentive to substitute capital for labor, a realignment of currency rates did not lead to a decline in American trade deficits. Moreover, greater Japanese investments in Asia had led to a decline in Japanese capital outflows to the US, thereby compromising the ability of the US to finance its deficits. Consequently, Japanese and West German governments agreed to lower their domestic interest rates to encourage capital outflows to the United States. Instead, lower interest rates fueled so rampant a speculative climate in Japan that even golf club memberships became tradable commodities and at the height of the bubble a single membership in the most expensive golf club (¥350 million) exceeded the cost of building an entirely new course in Britain (¥300 million) (Gao, 2001: 195; McCormack, 2001: 90)!

The resultant widening of the gaps in income and wealth, along with the loosening of the bonds between small and large enterprises, severely eroded the foundations of the social coalitions that had kept the LDP in power. As the Bank of Japan tried to ameliorate the situation by raising rates of interest, it triggered a cascading fall in the values of land and stocks, exposing the banking sector to fiercely devastating losses. To recoup their enormous losses, Japanese banks substantially increased their lending to industrial enterprises and financial institutions in East and Southeast Asia.

The transformations wrought in the social landscape of the Asian rimlands made local elites very receptive to overseas loans and they successfully lobbied their governments to deregulate cross-border flows of capital and to liberalize the financial sector. In South Korea, cheap loans enabled the *chaebol* to expand their investments overseas and thereby counter the growing workplace bargaining power of labor. In Thailand, capital inflows enabled provincial elites to enter new fields and challenge the dominance of the old Sino-Thai elite. In Indonesia and Malaysia, it permitted politically-connected entrepreneurs also to enter emerging high-profit sectors like telecommunications and purchase shares in the profitable state-owned enterprises that were being privatized. Governments in these states obligingly maintained high rates of interest and pegged their currencies to the US dollar to facilitate capital inflows and also offered off-the-book guarantees to provide additional security to overseas lenders.

Finally, the elimination of controls over capital flows eroded the national foundations of accumulation as corporate networks became progressively transnational in structure. Simultaneously, as innovations in transportation, communications, and manufacturing systems facilitated the segmentation of production into ever narrower and more widely dispersed part-processes and their integration within the technostructures of large conglomerates, the installation of factory complexes are not accompanied by the backward and forward linkages within states that had accrued during earlier phases of industrialization.

If this led to a massive inflow of capital into East and Southeast Asia, especially after the Mexican crisis of 1994 triggered a capital flight from Central and Latin America, it also constrained governments' options in macro-economic management and elevated inflation control above strategic planning. The dependence of Southeast Asian states on large inflows of private foreign capital for their export-oriented industrialization programs also underlined their vulnerability in contrast to the 'dragon' economies – with the partial exception of South Korea – which had relied on inflows of official US aid and their own domestic savings (Phongpaichit and Baker, 1999: 201). While firms continued to pursue debt-led strategies of growth, elevating capture of market share above profits, the dispersal of export-oriented manufacturing to low-wage sites did not entail a proportionate expansion of markets. The resulting overproduction chipped away at the roots of debt-led strategies of industrialization. Singapore was an exception to these trends because divestment of state-owned enterprises did not lead to a dilution in the government's role as it created a plethora of GLCs and a coterie of senior bureaucrats could coordinate the island-state's investment strategies through a system of interlocking directorships (Rodan, 2001: 151–3).

For most other states, pegging currencies to the US dollar was a double-edged sword. After the bubble burst, Japanese investors began to liquidate the US assets they had bought in the 1980s and bring their capital home. The greater demand for yen had steadily increased its value relative to the greenback and eroded the ability of the Japanese to finance the US current account deficit. Consequently, the United States monetary authorities in cooperation with their German and Japanese counterparts helped to lower the value of the yen. Coming on the heels of a substantial devaluation of the Chinese currency, this caught producers along the rimlands in a deadly vise. The depreciation of the yen made their technologically more sophisticated products uncompetitive and the depreciation of the reminbi made them less competitive against producers from China as well as other low- and middle-income economies in less technologically-demanding commodities.

However, rather than scaling back production, easy access to capital through short-term loans led enterprises to compete against each other in capturing market shares and thereby exacerbated the problem of overproduction. Eventually, once Thailand's ability to maintain its currency peg with the dollar was compromised, short-term loans were rapidly recalled as lenders stampeded to get out before the going got worse in a self-fulfilling prophesy. Differently put, while close economic integration may have insulated these economies from the debt-crisis of the early 1980s, the integration of production and procurement structures by the mid-1990s acted as a transmission belt for the crisis to spread across Southeast and East Asia. In contrast, the insular, inward-looking industrial structures of the Latin American economies acted as firewalls in the late 1990s. Until 1990, for instance, Brazilian regulations mandated that the domestic content in manufacturing had to be 98 percent by value and 95 percent by weight (Lissakers, 1991: 59). By 1990, even after the Collor Government had liberalized domestic content requirements in Brazil, intra-regional trade in Latin America accounted for a mere 0.4 percent of world trade as opposed to 4 percent for East and Southeast Asia.

Higher interest rates and more prudential lending standards mandated by the IMF so abruptly turned off the financial spigot to some of the most enterprising companies in the world because their high debt-to-equity ratios meant that they could neither pay the extra interest charges nor recapitalize their debt since they could get no further loans. Not only did the cash-flow crunch virtually paralyze their manufacturing arms but the decline in aggregate demand further undermined immediate prospects of recovery. Completing the vicious cycle, plunging values of local currencies exponentially aggravated the burden of short-term debts they had incurred (Wade and Veneroso, 1998a).

To recapitulate, the creation of a dense network of intra-regional link-ages debilitated the coherence of national industrial policies precisely when these policies were also under pressure from changes in the political ecology of world production, trade, and investment. Thorough-going deregulation of cross-border flows of trade and investments in the United States and Western Europe in the 1980s fractured domestic coalitions underpinning the 'developmental state' in Japan and the 'Four Dragons' as large conglomerates relocated their production operations to circum-vent protectionist barriers and to better exploit cost and wage differentials in conditions of kaleidoscopic realignments of exchange-rates. The cre-ation of transnational corporate structures diluted the dependence of cor-porations on their domestic state apparatuses while the progressive elimination of controls over capital flows provided access to large volumes of cheap credit. Cumulatively, these conditions provided propitious con-ditions for corporations to pursue a debt-financed strategy of expansion, aimed at increasing their market share, without being constrained by authoritative economic bureaucracies. The simultaneous pursuit of similar strategies of expansion, however, reduced the benefits accruing to each enterprise and thereby compounded the problem of indebtedness. The 'developmental state' was in short the victim of its own success.

6 A bonfire of illusions

The crisis consists precisely in the fact that the old is dying and the new cannot be born; in this interregnum a great variety of morbid symptoms appear.

Antonio Gramsci, *Prison Notebooks*

As the crisis hop-scotched over some of the fastest growing economies in history, in a cover story in 1999, *Businessweek* predicted the emergence of a new 'Atlantic Century' (Warner *et al.*, 1999). Despite the unwarranted substitution of the geomancy of one ocean for the geomancy of another in prognostications for the future, it underlined the extent to which bankruptcies and foreclosures had devastated the institutional fabric of the once-miraculous economies on the Asian rimlands and undermined the class coalitions that had ensured relative social peace in an era of breakneck economic growth.

Portraying the economic collapse as a financial crisis, the IMF mandated that governments of the economies placed on its life-support systems hike interest rates to stabilize their currencies, liquidate insolvent financial institutions, ensure central bank independence with price stability as its prime objective, open up capital markets and remove restrictions on the operations of foreign corporations including the right to engage in hostile takeovers (International Monetary Fund, 1997a; International Monetary Fund, 1998; Palat, 1999: 32–8; Bernard, 1999: 198–9). By applying the same recipe it had prescribed during the debt crisis of the 1980s to Latin American economies, the IMF ignored the very different configurations of production structures and class alliances and conflicts in the several economies along Asia's Pacific perimeters. Even Henry Kissinger observed that the IMF was like 'a doctor specializing in measles [who] tries to cure every illness with one remedy' (quoted in Cumings, 1999: 18). Rather than providing a tourniquet to stop the currency hemorrhage, the Fund's inappropriate diagnoses, prescriptions, and remedies aggravated the currency outflows and intensified the crisis.

In the first instance, by attributing the crisis to imprudent financial practices, lack of transparent accounting practices, and 'crony capitalism,' the IMF signaled that economic recovery would occur only after these deep-seated problems had been tackled. This led to a stampede as investors sought to pull their capital out before it was too late and the IMF's insistence that economies hooked up to its life-support systems liberalize capital controls facilitated this capital flight. In this sense, the money transfusions provided by the Fund were really a bailout for the overseas bankers who had lent money to industrial enterprises and financial institutions in East and Southeast Asia (Stiglitz, 2002: 95–7). Additionally, by highlighting loose financial and accounting practices in the debtor countries, the IMF exonerated the lenders from all blame (Radelet and Sachs, 1998).

The suggestion that economic 'fundamentals' were suspect in the ailing economies also contributed to the crisis in South Korea, where it was triggered by banks refusing to rollover short-term loans. The IMF's demand that governments accepting transfusions of money and loan guarantees raise interest rates from 25 to 50 percent to stem the currency hemorrhage further hollowed out some of the most enterprising enterprises in history. When the won had reached historic lows against the US dollar, the IMF's insistence that the South Korean government increase the ceiling on foreign equity ownership from 26 percent to 50 percent by the end of 1997 and to 55 percent by 1998 and eliminate all restrictions on foreign ownership of banks made South Korean companies potential bargains for foreign corporations (Palat, 1999).

Finally, unlike the debt-crisis of the early 1980s when loans had been incurred by governments, in the economic crisis engulfing the Asian rimlands in the mid-1990s, loans had been incurred mainly by private enterprises. In these circumstances, by imposing conditions on governments, the IMF's rescue program led to the nationalization of private corporate debt. Demands for draconian cuts in government expenditure including the privatization of state-owned enterprises and elimination of subsidies on essential items in states without well-developed social security nets severely weakened aggregate demand. The wave of bankruptcies, joblessness, and currency turmoil submerging these economies implied that intra-Asian trade which had accounted for 53 percent of all Asian trade in the early 1990s could no longer be the motor for regional growth and recovery and the whole regional edifice began to unravel at a dizzying pace (Bello, n.d.; Bello, 1998b: 15). Estimates suggest that Indonesia, Malaysia, South Korea, and Thailand suffered import declines ranging from 30 to 40 percent in 1997. Almost three years after Thailand was caught in the economic riptide, it was reported that less than one-third of the 2.5 million Thais who lost their jobs had received any kind of compensation (Crispin, 2000). In Indonesia, the number of unemployed was officially estimated to have increased from 13.7 million at the end of 1997 to 27.9 million at the end of February 1998 and some 79.4 million, or 40 percent of the population, were reckoned to be below the poverty level by early July 1998 (Robison and Rosser, 2000: 171–2; see also Stiglitz, 2002: 97, 99, 121).

The high growth rates registered by these economies, before the collapse of the baht sent their currencies into a free-fall, magnified the impact of the sharp turnaround in their fortunes. South Korea's per capita growth rate fell by almost 15 percent in 1997–98, Malaysia's and Thailand's by more than 20 percent, and Indonesia's by about 25 percent:

> Sudden collapses of these orders of magnitude . . . [had] no parallels in these countries' own histories. According to Suk Bum Yoon, some Koreans believe that the pain and economic loss associated with the crisis was worse than those experienced during that country's traumatic civil war of 1950–53. The convulsion in Indonesia during 1965–66, which led to the emergence of President Soeharto's so-called New Order regime, were associated with a decline of economic growth of no more than 2 percent of GDP. . . . Thailand had not experienced a year of negative growth since 1960. Malaysia's last recession, of 1985–86, saw negative growth of no more than 2 percent.
>
> (Hill and Chu, 2001: 6)

The breathtaking velocity and intensity of the meltdown mercilessly exposed the rifts in the social coalitions underpinning the developmental state that had been camouflaged by the fevered pace of growth in the pre-crisis years. If the Japanese government had been able to compensate for the retraction of corporate investments after the Japanese bubble burst in 1990, the smaller economies caught in the cascade of currency values and unsustainable levels of corporate debt had no such options. Even the resources of the Japanese government, strained by years of budgetary deficit, were insufficient to bail out insolvent banks, financial institutions, and industrial enterprises.

As social actors jostled for advantage, bureaucrats and opposition politicians in some jurisdictions initially welcomed IMF intervention since it provided opportunities to implement measures that had hitherto been politically unfeasible and because it could potentially prise open corrupt and authoritarian structures of government. More importantly, as the crisis wreaked havoc on corporate structures and massive layoffs undermined the power of organized labor, the implementation of policies force fed by the IMF to the governments of the ailing economies also changed the relative balance of forces between governments and enterprises. If it was the trans-border expansion of corporate networks and the ensuing anachronism of regulatory controls that had led to conditions of overproduction, the nationalization of private corporate debt and the infusion of public funds to stabilize financial institutions conferred a great degree of relative autonomy on state apparatuses in several jurisdictions. With the signal exception of Indonesia – where the combination of a resurgence of ethnic and religious rivalries with the implosion of the federal government has made political fragmentation a real possibility – after an initial phase of disarray, governments in the region have begun to institute regional mechanisms not only to blunt the impact of speculative attacks on currencies but also to jump-start economies along the region without relying on the United States as a market of last resort, as we shall see in the Epilogue.

In the first section here, we will chart the impact of the crisis and the ongoing processes of restructuring that wreaked havoc on corporate structures all across the Asian rimlands: *keiretsu* structures loosened and even unraveled, the *chaebol* were dismembered, mergers and acquisitions saw the wholesale transfer of corporate assets to overseas investors in some locations, the relentless transfer of production overseas hollowed out industrial sectors in the 'dragons' and many neighboring economies. Worsening economic conditions also undercut the power of labor and where structural collapse had not fatally compromised centralized government control – as in Indonesia – the weakening of major social classes once again conferred a degree of autonomy on the state apparatus, albeit on a basis far different from the developmental states of the Cold War era. The greater role of the state was underlined when the Hong Kong administration fended off speculative attacks on the Hong Kong dollar by spending some US$15.2 billion in the acquisition of stocks and became the single largest shareholder in the Hong Kong and Shanghai Banking Corporation in 1998. Subsequently, as we shall see, the Tung Chee-hwa administration adopted plans to transform the Special Administrative Region into an innovation-led, technology-intensive economy – adopted, that is, the functions of a developmental state (So and Chan, 2002). Bluntly put, while the IMF seized the crisis to excoriate activist state intervention, its own prescriptions have ironically strengthened the ability of governments to intervene along the Asian rimlands.

If the headlong descent of the Asian 'miracle' economies in 1997 and 1998 led to a retrospective indictment of administratively guided industrialization strategies by international financial institutions and Western governments, the compression of export prices from the ailing economies adversely impacted on manufacturing profits in the United States and Western Europe as we shall see in the second section. While constraints of space preclude a detailed analyses of these economies, even the thumbnail sketches presented here indicate that neither the United States economy nor the European Union were strong enough to pull the world economy out from the deepening recession. Though equity prices became hugely inflated in the United States, this asset-price inflation was not accompanied by a strong growth in production or profits and accordingly led to sharp falls in equity prices since mid-2000. Meanwhile, the costs of German reunification and difficulties entailed by the creation of a common currency had sapped the vitality of the European Union. If the relentless rise of stock prices in the United States had led to an influx of capital – especially from the Asian rimlands where the IMF's conditionalities eased capital flight –

the collapse of the speculative bubble facilitated a reorientation of macro-economic policies in East and Southeast Asia that may lead to an economic revitalization – a possibility we shall explore in the Epilogue.

A brave new world

In analyzing the ongoing restructuring of power relations in Indonesia, Vedi Hadiz (2001) aptly invokes Lenin's acute insight that a revolutionary situation arises only when two conditions are satisfied: the refusal of new forces to continue living in the old way and the inability of dominant classes to continue asserting their dominance. The tragedy of rapid economic growth along Asia's Pacific coasts was that while the developmental state had been rendered anachronistic by the trans-border expansion of production and procurement networks, embryonic new social forces remained unable to dislodge the post-Second World War social order. Regional economic collapse cast into sharp relief all the problems – the changing balance of class forces, tensions associated with increasing inequalities in income and wealth, the greater prominence of industrialists of Chinese ancestry in several jurisdictions, as well as social dislocations caused by migrant labor, and environmental degradation (Pempel, 1999a: 225) – that had hitherto been submerged by the breakneck pace of growth, just as policy options for governments became tightly constrained and the end of the Cold War meant that the United States had no incentive to prop up authoritarian regimes.

As the crisis impacted unevenly across Asia's Pacific Rim, the restructuring of political economies was conditioned by the specific constellations of power and privilege in each jurisdiction. Though Thailand and South Korea were pressured by the IMF into accepting greater foreign ownership of their corporate assets, the Thai government increased its stake in the banking sector while capitalists based in new sectors exploited opportunities presented by the eclipse of banking capital to transform power relations between capitalist factions. The reformist government in South Korea used the IMF conditionalities to undercut the power of the *chaebol* and organized labor with some success. In Indonesia, though, initial resistance by the Suharto regime and the weakening of central authority led to a far more anarchic situation while Malaysian Prime Minister Mahathir was able to evade IMF guidelines altogether by imposing capital controls in defiance of the Fund. Exposure of Japanese banks to large losses not only led to a spate of bank failures and takeovers by foreign interests but also to a thorough-going transformation of industrial organization. If government control of the commanding heights of the economy enabled Taiwan and Singapore to withstand the meltdown of neighboring economies, the serial transfer of manufacturing facilities to China increasingly jeopardizes Taiwan's industrial structure. Faced with a similar hollowing out of the industrial structure of Hong Kong, its government has even formally abandoned its laissez faire policy in favor of strategic economic planning. We examine these patterns in more detail below before turning to the impact of the Asian crisis on economies in Western Europe and the United States in the next section.

The most emergent arena of restructuring was the banking sector where financial liberalization had exposed the weakness, inexperience, and downright backwardness of banks all across a region where manufacturing, rather than finance, had occupied center-stage. Though Japanese banks were among the world's largest by market value, they lagged behind European and American banks in computerization and risk and asset management strategies. The most profitable Japanese banks earned a 2 percent return on equity compared with the 10 to 20 percent earned by their Western competitors. Some of the largest banks did not even have investment banking operations while others were without retail banking arms. Unlike American and European banks, the association between industrial enterprises and 'lead' banks meant that Japanese banks also rarely made syndicated loans to corporations to spread the risk (Kahn, 1999).

Insulated from foreign competition, able to freely access capital from world financial markets, and unbound by cash reserve constraints imposed by regulators elsewhere, banks represented a virtual gold mine for influential families especially in Indonesia, Malaysia, and Thailand. Hence, some bureaucrats and opposition leaders welcomed international pressure for providing a politically convenient cover to implement some long-needed changes, and to selectively punish opponents (Murphy, 2000; Bernard, 1999). John Matthews (1998: 752–3) even suggests that some elements of the IMF's stabilization package – relating to restructuring of the *chaebol*, and the institutional separation of the Bank of Korea from the Ministry of Finance – were instigated by South Korean bureaucrats themselves.

Even in Malaysia, where the central bank had greater autonomy from influential families and the personal interests of the political leadership were not so intertwined with the fortunes of particular institutions, attempts to exercise discipline over banks had largely been ineffective until the crisis set in. The economic meltdown, at the same time, triggered a confrontation between Prime Minister Mahathir representing what Edmund Gomez and K. S. Jomo (1997) have called the 'politicized oligopolies,' and his anointed heir, Deputy Prime Minister Anwar Ibrahim, representing technocrats, small businesses, and sections of the Malay and non-Malay middle classes. The latter attributed the crisis to nepotism and lack of transparency and supported the IMF's recommendations for higher interest rates, fiscal restraint, and currency stabilization as a restoration of 'economic fundamentals.' However, the former saw higher interest rates and further economic liberalization as the path to transferring national assets to foreign owners and viewed with alarm the experiences of South Korea, Thailand, and Indonesia after they had been subject to the IMF's ministrations. Most notably a wholesale accession to

IMF demands would have cracked the social compact that had preserved inter-ethnic peace for three decades and Mahathir's ability to play the nationalist card and prevent large-scale unemployment helped him triumph over his former deputy.

Defying the IMF, Mahathir sought to stem the currency hemorrhage by reimposing controls in August 1998 over capital flows, pegged the ringgit at 3.80 to the dollar, cut interest rates, decreed that all offshore ringgit be repatriated by the end of September, and declared a freeze on the repatriation of overseas portfolio capital for a year. Despite condemnation from the IMF and US Treasury Secretary Robert Rubin – and the resignation of Malaysian Central Bank governor, Ahmad Mohamed Don and his deputy, Fong Weng Phak, in protest – these measures reversed the tide and capital controls were rolled back within twelve months. Rather than retreating to an insulated economic environment, these regulations were designed to severely restrict currency speculation and did not expose Malaysia to the ravages experienced by states which were subject to the IMF's ministrations. In this endeavor, Mahathir was aided by the Japanese government – still smarting after it was forced to shelve its proposal for an AMF – guarantee of $570 million in Malaysian government bonds in December 1998 (Wade and Veneroso, 1998b: 21; Stiglitz, 2002: 123–5; Hughes, 2000: 222).

Simultaneously, Mahathir launched a restructuring plan that was carefully calibrated to punish his opponents and to maximize electoral mileage for the ruling party. After sinking some $15.8 billion in public funds to take over bad loans and recapitalize insolvent institutions, in August 1999, the government decreed that the country's 21 commercial banks, 12 merchant banks, and 25 finance companies merge into six 'superbanks' within a year. In mandating this restructuring of financial institutions, the government victimized institutions like Hong Leong and Phileo Allied associated with Anwar and mollified the Chinese by expanding the number of anchor institutions (Jayasankaran, 1999; Fuller, 1999).

By refusing to subject the economy to the ministrations of the IMF, unlike other ailing economies, Mahathir was also free to directly support a number of non-financial enterprises. However, once again political considerations loomed large, and while the state-owned oil company, Petronas, was enlisted to bail out the national car project, a number of companies with prior experience in the automobile sector were excluded from the project because these were owned by members of the Chinese minority (Gomez and Jomo, 1997: 180; Khoo Boo Teik, 2000; Haggard, 2000: 164–70).

For over a decade, as internal conflicts, mismanagement, and corruption plagued the Thai financial sector, successive governments had tried in vain to rein in the prominent families. The crisis finally helped corral them and by November 1997 the financial sector was almost completely transformed. Debt-for-equity swaps saw the virtually wholesale transfer of banking and financial sectors to American, European, Japanese, and Singaporean investors – by October 1998, one-third of the companies in the financial sector had been closed down and only five banks (Bangkok Bank, Thai Farmer's Bank, Bank of Ayudhaya, Siam Commercial Bank, and the Thai Military Bank) have survived with majority Thai ownership. Even so, by the end of 1999 total state investment in Thai banks approached US$12 billion, or almost 10 percent of GDP. The hollowing out of the banking and financial sectors propelled capitalists based in newer sectors to the top of the list of wealthiest families in Thailand, and Thaksin Shinawatra, the head of the wealthiest family, was elected prime minister in January 2001. His Thai Rak Thai ('Thai Love Thai') party won the support of all major big businesses and is seeking to get a breathing space by suspending reforms so that these businesses can regroup in the changed conditions of accumulation (McDonald, 2001; Hewison, 2001; Bello *et al.*, 1998: 47–8; Arnold, 1999b; Hewison, 2000: 203–4).

There had been much greater resistance to restructuring in Indonesia because it adversely affected the interests of the Suharto clan. President Suharto's initial reluctance to agree to the Fund's terms spread apprehension among investors and even after the government accepted the stringent conditions attached to a $43 billion rescue plan, the rupiah continued its headlong descent. Between January 15, 1998 when the agreement between the Indonesian government and the IMF was reached and January 22, the rupiah plunged from 8,500 to the US dollar to 16,500. Such savage volatility in exchange-rates made a mockery of the agreement, which had been premised on an exchange-rate of 5,000 rupiah to the dollar. When the rupiah had been trading at 2,400 to the dollar six months earlier, the currency's fall was so drastic that only 22 of the country's 228 publicly traded companies had assets exceeding their liabilities (Mydans, 1998; Bremner, 1997).

An economic contraction of this magnitude – by the end of 1998 almost 50 percent of the population was below the poverty line (Hill, 2000: 264)[1] – fueled ethnic tensions and re-ignited separatist movements that President Suharto's New Order Indonesia was ill equipped to contain. On the one hand, the cohesion and prestige of the military had been shattered by the exposure of its activities in East Timor and its role in fomenting anti-Chinese riots as well as by power struggles between the top brass. On the other hand, the insolvency of large conglomerates had undermined the social base of the ruling coalition while the heavy bias toward Java has spawned a variety of ethnic and separatist movements that might yet lead to the break-up of the world's fifth most populous state (Robison and Rosser, 2000).

The first manifestations of a rupture in the social order appeared in the form of brutal attacks on the Chinese minority. Unlike in Malaysia and Thailand, where Chinese minorities also controlled a disproportionate share of wealth, Sino-Indonesians were more vulnerable as they constituted a far smaller percentage of the population than in the other two jurisdictions. Hence, though a few prominent Sino-Indonesians had gained access to President Suharto's inner circle, the ruling Golkar party had not sought to integrate them into the power structure. In contrast, a variety of Islamic groups that had gained access to power sought to blame the wealthy minority for the crisis. Deprived of political cover, the Sino-Indonesian bourgeoisie sought to transfer funds overseas and thus aggravated the currency hemorrhage (Haggard, 2000: 116).

As the economic meltdown intensified, popular protests spearheaded by students but also manifested in the resurgence of militant separatist movements, eventually led to the fall of the Suharto regime after massive demonstrations rocked Jakarta in May 1998. Whatever else it might have connoted, the succession of Suharto's long-term confidante – Bachruddin Jusuf Habibie – to the presidency could not resolve the situation. Tied as the new president was to the New Order's elite, he could not uproot their privileges, while his own political survival demanded creating a space for new social forces thrown up by the crisis. Without Suharto's control over the military and government institutions, Habibie could not manage the accommodation of new social actors while preserving the scaffolding of the New Order. Precisely because 30 years of authoritarian rule had ensured that emerging social forces were not all equally well positioned in the ensuing contest for power, the erosion of centralized institutional frameworks was accompanied by the rise of coalitions of business and bureaucratic–political elites for power by creating competing networks of patronage. The breakdown of centralized political authority was also accompanied by the deployment of paramilitaries, directly or indirectly linked to political parties, as intra-elite groups sought to hijack democratic processes to feather their own nests (Tornquist, 2000; Hadiz, 2001).

By the time the government was able to seriously address the question of restructuring the banking sector after Suharto's ouster in May 1998, it was estimated that non-performing loans amounted to at least half of all outstanding credit and that most banks were insolvent. Compounding the situation, it became apparent that most banks had misrepresented their assets and hence overstated their ability to recapitalize. Government cash injections of some $10 billion implied that the government held 75 percent of the liabilities and 90 percent of the negative net worth of all Indonesian banks as over 66 banks were liquidated and 12 taken over by the state between September 1998 and March 1999 (Asian Development Bank, 1999: 25–7; Robison and Rosser, 2000: 185–8).

Despite plummeting asset values, bouts of political instability – such as persistent violence and the removal through impeachment of President Abdurrahman Wahid after he had maneuvered to succeed Habibie – meant that the tidal wave of foreign investments submerging domestic capital in the other ailing economies in the region has been conspicuously absent in Indonesia. This has enabled the elite to sell their non-performing assets at overvalued prices to the government and then buy them back at a heavy discount since there were no other potential purchasers (Hadiz, 2001). In Indonesia, therefore, while popular forces had dislodged centralized authority, they were unable to capture power and local 'big men' were able to step into the breach.

Conversely, there was less official resistance to restructuring in South Korea since the IMF mandates nicely dovetailed into the reform agenda of Kim Dae-Jung, the country's most famous dissident who had been elected president in the midst of the crisis. However, despite President Kim's predisposition to implement the IMF's plans because of his opposition to the *chaebol*, the better organization and strength of the labor movement and fierce resistance by heads of *chaebol* often stymied reforms. The insolvency of these conglomerates had catapulted financial restructuring to the top of the agenda and the government nationalized merchant banks with massive problem loans – spending some 115 trillion won ($117.3 billion) over four years to recapitalize the banks and other financial institutions – and then sought to liquidate, merge, or sell 15 of them. This opened the way for several overseas institutions to acquire a foothold in the country's financial system. Additionally, while separating the Bank of Korea from the Ministry of Finance, the government transferred oversight responsibilities to a new institution, the Financial Supervisory Commission (FSC), located within the prime minister's office. Finally, like the cases of Thailand and Indonesia, assets of shaky or insolvent financial institutions were transferred to a newly created Korea Asset Management Corporation (Strom, 1999; Matthews, 1998: 753–4; Larkin, 2002).

Plans for corporate reform proceeded in tandem with these measures. Medium-sized *chaebol* (those below the top five) were especially vulnerable due to their exceedingly high debt to equity ratios. Like their larger counterparts, these *chaebol* had also resorted to cross-subsidiary loan guarantees, cross-investments, and intra-group sales to expand and diversify their operations by borrowing with minimal collateral. Their greater inexperience and lower technical proficiency combined with their smaller size meant that the failure of one marginal affiliate could more easily jeopardize all other units, as demonstrated by the cases of the Kia and Halla *chaebol*. The government consequently used medium-sized *chaebol* as a testing ground for a raft of legislation which were then selectively applied to the Big Five. In the first instance, cross-subsidiary loan guarantees, cross-investments, and other similar financial arrangements were prohibited and internationally accepted accounting protocols were instituted. Ceilings on foreign investments were raised from 26 to 50 percent and the proportion of shares that could be acquired without board approval was increased to ease foreign takeovers and mergers. The government also strongly encouraged creditors and debtors to work out differences through arbitration, debt-equity swaps, extending terms for repayment, new equity issues, and other arrangements (Cumings, 1999: 26; Matthews, 1998: 750–1, 755–6; Woo-Cumings, 1999: 132–3). Market liberalization and the transfer of corporate assets to overseas investors is reflected in the rise of foreign investments from $1 billion in 1992 to an estimated $20 billion in 2000, all the more significant given the fall in the value of the won (Strom, 2000a).

Since the top five *chaebol* had lost their gilt-edged credit ratings, the government used the threat of cutting off credit to pressure them to streamline their operations by shedding loss-making subsidiaries and focusing on their 'core competencies' to retain their positions as internationally-competitive enterprises. To dampen overproduction, the government negotiated a series of business swaps and mergers: Daewoo trading its electronics firm for Samsung's automobile unit, or the consolidation of the memory-chip manufacturing arms of Hyundai and LG to create the world's second largest manufacturer of DRAM chips after Samsung (Woo-Cumings, 1999: 133). Perhaps most strikingly, the government authorized Hyundai Motors to spin-off from the country's largest *chaebol* in August 2000 and Hyundai Heavy Industries in March 2002, reducing Hyundai to a small collection of distressed companies (Burton, 2000; Ward, 2002a).

Despite the winnowing of weak performers, economic recovery is still faltering. After almost five years of restructuring, in April 2002 several major conglomerates still had very high debt–equity ratios, as indicated by Table 6.1, and the earnings of almost 24 percent of the manufacturers listed in the Kospi share index were not enough to cover interest payments on their debts (Ward, 2003).

The South Korean government also used international pressure as a convenient cover to discipline labor. When workers had forced the Kim Young Sam government to rollback measures introduced to dilute employment security in early 1997, Kim Dae-Jung, backed by an IMF mandate, was able to do what his predecessor could not. The dismissals that followed tripled the country's unemployment rate – with the number of jobless workers increasing from 658,000 to 1,700,000 between December 1997 and December 1998 (Koo, 2001: 201–2; Cumings, 1999: 26–7; Bernard, 1999: 197–200). Unemployment and the threat of unemployment undercut the power of organized labor, as indicated by the failure of the Hyundai Motors strike in the summer of 1998, the Seoul Metropolitan Subway Workers' Union the following May, and Daewoo Motors' strike in February 2001 (Neary, 2000; Kirk, 2001a).

Early initial successes, including the swap of subsidiaries among the bigger *chaebol*, mergers and acquisitions, however, soon ran aground because the pride of the owners of these behemoths was tied to their expansion into certain prestigious sectors. The higher capital-intensities of South Korean enterprises also enabled small groups of strategically placed workers to cripple production, and when unemployment rates had reached 8.6 percent by February 1999, prospects of further layoffs led them to join *chaebol* heads in frustrating plans to allow foreign firms to acquire South Korean firms. A report issued by a government research institute, the Korea Institute of Finance, acknowledged that by 2001, the four largest *chaebol* – Samsung, LG, SK, and Hyundai – had allocated only 17.5 percent of their

Table 6.1 Major South Korean conglomerates as of April 2002

	No. of affiliates	Debt-equity ratio (%)	Assets (000 billion won)
Korea Electrical Power Corp[a]	14	72.1	90.9
Samsung	63	240.6	72.4
LG	51	206.8	54.5
SK	62	156.4	46.8
Hyundai Motors	25	168.0	41.3
Korea Telecom[a]	9	101.7	32.6
Korea Highway Corp[a]	4	100.4	26.4
Hanjin	21	294.4	21.6
Korea Land Corp[a]	2	373.4	14.9
Korea National Housing Corp[a]	2	185.2	14.5
Hyundai	12	977.6	11.8
Gumho	15	503.1	10.6
Hyundai Heavy Industry	5	219.4	10.3
Hanwa	26	238.3	9.9
Korea Water Resources Corp[a]	2	27.2	9.5
Korea Gas Corp	2	256.0	9.1
Doosan	18	191.4	9.0
Dongbu	21	312.1	6.1
Hyundai Oilbank	2	837.1	5.9

Source: Adapted from Ward (2003).

Note
a State-owned enterprises.

investments to their core companies (Kirk, 2001b). However, sharp falls in imports as well as a steep decline in the value of the won stimulated favorable trade balances, and by January 2000 the jobless rate had fallen to a post-1997 low of 4.4 percent (Bridges, 2001: 75–84).

Mired in financial doldrums since the speculative bubble burst in 1990, the deepening crisis along Asia's Pacific Rim revealed the full extent of problems in the Japanese banking sector and prompted the government to promote a thoroughgoing reform. Though Japanese banks had been able to cover up the extent of domestic non-performing loans by lending overseas, with Japanese banks holding some 37 percent of private external liabilities of the 'newly industrializing economies' in Asia,[2] the collapse of East and Southeast Asian economies highlighted their lending practices. Intense pressure from international financial organizations, Western governments, and international investors, compelled the Japanese government to admit that potentially bad loans held by Japanese banks amounted to approximately ¥76.7 trillion yen or $583 billion in January 1998 – more than twice the previous estimate. By March 2001, a government report estimated that some $150 billion of this amount was fully unrecoverable (Tabb, 1995; Bennett, 1997; Leyshon, 1994: 134–5; *The Economist*, 1997e; Tett and Wighton, 1998; Chandler, 2001b).

Stretched as Japanese government finances were by high expenditures – by the end of 2001, the *Wall Street Journal* estimated that Japanese central and local government debt would account for 36 percent of global debt, or more than one and a half times the corresponding figure for the United States (McCormack, 2001: xiii) – to maintain low rates of unemployment and to compensate for low rates of corporate investments, it was unable to prevent a spate of high-exposure bank failures. With the regional economic collapse tightening credit, Japan's oldest brokerage house (Yamaichi Securities) and two of the largest 20 banks (Hokkaido Takushoku and Tokyu City banks) collapsed in November 1997. At the same time, five of the top ten banks reported huge losses (Bennett, 1997; *The Economist*, 1997b), and the yen dipped to its lowest rate against the US dollar in more than five years. In September 1999, the venerable Long-Term Credit Bank – the primary vehicle through which the government had bankrolled postwar reconstruction – was acquired by New York-based Ripplewood Holdings L.L.C. Even before Ripplewood's acquisition of a toehold in the financial sector, the first time that foreign investors secured control of a Japanese bank, and to insure themselves against similar takeovers, Japanese banks began to combine forces. In August 1999, Dai-Ichi Kangyo (DKB), Fuji, and Industrial Bank of Japan announced their merger to create Mizuho Holdings, the world's largest bank with assets of ¥141,000 billion (US$1,257 billion). With other mergers, the consolidation of operations in the Japanese banking sector led to substantial declines in employment (*New York Times*, 1999; Sims, 1999a; Tett, 1999; Tett and Harney, 1999; Kahn, 1999; Sims, 1999b).

While there had been mergers in the Japanese banking sector before, the current wave is significant for several reasons. Under pressure from the government – which channeled some ¥7,450 billion in public funds to help 15 major banks resolve their problem loans in early 1999, and a series of supplementary budgetary allocations every year since then – to restructure banking operations, it is expected that these mergers will consolidate overlapping facilities and pool resources to develop more effective risk management and banking strategies, including the investment of up to ¥150 billion a year in systems technologies. This was in sharp contrast to previous mergers where there had been stiff resistance to consolidating duplicate operations, cutting staff and severing unprofitable alliances (Harney and Tett, 1999; Sims, 1999a; Sims, 1999b; Tett and Harney, 1999)!

Since companies in rival *keiretsu* were competitors, the merger of banks further eroded the close relationships between the banking and industrial wings of the group and may indeed undermine the whole structure of postwar industrial relations (Tett and Naoko Nakamae, 1999).[3] Underlying this change, Japan's third-largest company by market capitalization, Toyota, listed its shares in the London and New York stock markets in September 1999 to increase its investor base and unwind the cross-shareholdings that had insulated Japanese companies from outside scrutiny (Nakamoto and Abrahams, 1999; Harney, 1999). Even more significantly, in March 1999, France's Renault acquired operational control over Nissan and subsequently Ford and DaimlerChrysler followed suit, acquiring control over Mazda and Mitsubishi Motors respectively. GM also increased its stake in Suzuki, Isuzu, and Subaru (Tanikawa, 2000).

These trends portend a further 'de-territorialization' of the techno-structures of Japanese corporations. As we have already seen, earlier waves of the cross-border expansion of production networks had either been spearheaded by Japanese small- and medium-scale enterprises, or parts suppliers had followed major manufacturers as they installed production facilities overseas. Especially after the collapse of the speculative bubble, the transnational expansion of Japanese capital had led to a loosening of *keiretsu* structures and jeopardized domestic multi-layered subcontracting networks. In the 1990s, as manufacturing shipments from Japan fell by 10 percent, some 20 percent of manufacturing jobs were eliminated and it is estimated that some 45 percent of manufacturing operations of Japanese multinationals occur outside Japan (Brooke, 2001a; Nakamoto and Pilling, 2002).[4] The transfer of production overseas has serially reduced the large surpluses that the Japanese economy reaped from its trade with Asia, with its trade balance with China (including Hong Kong) turning into a deficit by 2000. The fact that more than half of the China–Japan trade occurs within Japanese corporations – as production is sourced out to subsidiaries and joint ventures in China to gain cost advantages – forcefully underscores the dissolution of ties that had bound large and small businesses (Brooke, 2001b). In Japan itself, year-to-year bankruptcies were 21 percent higher in July 2000 (Strom, 2000b).

Another strand in the strategy to revamp Japanese industry is indicated by Sony's decision to bring its camcorder production back to Japan from China in the summer of 2002. While it is too early to tell whether this is a harbinger of a more general trend, it does suggest the impact of digitization, which shortens product life cycles to three and six months and increases pressures to calibrate production volumes more closely to market demand and to reduce shipping times. Responding to these pressures, Sony revamped its manufacturing operations in Japan by replacing product-based groups with cell-based manufacturing. When the company makes 200 to 300 models of camcorders, producing them in small batches by small groups of workers enables Sony to respond more nimbly to changes in market demand. This is because it can exercise better control over the volume of production than previously as assembly lines are notoriously difficult to stop once they are set in motion. Underpinning the system was the creation of four Sony Engineering, Manufacturing, and Customer Service (EMCS) companies – one each for Japan, Europe, the United States, and China – which consolidated activities carried out by separate manufacturing companies. By consolidating its separate manufacturing companies that had hitherto been divided along product lines, it has streamlined supply chains and ensured the optimal allocation of resources between its product lines. For instance, factories producing television sets in Japan had their peak production periods in the spring and autumn to meet high market demand at the start of the business and school year in April and for Christmas, while their slack periods were in the early summer and early autumn, which were the peak production times for camcorders to meet high demands for the holiday season. By consolidating operations, Sony's EMCS companies could share their resources between different product lines more optimally. Indeed, Sony has so streamlined its operations that it can now deliver a product to the United States within 48 hours of the order being received and the company has even closed its warehouses in the United States and Japan (Nakamoto, 2003).

Industrial restructuring by large Japanese companies and the establishment of direct relations with foreign suppliers and customers was accompanied by a steady decline in their reliance on the *sogo shosha*. Complicating matters for the *sogo shosha*, since they had often provided financing for infrastructural development – oil exploration, gas pipelines, mining – connected with their commodity trade, falling raw materials prices saddled them with substantial debt burdens. At the end of March 2001, all six of the largest *sogo shosha* had high liabilities – Nissho Iwai's debt including off-balance-sheet loan guarantees stood at 2,170 percent of its equity, Marubeni's at 1,100 percent, Itochu's at 1,050 percent, Mitsubishi's at 510 percent, Sumitomo's at 500 percent, and Mitsui's at 460 percent. To reduce their liabilities, the *sogo shosha* have also begun to merge their trading operations – Nissho Iwai and Mitsubishi agreed to combine their steel-trading operations for instance, while Sumitomo Chemicals and Mitsubishi Chemicals negotiated a merger – and to slash jobs (Hijino, 2000; Belson, 2002).

Just as a rising yen led to a spate of Japanese takeovers of US companies in the 1980s, continuing asset-price deflation – the Nikkei average of Japanese stocks dipped below the 10,000 benchmark for the first time in 17 years on November 13, 2001 – led to a stunning 129 percent increase in foreign direct investments in 1999 as overseas investors bought up ailing Japanese firms. The number of mergers and acquisitions initiated by foreign firms similarly grew by a record 34.7 percent in 2000 (*South China Morning Post*, 2001b).[5] Inflows of foreign investment grew by a further 30.3 percent in 2000 and US firms accounted for one-third of all foreign investments in Japan (*South China Morning Post*, 2001a). By another measure, the share of foreign firms in Japanese mergers and acquisitions in 2001 rose to one-third of the total volume – compared with 13 percent in 1999 and 2000 – and the Tokyo Stock Exchange reported that for the first time foreigners accounted for 51.8 percent of trading by value (Brooke, 2002; Ibison and Leahy, 2002).

Put differently, whereas Japan alone accounted for 45 percent of the global aggregate stock of market capitalization at the end of 1987 and the

United States for 30 percent, by 1999 Japan's share had shrunk to 11 percent while the US share had increased to 52 percent (Clairmont, 2001; Tabb, 1999: 77–8). The closest contemporary parallel to the Japanese asset deflation, which the OECD estimates reduced the nation's assets by $8 trillion in the 1990s, is the parallel annihilation of Soviet assets. Japanese business debt is hovering at close to 97 percent of GDP and even after bad debts of ¥60 trillion were written off, Japanese banks are still saddled with unrecoverable debts estimated to be worth ¥35 trillion. Despite the government launching 13 major spending packages worth a total of ¥135 trillion (Clairmont, 2001; McCormack, 2001: xiii), there has been no sign of an economic revival.

Compensating for the retraction of corporate investments, the rise in Japanese government expenditures had turned a budget surplus of 2 percent of GDP into a deficit of 7 percent of GDP by 2001 (Redding, 2002). Any attempt to restructure the economy by trimming government expenditure would inevitably lead to an explosive growth of unemployment which, at 5.6 percent, is already at a post-Second World War high. In these conditions, if the government were to cut its outlays on construction, which constituted some 43 percent of the national budget in 1993 and employed some 10 percent of the workforce (McCormack, 2001: 33), the social dislocations would be all the more catastrophic.

Finally, unlike the 'hollowing out' of Japanese industries in the 1980s when the high value of the yen led to a spurt in Japanese investments in Southeast Asia, since the onset of the current economic crisis employment cutbacks and factory closures in Southeast Asia have paralleled those in Japan, as major corporations have redirected their investment flows to China where production costs are significantly lower. Since 1990, China has accounted for 45 percent of the $719 billion in foreign direct investment flowing to Asia. While Great Britain overtook Japan as the largest investor in Southeast Asia in 1998, Japanese investments to China more than doubled in the 1990s and its trade with China (including Hong Kong) in 2000 was three times its level the previous year. Thus, even as compression of export prices following the depreciation of the yen led to the re-emergence of high trade surpluses with the United States in 1998, its surplus with Asia fell by 36 percent (Abrahams, 1999; Arnold, 1999a; Arnold, 2001; Brooke, 2001b; Chandler, 2001a; Gilpin, 2000: 169–79; McDonald, 2001).

If the cannibalization of the *chaebol* and the weakening of *keiretsu* ties in Japan eroded the position of small parts suppliers all along the Pacific coasts of Asia, in certain technologically-sophisticated sectors, some three decades of sustained economic growth and affiliative ties as OEM suppliers for major enterprises had created strong research-based small enterprises like laptop computer parts in Taiwan and audiocard and multimedia components in Singapore. In these cases, tie-ups with major manufacturers had helped to compensate for small domestic markets (Wong Poh-Kam *et al.*, 1997). Agglomeration economies enabled Taiwan's

Quanta Computer to emerge as the world's largest maker of notebook computers, overtaking Toshiba in 2001, producing computers for seven of the top ten notebook companies. With the development of a large supplier base – with companies such as Compal, Asutek, Arima, and Taiwan Semiconductor – Quanta can assemble laptops in 48 hours from receiving orders and has now also diversified into desktops by putting together Apple's sleek new iMac system (Landler, 2002).

Taiwan's smaller and more decentralized industrial sector also implied that its industries were not burdened with the high debt–equity ratios of the *chaebol*. While the push toward industrial upgrading had led to a steady rise in royalty payments for South Korean enterprises – between 1962 and 1996, the government estimated these amounted to $13.2 billion, while total Taiwanese imports of technology amounted to a mere $500 million by 1993 (Noble and Ravenhill, 2000: 85–6). Unlike South Korea and the other hemorrhaging economies in the region, Taiwan was a net exporter of capital and was hence less vulnerable to the rapid withdrawal of capital. The dominance of state- and GMD-controlled companies also meant that the Taiwanese government could formulate a more coordinated strategy toward overseas expansion of its production networks. However, increasing competitive pressures in the form of falling exchange values in the region contributed to a relentless outflow of manufacturing investments especially to China – in 2000, China received some $26 billion of Taiwan's total overseas investment of $76 billion (Cheng, 2001) – and to a corresponding fall of Taiwan's GDP as its unemployment rates reached record highs. Even in computers, Taiwanese manufacturers are shifting production to China and by the end of 2003, it is estimated that over two-thirds of notebook computers made by Taiwanese companies will be assembled in China (Landler, 2002).

The dominance of government-controlled companies in its economy also insulated Singapore from the growing trans-border expansion of production and procurement networks. Whereas the transnational expansion of corporations based in Japan or South Korea undermined the coherence of national economy-making, the Singapore government saw the overseas expansion of its companies – such as DBS Bank's purchase of Hong Kong's Dao Heng Bank in April 2001, or SingTel's acquisition of Australia's Cable and Wireless Optus – as extending the island-state's 'global reach' (Wee, 2001: 997).

Singapore was also fortunate that Seagate Technologies chose it as the site for its disk drive manufacturing operations in the early 1980s. The swift development of a number of related industries and the creation of a pool of skills in subassembly operations associated with precision engineering which was industry-specific but not firm-specific meant that the island-state soon accounted for some 40–50 percent of the global production of disk drives. Despite the transfer of some lower value-added subassembly operations to neighboring lower-wage sites, as components for hard disk drives have very stringent precision and quality requirements, firms that had developed the capacity to supply these components also had the capacity to provision other electronics assemblers as well (Wong Poh-Kam, 2001). Nevertheless, Singapore's small population base and compact size suggests that this model has extremely limited relevance for other states.

Moreover, as theorists of 'late development' have argued, a central strategy of successful rapid industrialization has been the protection of infant industries and the disproportionate allocation of resources to flag-ship industrial sectors such as steel and other heavy industries. In such allocations, the profitability or comparative advantage of strategic indus-tries was less important than product quality and technological prowess. It is by no means certain that the same policies are possible in technologies based not on mass production but on innovation and knowledge-intensity – software and the Internet, for instance. If a 'shop-floor' focus enabled Japanese and South Korean corporations to reverse-engineer automobiles and consumer electronic products and devise cheaper ways to manufac-ture them, such techniques are less significant when the rapid pace of innovations in information technologies create new products in approxi-mately 18 months or less! The South Korean EPB's refusal to see the potential of semiconductors in the late 1980s dramatically silhouetted the inadequacies of administrative guidance when the economic environment had been radically transformed by new technologies (Yeon-ho Lee and Hyuk-Rae Kim, 2000: 122). Similarly, though Japanese manufacturing industries continued to be at the leading edge, they have been reduced to the status of price-takers in computer and semiconductor industries, and the competitive pace in finance, insurance, and software in Japan is increasingly set by foreign firms such as Citicorp, GE Capital, and Microsoft (Pempel, 1998: 140–1; Murphy, 2000: 35).

Notwithstanding these concerns, after its restoration to Chinese sover-eignty, the Tung Chee-hwa Administration has adopted a policy to trans-form Hong Kong into a high-technology hub to compensate for the inexorable drain of manufacturing jobs from the Special Administrative Region (SAR). Envisaging Hong Kong to become a center for food and pharmaceuticals based on Chinese medicine, as well as a leading supplier of high value-added components and a regional center for information and entertainment based on multimedia formats, the SAR government in 1999 unveiled plans to create a US$1.7 billion technology park or Cyberport to create a strategic cluster of information technology industries. Nevertheless, whether Hong Kong has, or can attract, a sufficient pool of people with the necessary skills remains to seen (So and Chan, 2002; So, 2002; So, n.d.).

In short, though the sharp currency depreciations experienced by several East and Southeast Asian economies appear to have been arrested, the hollowing out of their industrial bases has led to widespread unem-ployment, bankruptcies, and distress sales of otherwise viable enterprises.

Relaxation of ceilings and restrictions on foreign investments in the context of plunging currency values have seen the sale of corporate crown jewels to overseas investors at fire-sale prices. By shifting the relative balance of power between governments and enterprises in favor of the former, the crisis has endowed bureaucratic state apparatuses with a greater degree of autonomy, especially since a wave of foreclosures and layoffs also weakened the power of organized labor. In this changed ecology of production, trade, and investment, the greater prominence of governments is manifested in the emergence of a new institutional arma-ture for regional integration along Asia's Pacific shores as outlined in the Epilogue. But before turning to that, we need to survey how the depreciat-ing currency values and a decline in effective demand in the erstwhile 'dragons' has exacerbated the problem of overproduction just as workers in Western Europe and North America face increasing pressure from low-cost imports from the Asian economies.

Houses of glass

Though the United States and Western Europe appeared to have weath-ered the storm, as the economic crisis ricocheted from the Asian rimlands to cause capital flights from Russia and Latin America in 1998, compres-sion of export prices from economies in East and Southeast Asia soon dev-astated the manufacturing sector in the United States. As we shall see below, the end of the Cold War had parallel and contradictory effects on the United States and Western Europe. While a decline in military expen-ditures following the end of the Cold War and corporate tax cuts had stim-ulated fresh investments in manufacturing in the United States, the reverse Plaza Accord of 1995 once again shifted competitive pressures onto US manufacturers. However, rising equity prices meant that overseas investors continued to pump money into US stocks and the stock market boom helped turn the federal deficit into a small surplus by 1998. Perhaps more impressively, soaring stock prices sent technology stocks sky-high and irresistibly drew ever-increasing capital flows to the United States. At the same time, the attendant asset-price inflation led to widening income inequalities in the United States as well as a parallel expansion of consumer expenditures. When manufacturers, buoyed by higher levels of expenditure and the ease of raising money, undertook a new bout of investments, it exacerbated the problem of overproduction precisely when demand con-tracted in the Asian rimlands and exports from the region undercut prices. Low rates of capacity utilization, in turn, drove profits downwards and pulled stock prices sharply lower. Conversely, the fall of the Berlin Wall had saddled Germany with the huge cost of political reunification with the erst-while German Democratic Republic and threatened to undermine moves toward a common European currency. The high interest rates necessary to preserve the latter project resulted in high levels of unemployment and the stringent conditions negotiated for the common currency constrained macroeconomic options for governments. If the rise of the dollar provided a respite, the break was fleeting since the compression of export prices from the Asian rimlands constrained an expansion of manufacturing.

In the first place, the collapse of the Soviet Union and the reunification of Germany had yielded a significant 'peace dividend' for the United States as the numbers of its troops garrisoned in Western Europe were slashed from some 300,000 in 1989 to about 122,000 in 1997–98. Defense expenditures fell correspondingly by 30 percent in real terms during the same period (Calleo, 1998). The extent of this fall in defense spending is partly exaggerated by the extraordinary rise in military expenditure during Ronald Reagan's presidency and defense spending in 1997 well exceeded spending levels during most of the Cold War years before 1980 (Achcar, 2000: 103). Nevertheless, the decline was significant enough that, along with a long-term fall in interest rates,[6] it permitted the Clinton administration to reduce the annual fiscal deficit from 4.6 percent of GDP in 1993 when it came into office to 1.2 percent of GDP by January 1998 (Calleo and Rowland, 1973; Brenner, 2002).

Combined with the prior corporate tax cuts initiated by the Reagan Administration – by the early 1990s, corporate taxation was at 23 percent of pre-tax profits compared with 52 percent between 1960 and 1964 (Brenner, 2002: 70) – the fall in real wages during the 1970s and 1980s and a low dollar stimulated a fresh wave of manufacturing investments in the United States. From languishing at an annual average rate of just 1.3 percent between 1982 and 1990, manufacturing investment rose steeply to an average annual rate of 9.5 percent between 1993 and 1997 and to 10.5 percent by 1999. In the context of the decommissioning of obsolete plant and equipment in the 1980s, and the accompanying shrinkage of the manufacturing labor force, this spurt of new investments and the reorganization of production processes also led to an annual average increase of 4.4 percent in labor productivity between 1993 and 1997 (Brenner, 2002: 76–7).

However, though US manufacturers were able to hold wages down, the rise in labor productivity did not compensate for an average annual rate of 6 percent rise in the value of the dollar following the reverse Plaza Accord of 1995. Consequently, as export prices declined by an average of 2.6 percent in both 1996 and 1997 to flatten profit rates in the manufacturing sector, there was increased speculation in equities. Simultaneously, to maintain a high dollar, the Japanese government as well as investors from all over the world poured money into US government securities – the purchase of US government securities in 1995 being more than double the average of the previous four years. Between 1995 and 1997, investors from overseas bought $700 billion in US government securities – a figure that exceeded not only the total new debt issued by the US Treasury during this period but also $266.2 billion of US government debt previously held by US residents. This torrent of cash inflows pushed down interest rates on 30-year Treasury bonds and led to a stratospheric growth in stock prices: the New York Stock Exchange index rising by 80 percent between 1994 and 1997 while the Standard and Poor index more than doubled. Indeed, by the spring of 1997, the value of US stocks was greater than the value of the US GDP of about $8 trillion. After peaking at 180 percent of the US GDP in 2000, it fell back to 150 percent by early 2000 (Brenner, 2002: 135–48; Gowan, 1999: 119; Therborn, 2001: 97).

This extraordinary rise of equity prices was driven in particular by corporations taking advantage of low interest rates to borrow money to buy back their own stocks so as to raise their value even further. Since corporate executives and even employees increasingly received compensation in stock options, bidding up stock prices was to their advantage while selling stock and using the proceeds to finance investments would work against them by lowering the value of their stock holdings. Thus, whereas the highest annual total for stock purchases before the mid-1990s had been the $51.4 billion recorded in 1989, the value of stock repurchases was $134.3 billion in 1997, $169.1 billion in 1998, and $145.5 billion in 1999 (Brenner, 2002: 148).

For purposes of the present discussion, this mercurial growth in equity prices had six major consequences. In the first instance, the rise in capital gains tax receipts as a result of skyrocketing equity prices from $44 billion in 1995 to $100 billion in 1998 directly contributed to the transformation of the US federal deficit into a small surplus in fiscal 1998 (Gowan, 1999: 120; Pollin, 2000: 24; Phillips, 2002: 103). Second, firms could meet their pension fund obligations by rising portfolio values rather than by channeling funds into retirement accounts and hence release cash for distribution as dividends (Pollin, 2000: 40). Third, rising equity prices were crucial for start-up firms, especially in the technology sector, and they were, albeit briefly, the brightest stars in an asset-inflated firmament. From an annual average of $3 billion for initial public offerings (IPOs) between 1980 and 1994, the annual gross proceeds from IPOs reached stratospheric heights: $30 billion between 1994 and 1998, $60 billion per annum in 1999 and 2000 (Brenner, 2002: 195). The results of this extraordinary infusion of funds into new start-up technology stocks was spectacular:

> The Internet stocks that have headlined the mania over the last year [1998] are without known precedent in US financial history. At its highs in early April, the market capitalization of Priceline.com, which sells airline tickets on the web and has microscopic revenues, was twice that of United Airlines and just a hair under American's. America Online was worth nearly as much as Disney and Time Warner combined, and more than GM and Ford combined. Yahoo was capitalized a third higher than Boeing, and eBay nearly as much as CBS. At its peak, AOL sported a price/earnings ratio of 720, Yahoo! of 1,468 and eBay of 9,751 ... previous world-transformative events had never been capitalized like this ... RCA peaked at a P/E of 73 in 1929.

Xerox traded at a P/E of 123 in 1961, Apple maxed out at a P/E of 150 in 1980. And all these companies were pretty quick to turn a profit, and once they did, their growth rates were ripping. In the so-called Nifty Fifty era of the early 1970s, the half-hundred glamour stocks that led the market sported P/Es of forty to sixty. . . . And those evaluations were once legendary for their extravagance.

(Doug Henwood, quoted in Pollin, 2000: 41)

This 'irrational exuberance' of the stock market, as Greenspan once characterized it, magnetically attracted foreign investments, especially after the meltdown in East Asia – and the ensuing flights of capital from Latin America and Russia in 1998 (Wade and Veneroso, 1998b: 15–18; *The Economist*, 1999). From accounting for just 4 percent of the total net purchases of US corporate equities in 1995, private investors from overseas accounted for 25.5 percent by 1999 and for 52 percent by the first half of 2000, while their share of total corporate bond purchases rose from 17 percent to 44 percent during the same period. By the first half of 2000, holdings of gross US assets by overseas investors amounted to $6.7 trillion or 78 percent of US GDP and since these assets could be liquidated relatively easily, the US economy was more vulnerable to capital flows than ever before (Brenner, 2002: 208–9).

The fourth consequence of the growth in equity prices was that the market capitalization of shares held by households increased from $4 trillion to $12.2 trillion between 1994 and the first quarter of 2000. This stimulated an unprecedented wave of consumer borrowing, and by 2000 household outstanding debt (including mortgages and consumer debt) as a percentage of personal disposable income had attained a hitherto-unimaginable level of 97 percent. Corporate debt rose in tandem, quadrupling between 1994 and the first half of 2000. Conversely, the personal savings rate which had averaged around 10.9 percent between 1950 and 1992 plunged from 8.7 percent in 1992 to −0.12 percent in 1990 (Brenner, 2002: 189–92; Pollin, 2000: 32–3). With debts growing faster than assets, the Federal Reserve Bank's triennial survey of consumer finances indicated that the median US household's net worth (including home equity) declined from $51,640 to $49,900 between 1989 and 1995 (Phillips, 2002: 107).

From this perspective it can be seen that US opposition to any attempt to rollback financial liberalization in the crisis-hit Asian economies rose from the need to draw on savings in other economies to compensate for its very low domestic savings rates, and to maintain its high rates of consumption and investment (Wade and Veneroso, 1998b: 35–8; Wade, 1998a: 1540). The greater the degree of world financial integration, the greater the ability of Wall Street firms to use the American dollar's role as the international reserve currency to their advantage. Since US Treasury bills offer a means to borrow money cheaply from world markets, the intermediated funds can be recycled as FDI outflows, portfolio investments, and loans at much higher rates of interest. Thus, support for the IMF packages that used bail out funds to sustain exchange-rates at unsustainable levels allowed the rich to convert their money into dollars and whisk it away to safe havens in the United States rather than to stem the currency hemorrhage as it was intended to do (Stiglitz, 2002: 95–6).

Fifth, a corollary to the asset price inflation and the parallel plunge in the US domestic rates of savings was a widening in inequalities in income and wealth. In 1999, an article in the *New York Times* put it starkly: 'The gap between the rich and the poor has grown into an economic chasm so wide that this year the richest 2.7 million Americans, the top 1 percent, will have as many after-tax dollars to spend as the bottom 100 million' (quoted in Phillips, 2002: 103; Brenner, 2002: 191). Most notably, inequalities in income and wealth widened not merely because the rich were getting richer at a faster rate: it was also because the poor were becoming poorer! Though the federal minimum wage was hiked from $4.25 an hour to $5.15 in 1996, the real value of the new minimum wage was 30 percent less than its real value in 1968 (Pollin, 2000: 21; Brenner, 2002: 220). The average real after-tax income of the middle 60 percent of the population was lower in 1999 than it had been in 1977. To maintain their household incomes, increasing numbers of women were thrust into the job market: in the workforce, the percentage of women with children under six rose from 19 percent in 1960 to 64 percent in 1995, a figure higher than in any other OECD member-state. Between 1989 and 1999, the average work year increased by 184 hours and the Bureau of Labor Statistics indicated that a typical worker in the US worked the equivalent of nine work weeks more than the typical worker in Western Europe (Phillips, 2002: 111–13). From this perspective, the low unemployment rate of only 4.3 percent in 1996 was due more to low wages making it necessary for people to work more rather than to its inherent dynamism. Indeed, Bruce Western and Katherine Beckett (1999) have argued that if the effects of the high rates of incarceration in the United States are included – being 5 to 10 times larger than the OECD average in 1993 – the rate of unemployment in the mid-1990s would be around 8 percent, and even worse if the long-term effects of incarceration are factored in.

Finally, by inflating the value of household assets, soaring equity prices triggered a parallel expansion in consumer expenditures: from an average annual rate of 12 percent between 1992 and 1997, consumer expenditures on durable manufactured goods surged to an average annual pace of 12 percent between 1997 and the first half of 2000. High consumer demand and easy access to capital, due to the powerful attraction posed by equity prices in the US, led to a sustained growth in manufacturing investments – by an annual average of 12 percent between 1991 and the first half of 2000, with investments disproportionately concentrated in information technology (Brenner, 2002: 202, 205–34).

However, the rise of the dollar since 1995, and especially after East and Southeast Asian currencies plunged in value since 1997, provided a devastating blow to manufacturing profits in the United States. Increased capacity, as we have already seen in the previous chapter, had been exerting a steady downward pressure on profits. In dollar terms, manufacturing prices in the world market fell by an annual average rate of 4 percent between 1995 and 2000 as a result both of rampant overproduction and of East and Southeast Asian producers selling at distress prices. The temporal coincidence of the rise of consumer expenditures in the US and the appreciation of the dollar also facilitated a rapid expansion of imports – and the US manufacturing trade deficit increased by two and a half times between the onset of the crisis in the Asian rimlands in 1997 and 2000. Correspondingly, the US corporate manufacturing rate fell by 20 percent during this three-year period (Brenner, 2002: 204–5, 209, 214–15, 237).

Conversely, steep devaluations of the currencies of Japan and of the East and Southeast Asian NICs have led them to register record surpluses in their trade with the United States, Western Europe, and Latin America. In 1998, Japan's politically contentious trade surplus with the United States grew by 23 percent over the previous year: at ¥6,700 billion, it was the highest since 1987. As a result of the IMF-mandated structural reforms and the ensuing cutbacks in imports, South Korea's foreign exchange reserves stood at an all-time high of $41 billion by August 1998 and were estimated to reach $50 billion by the end of the year (Wade and Veneroso, 1998b: 25; Cumings, 1998: 70; Abrahams, 1999).

Yet, propelled by steady infusions of capital by overseas investors, equity prices continued to rise in 1999 and 2000 – inflows of non-residential investments rose by 11 percent in 1999 and by an annualized rate of 14 percent in the first half of 2000 – as the NASDAQ index of high-technology stocks more than doubled. Driven by returns on venture capital which reached 165 percent in 1999, net purchases of US stocks by overseas investors reached a new high of $172.9 billion the following year. While the scale and velocity of such asset-price inflation stimulated further investments, it exacerbated the problem of over production and Walden Bello and Robert Brenner note that by April 2001, the utilization capacity of telecommunications networks languished at a mere 2.5 percent, leading to massive declines in stock prices of industry giants like AT&T, Sprint, and Worldcom. These declines ricocheted onto makers of telecommunications equipment – switching routers, fiber-optic cables, etc. – while computer makers announced substantial layoffs. Non-technology sectors had of course been plagued by overcapacity for much longer – according to Federal Reserve estimates, manufacturing plants in the US were operating at only 73 percent of capacity in December 2001. Even when factories are operating at full capacity, appearances may be deceptive. Contracts between the United Auto Workers and the US automobile companies – valid until September 2003 – require the automakers to pay their employees their full salary whether they are working or not. Hence, it was more economical for GM, Ford, and Chrysler to produce and sell cars at a small loss rather than to shut plants down completely. When the contract expires however, current estimates suggest that some 15,000 workers would be laid off – and as each job lost at a final assembly plant could lead to the loss of four jobs for part suppliers, the effects would be magnified. By early 2001, the economic slowdown began to deflate the stock market bubble and the value of household-owned equities fell by 31 percent between the first quarter of 2000 and the first quarter of 2001. This steep decline was almost immediately telegraphed by a significant dampening of consumer expenditures on durable goods which further depressed stock prices in a vicious cycle (Bello, 2001; Brenner, 2002: 225–6, 244–5, 249, 251–2, 256–9; Pearlstein, 2002).

Meanwhile, across the Atlantic, though the collapse of the Berlin Wall and the withdrawal of the Red Army had rendered Germany less susceptible to US pressure, the cost of reunification meant that Germany enjoyed no 'peace dividend.' Instead, Chancellor Helmut Kohl's decision to override Bundesbank recommendations and permit the conversion of ostmarks on a one-to-one basis to deutsche marks not only led to higher budgetary deficits but also put increasing pressure on weaker currencies in the European Monetary System (EMS). Since raising taxes was politically unfeasible, German monetary authorities had raised interest rates to finance the deficit. This was not accompanied by a revaluation of the deutsche mark because it would have come up against the determination of the French government to maintain a strong franc, and undermined French support for a common European currency. Abnormally high interest rates in France and Germany forced Britain, Italy and Portugal to abandon the EMS altogether in 1992. High interest rates in France also lifted unemployment levels above 10 percent, and ballooning unemployment benefits led to high fiscal deficits. At the same time, the depreciation of the dollar against the deutsche mark exerted pressures on all European currencies. If the slide of the pound and the lira after Britain and Italy left the EMS enabled these economies to experience an export boom and enjoy relatively low unemployment rates, it jeopardized monetary union across the continent. Relatively high costs undermined the competitiveness of the German economy – the annual average GDP growth rate being a mere 0.9 percent between 1991 and 1995 – and the slower growth of the German economy exerted a downward pressure on other European economies. The rate of unemployment in the eleven European Union countries averaged 11.3 percent in 1996 when the average annual rate of unemployment in the 16 leading economies during the Great Depression between 1930 and 1938 had only been 10.3 percent. Moreover, as the dollar began to rise after 1995, while the deutsche mark and the franc lost between 20 and 23 percent of their value, competitive pressures were shifted onto Britain where the pound, outside the EMS, tended to shadow the dollar. However, stringent conditions for the common European currency negotiated under the Maastricht Treaty limited macroeconomic options for other European states. Finally, compression of export prices in East and Southeast Asia limited the growth of manufactures in Western Europe even after the rise of the US dollar. For instance, the Japanese trade surplus with the European Union grew by 26 percent in 1998 (Brenner, 1998: 3; Brenner, 2002: 124–6; Strange, 1998: 70–1, 81, 152; Abrahams, 1999; Calleo, 2001: 189–95).

In the first half of the 1990s, then, as indicated by Table 6.2, the three major blocs of core states – Japan, the United States, and Western Europe – experienced their lowest rates of growth in half a century. Though GDP growth in the US picked up marginally in the latter half of the decade, there was no parallel recovery in Japan and Western Europe and, on the whole, persistent overproduction dampened possibilities of a smooth recovery: none of the major capitalist engines was capable of pulling the world economy from the rut (Pollin, 2000: 28–31; Brenner, 2002: 46–7).

To recapitulate, the meltdown of several East and Southeast Asian economies in 1997–98 was so unexpected that as their governing elites groped for lifelines, Western governments used the emergency cash infusions from the IMF as a battering ram to restructure the ailing economies. The standard IMF prescription of raising interest rates to stabilize currencies wreaked havoc on companies which depended on short-term loans even for routine operating costs. Contrary to the usual practice of restricting foreign access to a country's assets when its credit has dried up, the IMF even pressured governments accepting its emergency loans and loan guarantees to accepting greater foreign ownership of assets. And the insistence on maintaining open capital markets facilitated capital flight as investors rushed to pull their capital out of the ailing economies before the situation deteriorated even further.

Except in Indonesia – the weakest of the 'mini-dragons' – these measures had the unexpected outcome of bolstering the relative autonomy of governments. The nationalization of private corporate debt and the insistence on closing down insolvent enterprises increased governments' stake in the economy, while the layoffs and cutbacks in government welfare expenditure severely weakened organized labor. Meanwhile, the acquisition of corporate assets at firesale prices by foreign capital – except in Indonesia where political and economic instability discouraged investments and Malaysia which was not subject to the IMF regimen – contributed to a restructuring of industrial organization. In Japan, it was signaled by the loosening of *keiretsu* networks and of the interdependence between enterprises, 'lead' banks, and *sogo sosha*. In South Korea, the high debt–equity ratios of the *chaebol* provided the Kim Dae-Jung administration with the perfect opportunity to force them to downsize their operations. The continued drain of manufacturing jobs to China further hollowed out industrial structures everywhere though some economies – notably Singapore – were relatively successful in moving toward more technology-intensive sectors.

Table 6.2 Declining economic dynamism: Japan, United States, and Western Europe (average annual percentage change)

	1960–69	1969–79	1979–90	1990–95	1995–2000	1990–2000	2001
GDP							
US	4.60	3.30	2.90	2.40	4.10	3.20	0.30
Japan	10.20	5.20	4.60	1.70	0.80	1.30	−0.30
Germany	4.40	3.60	2.15	2.00	1.70	1.90	0.60
Euro-12	5.30	3.70	2.40	1.60	2.50	2.00	1.95
G-7	5.10	3.60	3.00	2.50	1.90	3.10	1.10
GDP per capita							
US	3.30	2.50	1.90	1.30	3.40	2.35	−0.80
Japan	9.00	3.40	4.00	1.10	1.10	1.10	0.20
Germany	3.50	2.80	1.90	7.00	1.60	4.30	0.40
G-7	3.80[a]	2.10[b]	1.90	1.20	2.50	1.80	0.60
Labor productivity total economy (GDP/worker)							
US	2.50	1.30	1.15	1.20	2.30	1.80	0.20
Japan	8.60	4.40	3.00	0.70	1.20	0.90	0.00
Germany	4.30	3.00	1.50	2.10	1.20	1.70	0.00
Euro-11	5.20	3.20	1.90	1.90	1.30	1.60	0.24
G-7	4.80[a]	2.80[b]	2.55	1.70	–	–	0.33
Real compensation total economy (per employee)							
US	9.70	2.80	0.70	0.60	1.90	1.30	2.30
Japan	7.30	5.00	1.60	0.60	0.20	0.50	−0.10
Germany	5.10	4.30	1.10	2.00	0.10	0.95	1.80
Euro-11	5.60	4.00	0.80	1.00	0.30	0.60	4.69
Unemployment rate							
US	4.80	6.20	7.10	5.90	4.60	5.25	4.80
Japan	1.40	1.70	2.50	2.90	4.10	3.50	5.00
Germany	0.80	2.05	5.80	8.20	8.60	8.20	7.70
Euro-15	2.30	4.60	9.10	9.80	9.90	9.90	7.40
G-7	3.10[a]	4.90[b]	6.80	6.70	6.40	6.60	6.80
Non-residential capital stock (private business economy)							
US (net)	3.90	3.80	3.00	2.00	3.80	2.90	−5.20
Japan (gross)	11.30	9.50	6.90	5.30	4.50	5.00	−0.10
Germany (gross)	6.60	4.50	3.00	3.00	3.10[c]	–	−4.50
G-7 (gross)	4.80	4.60	3.90	–	–	–	−5.70

Sources: Brenner (2002: 47, table 1.10); IMF, *World Economic Outlook*, April 2003; OECD, *Economic Outlook*, 2003 (Annex 1, 6, 13, 15).

Notes
a 1960–73.
b 1973–79.
c 1990–93.

Epilogue

A future imperfect: Remaking a regional economy

It is better to be vaguely right than precisely wrong.

Wildon Carr[1]

Obituaries to the 'Asian economic miracle' published in the wake of the financial crisis, and self-congratulatory proclamations of the 'triumph of Western capitalism,' obscure a fundamental restructuring of economic and political relationships in East and Southeast Asia since 1997–98. Most notably, widespread perceptions that the IMF had acted as a 'creditor cartel, not an institution sensitive to its members' needs' (Dieter and Higgot, 2000) reversed long-standing apprehensions regarding closer regional economic integration among governing elites.

Abiding animosities against the Japanese for their colonial occupation of Korea and Taiwan and for the atrocities their forces committed against the Chinese and most peoples of Southeast Asia during the Second World War, and more than a quarter-century of American aggression in the Korean peninsula and Indochina, had hitherto conditioned processes of regional integration along the Pacific coasts of Asia. Acknowledging these sensitivities, as Japanese leaders sought recognition as an emerging regional powerhouse by proposing the creation of an Asian Development Bank (ADB) to promote subsidized loans to low-income states, they included a provision giving the United States an equal equity position with Japan (Lincoln, 2002: 206–7). Since the ADB itself was too large to promote regional integration,[2] Japanese government and business elites launched several initiatives to institute formal mechanisms for greater regional integration. Though none of them led to fruition, they were nevertheless important means to socialize policy makers in the region. Later, when a major initiative launched in Canberra in November 1989, the Asia Pacific Economic Cooperation (APEC), it even eschewed a noun to describe its institutional form. Stretching from the eastern borders of Poland to the Atlantic coasts of New England, APEC was of course more of a transregional forum and conceptions of 'open regionalism' associated with it meant little more than unilateral liberalism rather than a government-directed process to construct a free trade region

(Ravenhill, 2002a). Instead, as we have seen, economic integration along Asia's Pacific perimeters was achieved primarily by the transborder expansion of corporate networks.

If regional integration had been stymied by animosities against Japan and intra-regional tensions stemming from the Soviet–American rivalry and unresolved conflicts – most notably in the Korean peninsula and across the Taiwan Straits – as well as the imbrication of the United States in regional security and economic arrangements, the financial crisis of 1997–98 sharply changed perceptions concerning closer regional integration among governing elites. Echoing a widespread sentiment in the region, Walden Bello (1998c) observed that never before has the IMF's 'connection to its principle "stockholder" been displayed as prominently as it is today when the words of wisdom coming from US Treasury Secretary Robert Rubin and IMF Managing Director Michael Camdessus have become virtually indistinguishable.'

After the United States thwarted a Japanese-led regional resolution to the financial crisis – the AMF – the fact that Japan was the largest donor of financial assistance, committing $42 billion in the multilateral packages put together by the IMF, received scant attention. It was all the more egregious that though the US contributed only $8 billion – less than a fifth as much as Japan – it determined the conditions attached to the IMF loans and loan guarantees and as Christopher Hughes (2000) noted, 'the currency crises have looked to be a repeat of the Gulf crisis of 1990–91, when, despite talk of global partnership, the USA dictated policy and Japan was expected to pay for it.'

In these circumstances, the Japanese leadership welcomed greater receptiveness to an institutional framework for regional economic integration also because the absence of such a mechanism had meant that they had been at a disadvantage in negotiations over multilateral trade agreements since they had no experience in negotiating regional trade agreements, unlike the US and the European Union who could draw on 'reams of legal text' (Bowles, 2002: 247). Precisely because regional economic integration along Asia's Pacific coasts had been initiated and largely sustained by the transborder expansion of Japanese corporate networks, no regionally-accepted accounting standards or protocols for the legal treatment of financial activity had evolved and Japanese governing elites complained that international standards were nothing but American ones that would wreck Japan's unique systems of regulation.[3]

If Japanese business and government leaders had incentives to revive their initiatives for a regional institutional armature, the Chinese leadership too came to regret its role in blocking the creation of an AMF. Beijing had opposed it not only because of worries about a 'yen hegemony' but also because it was seeking to play by the rules of the reigning international financial order to ease its membership to the World Trade Organization (Bowles, 2002: 241). However, when no such concessions were made in this regard despite China maintaining its exchange-rate and not succumbing to pressures to devalue the renminbi (RMB), and despite injecting a measure of stability by launching a massive infrastructural development program, Chinese leaders felt slighted. Relations between Beijing and Washington worsened when US airplanes bombed the Chinese Embassy in Belgrade during the NATO assault on Yugoslavia in 1998, and the Chinese refused to accept the 'wrong map' explanation proffered by the Clinton administration. They were further enraged when the US House of Representatives' Cox Report in 1999 accused China of stealing US nuclear weapons technology and of penetrating US nuclear weapons laboratories. The continued 'demonization' of China, Paul Bowles (2002: 242–3) plausibly suggests, convinced its leadership to look more favorably toward emerging forms of regional integration that excluded the United States.

If smaller economies in the region were disappointed by China's opposition to the creation of an AMF, the Chinese leadership's refusal to devalue the RMB and its willingness to accept the adverse impact on the competitiveness of Chinese exports when regional currencies were plummeting had also won China much political goodwill in the region (Wang, 2000: 154–6). Japanese proposals to stabilize regional currencies by creating a regional financing facility also tempered deep-seated suspicions of Japanese motives among smaller economies in the region. Finally, the emergence of China as a regional counterweight to Japan has led to a greater willingness to enter into bilateral and plurilateral trade agreements among government and business elites in smaller East and Southeast Asian economies. Closer regional trade and financial arrangements even diminished interstate political tensions along Asia's Pacific perimeters.

Precisely because the crisis did not throw up new social forces, as we saw in Chapter 6, governing elites in the region sought to reconsolidate their power by reviving their export engines while trying to insulate their currencies from raids by currency speculators. This strategy was predicated on the assumption that the crisis stemmed not from structural problems as alleged by the IMF and Western governments but from temporary liquidity problems generated by declining export growth (Hughes, 2000: 242). For government and business elites, a regional solution to the crisis confronting them primarily entailed an insulation from speculative raids on their currencies and promoting intra-regional trade and consumption. Prefiguring this strategy, in September 1997, Joseph Yam, the Chief Executive of the Hong Kong Monetary Authority, had forcefully questioned the wisdom of repatriating regional surpluses to the United States through the purchase of US Treasury instruments:

[M]ore than 80% of total Asian foreign exchange reserves amounting to US$600 billion are invested largely in North America and Europe. . . .

It can be argued therefore that Asia is financing much of the budget deficit of developed countries, particularly the United States, but has to try hard to attract money back into the region through foreign instruments. And the volatility of foreign portfolio investments has been a major cause of disruptions to the monetary and financial systems of the Asian economies. Some have even gone so far as to say that the Asian economies are providing the funding to hedge funds in non-Asian countries to play havoc with their currencies and financial markets.

(quoted in Nordhaug, 2002: 525)

As regional governing elites turned away from the United States and began to create an institutional framework for closer regional integration, it implied a reversal of the repatriation of trade surpluses earned by East and Southeast Asian states to the United States to fund US federal deficits and to maintain its high levels of consumption with low levels of domestic savings.

In the first instance, after its AMF initiative had been thwarted, the Japanese government announced a new initiative offering $30 billion in aid denominated in yen to the five economies most adversely affected by the financial crisis – Thailand, Indonesia, the Philippines, South Korea, and Malaysia – without the stringent conditions attached to typical IMF bail outs. In addition, the New Miyazawa initiative, as this proposal has come to be known, also pledged an additional $20 billion to Vietnam to support economic reforms (Amyx, 2000: 148–9; Nordhaug, 2002: 529). In November 1998, the Japanese government also provided $22.5 billion through the Export-Import Bank of Japan to foster private sector trade in the region. As its budgetary problems forced a cutback in its overseas development aid, the Japanese government shifted its emphasis from big-ticket projects to human resource development, promising some $32 million toward human resource development in ASEAN states and stationing finance ministry officials in Thailand and Vietnam to provide assistance in the use of yen loans and overseas debt management (Bowles, 2002: 240; Hughes, 2000: 244–5).

This was followed by an inaugural meeting of East Asian Finance Ministers representing the ten ASEAN member-states as well as China, Japan, and South Korea on May 13, 2000 when they agreed to create a network of currency swaps. By agreeing to work toward the creation of a regional liquidity fund, they envisaged a system whereby member-states can cushion the impact of currency fluctuations by having access to some of their partners' foreign exchange reserves. Central banks of the ASEAN members, plus China, Japan, and South Korea were estimated to have reserves of more than $800 billion in March 2000. Even if only a fraction of this were to be available, it could easily overcome liquidity crises without having to resort to the IMF or to US or European banks. Chinese membership in the currency swap network also provided a counter-balance to Japanese influence as the Chinese central bank together with the Hong Kong monetary authority controlled over $250 billion in reserves while being insulated against volatile exchange-rate fluctuations by comprehensive controls over capital flows. Moreover, as monetary arrangements are not discriminatory toward other states, they do not attract sanctions from the WTO (Montagnon, 2000; Dieter and Higgot, 2000; Bergsten, 2000). Crucially then, whereas corporate networks were the main mechanisms for regional integration before the crisis of 1997–98, intra-governmental negotiations are proving to be the main driving force for the new phase of regional integration in East and Southeast Asia.

These beginnings suggested a significant turn away from the hitherto accepted practice in East and Southeast Asia – with the exception of ASEAN which remained the only free-trade agreement in the region – to pursue unilateral liberalization measures rather than discriminatory, preferential bilateral trade agreements. Japan, in particular, had feared that because of its extremely diverse range of export markets, negotiating bilateral or plurilateral trade agreements might make it vulnerable to discriminatory regional trade agreements. However, in a 1999 White Paper, the Ministry of International Trade and Industry explicitly endorsed the creation of a free trade agreement in Northeast Asia, noting that such agreements had led to an expansion of trade and investment flows in other cases, such as that of the European Union (EU) and the North American Free Trade Agreement (NAFTA); that the reduction of tariff and commerical barriers helped prepare participating economies become more competitive in a global economy; and that regional agreements were the building blocks of multilateral trade agreements (Ravenhill, 2002b: 179–80).

Accompanying government-directed efforts toward regional integration was a recovery of intra-Asian trade after it had collapsed in 1998. Between 1990 and 2000, intra-Asian merchandise exports grew at an annual rate of 10 percent, even after accounting for a 17 percent drop in 1998, and accounted for 48.9 percent of merchandise exports of Asian economies. North America, in contrast, accounted for only 25.6 percent of merchandise exports from Asia (World Trade Organization, 2001: table III.72). Central to the growth of this intra-Asian trade was the re-emergence of China as the 'workshop of the world.' Low wages, a virtually limitless supply of docile labor, and political stability led to a relentless inflow of FDI to China, which emerged in 2002 as the largest recipient of FDI, overtaking the United States. Conversely, inflows of FDI to South Korea fell by 63.7 percent in the last quarter of 2002 compared with the last quarter of the previous year, while Indonesia suffered an annual decline of 35 percent in 2002 (Rhoads, 2003; Roberts and Kynge, 2003).

China now makes 50 percent of cameras sold worldwide, 30 percent of air-conditioners, 25 percent of washing machines, and 20 percent of refrigerators (Legget, 2002). In comparative terms, while Chinese exports have doubled in just the last five years, it took 12 years after 1838 for British exports to double, ten years for Germany to double its exports in the 1960s, and seven years for Japan in the 1970s (Roberts and Kynge, 2003). Though large inflows of foreign investment to China have led to a loss of jobs in East and Southeast Asia in some sectors,[4] rapid economic growth in China also served to boost imports – in 2001 Chinese imports from Asia amounted to $42 billion or about 53 percent of Japanese imports from the region (Richardson, 2002). As Jim Walker, chief economist for CLSA Emerging Markets notes, 'People simplistically believe there will be a giant sucking sound as China absorbs Asian economies. The reality is that for every dollar of exports, China imports 92 cents' (quoted in Crampton, 2003). China has committed itself to creating a free trade region with ASEAN by 2010 (Eckholm and Kahn, 2002).

On another estimate, China's gross industrial output grew from 2.4 percent of global industrial production in 1993 to 4.7 percent in 2002. Chinese purchases of industrial products, however, also rose to 4.6 percent of world industrial production in 2002. This implies that the net increase in China's manufacturing exports amounted to only 0.18 percent of world manufacturing production (Andersen, 2003). Moreover, Chinese firms, mainly state-owned enterprises, have also begun expanding overseas. According to the *World Investment Report, 2002*, the top 12 Chinese TNCs controlled more that $30 billion in foreign assets and employed more than 20,000 employees in their overseas operations, which generated $30 billion in sales (Iyengar, 2003).

Rapid growth in manufacturing in China has seen urban incomes increase by an annual average of 17 percent since 1998 and rural incomes by 6 percent (Crampton, 2003). This rise in incomes has created a lower middle-income – defined as people with an annual average household income of $1,200 – market of 470 million, larger than in any country other than India. Thus the Chinese now buy more cellphones than consumers anywhere else, more film than the Japanese, more vehicles than the Germans. As a result, foreign companies that once used China as an export base now sell most of their China-based production in the country itself (Kahn, 2003). Relatedly, in South Korea, after the close relations between banks and politically-connected enterprises were severed by the economic meltdown, the restructured banks have pursued consumer banking. The collapse of the asset bubble in the US economy since mid-2000 shifted investment strategies and contributed to a greater density in intra-regional capital flows. In 2001, the region's largest credit card issuer, Visa International, increased the numbers of cards issued by 25 percent to 310 million and the volume of sales and cash withdrawals in Asia using Visa cards grew by 44 percent to $310 billion. Increased consumer expenditure in South Korea was reflected in a more than 11 percent increase in retail sales in 2001 as household lending overtook corporate lending for the first time. The following year, South Korea's 18 commercial banks posted profits of $5 billion, an 11.4 percent increase over 2001 (Thornhill, 2002; Ward, 2002b; Kirk, 2003). Similarly, the World Bank estimates that private consumption increased at an average annual rate of 8.8 percent in China between 1990 and 2000 and though the corresponding rate in Malaysia was only 3.8, in 2000 personal consumption grew at a galloping rate of 10.7 percent. If successful, this could finally free economies along Asia's Pacific coasts from their dependence on the United States as a market of last resort.

To counteract the flight of manufacturing to China, the Japanese government sought to reorient its domestic industry to new growth sectors. In 1999, while Japanese imports of software totaled ¥720 billion, its exports were a meager ¥9.13 billion. Again, between 1991 and 2000, while Japanese companies registered 707 patents, the corresponding figure for US companies was 5,430. Recognizing the importance of rectifying this 'technology deficit,' the Ministry of Economy, Trade, and Industry – the new nomenclature for MITI after it was reorganized in 2001 – proposes to spend ¥24,000 billion over the next five years on information technology, environment, biotechnology, and nanotechnology. However, questions remain whether a rigid bureaucratic structure can be flexible enough to create high value-added products through science and technology. An apt illustration of the rigidity of the organizational structure of Japanese research is provided by the case of Yoshiahi Ito, who had done pioneering work on the genetic causes of leukemia and cancer. He was forced to move from Kyoto to Singapore with his entire research team in 2002 as he had reached the mandatory retirement age and the Japanese research establishment was not prepared to let him work any longer (Nakamoto and Pilling, 2002; see also Markoff, 2002)!

As governmental negotiations have begun to undergrid regional economic integration, political tensions in the region have begun to thaw as well and this has led to South Korea and Japan distancing themselves from US foreign policy positions in the region, notably with regard to North Korea. Elected on a pro-engagement platform, South Korean President Kim Dae-Jung made a historic trip to Pyongyang in June 2000. His 'Sunshine Policy' offered a beleaguered North Korean regime desperately needed economic assistance and a whole range of economic, cultural, and sporting exchanges were inaugurated. These included work toward reopening the Seoul–Pyongyang railway line, now nearing completion, which would connect South Korea to Europe, construction of a Special Economic Zone north of the demilitarized zone by Hyundai, and a joint tourist development project at Mount Kumgang. Despite Washington castigating the North Korean President Kim Jong Il as a charter member of an 'axis of evil,' between 60 and 70 percent of South Koreans do not see North Korea as a threat. Both Kim Dae-Jung and his successor, Roh Moo-Hyun, have rejected the Bush administration's confrontational approach toward Pyongyang. In September 2002, the Japanese Prime Minister Koizumi Junichiro also visited Pyongyang, despite opposition from Washington. In 2001, North Korea adopted sweeping economic reforms – coining Kaegon as the Korean equivalent of Perestroika, and according to Chinese authorities the North Korean leadership has determined that without security guarantees from the United States and access to economic assistance, the Democratic People's Republic of Korea will face economic collapse and social chaos. It is precisely the fear that such a collapse will trigger a flood of refugees south and pose an unbearable strain on its fragile economy that has led Seoul to publicly distance itself from Washington's increasingly belligerent posture toward Pyongyang. Rather than escalating tensions O. Wonchol, the architect of South Korea's industrial transformation under President Park Chung-Hee, has proposed a peninsula-wide divison of labor and resources to more optimally utilize North Korea's relative abundance of mineral resources and reserves of high-quality low-wage labor (McCormack, 2002; McCormack, 2003).

On another axis of regional tension, in November 2002, China reached agreement with ASEAN to prevent clashes in the South China Sea – concerning the Spratly Islands and other territorial disputes (Eckholm and Kahn, 2002). Finally, if the election of an opposition candidate, Chen Shui-bian, for the first time in the history of Taiwan has led to calls for a formal declaration of independence and raised tensions with China, the rapid growth of Taiwanese investments in China has also prompted leading businessmen to urge Taipei to rescind the ban on their joining the National People's Congress – China's parliament – and the Chinese People's Political Consultative Conference for them to have a formal voice in mainland politics (Lague, 2001).

Greater regional integration along Asia's Pacific coasts not only lessened the dependence of these economies on the United States as a market of last resort but also posed problems for the latter as it is in increasing need of foreign capital to compensate for its low rates of domestic savings and high rates of investment. In the context of the first foreign incursions on the US mainland since 1812 – the attacks on the World Trade Center and the Pentagon on September 11, 2001 – the Bush administration successfully pushed for an additional $48 billion for defense and the US military budget for 2002–3 equaled the combined defense outlays of the next 15 biggest military powers (Achcar, 2002: 75–6). Along with a prior $1.4 trillion tax cut, this transformed a projected cumulative $5.6 trillion federal budget surplus over 10 years when Bush took office to expectations in March 2002 of a $1.8 trillion deficit over the same period (Maddrick, 2003). To finance its current account deficit – estimated at $500 billion in 2002 and growing at an annual rate of 10 percent – the US requires capital inflows of some $1.9 billion every working day (Clairmont, 2003)! However, as the US equities bubble burst capital inflows have diminished – falling from $307.7 billion in 2000 to

$130.8 billion in 2001 and to just $30.1 billion in 2002 (Organization for Economic Cooperation and Development, 2003). This accounts in large part for the 9.7 percent fall in the value of the dollar between January 2002 and May 2003 against other major currencies. Moreover, higher federal deficits, unless counter-balanced by large capital inflows, would lead to higher interest rates and further dampen economic activity, especially when the euro and possibly the yen could emerge as alternatives to the US dollar as international reserve currencies. In short, while US governing elites proclaim their military invincibility, the material base of the US economy is far more vulnerable than they appear to realize.

Paradoxically, if the geopolitical ecology of the Cold War provided for the reconstruction of economies along Asia's Pacific seaboard, the dampening of lingering tensions stemming from those times now provides for the reconstruction of regional linkages on entirely new foundations. As we saw in Chapter 1, the relative impoverishment of US client states in East Asia – Japan, South Korea, and Taiwan – meant that rather than seeking to integrate them to foster the transnational expansion of US enterprises after the Second World War, postwar reconstruction was financed by massive injections of US aid and on export promotion. Large infusions of American aid and procurements funneled through the bureaucracies of its client states enabled them to pursue developmental goals through the implementation of national industrial policies determined by elite economic agencies. These policies were determined by the specific configurations of class forces in each jurisdiction as well as by its prior legacies of industrialization as we saw in Chapters 2 and 3. Meanwhile, though Hong Kong and Singapore had lost their entrepôt functions due to the Chinese Revolution and the failure of federation with Malaya respectively, as British colonies they were not recipients of US aid. If the flight of capital from China was crucial in Hong Kong's transformation into a manufacturing platform, Singapore relied on foreign investors by providing excellent infrastructural facilities and by brutally cauterizing a militant labor movement.

Fortuitously for Taiwan and South Korea, as the limits imposed by their narrow domestic markets on import-substituting policies were being reached in the mid-1960s, an increase in competitive pressures faced by Japan and other high-income economies led enterprises based in those jurisdictions to seek out low-waged labor overseas. When the pursuit of multiple, parallel patterns of industrialization serially eroded the advantages accruing to each of the low- and middle-income states that had pursed a strategy of import-substituting industrialization, a transborder expansion of Japanese production networks to East and Southeast Asian economies enabled them to withstand the collapse of low- and middle-income economies elsewhere in the early 1980s. Sustained rates of growth, however, radically transformed social topographies all across the region and rendered the coalitional logic of the developmental state anachronistic.

Ruling coalitions in these jurisdictions were able to largely accommodate these pressures from below by easing controls over capital flows and – except in Japan, Taiwan, Hong Kong, and Singapore – by adopting debt-led strategies of industrialization. However, this undermined national industrial policies since it conferred priority on inflation control and the resulting bout of overproduction led to the financial crisis of 1997–98. Ironically, if the IMF and Western governments blamed 'crony capitalism' for the meltdown of some of the fastest growing economies in history, and forced their governments to liberalize their economies, curb public spending, nationalize private corporate debt, dissolve bankrupt enterprises, break up heavily indebted conglomerates, and permit greater foreign ownership of assets, these very measures shifted the balance of power between states and local capital back to states.

Governing elites in the region, resentful of Western pressures during the crisis, have now begun to reintegrate their economies on an entirely different institutional basis as they seek to reduce their reliance on the United States as the market of last resort. Closer regional integration and an increase in consumption has begun to redirect capital flows away from the United States. Thus, contrary to the triumphalist rhetoric of US political and business leaders, the material foundations of the American economy are steadily eroding as capital continues to accumulate in great goblets along Asia's Pacific coasts.

Notes

Introduction

1 Robert Wade (1996) has argued that the World Bank report was a reflection of Japan's increased prominence in the world-economy. As much of Japan's overseas investment and assistance policies ran counter to the neo-classical orthodoxy professed by the Bank, Japan's Policy and Human Resource Development trust fund for the Bank substantially underwrote the costs of the report. However, stiff opposition from the Bank's staff so diluted the report that the London *Financial Times* was to report that 'Industrial policies to promote particular sectors or companies have been a failure in East Asia and do not explain the region's rapid growth in recent decades due to a World Bank study' (quoted in Wade, 1996: 28).

2 I use 'divisioning of labor' rather than the more usual 'division of labor' to indicate the ongoing, dynamic nature of the process rather than the static condition suggested by the latter term.

1 Geopolitical ecology of US hegemony

1 When General Douglas MacArthur noted in a speech in Seattle in 1951, 'the gradual rotation of the epicenter of world trade back to the Far East whence it started many centuries ago,' his concern was *not* the economic challenge posed by Japan and other economies on Asia's Pacific perimeters, but that '"the main problem" of the "next thousand years" would be "the raising of the sub-normal standards of life of its more than a billion people"' (quoted in Miles, 1990: 171).

2 The scarcity of dollars had become so acute by mid-1949 that Britain was compelled to devalue the pound by 30.5 percent, from $4.03 to $2.80, in an attempt to gain an advantage over European competitors and to end speculative pressures against the pound (Block, 1977: 98; McCormick, 1989: 90; van der Wee, 1986: 43).

3 By the end of 1952, the United States was footing 60 percent of the French war expenses in Indochina, with the US share rising to 80 percent at the time of the Geneva Conference. And as McCormick (1989: 113) notes, 'French fingers pulled the triggers, but American dollars loaded the guns.'

4 Other examples of the industrialization of previously non-industrialized parts of the core include the environs of Flanders in Belgium, the 'M4 Corridor' in southern England, Toulouse and other areas of southwestern France; and the Mezzogiorna in Italy (van der Wee, 1986: 55; Henderson, 1989: 6).

5 For a synoptic account of the increase of wages, real and nominal, in Western Europe and its impact on consumption, see van der Wee (1986: 236–45).

6 Though US aid to Taiwan was officially terminated in 1965, a considerable portion of the total of $1,467.7 million committed between 1951 and 1965 remained undelivered. Consequently, aid deliveries continued through to 1968 and may have amounted to a cumulative total of $1,489 million – the $8.7 million discrepancy between commitments and deliveries being due to discrepancies in sources (Jacoby, 1966: 38–44).

7 To put this in perspective, Soviet economic and military disbursements to all 'less developed countries' between 1954 and 1978 was only $7.6 billion, or only slightly more than US *economic* aid to South Korea alone (Cumings, 1987: 67; Woo, 1991: 45).

2 Strong states, weak societies

1 When the total exports from Britain to the United States were valued at $400 million in 1951, Malaya's rubber exports to the US alone were worth $405 million (Tremewan, 1994: 12).

2 In the first eight months of the Occupation, the rates of inflation were especially steep. If the index of prices in August 1945 is taken to be 100, it rose to 346.8 in September, to 548.9 in December, and to 1184.5 in March 1946 (Johnson, 1982: 177–8).

3 The consumer price index in Taiwan, which had risen by 10 percent annually between 1946 and 1949, soared to 500 percent in 1949–50 due to the victory of the CCP (Lundberg, 1979). By another reckoning, the wholesale price index increased 260 percent in 1946, 360 percent in 1947, 520 percent in 1948, and 3,500 percent in 1949 (Ho, 1978: 104).

4 According to one study, 91 percent of the large landowners, and more than 98 percent of the small landowners sold their shares in the corporations – Taiwan Cement Corporation, Taiwan Pulp and Paper Corporation, Taiwan Agriculture and Forestry Corporation, and the Taiwan Industrial and Mining Corporation – either in one or in several lots, often at a loss. The same study also indicates that only about 17 percent of the large, and 10 percent of the smaller, landowners used the proceeds of these sales to establish their own businesses (Ho, 1978: 167; Simon, 1988a: 147–8).

5 While acknowledging the existence of relatively equitable patterns of income distribution in these states, it must be borne in mind that institutional factors – the ability to open bank and postal savings accounts under assumed names in South Korea and Japan, for instance (Johnson, 1982: 210; Amsden, 1989: 16, 38) – severely distort conventional measures.

6 Typically, workers in the first tier of subcontracting companies tend to be unionized though they do not belong to the same unions as workers of the parent firms. Workers in the lower rungs were unlikely to be unionized (Shapira, 1993: 232).

7 By another indicator, with the rapid increase in war-related industries, 1.4 million Koreans were employed in factories by 1941. In contrast, there were only 2 million factory workers in all of China in 1933 (Cumings, 1981: 26–7)!

8 By 1941, factory employment (including miners) approached 181,000 in Taiwan.

9 Young-bum Park and Michael Lee (1995: 57, n. 1) estimate that 95 percent of Korean mines and 94 percent of factories were controlled by Japanese enterprises. Similarly, the Taiwanese were forbidden to form corporations without Japanese participation till 1924, and even after that they were largely confined to small-scale industry, trade, and land development. Only 31 percent of those with technical qualifications were native Taiwanese and more than one-third of these were physicians or pharmacists, while only 27 percent of government

employees were native islanders (Ho, 1978: 100–2; Gold, 1988a: 106–9; Haggard, 1990: 78–9).

10 In the absence of a central bank, central banking functions are performed by several separate agencies in Hong Kong. The Hongkong and Shanghai Bank and the Chartered Bank issue bank notes, act as the lender of last resort, serve as the government's banker, and hold large amounts of the cash reserves of other banks. To issue currency notes, the two major banks are required to deposit equivalent assets in non-interest bearing deposits with the Exchange Fund and hence the new Hong Kong dollars are still theoretically backed by foreign currency assets, though no longer in terms of British pounds alone. Supervision of private financial institutions falls under the purview of the Commissioner of Banking while the control of money and credit, the management of foreign exchange reserves and currency issue, and the stabilization of exchange-rates are the responsibility of the Secretary of Monetary Affairs. Both these officials, in turn, report to the colony's Financial Secretary (Jao, 1993: 140–3).

11 Between 1959 and 1963, a new group of industries – tobacco, wood and cork products, metal products, chemicals and petroleum products – had surpassed the industries that had been dominant at the time Singapore gained self-governing status: food, beverages, printing and publishing, and electrical machinery. However, the capital-intensive nature of the new industries, especially the chemical and petroleum sectors, did not alleviate the unemployment situation, which rose from 13.2 percent in 1959 to 14 percent in 1963 despite a 107.8 percent increase in industrial output and a fall in the population growth rate. Though the number of pioneer firms increased from 42 with a subscribed capital of S$163 million in June 1963 to 113 with a subscribed capital of S$233 million by the end of the year, 56 percent of this figure was accounted for by locally-based capital. The share of local capital is even greater, 69.4 percent of total subscribed capital, if the highly capital intensive sectors are excluded (Rodan, 1989: 74–6).

3 The making of industrial behemoths

1 Between 1970 and 1979, Taiwan had the highest ratio of savings to net national product in the world – an average of 30.5 percent between 1970 and 1979 as opposed to 17.5 percent for South Korea and 26.5 percent for Japan (Wade, 1990: 61–2).

2 Between 1966 and 1970, domestic bank lending rates in South Korea were 24.4 percent while the foreign interest rate was 6.4 percent, and when adjusted for exchange-rate depreciation and inflation, the real private cost of borrowing from abroad was −3.1 percent. Between 1971 and 1975, the domestic lending rate was 17.0 percent, foreign interest rate 7.9 percent, and the real cost of private borrowing abroad −3 percent (Amsden, 1989: 76, table 3.8, 94–5; Woo, 1991: 104, table 4.7; see also Kuznets, 1977: 157–8). Hagen Koo and Eun Mee Kim (1992: 129, table 5.1), however, present a different estimate: domestic bank lending rates between 1966 and 1970 being 25.04 percent on average, and the real interest rate being 9.72 percent on average, the corresponding figures between 1971 and 1975 being 16.8 percent and −2.92 percent respectively.

3 According to one analyst, only 40 percent of the 500 largest manufacturing concerns in Taiwan belonged to a business group, and only 40 percent of these groups have even a single firm listed on the stock exchange. This indicates that the overwhelming majority of enterprises remain single-unit firms (Wade, 1990: 66).

4 Since no *sogo shosha* has an equally good vantage point in every regional or product market, different *sogo shoshas* give clients access to different markets. Additionally, cost structures differ between *sogo shoshas* in different markets. Hence there is no strategic reason for a firm to ally itself solely with one *sogo shosha* (Yoshino and Lifson, 1986: 58–9; Womack *et al.*, 1990: 58–62).

5 Strapped for capital, and without the large market runs enjoyed by American and European manufacturers, Toyota was unable to imitate their methods of production. While experimenting with different methods, Taiichi Ohno at Toyota discovered that costs per part actually fell if components were made in small batches, as it eliminated the cost of carrying large inventories and because quality defects could be identified and corrected almost instantly. Since the erratic nature of orders often resulted in suppliers being compelled to stock large volumes of one type of a component before changing machinery to build the next part, the next step was to synchronize production schedules. This was achieved by creating functional tiers of subcontractors and leaving engineering decisions to them. By ensuring that the first-tier subcontractors did not compete with each other, they were also encouraged to cooperate with each other to improve the design process (Cusumano, 1985: 265–6; Womack *et al.*, 1990: 52–61; Lazoinick, 1995: 97).

4 Crisis of US hegemony and the growth of regional economic integration in Pacific-Asia

1 When US corporate investment overseas increased sixteen-fold beween 1950 and 1980, from $12 billion to $192 billion, domestic investment grew only at half the pace, from $54 billion to $400 billion (Bluestone and Harrison, 1982: 42).

2 As late as 1966, host country markets accounted for three-fourths of all sales by US transplants in Asia, and the remainder were primarily exported to other nearby markets. By 1977, exports to the United States constituted one-third of all sales by US subsidiaries in Asia and over 90 percent of this trade was intra-firm transfers within TNCs. Exports to third country destinations accounted for another 25 percent of all sales with Japan emerging as the principal market (Encarnation, 1992: 153, 156–68; Gold, 1988b: 195).

3 Tessa Morris-Suzuki (1991: 139) has estimated that average Japanese wages, which were 15 percent *lower* than in the Philippines in 1960, were four times as much by 1970.

4 Net profit share is derived by dividing net profits (including rent and interest) by net value added.

5 Between 1966 and 1971, when the volume of Japanese textile production in Indonesia grew from 250 to 600 million meters, the domestic industry lost over half its workforce as they were outproduced by Japanese transplants. The decline in production was most severe in the handloom and batik sectors where over 70 percent of the total workforce was laid off (Nester, 1990: 120).

6 Though ethnic Chinese amounted to only 29 percent of the population of Malaysia, they accounted for 61 percent of the share capital in the mid-1990s (Henderson, 1999: 336).

7 The average number of firms owned by the ten largest *chaebol* increased from 7.5 in 1972 to 25.4 in 1979. Measured by the two-digit industrial classification, during the same time, the number of different industrial sectors they operated in grew from an average of 7.7 per *chaebol* to 17.6. During this timeframe, gauged in terms of assets, these ten largest *chaebol* registered compound average annual growth rates of 47.7 percent when real GNP grew at an annual average rate of 10.2 percent (Koo and Kim, 1992: 136).

8 The number of Japanese investments in Taiwan accounted for 28 percent of cases, 26 percent of total foreign capital, and averaged $1.25 million (Gold, 1988b: 196).

9 These figures must be treated with some caution as Jeffrey Winters (Winters, 1996: 114, n. 45) reminds us that '[U]ntil very recently, an investment was categorized as "foreign" if there was as little as 1 percent foreign participation.'

5 Debts and delusions

1 Between 1975 and 1984, in the Japanese manufacturing sector, financial assets as a proportion of liabilities rose from 42.6 percent to 66.3 percent. By 1984, Toyota Motors and Matsushita Electric had annual financial earnings, unconnected to their manufacturing operations, of ¥48.9 billion ($211.7 million) and ¥57.7 billion ($249.8 million) respectively. And by 1987, profits from Toyota's financial operations had tripled from its 1984 level and its total cash holdings was enough to buy Honda. Continuing its mercurial rise, these holdings had reached over $25 billion by 1995 and Matsushita's performance was only slightly less spectacular (Calder, 1997: 19).

2 Without a thorough-going reform of US agricultural policies, the short-sighted policy of rapidly expanding acreage during the euphoria following the massive Soviet grain purchases of 1972 and 1973 led to a bout of farm failures in the 1980s that were as severe as in the 1930s (Summers *et al.*, 1990: 130–6; Friedmann, 1993: 40–2).

3 *Tobashi* accounts refer to an arrangement whereby losses of one privileged client of a brokerage house are shifted to another client on the understanding that the buyer would be provided with a similar accommodation should the stock's performance fail to enable the buyer to recoup its purchase price in the open market (Bennett, 1997).

4 Numbers of Japanese bank offices in Asia rose from 99 in 1980 to 313 in 1990 and 363 in 1994 and the Asian share of overseas loans by Japanese banks increased from 19 percent in 1991 to 26 percent in 1994 (Pempel, 1999b: 68).

5 Privatization in the Malaysian context encompasses even instances where less than 50 percent of the assets of state-owned enterprises were sold to private investors as well as cases where the government retained equity control. It also includes contracting-out, leasing, and build–operate–transfer arrangements (Jomo, 1995: 43).

6 Between 1990 and 1993, Japanese investment flows to Thailand dropped from $1.2 billion to $578 million; and total foreign direct investment fell from $2.4 billion in 1990 to $640 million in 1994 (Bello *et al.*, 1998: 17).

7 Crucially, while real hourly wages declined in industries where the US had lost its competitive edge – by 11 percent in steel between 1979 and 1993, or by 8.3 percent in textiles – wages rose in sectors where US industry retained its advantages, as in chemicals where real hourly earnings increased by 17.1 percent during the same period (Gordon, 1996b: 20, 28, 188, 193).

8 Despite the diversity of the small business sector, a 1953 law legalized cartels in several industries and the Japan Political League of Small and Medium Sized Enterprises became a vehicle to mobilize small businesses to support legislation favoring their interests. Similarly, Nōkyō provided such a comprehensive range of services that it was almost suicidal for farm families not to join the nominally voluntary organization.

9 Moreover, since many seats required only 12–15 percent of the ballot, this system fragmented opposition by favoring niche parties, especially since well-organized local candidates had advantages over candidates promoting wider national agendas (Pempel, 1998: 98).

10 Though the real magnitude of the devaluation is disputed, what was significant was that it was perceived as substantial and investment flows were switched accordingly (Wade, 1998a: 1541).

6 A bonfire of illusions

1 There is considerable dispute over the poverty figures, with the World Bank painting a much more optimistic picture. The Indonesian government's higher poverty figures is designed to win a breathing space from the structural reforms imposed by the IMF. Jan Breman's (1999) field study suggests that about 30 to 35 percent of the population were unable to fulfill their minimal needs after the crisis and that the adverse impacts were greater in Java than on the other islands.
2 Asian economies accounted for 19 percent of Japanese banks' overseas lending in 1991 and 26 percent in 1994. Additionally, Japanese banks provided about 75 percent of China's bilateral borrowings by the early 1990s (Pempel, 1999b: 68).
3 Sumitomo, for instance, had been linked to the Sumitomo group while Sakura had been associated with the Mitsui *keiretsu* that included Toshiba and Toyota.
4 The corresponding figure for the United States is 55 percent (Brooke, 2001a).
5 The size of inward foreign investments to Japan was, however, smaller than corresponding figures for the United States and the European Union. In 1999, inflows of FDI to Japan according to the IMF totaled US$12.3 billion as against US$282.5 billion for the United States and $359.2 billion for the European Union (*South China Morning Post*, 2001b).
6 The real rate of interest on 30-year US Treasury bonds fell from 8.1 percent in 1984 to 4.9 percent in 1988 and to 3.6 percent in 1993 (Brenner, 2002: 68).

Epilogue

1 This quote has been often attributed to John Maynard Keynes and even to Amartya Sen. The earliest reference to it comes from Gerald Shove (1942) who attributed it to Wildon Carr. I am grateful to Pulapre Balakrishnan and Geoff Harcourt for this reference.
2 At its formation it included 34 members including South Asian states and it has expanded its membership in recent years to include the former Soviet Central Asian republics. Though its member-states have increased to 58 today, the parity in voting shares between Japan and the United States – 13 percent each – has remained unchanged (Lincoln, 2002: 207–8).
3 A former Japanese vice-minister for finance, Sakakibara Eisuke, charged that global standards are nothing but 'American standards' while Kaneko Masaru argued that 'By politely acceding to international accounting standards in order to make it easy for American financial industry to invest in Japanese stocks, [Japan is] working hard for the destruction of its own system' (quoted in Grimes, 2000: 59).
4 In 2001 alone, Malaysia's industrial center in Penang lost some 16,000 high-paying electronics jobs to China (Eckholm and Kahn, 2002). The US Labor Department estimates that as a result of cheaper imports, especially from China, the price of TV sets has dropped by 9 percent each year since 1998 and the price of sports equipment by 3 percent each year. Drops of this magnitude have reduced the competitiveness of US manufacturers and contributed to the growth in US unemployment (Legget, 2002).

Bibliography

Abrahams, Paul (1999). 'Trade Surplus Climbs to Record $122 Billion,' *Financial Times*, 26 January.

Achcar, Gilbert (2000). 'The Strategic Triad: USA, China, Russia,' in T. Ali (ed.), *Masters of the Universe: NATO's Balkan Crusade*, London: Verso, 99–144.

Achcar, Gilbert (2002). *The Clash of Barbarians: Sept 11 and the Making of the New World Disorder*, New York: Monthly Review Press.

Aglietta, Michel (1987). *A Theory of Capitalist Regulation: The US Experience*, London: Verso.

Allen, George C. (1981a). *The Japanese Economy*, London: Weidenfeld & Nicolson.

Allen, George C. (1981b). *A Short Economic History of Modern Japan*, New York: St. Martin's Press.

Amsden, Alice H. (1989). *Asia's Next Giant: South Korea and Late Industrialization*, New York: Oxford University Press.

Amsden, Alice H. (1991). 'Big Business and Urban Congestion in Taiwan: The Origins of Small Enterprise and Regionally Decentralized Industry (Respectively),' *World Development*, XIX, (9 September), 1121–35.

Amsden, Alice H. (2001). *The Rise of 'The Rest': Challenges to the West from Late-Industrializing Economies*, New York: Oxford University Press.

Amyx, Jennifer A. (2000). 'Political Impediments to Far-Reaching Banking Reforms in Japan: Implications for Asia,' in G. M. Noble and J. Ravenhill (eds), *The Asian Financial Crisis and the Architecture of Global Finance*, Cambridge, Cambridge University Press, 132–51.

Andersen, Jonathan (2003). 'China is a Force to Reckon With But Not to Fear,' *Financial Times*, 25 February.

Anek Laothamatas (1994). 'From Clientalism to Partnership: Business-Government Relations in Thailand,' in A. MacIntyre (ed.), *Business and Government in Industrialising Asia*, Ithaca, NY: Cornell University Press, 195–215.

Aoki, Masahiko (1987). 'The Japanese Firm in Transition,' in K. Yamamura and Y. Yasukichi (eds), *The Political Economy of Japan, I, The Domestic Transformation*, Stanford, CA: Stanford University Press, 263–88.

Appelbaum, Richard P. and Jeffrey Henderson (eds). (1992). *States and Development in the Asian Pacific Rim*, Newbury Park, CA: Sage.

Armstrong, Philip, Andrew Glyn, and John Harrison (1984). *Capitalism Since World War II: The Making and Breakup of the Great Boom*, London: Fontana.

Arnold, Wayne (1999a). 'Japan's Light Dims in Southeast Asia,' *New York Times*, 26 December.

Arnold, Wayne (1999b). 'Thailand to Sell Troubled Bank to Standard Chartered,' *New York Times*, 4 September.

Arnold, Wayne (2001). 'Japan's Electronics Slump Takes a Toll on Southeast Asia,' *New York Times*, 1 September.

Arrighi, Giovanni (1982). 'A Crisis of Hegemony,' in Samir Amin, Giovanni Arrighi, André Gunder Frank and Immanuel Wallerstein (eds), *Dynamics of Global Crisis*, New York: Monthly Review Press, 55–108.

Arrighi, Giovanni (1990). 'The Three Hegemonies of Historical Capitalism,' *Review*, XIII, (3, Summer), 365–408.

Arrighi, Giovanni (1994). *The Long Twentieth Century: Money, Power, and the Origins of Our Time*, London: Verso.

Arrighi, Giovanni and Beverly J. Silver (1984). 'Labor Movements and Capital Migration: The US and Western Europe in World-Historical Perspective,' in C. Bergquist (ed.), *Labor in the Capitalist World-Economy*, Beverly Hills, CA: Sage, 183–216.

Arrighi, Giovanni, Satoshi Ikeda, and Alex Irwan (1993). 'The Rise of East Asia: One Miracle or Many?' in R. A. Palat (ed.), *Pacific-Asia and the Future of the World-System*, Westport, CT: Greenwood Press, 41–65.

Asian Development Bank (1999). *Key Indicators of Developing Asian and Pacific Countries, 1999*, Manila: Asian Development Bank.

Bank for International Settlements (various years). *Consolidated International Banking Statistics*, Basle: Bank for International Settlements.

Bardacke, Ted (1998). 'Origins: The Day the Miracle Came to an End,' *Financial Times*, 12 January.

Barrett, Richard E. (1988). 'Autonomy and Diversity in the American State on Taiwan,' in E. A. Winkler and S. Greenhalgh (eds), *Contending Approaches to the Political Economy of Taiwan*, Armonk, NY: M. E. Sharpe, 121–37.

Bello, Walden (1997). 'Addicted to Capital: The Ten-Year High and Present-Day Withdrawal Trauma of Southeast Asia's Economies,' Bangkok: Focus on the Global South.

Bello, Walden (1998a). 'The End of a "Miracle": Speculation, Foreign Capital Dependence and the Collapse of the Southeast Asian Economies,' *Multinational Monitor*, XIX, (2, January).

Bello, Walden (1998b). 'The Rise and Fall of South-east Asia's Economy,' *The Ecologist*, XXVIII, (1, January–February), 9–17.

Bello, Walden (1998c). 'What is the IMF's Agenda for Asia?' *Focus on Trade*, 22, (27, January).

Bello, Walden (2001). 'Genoa and the Multiple Crises of Globalisation,' Amsterdam: Transnational Institute, <http://www.tni.org/archives/bello/genoa2.htm>.

Bello, Walden (n.d.). 'The End of the Asian Miracle,' Bangkok: Focus on the Global South.

Bello, Walden and Stephanie Rosenfeld (1990). *Dragons in Distress: Asia's Miracle Economies in Crisis*, Harmondsworth: Penguin.

Bello, Walden, Shea Cunningham, and Li Kheng Poh (1998). *A Siamese Tragedy: Development & Disintegration in Modern Thailand*, London: Zed.

Belson, Ken (2002). 'Japanese Trading Company Plans Sharp Cutbacks,' *New York Times*, 30 January.

Bennett, Neville (1997). 'Japanese Economy in Danger of Meltdown,' *National Business Review*, 28 November.

Berger, Mark T. (1997). 'Old State and New Empire in Indonesia: Debating the Rise and Decline of Suharto's New Order,' *Third World Quarterly*, XVIII, (2), 321–61.

Berger, Peter L. and H.-H. Michael Hsiao (eds). (1988). *In Search of the East Asian Development Model*, New Brunswick, NJ: Transaction Books.

Bergsten, Fred (2000). 'Towards a Tripartite World,' *The Economist*, 15 July.

Bernard, Mitchell (1999). 'East Asia's Tumbling Dominoes: Financial Crises and the Myth of the Regional Model,' in L. Panitch and C. Leys (eds), *Global Capitalism Versus Democracy: Socialist Register, 1999*, Rendlesham: Merlin Press, 178–208.

Bernard, Mitchell and John Ravenhill (1995). 'Beyond Product Cycles and Flying Geese: Regionalization, Hierarchy, and the Industrialization of East Asia,' *World Politics*, XLVII, (2), 171–209.

Bevacqua, Ron (1998). 'Whither the Japanese Model? The Asian Economic Crisis and the Continuation of Cold War Politics in the Pacific Rim,' *Review of International Political Economy*, V, (1, Autumn), 410–23.

Bienefeld, Manfred (1989). 'The Lessons of History and the Developing World,' *Monthly Review*, XLI, (3, July–August), 9–41.

Block, Fred L. (1977). *The Origins of International Economic Disorder: A Study of United States Monetary Policy from World War II to the Present*, Berkeley, CA: University of California Press.

Bloomberg News (1998). 'Japanese Unload Their Foreign Bonds,' *New York Times*, 13 February.

Bluestone, Barry and Bennett Harrison (1982). *The Deindustrialization of America: Plant Closings, Community Abandonment, and the Dismantling of Basic Industries*, New York: Basic Books.

Blumberg, Evelyn and Paul Ong (1994). 'Labor Squeeze and Ethnic/Racial Recomposition in the U.S. Apparel Industry,' in Edna Bonachich, Lucie Cheng, Normal Chinchilla, Nora Hamilton and Paul Ong (eds), *Global Production: The Apparel Industry in the Pacific Rim*, Philadelphia, PA: Temple University Press, 309–27.

Bonacich, Edna and David V. Waller (1994). 'The Role of U.S. Apparel Manufacturers in the Globalization of the Industry in the Pacific Rim,' in Edna Bonacich, Lucie Cheng, Normal Chinchilla, Nora Hamilton and Paul Ong (eds), *Global Production: The Apparel Industry in the Pacific Rim*, Philadelphia, PA: Temple University Press, 80–102.

Borden, William S. (1984). *The Pacific Alliance: United States Foreign Policy and Japanese Trade Recovery, 1947–1955*, Madison, WI: University of Wisconsin Press.

Bowie, Alasdair (1994). 'The Dynamics of Business–Government Relations in Industrialising Malaysia,' in A. MacIntyre (ed.), *Business and Government in Industrialising Asia*, Ithaca, NY: Cornell University Press, 167–94.

Bowles, Paul (2002). 'Asia's Post-Crisis Regionalism: Bringing the State Back In, Keeping the (United) States Out,' *Review of International Political Economy*, IX, (2, Summer), 230–56.

Bowles, Paul and Brian MacLean (1996). 'Regional Blocs: Can Japan be the Leader?' in R. Boyer and D. Drache (eds), *States Against Markets: The Limits of Globalization*, London: Routledge, 155–69.

Breman, Jan (1999). 'Indonesia: Politics of Poverty and a Leaking Safety Net,' *Economic and Political Weekly*, XXXIV, (20, May 15–21).

Bremner, Brian (1997). 'Rescuing Asia,' *Businessweek*, 17 November.

Bremner, Brian (1998). 'An Exit Plan for Japan,' *Business Week*, 26 October.

Bremner, Brian (1999). 'The Bank Mergers and Forced Sales to Foreigners are Just the Start of Even Greater Upheaval,' *Businessweek*, 15 February.

Brenner, Robert (1998). 'The Economics of Global Turbulence,' *New Left Review*, (229, May–June), whole issue.

Brenner, Robert (2002). *The Boom and the Bubble: The US in the World Economy*, London: Verso.

Bridges, Brian (2001). *Korea After the Crash: The Politics of Economic Recovery*, London: Routledge.

Brooke, James (2001a). 'Factory Jobs Move Overseas as Japan's Troubles Deepen,' *New York Times*, 31 August.

Brooke, James (2001b). 'Tokyo Fears China may Put an End to "Made in Japan",' *New York Times*, 20 November.

Brooke, James (2002). 'Bad News Keeps Coming for Japanese Economy,' *New York Times*, 10 January.

Brus, Wlodzimiercz (1973). *The Economics and Politics of Socialism: Collected Essays*, London: Routledge & Kegan Paul.

Brus, Wlodzimiercz (1975). *Socialist Ownership and Political Systems*, London: Routledge & Kegan Paul.

Bunker, Stephen G. and Denis O'Hearn (1993). 'Strategies of Economic Ascendants for Access to Raw Materials: A Comparison of the United States and Japan,' in R. A. Palat (ed.), *Pacific-Asia and the Future of the World-System*, Westport, CT: Greenwood Press, 83–102.

Bunker, Stephen G. and Paul S. Ciccantell (1995). 'Restructuring Space, Time, and Competitive Advantage in the Capitalist World-Economy: Japan and Raw Materials Transport After World War II,' in D. A. Smith and J. Borocz (eds), *A New World Order? Global Transformations in the Late Twentieth Century*, Westport, CT: Greenwood Press, 109–29.

Burton, John (2000). 'Hyundai Motor Goes it Alone,' *Financial Times*, 31 August.

Burton, John and Gerrad Baker (1998). 'South Korea: The Country That Invested its Way Into Trouble,' *Financial Times*, 15 January.

Butler, Steven (1996). 'Is the Miracle Over?' *U.S. News*, 9 December.

Buttel, Frederick, H. (1989). 'The US Farm Crisis and the Restructuring of American Agriculture: Domestic and International Dimensions,' in D. Goodman and M. Redclift (eds), *The International Farm Crisis*, Basingstoke, Hampshire: Macmillan, 46–83.

Calder, Kent E. (1997). 'Assault on the Bankers' Kingdom: Politics, Markets, and the Liberalization of Japanese Industrial Finance,' in Michael Loriaux, Meredith Woo-Cumings, Kent E. Calder, Sylvia Maxfield, and Sofia Perez (eds), *Capital Ungoverned: Liberalizing Finance in Interventionist States*, Ithaca, NY: Cornell University Press, 16–56.

Calleo, David P. (1982). *The Imperious Economy*, Cambridge, MA: Harvard University Press.

Calleo, David P. (1998). 'A New Era of Overstretch? American Policy in Europe and Asia,' *World Policy Journal*, XV, (1), 11–25.

Calleo, David P. (2001). *Rethinking Europe's Future*, Princeton, NJ: Princeton University Press.

Calleo, David P. and Benjamin M. Rowland (1973). *America and the World Political Economy: Atlantic Dreams and National Realities*, Bloomington, IN: Indiana University Press.

Castells, Manuel, Lee Goh, and Reginald Y.-W. Kwok (1990). *The Shek Kip Mai Syndrome: Economic Development and Public Housing in Hong Kong and Singapore*, London: Pion.

Castles, Stephen (1984). *Here for Good: Western Europe's New Ethnic Minorities*, London: Pluto.

Champion, Steven R. (1997). *The Great Taiwan Bubble: The Rise and Fall of an Emerging Stock Market*, Berkeley, CA: Pacific View Press.

Chandler, Alfred D. (1977). *The Visible Hand: The Managerial Revolution in American Business*, Cambridge, MA: Belknap Press.

Chandler, Alfred D. (1990). *Scale and Scope: The Dynamics of Industrial Capitalism*, Cambridge, MA: Belknap Press.

Chandler, Clay (2001a). 'A Factory to the World: China's Vast Labor Pool, Low Wages Lure Manufacturers,' *Washington Post*, 25 November.

Chandler, Clay (2001b). 'Profits Fall Sharply at Banks in Japan,' *Washington Post*, 27 November.

Chang Ha-Joon (1998). 'South Korea: The Misunderstood Crisis,' in K. S. Jomo (ed.), *Tigers in Trouble: Financial Governance, Liberalisation and Crisis in East Asia*, London: Zed Books, 222–31.

Cheng, Allen T. (2001). 'Taiwan (In)dependence,' *Asiaweek*, 30 November.

Cheng, Lu-Lin and Gary Gereffi (1994). 'The Informal Economy in East Asian Development,' *International Journal of Urban and Regional Research*, XVIII, (2), 194–219.

Cheng, Tun-jen (1990). 'Political Regimes and Development Strategies: South Korea and Taiwan,' in G. Gereffi and D. L. Wyman (eds), *Manufacturing Miracles: Paths of Industrialization in Latin America and East Asia*, Princeton, NJ: Princeton University Press, 139–78.

Chiu, Stephen W. K. (1996). 'Unravelling Hong Kong's Exceptionalism: The Politics of Laissez-Faire in the Industrial Takeoff,' *Political Power and Social Theory*, X, 229–56.

Choi, Alex H. (1994). 'Beyond Market and State: A Study of Hong Kong's Industrial Transformation,' *Studies in Political Economy*, (45, Fall), 28–64.

Choi, Alex H. (1998). 'Statism and Asian Political Economy: Is There a New Paradigm?' *Bulletin of Concerned Asian Scholars*, XXX, (3), 50–60.

Choi, Alex H. (1999). 'State-Business Relations and Industrial Restructuring,' in Tai-Wing Ngo (ed.), *Hong Kong's History: State and Society Under Colonial Rule*, London: Routledge, 141–61.

Choi, Jang Jip (1993). 'Political Cleavages in South Korea,' in H. Koo (ed.), *State and Society in Contemporary Korea*, Ithaca, NY: Cornell University Press, 13–50.

Chon, Soohyun (1992). 'Political Economy of Regional Development in Korea,' in R. P. Appelbaum and J. Henderson (eds), *States and Development in the Asian Pacific Rim*, Newbury Park, CA: Sage, 150–75.

Chu, Jou-Juo (2000). 'Nationalism and Self-Determination: The Identity Politics in Taiwan,' *Journal of Asian and African Studies*, XXXV, (3), 303–21.

Chuk Kyo Kim and Chul Heui Lee (1983). 'Ancillary Firm Development in the Korean Automobile Industry,' in Konosuke Odaka (ed.), *The Motor Vehicle Industry in Asia: A Study of Ancillary Firm Development*, Singapore: Singapore University Press.

Chun, Allen (2000). 'Democracy as Hegemony, Globalization as Indigenization, or the "Culture" in Taiwanese National Politics,' *Journal of Asian and African Studies*, XXXV, (1), 7–27.

Chung In Moon and Sang-young Rhyu (2000). 'The State, Structural Rigidity, and the End of Asian Capitalism: A Comparative Study of Japan and South Korea,' in R. Robison, *et al.* (eds), *Politics and Markets in the Wake of the Asian Crisis*, London: Routledge, 77–98.

Chung, Young-Il (1990). 'The Agricultural Foundations for Korean Industrial Development,' in C. H. Lee and I. Yamazawa (eds), *The Economic Development of Japan and Korea: A Parallel with Lessons*, New York: Praeger, 137–49.

Clairmont, Frederic (2003). 'United States: The Debt Mountain,' *Economic and Political Weekly*, (1 February).

Clairmont, Frederic F. (2001). 'Implosion of Japanese Capitalism,' *Economic and Political Weekly*, (28 April).

Cobb, James C. (1984). *Industrialization and Southern Society, 1887–1994*, Lexington, KY: Lexington University Press.

Coggan, Philip and Clay Harris (1998). 'UK Main Foreign Owner of US Treasuries,' *Financial Times*, 9 April.

Crampton, Thomas (2003). 'A Strong China May Give Boost to its Neighbors,' *International Herald Tribune*, 23 January.

Crispin, Shawn W. (2000). 'Labour's New Clout,' *Far Eastern Economic Review*, 23 March.

Cumings, Bruce (1981). *The Origins of the Korean War: Liberation and the Emergence of Separate Regimes*, Princeton, NJ: Princeton University Press.

Cumings, Bruce (1987). 'The Origins and Development of the Northeast Asian Political Economy: Industrial Sectors, Product Cycles, and Political Consequences,' in F. C. Deyo (ed.), *The Political Economy of the New Asian Industrialism*, Ithaca, NY: Cornell University Press, 44–83.

Cumings, Bruce (1989). 'The Abortive Abertura: South Korea in the Light of Latin American Experience,' *New Left Review*, 173, (January–February), 5–32.

Cumings, Bruce (1998). 'The Korean Crisis and the End of "Late" Development,' *New Left Review*, 231, (September–October), 43–72.

Cumings, Bruce (1999). 'The Asian Crisis, Democracy and the End of "Late" Development,' in T. J. Pempel (ed.), *The Politics of the Asian Economic Crisis*, Ithaca, NY: Cornell University Press, 17–44.

Cusumano, Michael A. (1985). *The Japanese Automobile Industry: Technology and Management at Nissan and Toyota*, Cambridge, MA: Harvard University Press.

Daly, M. (1987). 'Rationalizaton of International Banking and the Implications for the Pacific Rim,' *Conference on International Capital and Urbanization of the Pacific Rim, Center for Pacific Rim Studies*, University of California at Los Angeles, March 26–28.

Daly, M. T. (1994). 'The Road to the Twenty-first Century: The Myths and Miracles of Asian Manufacturing,' in S. Corbridge *et al.* (eds), *Money, Power and Space*, Oxford: Blackwell, 165–88.

Damus, Renate (1981). 'The 1980 Polish Strike and the Strike Cycles in the 1970s,' *Telos*, 47, 104–10.

Davis, Mike (1986). *Prisoners of the American Dream: Politics and Economy in the History of the U.S. Working Class*, London: Verso.

Denker, Mehmet Sami (1994). 'The Evolution of Japanese Investment in Malaysia,' in K. S. Jomo (ed.), *Japan and Malaysian Development: In the Shadow of the Rising Sun*, London: Routledge, 44–74.

Deyo, Frederic C. (1989). *Beneath the Miracle: Labor Subordination in the New Asian Industrialism*, Berkeley, CA: University of California Press.

Deyo, Frederic C. (1990). 'Economic Policy and the Popular Sector,' in G. Gereffi and D. L. Wyman (eds), *Manufacturing Miracles: Paths of Industrialization in Latin America and East Asia*, Princeton, NJ: Princeton University Press.

Dicken, Peter (1991). 'The Changing Geography of Japanese Foreign Direct Investment in Manufacturing Industry: A Global Perspective,' in J. Morris (ed.), *Japan and the Global Economy: Issues and Trends in the 1990s*, London: Routledge, 14–42.

Dicken, Peter (1992). *Global Shift: The Internationalization of Economic Activity*, New York: Guilford Press.

Dieter, Heribert and Richard Higgot (2000). 'East Asia Looks to its Own Resources,' *Financial Times*, 16 May.

Dixon, Chris (1999). *The Thai Economy; Uneven Development and Internationalisation*, London: Routledge.

Donnelly, Michael W. (1984). 'Conflict over Government Authority and Markets: Japan's Rice Economy,' in E. S. Krauss *et al.* (eds), *Conflict in Japan*, Honolulu: University of Hawaii Press, 335–74.

Douglass, Mike (1991). 'Transnational Capital and the Social Construction of Comparative Advantage in Southeast Asia,' *Southeast Asian Journal of Social Science*, XIX, (1 & 2), 14–43.

Douglass, Mike (1993a). 'The "New" Tokyo Story: Restructuring Space and the Struggle for Place in a World City,' in K. Fujita and R. C. Hill (eds), *Japanese Cities in the Global Economy: Global Restructuring and Urban-Industrial Change*, Philadelphia, PA: Temple University Press, 83–119.

Douglass, Mike (1993b). 'Social, Political, and Spatial Dimensions of Korean Industrial Transformation,' *Journal of Contemporary Asia*, XXIII, (2), 149–72.

Dunning, John H. (1988). 'International Business, the Recession and Economic Restructuring,' in N. Hood and J.-E. Vahlne (eds), *Strategies in Global Competition*, Chippenham, Wilts: Routledge, 84–103.

Eccleston, Bernard (1989). *State and Society in Post-War Japan*, Cambridge: Polity Press.

Eckert, Carter (1993). 'The South Korean Bourgeoisie: A Class in Search of Hegemony,' in H. Koo (ed.), *State and Society in Contemporary Korea*, Ithaca, NY: Cornell University Press, 95–130.

Eckholm, Eric and Joseph Kahn (2002). 'Asia Worries About Growth of China's Economic Power,' *New York Times*, 24 November.

Economist, The (1997a). 'The Asian Miracle: Is It Over?' 1 March.

Economist, The (1997b). 'Burning Nicely,' 1 November.

Economist, The (1997c). 'The Coming Car Crash: Global Pile-up,' 10 May.

Economist, The (1997d). 'The Giants Stumble,' 18 October.

Economist, The (1997e). 'Japan Makes a Stand, Sort of,' 20 December.

Economist, The (1997f). 'Risks Beyond Measure,' 13 December.

Economist, The (1999). 'Emerging Market Indicators,' 30 January.

Edgington, David W. (1991). 'Japanese Direct Investment and Australian Economic Development,' in J. Morris (ed.), *Japan and the Global Economy: Issues and Trends in the 1990s*, London: Routledge, 173–94.

Edwards, Richard C. (1979). *Contested Terrain: The Transformation of the Workplace in the Twentieth Century*, New York: Basic Books.

Elger, Tony and Chris Smith (1994a). 'Global Japanization? Convergence and Competition in the Organization of the Labour Process,' in T. Elger and

C. Smith (eds), *Global Japanization: The Transnational Transformation of the Labour Process*, London: Routledge, 31–59.

Elger, Tony and Chris Smith (eds). (1994b). *Global Japanization? The Transnational Transformation of the Labour Process*, London: Routledge.

Encarnation, Dennis J. (1992). *Rivals Beyond Trade: America versus Japan in Global Competition*, Ithaca, NY: Cornell University Press.

England, Joe (1971). 'Industrial Relations in Hong Kong,' in K. Hopkins (ed.), *Hong Kong: the Industrial Colony – A Political, Social and Economic Survey*, Hong Kong: Oxford University Press, 207–59.

England, Joe and John Rear (1975). *Chinese Labour Under British Rule: A Critical Study of Labour Relations and Law in Hong Kong*, Hong Kong: Oxford University Press.

Evans, Peter B. (1987). 'Class, State, and Dependence in East Asia: Lessons for Latin Americanists,' in F. C. Deyo (ed.), *The Political Economy of New Asian Industrialism*, Ithaca, NY: Cornell University Press, 203–26.

Field, Norma (1991). *In the Realm of a Dying Emperor: Japan at Century's End*, New York: Random House.

Fitch, Robert (1993). *The Assassination of New York*, London: Verso.

Frieden, Jeff (1987). 'Third World Indebted Industrialization: International Finance and State Capitalism in Mexico, Brazil, Algeria, and South Korea,' in David G. Becker, Jeff Frieden, Sayre P. Schatz, and Richard L. Sklar (eds), *Postimperialism: International Capitalism and Development in the Late Twentieth Century*, Boulder, CO: Lynne Rienner, 131–59.

Friedman, David (1983). 'Beyond the Age of Ford: The Strategic Basis of the Japanese Success in Automobiles,' in J. Zysman and L. D. A. Tyson (eds), *American Industry in International Competition: Government Policies and Corporate Strategies*, Ithaca, NY: Cornell University Press, 350–90.

Friedman, David (1988). *The Misunderstood Miracle: Industrial Developmernt and Political Change in Japan*, Ithaca, NY: Cornell University Press.

Friedmann, Harriet (1982). 'The Political Economy of Food: The Rise and Fall of the Postwar International Food Order,' *American Journal of Sociology*, LXXXVIII, (Supplement), S248–86.

Friedmann, Harriet (1993). 'The Political Economy of Food: A Global Crisis,' *New Left Review*, 197, (January–February), 29–57.

Friedmann, Harriet and Philip McMichael (1989). 'Agriculture and the State System: The Rise and Decline of National Agricultures, 1870 to the Present,' *Sociologia Ruralis*, XXIX, (2), 93–117.

Fuerbringer, Johnathan (1997). 'How Asian Currencies Tumbled So Quickly,' *New York Times*, 10 December.

Fujita, Kuniko and Richard Child Hill (1993). 'Toyota City: Industrial Organization and the Local State in Japan,' in K. Fujita and R. C. Hill (eds), *Japanese Cities in the World Economy*, Philadelphia, PA: Temple University Press, 175–200.

Fujiwara, S. (1989). 'Foreign Trade, Investment, and Industrial Imperialism in Postwar Japan,' in T. Morris-Suzuki and T. Seriyama (eds), *Japanese Capitalism Since 1945*, Armonk, NY: M. E. Sharpe, 166–206.

Fuller, Thomas (1999). 'Malaysia's Merger Plan Stuns Bankers,' *International Herald Tribune*, 7 August.

Gao, Bai (2001). *Japan's Economic Dilemma: The Institutional Origins of Prosperity and Stagnation*, Cambridge: Cambridge University Press.

Gardner, Richard N. (1980). *Sterling-Dollar Diplomacy in Current Perspective: The*

Origins and Prospects of Our International Economic Order, New York: Columbia University Press.

Garon, Sheldon (1994). 'Rethinking Modernization and Modernity in Japanese History: A Focus on State–Society Relations,' *Journal of Asian Studies*, LIII, (2, May), 346–66.

George, Susan (1992). *The Debt Boomerang: How Third World Debt Harms Us All*, London: Pluto.

Gereffi, Gary (1990). 'Big Business and the State,' in G. Gereffi and D. L. Wyman (eds), *Manufacturing Miracles: Paths of Late Industrialization in Latin America and East Asia*, Princeton, NJ: Princeton University Press, 90–109.

Gerlach, Michael (1989). '*Keiretsu* Organization in the Japanese Economy: Analysis and Trade Implications,' in Chalmers Johnson, Laura D'Andrea Tyson, and John Zysman (eds), *Politics and Productivity: How Japan's Development Strategy Works*, New York: Ballinger.

Gerschenkron, Alexander (1962). *Economic Backwardness in Historical Perspective*, Cambridge, MA: Harvard University Press.

Gilpin, Robert (1975). *U.S. Power and the Multinational Corporation: The Political Economy of Foreign Direct Investment*, New York: Basic Books.

Gilpin, Robert (2000). *The Challenge of Global Capitalism: The World Economy in the 21st Century*, Princeton, NJ: Princeton University Press.

Glasmeier, Amy and Noriuki Sugiura (1991). 'Japan's Manufacturing System: Small Business, Subcontracting and Regional Complex Formation,' *International Journal of Urban and Regional Research*, XV, (3, September), 395–414.

Glyn, Andrew, Alan Hughes, Alain Lipietz and Ajit Singh (1991). 'The Rise and Fall of the Golden Age,' in S. A. Marglin and J. B. Schor (eds), *The Golden Age of Capitalism: Reinterpreting the Postwar Experience*, Oxford: Clarendon Press, 39–125.

Gold, Thomas B. (1986). *State and Society in the Taiwan Miracle*, Armonk, NY: M. E. Sharpe.

Gold, Thomas B. (1988a). 'Colonial Origins of Taiwanese Capitalism,' in E. A. Winckler and S. Greenhalgh (eds), *Contending Approaches to the Political Economy of Taiwan*, Armonk, NY: M. E. Sharpe, 101–17.

Gold, Thomas B. (1988b). 'Entrepreneurs, Multinationals, and the State,' in E. A. Winckler and S. Greenhalgh (eds), *Contending Approaches to the Political Economy of Taiwan*, Armonk, NY: M. E. Sharpe, 175–205.

Goldfield, David R. (1982). *Cotton Fields and Skyscrapers: Southern City and Region, 1607–1980*, Baton Rouge, LA: Louisiana State University Press.

Goldstein, Joshua S. and David P. Rapkin (1991). 'After Insularity: Hegemony and the Future World Order,' *Futures*, XXIII, (9, November), 935–59.

Gomez, Edmund Terence and Kwame Sundaram Jomo (1997). *Malaysia's Political Economy: Politics, Patronage, and Profits*, Cambridge: Cambridge University Press.

Gordon, Andrew (1985). *The Evolution of Labor Relations in Japan: Heavy Industry, 1853–1955*, Cambridge, MA: Harvard University Press.

Gordon, Andrew (1996a). 'Conditions for the Disappearance of the Japanese Working-Class Movement,' in E. J. Perry (ed.), *Putting Class in Its Place: Worker Identities in East Asia*, Berkeley: University of California Press, 11–52.

Gordon, David M. (1996b). *Fat and Mean: The Corporate Squeeze of Working Americans and the Myth of Managerial 'Downsizing'*, New York: Martin Kessler.

Gowan, Peter (1999). *The Global Gamble: Washington's Faustian Bid for World Dominance*, London: Routledge.

Greenhalgh, Susan (1988). 'Supranational Processes of Income Distribution,' in E. A. Winckler and G. Susan (eds), *Contending Approaches to the Political Economy of Taiwan*, Armonk, NY: M. E. Sharpe, 67–100.

Greenhalgh, Susan (1994). 'De-Orientalizing the Chinese Family Firm,' *American Ethnologist*, XXI, (4), 746–75.

Grieder, William (1997). *One World, Ready or Not: The Manic Logic of Global Capitalism*, New York: Simon & Schuster.

Grimes, William W. (2000). 'Japan and Globalization: From Opportunity to Restraint,' in S. S. Kim (ed.), *East Asia and Globalization*, Lanham, MD: Rowman & Littlefield, 55–79.

Gwynne, Robert (1991). 'New Horizons? The Third World Motor Vehicle Industry in an International Framework,' in C. M. Law (ed.), *Restructuring the Global Automobile Industry: National and Regional Impacts*, London: Routledge, 61–87.

Hadiz, Vedi R. (1997). *Workers and the State in New Order Indonesia*, London: Routledge.

Hadiz, Vedi R. (2001). 'Reorganising Power in Indonesia: National and Local Dynamics,' *Conference on Consolidating Democracy in Indonesia*, Ohio State University, Columbus, OH: 11–13 May.

Haggard, Stephan (2000). *The Political Economy of the Asian Financial Crisis*, Washington, DC: Institute for International Economics.

Haggard, Stephan and Chung-in Moon (1993). 'The State, Politics, and Economic Development in Postwar South Korea,' in H. Koo (ed.), *State and Society in Contemporary Korea*, Ithaca, NY: Cornell University Press, 51–93.

Haggard, Stephen (1990). *Pathways from the Periphery: The Politics of Growth in the Newly Industrializing Countries*, Ithaca, NY: Cornell University Press.

Haggard, Stephen and Tun-jen Cheng (1987). 'State and Foreign Capital in the East Asian NICs,' in F. C. Deyo (ed.), *The Political Economy of the New Asian Industrialism*, Ithaca, NY: Cornell University Press, 84–135.

Haggard, Stephen and Jongryn Mo (2000). 'The Political Economy of the Korean Financial Crisis,' *Review of International Political Economy*, VII, (2, Summer), 197–218.

Hamilton, Gary (1999). 'Asian Business Networks in Transition: or, What Alan Greenspan Does Not Know about the Asian Business Crisis,' in T. J. Pempel (ed.), *The Politics of the Asian Economic Crisis*, Ithaca, NY: Cornell University Press, 45–61.

Hamilton, Gary G. and Nicole W. Biggart (1989). 'Market, Culture, and Authority: A Comparative Analysis of Management in the Far East,' *American Journal of Sociology*, XCIV, (Supplement), S52–94.

Hanke, Steve H. (1997). 'The IMF: Immune From (Frequent) Failure,' *Wall Street Journal*, 25 August.

Harney, Alexandra (1999). 'Toyota President Will Welcome Foreign Criticism,' *Financial Times*, 21 September.

Harney, Alexandra and Gillian Tett (1999). 'The Semantics of Consolidation,' *Financial Times*, 21 August.

Harrison, Bennett (1984). 'Regional Restructuring and "Good Business Climates": The Economic Transformation of New England Since World War II,' in L. Sawers and W. K. Tabb (eds), *Sunbelt/Snowbelt: Urban Development and Regional Restructuring*, New York: Oxford University Press, 48–96.

Harrison, Bennett (1994). *Lean and Mean: The Changing Landscape of Corporate Power in the Age of Flexibility*, New York: Basic Books.

Harrison, Bennett and Barry Bluestone (1990). *The Great U-Turn: Corporate Restructuring and the Polarizing of America*, New York: Basic Books.

Hart-Landsberg, Martin (1993). *The Rush to Development: Economic Change and Political Struggle in South Korea*, New York: Monthly Review Press.

Hatch, Walter and Kozo Yamamura (1996). *Asia in Japan's Embrace: Building a Regional Production Alliance*, Cambridge: Cambridge University Press.

Hayami, Yujiro (1988). *Japanese Agriculture Under Seige: The Political Economy of Agricultural Policies*, New York: St. Martin's Press.

Henderson, Jeffrey (1989). *The Globalisation of High Technology Production: Society, Space, and Semiconductors in the Restructuring of the Modern World*, London: Routledge.

Henderson, Jeffrey (1993). 'Against Economic Orthodoxy: On the Making of the East Asian Economic Miracle,' *Economy and Society*, XXII, (2, May), 200–17.

Henderson, Jeffrey (1999). 'Uneven Crises: Institutional Foundations of East Asian Economic Turmoil,' *Economy and Society*, XXVIII, (3, August), 327–68.

Hewison, Kevin (1987). 'National Interests and Economic Downturn: Thailand,' in Richard Robison, Kevin Hewison, and Richard Higgott (eds), *Southeast Asia in the 1980s: The Politics of Economic Crisis*, Sydney: Allen & Unwin, 52–79.

Hewison, Kevin (2000). 'Thailand's Capitalism Before and After the Economic Crisis,' in Richard Robison, Mark Beeson, Kanishka Jayasuriya, and Hyuk-Rae Kim (eds), *Politics and Markets in the Wake of the Asian Crisis*, London: Routledge, 192–211.

Hewison, Kevin (2001). 'Pathways to Recovery: Bankers, Business and Nationalism in Thailand,' Hong Kong: City University of Hong Kong.

Hijino, Ken (2000). 'Japanese Chemical Groups to Merge,' *Financial Times*, 17 November.

Hill, Hal (2000). *The Indonesian Economy*, Cambridge: Cambridge University Press.

Hill, Hal and Yun-Peng Chu (2001). 'An Overview of the Key Issues,' in H. Hill and Y.-P. Chu (eds), *The Social Impact of the Asian Financial Crisis*, Cheltenham: Edward Elgar, 1–25.

Hill, Richard Child (1989). 'Comparing Transnational Production Systems: The Automobile Industry in the USA and Japan,' *International Journal of Urban and Regional Research*, XIII, (3, September), 462–80.

Hirschman, Albert (1958). *The Strategy of Economic Development*, New Haven, CT: Yale University Press.

Ho, Samuel P. S. (1978). *The Economic Development of Taiwan, 1860–1970*, New Haven, CT: Yale University Press.

Hobsbawm, Eric J. (1994). *The Age of Extremes: A History of the World, 1914–1991*, New York: Pantheon.

Hughes, Christopher W. (2000). 'Japanese Policy and the East Asian Currency Crisis: Abject Defeat or Quiet Victory?' *Review of International Political Economy*, VII, (2, Summer), 219–53.

Hutchcroft, Paul D. (1998). *Booty Capitalism: The Politics of Banking in the Philippines*, Ithaca, NY: Cornell University Press.

Hutchison, Jane (2001). 'Crisis and Change in the Philippines,' in G. Rodan *et al.* (eds), *The Political Economy of South-East Asia: Conflicts, Crises, and Change*, Melbourne: Oxford University Press, 42–70.

Ibison, David and Joe Leahy (2002). 'Foreign Share of Japanese M & A Trebles,' *Financial Times*, 17 January.

Ikenberry, G. John (1989). 'Rethinking the Origins of American Hegemony,' *Political Science Quarterly*, CIV, (2, Fall), 375–400.

Ingham, Geoffrey (1994). 'States and Markets in the Production of World Money: Sterling and Dollar,' in S. Corbridge *et al.* (eds), *Money, Power and Space*, Oxford: Blackwell, 29–48.

International Monetary Fund (1997a). 'Republic of Korea: IMF Stand-By Arrangement, Summary of the Economic Program, December 5, 1997,' Washington, DC: International Monetary Fund.

International Monetary Fund (1997b). *World Economic Outlook: An Interim Assessment*, Washington, DC: International Monetary Fund.

International Monetary Fund (1998). 'Statement by the Managing Director on the IMF Program with Indonesia,' Washington, DC: International Monetary Fund.

Iriye, Akira (1974). *The Cold War in Asia: A Historical Introduction*, Englewood Cliffs, NJ: Prentice-Hall.

Islam, Iyanatul and Anis Chowdhury (1997). *Asia-Pacific Economies: A Survey*, London: Routledge.

Itoh, Makoto (1990). *The World Economic Crisis and Japanese Capitalism*, New York: St. Martin's Press.

Itoh, Makoto (1992). 'The Japanese Model of "Post-Fordism",' in M. Storper and A. J. Scott (eds), *Pathways to Industrialization and Regional Development*, London: Routledge, 116–34.

Itoh, Makoto (1994). 'Is the Japanese Economy in Crisis?' *Review of International Political Economy*, I, (1, Spring), 29–51.

Itoh, Makoto (2000). *The Japanese Economy Reconsidered*, Basingstoke: Palgrave.

Iyengar, Jayanthi (2003). 'Wrong Turn seen in China's Economic Roadmap,' *Asia Times*, 1 April.

Jacoby, Neil H. (1966). *U.S. Aid to Taiwan: A Study of Foreign Aid, Self-Help, and Development*, New York: Praeger.

Jao, Y. C. (1993). 'The Financial Structure,' in D. G. Lethbridge (ed.), *The Business Environment in Hong Kong*, Hong Kong: Oxford University Press, 124–79.

Jayanth, V. (1998). 'Currency Turmoil, A Creation of the Private Sector,' *The Hindu*, 26 January.

Jayasankaran, S. (1999). 'Merger by Decree,' *Far Eastern Economic Review*, 9 September.

Johnson, Chalmers (1982). *MITI and the Japanese Miracle: The Growth of Industrial Policy, 1925–1975*, Stanford, CA: Stanford University Press.

Johnson, Chalmers (1987). 'Political Institutions and Economic Performance: The Government–Business Relationship in Japan, South Korea, and Taiwan,' in F. C. Deyo (ed.), *The Political Economy of the New Asian Industrialism*, Ithaca, NY: Cornell University Press, 138–64.

Johnson, Chalmers (1998). 'Economic Crisis in East Asia: The Clash of Capitalisms,' *Cambridge Journal of Economics*, XXII, 653–61.

Jomo, K. S. (1987). 'Economic Crisis and Policy Response in Malaysia,' in R. Robison *et al.* (eds), *Southeast Asia in the 1980s: The Politics of Economic Crisis*, Sydney: Allen & Unwin, 113–48.

Jomo, K. S. (ed.) (1995). *Privatizing Malaysia: Rents, Rhetoric, Realities*, Boulder, CO: Westview.

Jomo, K. S. (1998). 'Malaysia: From Miracle to Debacle,' in K. S. Jomo (ed.), *Tigers in Trouble: Financial Governance, Liberalisation and Crisis in East Asia*, London: Zed Books, 181–97.

Jomo, K. S., Chen Yun Chung, Brian C. Folk, Irfan Ul-Haq, Pasuk Phongpaichit, Batara Simatupang, and Mayuri Tateishi (1997). *Southeast Asia's Misunderstood Miracle: Industrial Policy and Economic Development in Thailand, Malaysia and Indonesia*, Boulder, CO: Westview Press.

Jones, Leroy P. and Il SaKong (1980). *Government, Business, and Entrepreneurship in Economic Development: The Korean Case*, Cambridge, MA: Harvard University Press.

Kahn, Joseph (1999). 'U.S. Bankers See No Threat in Planned Japanese Behemoth,' *New York Times*, 21 August.

Kahn, Joseph (2003). 'Made in China, Bought in China: Multinationals Succeed, Two Decades Later,' *New York Times*, 5 January.

Kasarda, John D. (1988). 'People and Jobs on the Move: America's New Spatial Dynamics,' in G. Steinlieb and J. W. Hugher (eds), *America's New Market Geography: Nation, Region, and Metropolis*, New Brunswick, NJ: Rutgers University Press, 217–42.

Katzenstein, Peter J. (1997). 'Asian Regionalism in Comparative Perspective,' in P. J. Katzenstein and T. Shiraishi (eds), *Network Power: Japan and Asia*, Ithaca, NY: Cornell University Press, 1–44.

Kenney, Martin and Richard Florida (1988). 'Beyond Mass Production: Production and the Labor Process in Japan,' *Politics & Society*, XIV, (1, March), 121–58.

Khoo Boo Teik (2000). 'Economic Nationalism and Its Discontents: Malaysian Political Economy After July 1997,' in Richard Robison, Mark Beeson, Kanishka Jayasuriya, and Hyuk-Rae Kim (eds), *Politics and Markets in the Wake of the Asian Crisis*, London: Routledge, 212–37.

Kirby, Stuart (1983). 'Towards the Pacific Century: Economic Development in the Pacific Basin,' London: Economist Intelligence Unit.

Kirk, Don (2001a). 'Daewoo Motors' Fate Tied to Labor Strife,' *New York Times*, 21 February.

Kirk, Don (2001b). 'South Korea Slips Away from Changes Imposed in Bailout,' *New York Times*, 17 December.

Kirk, Don (2003). 'Large Banks in South Korea Report a Big Jump in Profits,' *New York Times*, 23 January.

Kiyonari, Tadao (1993). 'Restructuring Urban–Industrial Links in Greater Tokyo: Small Producers' Responses to Changing World Markets,' in K. Fujita and R. C. Hill (eds), *Japanese Cities in the World Economy*, Philadelphia, PA: Temple University Press, 141–56.

Kobayhashi Chutaro (1987). 'The Hard Rain of American Grain: An Historical Overview of Japanese Agricultural Policy,' *AMPO: Japan-Asia Quarterly Review*, XIX, (2), 29–37.

Kojima Kiyoshi (1977). *Japan and a New World Economic Order*, Boulder, CO: Westview Press.

Koo, Hagen (1987). 'The Interplay of State, Social Class, and the World System in East Asian Development: The Cases of South Korea and Taiwan,' in F. C. Deyo (ed.), *The Political Economy of the New Asian Industrialism*, Ithaca, NY: Cornell University Press, 165–81.

Koo, Hagen (1990). 'From Farm to Factory: Proletarianization in Korea,' *American Sociological Review*, LV, (October), 669–81.

Koo, Hagen (1993). 'The State, *Minjung*, and the Working Class in South Korea,' in H. Koo (ed.), *State and Society in Contemporary Korea*, Ithaca, NY: Cornell University Press, 131–62.

Koo, Hagen (1996). 'Work, Culture, and Consciousness of the Korean Working Class,' in E. J. Perry (ed.), *Putting Class in Its Place: Worker Identities in East Asia*, Berkeley, CA: University of California Press, 53–76.

Koo, Hagen (2001). *Korean Workers: The Culture and Politics of Class Formation*, Ithaca, NY: Cornell University Press.

Koo, Hagen and Eun Mee Kim (1992). 'The Developmental State and Capital Accumulation in South Korea,' in R. P. Appelbaum and J. Henderson (eds), *States and Development in the Asian Pacific Rim*, Newbury Park, CA: Sage, 121–49.

Krueger, Anne O. (1979). *The Developmental Role of the Foreign Sector and Aid*, Cambridge, MA: Harvard University Press.

Kuznets, Paul W. (1977). *Economic Growth and Structure in the Republic of Korea*, New Haven, CT: Yale University Press.

Kwan, C. H. (1994). *Economic Interdependence in the Asia-Pacific Region: Towards a Yen Bloc*, London: Routledge.

Kwon, Seung-Ho and Michael O'Donnell (2001). *The Chaebol and Labour in Korea: The Development of Management Strategy in Hyundai*, London: Routledge.

Ladejinsky, Wolf Issac (1977). *Agrarian Reform as Unfinished Business: The Selected Papers of Wolf Ladejinsky*, New York: Oxford University Press.

LaFeber, Walter (1980). *America, Russia, and the Cold War*, New York: Alfred A. Knopf.

Lague, David (2001). 'Money Speaks,' *Far Eastern Economic Review*, CLXIV, (33, August 23), 24.

Landler, Mark (2002). 'Taiwan Maker of Notebook PCs Thrives Quietly,' *New York Times*, 25 March.

Larkin, John (2002). 'Korea Bites the Bullet,' *Far Eastern Economic Review*, 28 March.

Lash, Scott and John Urry (1987). *The End of Organized Capitalism*, Cambridge: Polity Press.

Lau, Ho-Fuk and Chi-Fan Chan (1994). 'The Development Process of the Hong Kong Garment Industry: A Mature Industry in a Newly Industrialized Economy,' in Edna Bonacich, Lucie Cheng, Normal Chinchilla, Norma Hamilton and Paul Ong (eds), *Global Production: The Apparel Industry in the Pacific Rim*, Philadelphia, PA: Temple University Press, 105–25.

Lauridsen, Laurids S. (1998). 'Thailand: Causes, Conduct, Consequences,' in K. S. Jomo (ed.), *Tigers in Trouble: Financial Governance, Liberalisation and Crisis in East Asia*, London: Zed Books, 137–61.

Lazoinick, William (1995). 'Cooperative Employment Relations and Japanese Economic Growth,' in J. Schor and J.-I. You (eds), *Capital, the Statem, and Labour: A Global Perspective*, Tokyo: United Nations University Press, 70–110.

Lee, Joseph S. (1995). 'Economic Development and the Evolution of Industrial Relations in Taiwan, 1950–1993,' in A. Verma *et al.* (eds), *Employment Relations in the Growing Asian Economies*, London: Routledge, 88–118.

Lee, Kim-Ming (1999). 'Flexible Manufacturing in a Colonial Economy,' in Tak-Wing Ngo (ed.), *Hong Kong's History: State and Society Under Colonial Rule*, London: Routledge, 162–79.

Lee, Su-Hoon (1998). 'Crisis in Korea and the IMF Control,' in E.-M. Kim (ed.), *The Four Asian Tigers: Economic Development and the Global Political Economy*, San Diego, CA: Academic Press, 209–28.

Leftwich, Adrian (1995). 'Bringing Politics Back In: Towards a Model of the Developmental State,' *Journal of Development Studies*, XXXVIII, (3), 400–27.

Legget, Karby (2002). 'The World's Factory Floor,' *Wall Street Journal*, 10 November.

Lethbridge, David G. and Ng Sek-Hong (1993). 'The Business Environment and Employment,' in D. G. Lethbridge (ed.), *The Business Environment in Hong Kong*, Hong Kong: Oxford University Press, 70–104.

Levin, David A. and Ng Sek-Hong (1995). 'From an Industrial to a Post-Industrial Economy: Challenges for Human Resource Management in Hong Kong,' in Anil Verma, Thomas P. Kochan, and Russell D. Lansbury (eds), *Employment Relations in the Growing Asian Economies*, London: Routledge, 119–57.

Leyshon, Andrew (1994). 'Under Pressure: Finance, Geo-Economic Competition, and the Rise and Fall of Japan's Postwar Growth Economy,' in S. Corbridge *et al.* (eds), *Money, Power and Space*, Oxford: Blackwell, 116–45.

Lim, Linda Y. C. (1999). 'Free Market Fancies: Hong Kong, Singapore, and the Asian Financial Crisis,' in T. J. Pempel (ed.), *The Politics of the Asian Economic Crisis*, Ithaca, NY: Cornell University Press, 101–15.

Lim, Linda and Pang Eng Fong (1986). *Trade, Employment, and Industrialisation in Singapore*, Geneva: International Labour Office.

Lin, Steven A. Y. (2002). 'Roles of Foreign Direct Investments in Taiwan's Economic Growth,' in P. C. Y. Chow (ed.), *Taiwan in the Global Economy: From an Agrarian Economy to an Exported of High-tech Products*, Westport, CT: Praeger, 79–94.

Lincoln, Edward J. (2002). 'The Asian Development Bank: Time to Wind it Up?' in M. Beeson (ed.), *Reconfiguring East Asia: Regional Institutions and Organizations After the Crisis*, London: RoutledgeCurzon, 205–25.

Lissakers, Karin (1991). *Banks, Borrowers, and the Establishment: A Revisionist Account of the International Debt Crisis*, New York: Basic Books.

Lui, Tai Lok and Stephen W. K. Chiu (2001). 'Flexibility under Unorganized Industrialism? The Experience of Industrial Restructuring in Hong Kong,' in Frederic C. Deyo, Richard F. Doner, and Eric Herschberg (eds), *Economic Governance and the Challenge of Flexibility in East Asia*, Lanham, MD: Rowman & Littlefield, 55–77.

Lundberg, E. (1979). 'Fiscal and Monetary Policies,' in W. Galenson (ed.), *Economic Growth and Structural Change in Taiwan*, Ithaca, NY: Cornell University Press, 263–307.

McCormack, Gavan (2001). *The Emptiness of Japanese Affluence*, Armonk, NY: M. E. Sharpe.

McCormack, Gavan (2002). 'North Korea in the Vice,' *New Left Review*, (18, Second series, November–December), 5–27.

McCormack, Gavan (2003). 'Sunshine, Containment, War: The Korean Options.' Unpublished manuscript.

McCormick, Thomas J. (1989). *America's Half Century: United States Foreign Policy in the Cold War*, Baltimore, MD: Johns Hopkins University Press.

McDermott, Darren and David Wessel (1997). 'Financial Sector Weaknesses are Roiling Asian Currencies,' *Wall Street Journal*, 6 October.

McDonald, Hamish (2001). 'Shrinking Japan Exposes Region to a New Meltdown,' *Sydney Morning Herald*, 17 March.

MacIntyre, Andrew (1999). 'Political Institutions and the Economic Crisis in Thailand and Indonesia,' in T. J. Pempel (ed.), *The Politics of the Asian Economic Crisis*, Ithaca, NY: Cornell University Press, 143–62.

McMichael, Philip (1993). 'Agro-Food Restructuring in the Pacific Rim: A

Comparative-International Perspective on Japan, South Korea, The United States, Australia, and Thailand,' in R. A. Palat (ed.), *Pacific-Asia and the Future of the World-System*, Westport, CT: Greenwood, 103–16.

McMichael, Philip and Chul-Kyoo Kim (1994). 'Japanese and South Korean Agricultural Restructuring in Comparative and Global Perspective,' in P. McMichael (ed.), *The Global Restructuring of Agro-Food Systems*, Ithaca, NY: Cornell University Press, 21–52.

Maddrick, Jeff (2003). 'A Deficit, Any Way it is Sliced,' *New York Times*, 17 April.

Mann, Michael (1986). *The Sources of Social Power: A History of Power from the Beginning to A.D. 1760*, Cambridge: Cambridge University Press.

Marer, Paul (1985). *Dollar GNPs of the U.S.S.R. and Eastern Europe*, Baltimore, MD: Johns Hopkins University Press.

Marglin, Stephen A. and Juliet B. Schor (eds). (1991). *The Golden Age of Capitalism: Reinterpreting the Postwar Experience*, Oxford: Clarendon Press.

Markoff, John (2002). 'Rebel Wants Japan's Inventors to Get Some U.S.-Style Rewards,' *New York Times*, 18 September.

Markusen, Ann, Scott Campbell, Peter Hall and Sabrina Dietrich (1991). *The Rise of the Gunbelt: The Military Remapping of Industrial America*, New York: Oxford University Press.

Mason, Edward Sagendorph, Kwang Suk Perkins, and Mahn Je Kim (eds). (1980). *The Economic and Social Modernization of the Republic of Korea, 1945–1975*, Cambridge, MA: Harvard University Press.

Matthews, John A. (1998). 'Fashioning a New Korean Model Out of the Crisis: The Rebuilding of Institutional Capabilities,' *Cambridge Journal of Economics*, XXII, 747–59.

Miles, Michael W. (1990). *The Odyssey of the American Right*, New York: Oxford University Press.

Miners, Norman J. (1993). 'Government and Politics,' in D. Lethbridge (ed.), *The Business Environment in Hong Kong*, Hong Kong: Oxford University Press, 105–23.

Mollenkopf, John H. (1983). *The Contested City*, Princeton, NJ: Princeton University Press.

Montagnon, Peter (2000). 'Disillusion Leads to Growing Spirit of Cooperation Among Asian Nations,' *Financial Times*, 21 July.

Morales, Rebecca (1994). *Flexible Production: Restructuring the International Automobile Industry*, Cambridge: Polity Press.

Moran, Michael (1991). *The Politics of the Financial Services Revolution: The USA, UK and Japan*, London: Macmillan.

Morgan, Dan (1980). *Merchants of Grain*, New York: Penguin.

Morgenson, Gretchen (1998). 'Beware of Japanese Bearing Gifts,' *New York Times*, 21 June.

Morishima, Michio (1982). *Why has Japan 'Succeeded?' Western Technology and the Japanese Ethos*, Cambridge: Cambridge University Press.

Morris-Suzuki, Tessa (1991). 'Reshaping the International Division of Labour: Japanese Manufacturing Investment in Southeast Asia,' in J. Morris (ed.), *Japan and the Global Economy: Issues and Trends in the 1990s*, London: Routledge, 135–53.

Morris-Suzuki, Tessa (1994). *The Technological Transformation of Japan: From the Seventeenth to the Twenty-First Century*, Cambridge: Cambridge University Press.

Muraoka, Teruzo (1991). 'Pursuing the New International Economic Order: Overseas Investment and trade of Japan, the Asian NIEs and ASEAN,' in J. Morris (ed.), *Japan and the Global Economy: Issues and Trends in the 1990s*, London: Routledge, 154–71.

Murphy, R. Taggart (1996). *The Weight of the Yen: How Denial Imperils America's Future and Ruins an Alliance*, New York: W. W. Norton.

Murphy, R. Taggart (2000). 'Japan's Economic Crisis,' *New Left Review*, II, (1, January–February), 25–52.

Mydans, Seth (1998). 'Indonesia's Currency Falls Hard, Clouding Recovery,' *New York Times*, 23 January.

Myers, Ramon H. (1984). 'The Economic Transformation of the Republic of China on Taiwan,' *China Quarterly*, (99), 500–28.

Nakamae, Naoko (1999). 'Stock Market Falls 4.2% on Year,' *Financial Times*, 1 April.

Nakamoto, Michiyo (2003). 'A Speedier Route from Order to Camcorder,' *Financial Times*, 12 February.

Nakamoto, Michiyo and Paul Abrahams (1999). 'Toyota to List in New York and London,' *Financial Times*, 8 September.

Nakamoto, Michiyo and David Pilling (2002). 'Japan Directs a Route to Recovery,' *Financial Times*, 8 August.

Nakane, Chie (1970). *Japanese Society*, Berkeley, CA: University of California Press.

Nakao, Shigeo (1995). *The Political Economy of Japan Money*, Tokyo: University of Tokyo Press.

Neary, Michael (2000). 'Hyundai Motors, 1998–1999,' *Capital & Class*, (70, Spring), 1–7.

Nester, William R. (1990). *Japan's Growing Power over East Asia and the World Economy: Ends and Means*, London: MacMillan.

New York Times (1999). 'Sumitomo, Sakura Banks to Merge,' 14 October.

Noble, Gregory M. and John Ravenhill (2000). 'The Good, the Bad and the Ugly? Korea, Taiwan and the Asian Financial Crisis,' in G. M. Noble and J. Ravenhill (eds), *The Asian Financial Crisis and the Architecture of Global Finance*, Cambridge: Cambridge University Press, 80–107.

Nordhaug, Kristen (2002). 'The Political Economy of the Dollar and the Yen in East Asia,' *Journal of Contemporary Asia*, XXXII, (3), 517–35.

Nuti, Domenico M. (1981). 'The Polish Crisis: Economic Factors and Constraints,' in R. Miliband and J. Saville (eds), *The Socialist Register, 1991*, London: Merlin Press, 104–43.

O'Connor, James (1973). *The Fiscal Crisis of the State*, New York: St. Martin's Press.

Odaka Konosuke, Ono Keinosuke, and Adachi Fumihiko (1988). *The Automobile Industry in Japan: A Study in Ancillary Firm Development*, Tokyo: Kokusaibunken Insatsusha.

Ofreneo, Rosalinda P. (1994). 'The Philippine Garment Industry,' in Edna Bonacich, Lucie Cheng, Normal Chinchilla, Nora Hamilton, and Paul Ong (eds), *Global Production: The Apparel Industry in the Pacific Rim*, Philadelphia, PA: Temple University Press, 162–79.

Ong, Aihwa (1990). 'Japanese Factories, Malay Workers: Class and Sexual Metaphors in West Malaysia,' in J. M. Atkinson and S. Errington (eds), *Power and Difference: Gender in Island Southeast Asia*, Stanford, CA: Stanford University Press, 385–422.

Ong, Aihwa (1991). 'Gender and the Politics of Postmodernity,' *Annual Review of Anthropology*, XX, 279–309.

260   *Bibliography*

Onis, Ziya (1991). 'The Logic of the Developmental State,' *Comparative Politics*, XXIV, (1, October), 109–26.

Organization for Economic Cooperation and Development (2003). 'Trends and Recent Developments in Foreign Direct Investment,' Paris: OECD.

Orru, Marc, Nicole W. Biggart, and Gary G. Hamilton (1991). 'Organizational Isomorphism in East Asia,' in W. W. Powell and P. J. DiMaggio (eds), *The New Institutionalism in Organizational Analysis*, Chicago: University of Chicago Press, 361–89.

Owen, Nicholas C. (1971). 'Economic Policy in Hong Kong,' in K. Hopkins (ed.), *Hong Kong: The Industrial Colony – A Political, Social and Economic Survey*, Hong Kong: Oxford University Press, 141–206.

Ozawa, Terutomo (1979). *Multinationalism, Japanese Style: The Political Economy of Outward Dependency*, Princeton, NJ: Princeton University Press.

Ozawa, Terutomo (1985). 'Japan,' in J. H. Dunning (ed.), *Multinational Enterprises, Economic Structure and International Competitiveness*, Chichester: John Wiley & Sons, 155–85.

Palat, Ravi Arvind (1996). 'Pacific Century: Myth or Reality?' *Theory & Society*, XXV, (3, June), 303–47.

Palat, Ravi Arvind (1998). 'Up the Down Staircase: Australasia in the "Pacific Century",' *Thesis XI*, (55, November), 15–40.

Palat, Ravi Arvind (1999). 'Miracles of the Day Before? The Great Asian Meltdown and the Changing World-Economy,' *Development and Society*, XXVIII, (1, June), 1–47.

Palat, Ravi Arvind (2001). 'Barbarians at the Gate: Restructuring Asia's Pacific Rim After the Crash of 1997–98,' *Economic and Political Weekly*, XXXVI, (48, December 1), 4473–84.

Pang Eng Fong and Linda Lim (1977). *The Electronics Industry in Singapore*, Singapore: Chopmen.

Parboni, Riccardo (1981). *The Dollar and Its Rivals*, London: Verso.

Park, Young-bum and Michael Byungnam Lee (1995). 'Economic Development, Globalization and Practices in Industrial Relations and Human Resource Management in Korea,' in Anil Verma, Thomas P. Kochan, and Russell D. Lansbury (eds), *Employment Relations in the Growing Asian Economies*, London: Routledge, 27–62.

Passell, Peter (1998). 'Foreign Banks Seen as Winners in South Korean Economic Debacle,' *New York Times*, 8 January.

Pearlstein, Steven (2002). 'Too Much Supply, Too Little Demand: Businesses Have Few Incentives to Expand or Hire, Economists Say,' *Washington Post*, 25 August.

Pempel, T. J. (1997). 'Regime Shift: Japanese Politics in a Changing World Economy,' *Journal of Japanese Studies*, XXIII, (3), 333–61.

Pempel, T. J. (1998). *Regime Shift: Comparative Dynamics of the Japanese Political Economy*, Ithaca, NY: Cornell University Press.

Pempel, T. J. (ed.) (1999a). *The Politics of the Asian Economic Crisis*, Ithaca, NY: Cornell University Press.

Pempel, T. J. (1999b). 'Regional Ups, Regional Downs,' in T. J. Pempel (ed.), *The Politics of the Asian Economic Crisis*, Ithaca, NY: Cornell University Press, 62–78.

Phillips, Kevin (2002). *Wealth and Democracy: A Political History of the American Rich*, New York: Broadway Books.

Phongpaichit, Pasuk and Chris Baker (1998). *Thailand's Boom and Bust*, Chiang Mai: Silkworm Books.

Phongpaichit, Pasuk and Chris Baker (1999). 'The Political Economy of the Thai Crisis,' *Journal of the Asia-Pacific Economy*, IV, (1), 193–208.

Phongpaichit, Pasuk and Chris Baker (2000). *Thailand's Crisis*, Chiang Mai: Silkworm Books.

Pollack, Andrew (1997). 'Despite World-Class Economy, Sense of Decline,' *New York Times*, 4 February.

Pollin, Robert (2000). 'Anatomy of Clintonomics,' *New Left Review*, II, (3, May–June), 17–46.

Radelet, Steven and Jeffrey Sachs (1998). 'The East Asian Financial Crisis: Diagnosis, Remedies, Prospects,' *Brookings Papers on Economic Activity*, (1), 1–90.

Rasiah, Rajah (1993). 'Free-Trade Zones and Industrial Development in Malaysia,' in K. S. Jomo (ed.), *Industrialising Malaysia: Policy, Performance, Prospects*, London: Routledge, 118–46.

Ravenhill, John (2002a). 'Institutional Evolution at the Trans-Regional Level: APEC and the Promotion of Liberalisation,' in M. Beeson (ed.), *Reconfiguring East Asia: Regional Institutions and Organizations After the Crisis*, London: RoutledgeCurzon, 227–46.

Ravenhill, John (2002b). 'A Three Bloc World? The New East Asian Regionalism,' *International Relations of the Asia-Pacific*, II, (2), 167–95.

Redding, Brian (2002). 'Japan's Way Out May be to Spend,' *Financial Times*, 15 September.

Rhoads, Christopher (2003). 'Foreign Investment in U.S. Plunges Nearly 80%,' *Wall Street Journal*, 20 June.

Richardson, Michael (2002). 'Southeast Asia Sees China as Export Boon: ASEAN is Ready to Embrace Market,' *International Herald Tribune*, 27 April.

Ridding, John and James Kynge (1998). 'Thailand: Complacency Gives Way to Contagion,' *Financial Times*, 13 January.

Roberts, Dan and James Kynge (2003). 'The New Workshop of the World,' *Financial Times*, 3 February.

Robison, Richard (1987). 'After the Gold Rush: The Politics of Economic Restructuring in Indonesia in the 1980s,' in Richard Robison, Kevin Hewison, and Richard Higgott (eds), *Southeast Asia in the 1980s: The Politics of Economic Crisis*, Sydney: Allen & Unwin, 16–51.

Robison, Richard (1993). 'Indonesia: Tensions in State and Regime,' in Kevin Hewison, Richard Robison, and Garry Rodan (eds), *Southeast Asia in the 1990s: Authoritarianism, Democracy & Capitalism*, St. Leonard's, NSW: Allen & Unwin, 39–74.

Robison, Richard and Andrew Rosser (2000). 'Surviving the Meltdown: Liberal Reform and Political Oligarchy in Indonesia,' in R. Robison *et al.* (eds), *Politics and Markets in the Wake of the Asian Crisis*, London: Routledge, 171–91.

Rodan, Garry (1989). *The Political Economy of Singapore's Industrialization: National State and International Capital*, Kuala Lumpur: Forum.

Rodan, Garry (1997). 'State–Society Relations and Political Opposition in Singapore,' in G. Rodan (ed.), *Political Oppositions in Industrializing Asia*, London: Routledge, 95–127.

Rodan, Garry (2001). 'Singapore: Globalisation and the Politics of Economic Restructuring,' in Garry Rodan, Kevin Hewison, and Richard Robison (eds), *The Political Economy of South-East Asia: Conflicts, Crises, and Change*, Melbourne: Oxford University Press, 138–77.

Roddick, J. (1988). *The Dance of Millions: Latin America and the Debt Crisis*, Birmingham: Third World Publications.

Saravanamuttu, Johan (1988). 'Japanese Economic Penetration in ASEAN in the Context of the International Division of Labour,' *Journal of Contemporary Asia*, XVIII, (2), 139–64.

Sassen, Saskia (1988). *The Mobility of Labor and Capital: A Study in International Investment and Labor Flow*, Cambridge: Cambridge University Press.

Sassen, Saskia (1991). *The Global City: New York, London, Tokyo*, Princeton, NJ: Princeton University Press.

Schiffer, Jonathan R. (1991). 'State Policy and Economic Growth: A Note on the Hong Kong Model,' *International Journal of Urban and Regional Research*, XV, (June), 180–96.

Schive, Chi (1995). *Taiwan's Economic Role in East Asia*, Washington, DC: Center for Strategic and International Studies.

Schonberger, Howard B. (1982). 'U.S. Policy in Post-War Japan: The Retreat from Liberalism,' *Science & Society*, XLVI, (1), 39–59.

Schonberger, Howard B. (1989). *Aftermath of War: Americans and the Remaking of Japan, 1949–1952*, Kent, OH: Kent State University Press.

Schurmann, Franz (1974). *The Logic of World Power: An Inquiry into the Origins, Currents, and Contradictions of World Politics*, New York: Pantheon.

Segal, Gerald (1990). *Rethinking the Pacific*, Oxford: Clarendon Press.

Seiyama, T. (1989). 'A Radical Interpretation of Japanese Economic Policies,' in T. Morris-Suzuki and T. Seiyama (eds), *Japanese Capitalism Since 1945: Critical Perspectives*, Armonk, NY: M. E. Sharpe, 28–73.

Selden, Mark (1983). 'The Proletariat, Revolutionary Change, and the State in China and Japan, 1850–1920,' in I. Wallerstein (ed.), *Labor in the World Social Structure*, Beverly Hills, CA: Sage, 28–73.

Selden, Mark (1997). 'China, Japan, and the Regional Political Economy of East Asia, 1945–1995,' in P. J. Katzenstein and T. Shiraishi (eds), *Network Power: Japan and Asia*, Ithaca, NY: Cornell University Press, 306–40.

Shapira, Philip (1993). 'Steel Town to Space World: Restructuring and Adjustment in Kitakyushu City,' in K. Fujita and R. C. Hill (eds), *Japanese Cities in the World Economy*, Philadelphia, PA: Temple University Press, 224–54.

Sheard, Paul (1983). 'Auto-Production Systems in Japan: Organisational and Locational Features,' *Australian Geographical Studies*, XXI, (1 April), 49–68.

Shibusawa, Masakide, Zakari Haji Amman, and Brian Bridges (1992). *Pacific Asia in the 1990s*, London: Routledge.

Shove, Gerald (1942). 'The Place of Marshall's Principles in the Development of Economic Theory,' *Economic Journal*, LII, 294–329.

Sik, Ota (1976). *Plan and Market Under Socialism*, White Plains, NY: International Arts and Sciences Press.

Silver, Beverly J. (1997). 'Turning Points of Workers' Militancy in the World Automobile Industry, 1930s–1990s,' *Research in the Sociology of Work*, VI, 43–71.

Silver, Beverly J. (2003). *Forces of Labor: Workers' Movements and Globalization since 1870*, New York: Cambridge University Press.

Simon, D. F. (1988a). 'External Incorporation and Internal Reform,' in E. A. Winckler and S. Greenhalgh (eds), *Contending Approaches to the Political Economy of Taiwan*, Armonk, NY: M. E. Sharpe, 138–50.

Simon, Dennis F. (1988b). 'Technology Transfer and National Autonomy,' in E. A. Winckler and S. Greenhalgh (eds), *Contending Approaches to the Political Economy of Taiwan*, Armonk, NY: M. E. Sharpe, 206–23.

Sims, Calvin (1999a). 'Three Japanese Banks Unite to Form World's Largest,' *New York Times*, 21 August.

Sims, Calvin (1999b). 'Japan Bank Merger Carries Old Burdens,' *New York Times*, 7 September.

Sit, Victor F.-S., Sin Liu Wong, and Tsiu-Sing Kiang (1979). *Small Scale Industry in a Laissez-Faire Economy: A Hong Kong Case Study*, Hong Kong: University of Hong Kong Press.

Smitka, Michael J. (1991). *Competitive Ties: Subcontracting in the Japanese Automotive Industry*, New York: Columbia University Press.

So, Alvin Y. (2002). 'Beyond Colonial Governance? The Making of the SAR State in Hong Kong,' *Revisiting Asian States*, University of Leiden, 28–30 June.

So, Alvin Y. (n.d.). 'Hong Kong's Pathway to Becoming a Global City: A Regional Analysis,' in J. Gugler (ed.), *World City in Poor Countries*, Cambridge: Cambridge University Press.

So, Alvin Y. and Sai-Hsin May (1993). 'Democratization in East Asia in the Late 1980s: Taiwan Breakthrough. Hong Kong Frustration,' *Studies in Comparative International Development*, XXVIII, (2, Summer), 61–80.

So, Alvin Y. and Ming K. Chan (2002). 'Crisis and Transformation in the Hong Kong SAR,' in M. K. Chan and A. Y. So (eds), *Crisis and Transformation in China's Hong Kong*, Armonk, NY: M. E. Sharpe, 363–84.

Soja, Edward W. (1989). *Postmodern Geographies: The Reassertion of Space in Critical Social Theory*, London: Verso.

South China Morning Post (2001a). 'Firms invest record $201 billion,' 8 June.

South China Morning Post (2001b). 'Japan Ripe for Picking,' 31 May.

Steven, Rob (1990). *Japan's New Imperialism*, London: Macmillan.

Steven, Rob (1996). *Japan and the New World Order: Global Investments, Trade and Finance*, Basingstoke: Macmillan.

Stiglitz, Joseph E. (2002). *Globalization and Its Discontents*, New York: W. W. Norton.

Strange, Susan (1998). *Mad Money: When Markets Outgrow Governments*, Ann Arbor, MI: University of Michigan Press.

Strom, Stephanie (1997). 'Japanese Companies Buffer Themselves Against Currency Swings,' *New York Times*, 25 October.

Strom, Stephanie (1999). 'U.S. Firm Buys Control of Korea First Bank,' *New York Times*, 18 September.

Strom, Stephanie (2000a). 'Barbarians at the Toll Booth,' *New York Times*, 16 September.

Strom, Stephanie (2000b). 'Rickety Japanese Banks: As Borrowers Collapse Is New Bailout Needed?' *New York Times*, 8 September.

Summers, George F., Francine Horton, and Christina Gringeri (1990). 'Rural Labour-Market Changes in the United States,' in T. Marsden *et al.* (eds), *Rural Restructuring: Global Processes and Their Responses*, London: David Fulton, 129–64.

Sung, Y. W. (1982). 'Public Finance and Economic Policies in Hong Kong,' in J. Y. S. Cheng (ed.), *Hong Kong in the 1980s*, Hong Kong: Summerson, 45–59.

Tabb, William K. (1995). *The Postwar Japanese System: Cultural Economy and Economic Transformation*, New York: Oxford University Press.

Tabb, William K. (1999). 'The End of the Japanese Postwar System,' *Monthly Review*, LI, (3, July–August), 71–80.

Tanikawa, Miki (2000). 'G.M. Doubles Its Stake in Suzuki Motors to 20%,' *New York Times*, 15 September.

Taplin, Ian M. (1994) 'Recent Manufacturing Changes in the U.S. Apparel Industry: The Case of Corth Carolina,' in Edna Bonacich, Lucie Cheng, Normal Chinchilla, Nora Hamilton, and Paul Ong (eds), *Global Production: The Apparel Industry in the Pacific Rim*, Philadelphia, PA: Temple University Press, 328–44.

Tett, Gillian (1999). 'Japanese Banks Join Rush to Merge,' *Financial Times*, 8 October.

Tett, Gillian and Alexandra Harney (1999). 'Japan Looks to Ride on Reform Rollercoaster,' *Financial Times*, 15 October.

Tett, Gillian and Naoko Nakamae (1999). 'The Last Tango in Tokyo,' *Financial Times*, 15 October.

Tett, Gillian and David Wighton (1998). 'Tokyo And Its Scale of Bad Loans,' *Financial Times*, 13 January.

Therborn, Goran (2001). 'Into the 21st Century: The New Parameters of Global Politics,' *New Left Review*, II, (10, July–August), 87–110.

Thornhill, John (2002). 'Asia Awakes,' *Financial Times*, 1 April.

Tokunaga, Shojiro (1992). 'Japan's FDI = Promoting Systems and Intra-Asia Networks: New Investment and Trade Systems Created by the Borderless Economy,' in S. Tokunaga (ed.), *Japan's Foreign Investment and Asian Economic Interdependence*, Tokyo: University of Tokyo Press, 5–47.

Tornquist, Olle (2000). 'Dynamics of Indonesian Democracy,' *Economic and Political Weekly*, XXXV, (18, April 29), 1559–75.

Toshihiko Kawagoe (1993). 'Deregulation and Protectionism in Japanese Agriculture,' in Juro Teranishi and Y. Kosai (eds), *The Japanese Experience of Economic Reforms*, New York: St. Martin's Press, 366–91.

Tracy, Constance Lever and Noel Tracy (1999). 'The Three Faces of Capitalism and the Asian Crisis,' *Bulletin of Concerned Asian Scholars*, XXXI, (3, July), 3–18.

Tremewan, Christopher (1994). *The Political Economy of Social Control in Singapore*, New York: St. Martin's Press.

Trimberger, Ellen Kay (1978). *Revolutions from Above: Military Bureaucrats in Japan, Turkey, Egypt, and Peru*, New Brunswick, NJ: Transaction Books.

Tubiana, Laurence (1989). 'World Trade in Agricultural Products: From Global Regulation to Market Fragmentation,' in D. Goodman and M. Redclift (eds), *The International Farm Crisis*, Basingstoke: Macmillan.

Tuma, Elias H. (1965). *Twenty-Six Centuries of Agrarian Reform: A Comparative Analysis*, Berkeley, CA: University of California Press.

Turnbull, Constance M. (1989). *A History of Singapore, 1819–1988*, Singapore: Oxford University Press.

Uchitelle, Louis (1997a). 'Borrowing Asia's Trouble,' *New York Times*, 28 December.

Uchitelle, Louis (1997b). 'Global Good Times, Meet the Global Glut,' *New York Times*, 16 November.

Uchitelle, Louis (1997c). 'Korean Bailout Could Set Questionable Precedent,' *New York Times*, 4 December.

United Nations (1990). *World Economic Survey, 1990*, New York: United Nations.

van der Wee, Herman (1986). *Prosperity and Upheaval: The World Economy Since 1945–1980*, Berkeley: University of California Press.

Wade, Robert (1990). *Governing the Market: Economic Theory and the Role of Government in East Asian Industrialization*, Princeton: Princeton University Press.

Wade, Robert (1992). 'East Asia's Economic Success: Conflicting Perspectives, Partial Insights, Shaky Evidence,' *World Politics*, LIV, (2 January), 270–320.

Wade, Robert (1996). 'Japan, the World Bank, and the Art of Paradigm Mainte-nance: *The East Asian Miracle* in Political Perspective,' *New Left Review*, (217, May–June).

Wade, Robert (1998a). 'The Asian Debt-and-development Crisis of 1997–?: Causes and Consequences,' *World Development*, XXVI, (8), 1535–53.

Wade, Robert (1998b). 'From "Miracle" to "Cronyism": Explaining the Great Asian Slump,' *Cambridge Journal of Economics*, XXII, 693–706.

Wade, Robert and Frank Veneroso (1998a). 'The Asian Financial Crisis: The Unrec-ognized Risk of the IMF's Asia Package,' New York: Russell Sage Foundation.

Wade, Robert and Frank Veneroso (1998b). 'The Gathering World Slump and the Battle Over Capital Controls,' *New Left Review*, 231, (September–October), 13–42.

Wang, Hongying (2000). 'Dangers and Opportunities: The Implications of the Asian Financial Crisis,' in G. M. Noble and J. Ravenhill (eds), *The Asian Financial Crisis and the Architecture of Global Finance*, Cambridge: Cambridge University Press, 152–69.

Ward, Andrew (2002a). 'Hyundai Heavy Cuts Ties to Parent Company,' *Financial Times*, 3 March.

Ward, Andrew (2002b). 'Shoppers turn South Korea's economy around,' *Financial Times*, 9 August.

Ward, Andrew (2003). 'Transparency Should by Now be a Given in Korea. But Foreign Investors Still Face Uncertainties and Surprises,' *Financial Times*, 9 July.

Warner, Joan, Pete Engardio, and Thane Peterson (1999). 'The Atlantic Century,' *Businessweek*, 8 February.

Watts, Michael (1992). 'Peasants and Flexible Accumulation in the Third World: Producing Under Contract,' *Economic and Political Weekly*, XXVII, (30, July 25, Review of Political Economy), PE-90–7.

Wee, C. J. W.-L. (2001). 'The End of Disciplinary Modernisation? The Asian Eco-nomic Crisis and the Ongoing Reinvention of Singapore,' *Third World Quarterly*, XXII, (6), 987–1002.

Western, Bruce and Katherine Beckett (1999). 'How Unregulated is the U.S. Labor Market? The Penal System as a Labor Market Institution,' *American Journal of Sociology*, CIV, (4, January), 1030–60.

Whitley, Richard D. (1990). 'Eastern Asian Enterprise Structures and the Compar-ative Analysis of Forms of Business Organization,' *Organization Studies*, XI, (1), 47–74.

Wilkins, Mira (1974). *The Maturing of Multinational Enterprise: American Business Abroad from 1914 to 1970*, Cambridge, MA: Harvard University Press.

Wilkins, Mira (1980). 'Multinational Automobile Enterprises and Regulation: An Historical Overview,' in D. H. Ginsburd and W. J. Abernathy (eds), *Government, Technology, and the Future of the Automobile*, New York: McGraw Hill, 221–58.

Winters, Jeffrey A. (1996). *Power in Motion: Capital Mobility and the Indonesian State*, Ithaca, NY: Cornell University Press.

Winters, Jeffrey A. (2000). 'The Financial Crisis in Southeast Asia,' in R. Robison, *et al.* (eds), *Politics and Markets in the Wake of the Asian Crisis*, London: Routledge, 34–52.

Wolf, Diane Lauren (1992). *Factory Daughters: Gender, Household Dynamics, and Rural Industrialization in Java*, Berkeley: University of California Press.

Womack, James P., Daniel T. Jones, and Daniel Roos (1990). *The Machine that Changed the World*, New York: Columbia University Press.

Wong Poh-Kam (2001). 'Flexible Production, High-Tech Commodities, and Public Policies: The Hard Disk Drive Industry in Singapore,' in Frederic C. Deyo, Richard F. Doner, and Eric Hershberg (eds), *Economic Governance and the Challenge of Flexibility in East Asia*, Lanham, MA: Rowman & Littlefield, 191–216.

Wong Poh-Kam, Phang Sock-Yong, Yong Jong-Say, and Chng Meng-Kng (1997). 'Development of Internationally Competitive Indigenous Manufacturing Firms in Singapore,' Tokyo: Foundation for Advanced Studies on International Development.

Woo, Jung-en (1991). *Race to the Swift: State and Finance in Korean Industrialization*, New York: Columbia University Press.

Woo-Cumings, Meredith (1999). 'The State, Democracy, and the Reform of the Corporate Sector in Korea,' in T. J. Pempel (ed.), *The Politics of the Asian Economic Crisis*, Ithaca, NY: Cornell University Press, 116–42.

World Bank (1993). *The East Asian Miracle: Economic Growth and Public Policy*, New York: Oxford University Press.

World Trade Organization (2001). *International Trade Statistics, 2001*, Geneva: World Trade Organization.

WuDunn, Sheryl (1998a). 'Japanese Government Downplays Fear Over Bad Bank Loans,' *New York Times*, 13 January.

WuDunn, Sheryl (1998b). 'Japan's Wobbly Banks Prepare for the Unthinkable,' *Financial Times*, 3 February.

WuDunn, Sheryl (1998c). 'Japanese Banks Report Biggest Losses Ever,' *New York Times*, 23 May.

WuDunn, Sheryl (1998d). 'Japan Has Slid into Recession, New Data Confirmed,' *New York Times*, 13 June.

WuDunn, Sheryl and Nicholas D. Kristoff (1997). 'Japan Seems Paralyzed by Asian Crisis,' *New York Times*, 17 December.

Yang, Martin M. C. (1970). *Socio-Economic Results of Land Reform in Taiwan*, Honolulu: East-West Center Press.

Yeon-ho Lee and Hyuk-Rae Kim (2000). 'The Dilemma of Market Liberalization,' in Richard Robison, Mark Beeson, Kanishka Jayasuriya, and Hyuk-Rae Kim (eds), *Politics and Markets in the Wake of the Asian Crisis*, London: Routledge, 116–29.

Yeung, Henry Wai-chung (2000). 'Neoliberalism, *Laissez-Faire* Capitalism and Economic Crisis: The Political Economy of Deindustrialization of Hong Kong,' *Competition & Change*, VI, 121–69.

Yonekura, Seiichiro (1993). 'Postwar Reform in Management and Labor: The Case of the Steel Industry,' in Juro Teranishi and Yutaka Kosai (eds), *The Japanese Experience of Economic Reforms*, New York: St. Martin's Press, 205–38.

Yoshihara, Kunio (1978). *Japanese Investment in Southeast Asia*, Honolulu: University of Hawaii Press.

Yoshihara, Kunio (1988). *The Rise of Ersatz Capitalism in Southeast Asia*, Singapore: Oxford University Press.

Yoshino, Michael Y. and Thomas B. Lifson (1986). *The Invisible Link: Japan's Sogo Shosha and the Organization of Trade*, Cambridge, MA: MIT Press.

You-tien Hsing (1998). *Making Capitalism in China: The Taiwan Connection*, New York: Oxford University Press.

Index

eBooks – at www.eBookstore.tandf.co.uk

A library at your fingertips!

eBooks are electronic versions of printed books. You can store them on your PC/laptop or browse them online.

They have advantages for anyone needing rapid access to a wide variety of published, copyright information.

eBooks can help your research by enabling you to bookmark chapters, annotate text and use instant searches to find specific words or phrases. Several eBook files would fit on even a small laptop or PDA.

NEW: Save money by eSubscribing: cheap, online access to any eBook for as long as you need it.

Annual subscription packages

We now offer special low-cost bulk subscriptions to packages of eBooks in certain subject areas. These are available to libraries or to individuals.

For more information please contact webmaster.ebooks@tandf.co.uk

We're continually developing the eBook concept, so keep up to date by visiting the website.

www.eBookstore.tandf.co.uk

For Product Safety Concerns and Information please contact our EU
representative GPSR@taylorandfrancis.com
Taylor & Francis Verlag GmbH, Kaufingerstraße 24, 80331 München, Germany

www.ingramcontent.com/pod-product-compliance
Lightning Source LLC
Chambersburg PA
CBHW070607270326
41926CB00013B/2452